Why Do You Need This New Edition?

If you're wondering why you should buy this new edition of *Creative Writer's Handbook, Fifth Edition,* here are 10 good reasons!

1. **NEW**—Fresh writing exercises for each of the four genres.

2. **NEW**—Research tips reflecting technological and media advances in Chapters 2 and 15 to help with your online writing.

3. **NEW**—Writing quotations from renowned writers relating to key topics to provide a professional's viewpoint on writing.

4. **NEW**—Selections in poetry, fiction, non-fiction, and drama.

5. **NEW**—Revised journal-keeping chapter incorporating Internet research to provide new journaling techniques.

6. **NEW**—Information on receiving feedback in Chapter 15.

7. **NEW**—Using the Internet to sell your writing.

8. **NEW**—Updated illustrations of techniques and tricks of the trade.

9. **NEW**—Increased demonstration of skills useful for writing all genres to help you become a stronger writer.

10. **NEW**—Chapter- and part-opening images relevant to chapter topics.

PEARSON

Creative Writer's Handbook

FIFTH EDITION

PHILIP K. JASON

Emeritus Professor of English, United States Naval Academy; Director,
The Writing Program, Naples Center of Florida Gulf Coast University

ALLAN B. LEFCOWITZ

Artistic Director Emeritus, The Writer's Center; Emeritus Professor of English,
United States Naval Academy

Longman

New York   San Francisco   Boston
London   Toronto   Sydney   Tokyo   Singapore   Madrid
Mexico City   Munich   Paris   Cape Town   Hong Kong   Monreal

Senior Editor: Vivian Garcia
Senior Supplements Editor:
Donna Campion
Executive Marketing Manager:
Joyce Nilsen
Production Manager: Jacqueline A. Martin
Project Coordination and Text Design:
Elm Street Publishing Services
Electronic Page Makeup: Integra Software
Services Pvt. Ltd.
Cover Designer/Manager:
Wendy Ann Fredericks

Cover Art: Munson-Williams-Proctor Arts
Institute/Art Resource, NY
Visual Researcher: Rona Tuccillo
Senior Manufacturing Buyer: Roy L.
Pickering, Jr.
Printer and Binder: RR Donnelley & Sons
Company/Harrisonburg
Cover Printer: RR Donnelley & Sons
Company/Harrisonburg

For permission to use copyrighted material, grateful acknowledgment is made to the copyright
holders on pp. 396–402, which are hereby made part of this copyright page.

Library of Congress Cataloging-in-Publication Data

Jason, Philip K.
  Creative writer's handbook / Philip K. Jason, Allan B. Lefcowitz. —5th ed.
    p. cm.
  Includes index.
  ISBN 978-0-13-605052-0
I. Lefcowitz, Allan B.   II. Title.
PN145.J37 2010
808'.02–dc22   2008043024

Longman
is an imprint of

www.pearsonhighered.com

1 2 3 4 5 6 7 8 9 10—DOH—12 11 10 09

ISBN-13: 978-0-13-605052-0
ISBN-10: 0-13-605052-2

CONTENTS

◀━━━━━▶   **PART TWO**   THE CONCERNS OF THE POET

PART THREE   THE CONCERNS OF THE
STORYTELLER

PART FOUR   THE CONCERNS OF THE
PLAYWRIGHT

• • ANTHOLOGY OF POEMS • •

Because the many illustrative poems in this text are not found in a single chapter, we provide the following list for convenience.

See also excerpts from works by A. R. Ammons, Sterling Brown, Robert Browning, John Ciardi, Margaret Gibson, Philip Levine, Audre Lorde, Andrew Marvell, Marianne Moore, Alexander Pope, Wyatt Prunty, John W. Saxe, William Shakespeare, J. B. Smiley, Dave Smith, Andrien Stoutenburg, Dylan Thomas, Walt Whitman, and many student poets (page references in index).

• PREFACE TO FIFTH EDITION •

When Phillip Jason and I first designed the *Creative Writer's Handbook*, the landscape for writers was much different: Most students still used typewriters; there was no Internet; undergraduate majors in creative writing were almost non-existent; secondary schools offered few courses focused on any type of writing. Though the basic skills a writer needs have not changed, the tools have. This edition has been revised to respond to the impact of changed technical and educational conditions, feedback of our peers and students, and twenty years of additional experience in teaching creative writing.

———————•———————

The *Creative Writer's Handbook* is designed to help beginners. Although creativity cannot be taught, you can learn to tap and shape your creative energies. We do not hold with that popular image of the creative artist as a solitary, inspired soul who spins out a sublime work without sweat and labor.

Just as people with physical gifts can be coached so that these gifts are perfected, people with creative imaginations can be led to exercise and develop that creativity. They can be "coached" in the intricacies of language and literary structure. Our experience with hundreds of students in creative writing classes and workshops has shown us that most people have more creative talent than they realize. When they first begin to practice the craft, however, they need some direction about conventions, forms, and procedures. Each writer need not invent the game for him- or herself.

This book began because we felt that the texts available to us, though admirable, were too advanced for beginners. They were like calculus to those who need algebra. We wanted a text that responded to the issues we faced in the classroom and the workshop with novice writers who needed to know everything from the rules of the game, to the proper formats, to the professional lingo, to the tricks of the trade. We had in mind a text that students could refer to for specific information about basic issues and problems.

In each chapter, we combined theory, practical advice, and examples. The many questions and exercises are designed to involve you in the issues and practice of literary craft. Some of them may even spark results worth developing into poems, stories, or plays.

Another premise of the book is that *any* successful writing is, finally, the result of rigorous editing. As important as it is to get something down on paper in the first place, it is equally important to learn how to shape and reshape, how to spot your problems, and how to work out your solutions. Every writer must learn how to take and use criticism and, at some point, every successful writer must take on the role of self-editor.

In the *Creative Writer's Handbook*, Fifth Edition, we have provided a series of occasions for you to think, read, investigate, *write*, write again, and rewrite—and also to imitate, invent, respond, discover, and surprise yourself. However, even though we have given the order of presentation considerable thought, there can be as many paths through the book as there are readers. Although this text is aimed at the student in the creative writing course, we have kept in mind the needs of the writer who wants to go at it solo.

The four chapters of "Part One: A Writer's Concerns" take up bedrock issues of importance to every creative writer; the next ten chapters—Parts Two, Three, and Four—focus on specific issues in the major genres; and the final chapter, Part Five, contains summary and professional material useful for revision and submission of manuscripts to teachers and for publication or presentation. We stress the essential interrelationships among the genres because they are all narrations of emotions, observations, and stories.

Chapter 1 provides an opportunity for you to assess your motives and attitudes as a student of writing. We suggest ways that will help you become assertive, disciplined, and ready for work. We encourage you to be serious but not sour. Once you are "Working Like a Writer," you have a fighting chance of doing the work of a writer.

Chapter 2, "Journal/Research/Invention," aims to show ways that a writer forces commitment. Writers write. We provide a full box of suggestions to keep you working, but the goal is for you to strike off on your own. The journal is your lab, your practice field, where you can make false starts, mistakes, and discoveries. However, commitment to writing also involves commitment to learning about the world into which and from which you draw your narratives.

Chapter 3 contains the exploration of "Point of View." In the journal, a person very close to the intimate "I" does almost all of the recording. Literary creations, however, often involve a less literally autobiographical "I." Who is the speaker in the story or poem? What difference does it make? Exploring these key questions requires careful reading and a number of exercises—occasions—to help you become confident in handling this complex, unavoidable issue.

In Chapter 4, "Language Is Your Medium," you have an opportunity to exercise all the muscles in the body of words that you need to command and to get them working in harmony. You don't expect a landscape painter to succeed without knowing anything about lines, shapes, and colors, and about brushes, pigments, and canvas. The writer too must master the materials, in this case the materials of language. Most of us take language for granted—it's something we're born to. Remember, however, that the demands put on your language skills are now heightened and your attention to language must be similarly heightened if you are to develop a useful style. We think you will enjoy these jumping jacks, push-ups, and other language calisthenics.

These first chapters are grounded in general issues so you can come to understand the ways in which any writing task can be creative. In the next ten chapters, you will explore the specific conventions and special concerns of the major genres: poetry, prose narrative, and drama. Wherever possible, we also show how the genres leap their boundaries and how techniques useful in one may be useful in another.

The genre chapters combine information, examples, and exercises and contain both professional and student work to show various levels of achievement. We have isolated the major problems that beginners have and examined the nature and causes of those problems. Often we suggest solutions. We are convinced that effective creative writing is a network of solved problems.

Each of the three parts devoted to genre exploration begins with a chapter focusing on the conventions through which that genre defines itself. Our bias here is that without coming to grips with the conventions, you cannot reach an audience, nor can you ever become effectively unconventional. We deal with foundations on which a variety of houses may be built.

In this book, *conventional* refers to the customs or protocols of a literary type. Just as religious groups have set patterns of observance and just as a formal meeting has its way of getting things done (following, for instance, *Robert's Rules of Order*), so literary genres have their conventional—customary—methods of expression. Conventions enable everyone to start off with an agreement about the ground rules, and so, it is *through* these conventions, not *despite* them, that creative expression takes place. Through them, you meet the audience halfway.

Part V provides a writer's toolbox. Chapter 15, "From Drafting to Revision to Submission," aims at further development of editorial skills. It also explains and illustrates the conventions of manuscript form and discusses strategies for submitting work to editors. We have included useful Web sites. The book concludes with a glossary of key terms we use in the book.

As much as possible we have followed our own classroom practice, which focuses on providing an opportunity to write and receive feedback. Our approach is more like that of writers and editors than of critics. We have tried to give a realistic picture of the processes, demands, and rewards of the game. We cannot, of course, touch on everything. You will need someone—a teacher, workshop leader, or editor—to deal with the exceptions and complications, of which there are many. We want to stress again that this book is about showing useful techniques for the beginner. No book teaches; practice does.

For a Teacher or Workshop Leader

So that both you and your students might have a variety from which to choose, we have included many more examples and exercises than anyone could use, even in a year-long course or workshop.

We invite you, as we do all our readers, to send us the results of these exercises for possible inclusion in future editions, as well as exercises of your own. On one hand, we would also like to hear about aspects of craft you would like to see treated more fully. On the other hand, where do you think we could cut back? Remembering that this text is for beginning creative writers, please let us know what elements we missed completely. As an editor out in the field, you become our best source for improving the book.

———————●———————

Though the voice in the *Creative Writer's Handbook* remains in the first person plural, Phil Jason is not responsible for any flaws in this revision. Still, a good deal of his thinking underpins the book. I am grateful for his friendship over thirty years. Without him, the book would not exist.

I would also like to thank the many colleagues and students who have contributed to all the previous and present editions. I especially thank Vivian Garcia of Longman, who has constantly encouraged me as well as given me direction. I thank the many friends in the field who have let me use their work or read and commented on sections: Kate Blackwell, Phillip Gerard, Bob Hicok, John Kern, Lee Lawrence, Alice McDermott, E. Ethelbert Miller, Linda Pastan, Marjorie Schwarzer, and the many workshop students upon whom I beta-tested exercises and portions of the text. Above all, I thank my wife, Jane Fox, who has read, edited, and lived through this revision so many times that her name also should be on the cover.

Allan B. Lefcowitz

PART ONE

• • A WRITER'S CONCERNS • •

MODEL JOURNAL ENTRIES

Selections from *Creative Writer's Handbook* Journal

8/31/07: Start. Goal a chapt a wk. Focus on text for 21st century. Update many examples (read poetry especially) and work in connections with computers and Internet. From this point of view the hill looks long and steep. Happy birthday to me.

9/15/07: Send Phil revision for chapt 1 with suggestions for inset advice on how to respond to reader feedback. Can't cover all the bases. Beginning writers will feel personally injured if their work is not loved. I always feel as if I'm sticking a pin in a balloon. The thin-skinned ones burst but the serious ones understand that they have to patch the holes and blow more air in. I'm not sure I like the image . . . suggests hot air.

10/08/07: Already two chapts behind since Phil decided to take his life in a different direction. I'll have a greater burden for the poetry sections. Already started to read a ton of poetry. Want to work in the Bob H's poem about the VT massacre. Too early to think about poetry. Catch up on Journal. I'm sure I want to cut separate chapt on research and combine all into one. Beginning writers, I suspect, will do most of their research on the Internet. Work it in and also the dangers. Journal/research all about stoking the fire. At least I'm taking my own advice. Do as I do.

11/22/07: Sisyphus should have had a book to push uphill. Thought I was on a good pace but realized yesterday that need to do more linkage between genres. In a way, it's all one giant category of literature with poetry, fiction, etc., as sub-genre. The foundation is love of storytelling and language with bricks of point of view, voice, etc. Beginning writers may be led to see false boundaries because of the way we talk about genres academically. Need a few days off to recharge the batteries.

12/31/07: Four weeks behind but starting to feel that direction of new ed. is clearer. Still I feel "time's chariot rushing near." Work in the poems on dinosaurs. Bob's poem will go in the practice chapter as sample of poetic response to immediate events. What with Iraq, there are plenty of events to respond to. I got to thinking about Owen's "Dulce et Decorum Est." To work. To work.

2/27/08: Only two weeks behind. Fiction is going faster since I decided to cut the amount of new work. If I were smart I'd just change the schedule. But then I'd probably get behind the new one. E-mail Gerard to get permission on his piece. I wonder if it would make a good summation for the nonfiction chapter.

3/6/08: E-mail editor (Vivian) about progress. Mention in nonfiction something about the recent hullabaloo. How much fiction can you let creep into your nonfiction? Modern epistemology including deconstructivism would suggest that anything can go since nothing is certain once it goes into words. Everything is point of view and shifts and we only share on the margins, if at all. But I don't think that's much help to writers since, in the final analysis, the same old problems exists for them of shaping something to take in. It's the problem solving that occupies the writer and that, in the last analysis, is what the book is about.

3/14/08 Ides of March: About two months to go before due date. I work well under pressure, as do many writers. Though I recommend to students that they find a time to write everyday, I often don't follow my own advice and put in long days followed by neglect. Perhaps I should mention in chapt 1 an interesting aspect about the writing process: how a writer suddenly realizes that he has pushed the rock over the crown of the hill and is on the down slope of the work. It doesn't occur when 50% of the work is done; it occurs when your eyes can see where you are going. Very mysterious, especially in plotted pieces. You see the end of the voyage and, though lots of writing is still to be done, you feel a burden lifted, your steps quicken, and your steps become surer.

3/20/08: Almost done with drama section. Decided to use a student play I found in *Perfect Ten* because it is closer to what the beginning playwright can manage. The problem with longer plays for CWH is that a student writer simply doesn't have the time to do the development work. On the same principle, perhaps I should consider dropping the novel discussion. Onward!

4/1/08: Definitely have dropped the section on "Tools and Resources" because the Internet has become the resource of preference for my students. I'll put some of the material in the Instructors Manual and teachers can hand it out if they feel the need. So much has changed about writing and research since we first conceived of CWH. I guess I'll start saying to my students: "In the old days we had to walk to school uphill, both ways." Or something similar about the card catalogue, typewriters, and no air conditioning in the classroom. Just 45 days left before the manuscript is due. I'm going to make the finish line on time.

CHAPTER 1

WORKING LIKE A WRITER

"Finish it? Why would I want to finish it?"

"Writing remains my unshakable morning habit.
I am still trying to learn my trade, and with
advancing age see more clearly than ever how
much there is still to learn."

John Updike

Pleasure and Passion

Throughout *The Creative Writer's Handbook,* we focus on the craft of writing. We stress the importance of understanding conventions and mastering techniques in order to create a successful work. Since we do not say much in other chapters about the pleasure a writer receives, we'll do that here.

Some of you will delight in writing to express an emotion or idea. You will have built up a head of steam about something, and only a poem or play will release that energy. Some of you will write to wrestle with personal demons. Others because it pleases you to amaze people or to make them laugh. Many of you will enjoy playing and working with words and forms, and in those moments of "getting it right," of solving the endless series of challenges that each piece of writing presents. Mostly you will write for a blend of these pleasures.

Even if you hope that you can make a living by doing something that appears on the surface easier than laying bricks or selling them (but is actually much more demanding), you still need to start with a sense that setting words on paper pleases you and that pleasing an audience pleases you.

Few accomplishments are as rewarding and meaningful as creating a literary work through which you share your visions of the human experience or, at a more modest level, through which you entertain and divert people for a moment. When that sharing happens, the world is a better place—if only because it is a little less lonely. These are lofty and distant goals. On a day-to-day basis, writers learn to find satisfaction in the pains of creation.

What can we do about stoking the fire? Not much. The passions, the needs, the ongoing or anticipated pleasures that fuel the urge to write are as individual as each writer. Without the fire, nothing happens. But desire is not enough. Having passion without technique is one sure way to dampen the fire.

Attitudes

> "*What is written without effort
> is in general read without pleasure.*"
>
> Samuel Johnson

The desire to be a writer is not sufficient. You need to develop the attitudes that can help carry you from the desire to the reality. This chapter focuses on one attitude in particular—*taking a professional stance* to your work, to your audience, and to your editor.

Unlike the writer who may have many motives for writing, the reader usually has one motive for reading: to experience writing that pleases both in its shape and subject. Of course, experts and students in a field—let us say nuclear physics—might slog their way through a jungle of poor prose to acquire the information they need to understand the Big Bang. Most of us would not. To satisfy the readers' desire for writing that pleases, you have to be aware of their needs and then take pains to satisfy them. In fact, 90 percent of what is "creative" in creative writing grows from a professional attitude toward taking pains over fine points that the amateur thinks of as impeding details.

For most of us, achieving a mature stance toward writing does not simply happen.

You need to understand that "good" creative writing is a subset of good writing in general. In all effective writing, the conventions of English mechanics and usage (grammar, punctuation, spelling, word order) remain relevant. You cannot think of these conventions as a drag on your creativity; in fact, they are the very bedrock that allows others to share your creativity. For example, conventional spelling allows you and the reader to share a way of immediately recognizing a word. Misspell two meny words and sea how rapidly the godwill of your redear disappears.

Certainly, you may take license with conventions for special purposes. You may develop a character who speaks ungrammatically, or you may decide not to use capitals or punctuation for special effects, as did e e cummings. However, flawed prose does not automatically become good poetry. Carelessness, slovenliness, and ignorance do not become virtues just because you are trying to be creative.

A professional writer is not satisfied with self-expression alone. If you write only for yourself, you have severely limited your audience. Even if you do not hope to make a living from writing (few writers do so anyway), your writing will become more effective when you are aware that you must please, involve, awaken, provoke, excite, move other people. The sense of a potential audience should create in you both energy and a feeling of obligation. Unless you make something happen to a reader, you are not doing anything worthwhile as a writer. (There are therapeutic uses of writing in psychiatry, of course, but those are not the concerns of this book.)

How do you determine your success? One way is by being in a course, workshop, or writer's group that will provide feedback from an instructor and the other participants. They are your first sounding boards, to be replaced at some point by editors or directors and by your own developed editorial ability. Learning to invite and make positive use of this feedback—even of harshly negative commentary—is essential to your growth as a writer.

"I love criticism just so long as it's unqualified praise."
Noel Coward

Most of us would agree with Coward. However, we are not likely to get unqualified praise from anyone—except loved ones, we hope. Most of us will get *criticism,* a word we will avoid in *The Creative Writer's Handbook.* We use *feedback* instead of *criticism* because the latter has—unfortunately—acquired a negative connotation, especially in workshop situations. More to the point, *feedback* describes the process much more accurately. You "feed" the poem, short story, play, or whatever to one or more people in the hope that it will give them pleasure. In turn, you hope that they will have something useful to feed "back" to you—praise, certainly, but for the writer who takes a professional stance, suggestions on how to improve the manuscript. In the case of longer works, such as a play or novel, the creation may be still in progress, and you seek feedback about relatively smaller units to see if there are any problems before you invest more time and energy.

The glow you feel when your work is praised generally or in detail should always be tempered by the knowledge that the person who is praising the, let us say, poem may be someone who is practicing the better part of valor by giving you what you want or who was simply amazed that you could attempt to write a poem in the first place ... or who has low standards. They cannot discern the effective from the ineffective. You may, of course, simply have written something praiseworthy and, if so, you should modestly say "thank you" and get back to writing your next piece. And if the feedback is totally negative, shrug your shoulders and say to yourself, "*Non disputandum est gustibus.*" (There is no arguing about taste.) Never, never attempt to bludgeon the person into telling you that your work is perfect. It's undignified and wasted effort. We are only half joking.

More essential to your development as a writer is learning how to respond to the feedback that falls short of total praise. If, for example, someone tells you to expand, subtract, explain, change the word order, modify a plot element, or any of the apparent or real problems that can occur in a work, your proper response is to thank him or her, take down notes, read written comments carefully, and either edit the work or ignore the feedback. You change your text in response to the feedback when it is clearly useful; you ignore it when your gut feeling is that the responder is wrong. In Chapter 15, "From Drafting to Revision to Submission," we present some scenarios about ways to accept and reject various types of feedback.

Good feedback leads you to reconsider what appears on the page and to look at it through another set of eyes. In the end, though, the work is yours and you are the one who will suffer if you change something just because of a criticism. In our experience, well-considered feedback allows us to locate some flaw we either had not seen or had seen but hoped others would not because we did not want to do the difficult work of rewriting. The fix recommended may not be the one we need but is likely to lead to the one that will be a success.

In a group feedback situation, do unto others as you would want done unto yourself. Give praise where praise is due, and give help where you think it would help improve a reader's pleasure in the work that has been fed to you. If you see nothing interesting in the work, silence is the most effective strategy because it sends an indirect message to a serious writer.

It is most useful to begin any feedback by applauding the interesting and/or effective aspects of the work before launching into the problems you see. You always need to let the writer know specifically what aspects of the work pleases, and why they are effective or interesting, and what aspects displease and why. It is not useful to state that some aspect of a work is a problem unless you can give the reason it is or may be a problem. Here are two formulas:

1. I liked X because...
2. I had a problem with Y because...

In short, the most valuable feedback stays focused on the work.

Whether you receive feedback in a workshop or from an editor (workshop leader), after your first draft, one of your revisions should be in response to technical feedback. This book gives you the tools to identify and talk professionally about something you or someone else has written.

 THE WRITER PARTICIPATES IN WRITING

> *"The more that you read,*
> *The more things you will know.*
> *The more that you learn,*
> *The more places you'll go."*
>
> Dr. Seuss

Participation means reading, listening, and going to plays and movies. Experience as many and as varied instances as possible of the genre you want to create. Being a writer means being more conscious of how the game is played. Almost without exception, great athletes are fans of their sport; artists visit galleries and museums; musicians attend concerts. It is reasonable for writers to read, both for pleasure and for professional development. (In Chapter 13, "Dialogue and Its Problems," we have something to say about a special burden placed on playwrights.)

Existing stories, plays, and poems are the inescapable context for new work in each genre. You must know genre conventions, the scope of literature, and the contemporary literary environment. If you have aspirations to write poetry, you should be constantly reading poetry. You need to read your contemporaries as well as the major voices of past literary periods. Read, analyze, ponder, imitate, and record your impressions. Just as important, read work that opens new vistas. Don't stick to only one genre, subgenre, or time period. Perhaps you only intend to write science fiction. Still, your stories are likely to benefit from reading Homer, William Faulkner, and Joyce Carol Oates.

As you read or see plays, keep your eyes open for blunders you think the writer has made. Work out how you might have handled the writing problem differently. Look for techniques that you can borrow and apply to your own writing. Imagine your own variation on another writer's characters, images, themes, or premises. Writing is a response to other writing just as much as it is a response to life.

 ## A DIGRESSION: FOR THE CLASSROOM USER

- You always wanted to try writing something, so you thought you would take this course or a workshop. A good enough reason. Your desire to experiment, to try something new, needs an outlet. Take maximum advantage. Though you may never go further with your writing than this course, you will have satisfied your curiosity. You will come away with a sense of the demands placed on a creative writer, and your appreciation of literature should be enhanced by the fact that you have faced the series of complex problems that a successful writer must solve.

- You always had trouble with writing, so you thought you would take a course that focuses on it. A good motive, but perhaps this is the wrong course. A course in creative writing is not intended to remediate grammar and mechanics, sentence structure, and organization. This course assumes you have a firm control over the basic conventions of the written language. On the other hand, if you write without error but not *effectively,* a creative writing course can help you. The attention to writing strategies, diction, flow, figurative language, and other issues can become a practice field for any writer. All writing becomes creative when it escapes being bland, meandering, and impersonal. In fact, from that point of view, all effective writing is creative. So, yes, your efforts will contribute to your general writing ability—though only if the fundamentals are well in hand.

- You need to fulfill a distribution requirement and this was the only humanities course that wasn't at an hour before you hate to rise. A practical reason, certainly, but not an impressive one. The key to what happens now is your attitude. Get the most out of the situation. Write, even if you only write imitations. You will meet some interesting people, and you will have fun reading their work as well as the work of accomplished, published writers. Remember also that everyone can benefit from the kind of engagement with the language and human issues that this course will offer.

◄━━━━━► WORKING HABITS

As we indicated earlier, assuming a professional posture keeps you focused on improving your writing. Professionals understand the need to take pains with the details and to approach their task with energy and discipline.

You have to commit time to writing. We know one writer who pretends she is going to a job. She dresses, has breakfast, packs a lunch, and then is off to her writing space for a set time. She will not take phone calls unless they are associated with her writing work. (The answering machine is her gatekeeper.) She leaves her cell phone on silent mode or checks incoming callers on the screen before answering. If the muse doesn't visit, she writes in her journal. As rigorous as that discipline may seem, she validates for herself (and others) that she takes her writing seriously. Another friend, who has a full-time job in local government, rises at 5:00 a.m. to cram in an hour of writing before leaving for work.

Many writers set up reward systems to help them get through a scheduled writing period. Promise yourself that after an hour (or five pages, or a draft of a chapter) that you can have a snack, or surf the Internet, or browse the newspaper.

For some people, such bribes or routines are unnecessary. These lucky people either have discipline built into their souls or are so rewarded by the writing process itself that they can hardly pull themselves away from it. Most of us, however, need to impose a routine on ourselves so that we will write even when we are not in the mood. Once writing is a daily habit, just like an athlete you will not feel comfortable when you skip a session. When "it's time to write," you will be ready—just like when it's time to jog your five miles. When you find that your routine no longer works, try something new. Shift the time, rearrange where you work or work someplace else, accelerate or slow down the revision process.

Still, the commitment to writing time needs reinforcement and support. Here are some hints for keeping you feeling like a professional and growing as a writer:

1. Make your writing space as inviting and efficient as possible. We assume that most of our readers will be working on a computer, so it makes sense to have a well-organized setup for the monitor, mouse, keyboard, CPU, and printer (and paper). Given that a slip of the finger or power outages will happen, back up constantly. (We even know some writers who are so concerned about the possibility of a disaster that they keep a copy of their backup in another place plus hard copy.) Have the old technology also conveniently available: pencils, pens, and paper. This practice is obviously true of those who still write first drafts by hand or those who keep notes as they go along, even notes from information gleaned from the Internet. One blessing of the Internet is that you can copy information directly into the pieces on which you are working or keep it handy in a separate file. Out of habit, we have dictionaries, handbooks, and style manuals within arm's reach, but the ease with which the essential reference tools can be

accessed on your computer probably will allow you to keep your working surface a bit less cluttered.

2. If you need to be away from your writing space during writing time, be ready to write anyway. Have your notebook (or laptop) with you or a PDA, Bluetooth, or other handheld device. If you have an inspiration, you can always message yourself on your cell phone. If you're more comfortable with the old technology, be sure to have a pen or pencil to write in your notebook. Some writers we know even keep a pad and pencil by their bed ready for the idea that springs from a dream or sleeplessness.

3. Even when you are running hot on a piece of writing, a moment will come when you feel your inspiration or energy run dry. Rather than continue writing until you have squeezed all the juices from that session, stop in the middle of a sentence, or scene, or line that you are fairly sure you know how to finish. In your next writing session you will have some work that you can complete easily—a running start.

4. While you are writing, do not talk specifically about your work to friends, family, or teachers. Telling your story or writing plans over a brandy to a fascinated lover has one doubtful benefit attached to two certain downsides. Talking out your idea does get you immediate feedback. If the feedback pumps you up, however, it also may remove the inner urge to communicate the hard way—in writing. And if the feedback is unenthusiastic, you might abandon an idea that is, in fact, a good one but just doesn't "sound" good in a crowded bar. Your job is not to talk about but to write about.

5. Don't keep yourself from starting to write or moving on in a piece by looking for an ideal beginning, ideal phrasing, or ideal structure. The answer to the question "Where should I begin?" is that same answer you give to the question "Where does a 800-pound gorilla sleep?" In fact, not only can you begin writing your poem, story, or play any place you want to, but you also need not be concerned about the conventions, coherence, logic, or any other responsibility to the reader *just so long as you are creating a draft*.

(This paradox is only apparent. It makes no difference where you begin or by what fits and start you proceed. What counts is where you decide to have your reader begin—in other words, what matters is the final draft. It is as likely as not that you won't discover the most effective beginning until you have written for a time. Don't try to be perfectly polished as you go along, thinking you can avoid rewriting. Remember the fate of Grande, a character in Camus's *The Plague* who believed he would write the perfect novel if only he could find the ideal opening sentence. He never got beyond it as he wrote and presented to friends a variation of the opening sentence over and over again. So don't be afraid of letting the material flow undisturbed. In later drafts your editor–self can take over from your writer–self and channel the flow in useful directions. A corollary of this recommendation is to keep moving forward even when you realize that you will have to change something earlier in your draft. You are going to discover that you will have to change more and going backward over and over again can be an infinite regress. When you realize that a change will be needed, just drop a note to yourself to that effect right at that point. And charge forward.)

6. Some writers occasionally have "writer's luck" and produce a perfect draft without revision. But most effective writing is the result of rewriting and then rewriting. (We might note that contemporary writers are blessed because computers allow them the opportunity to produce dozens of drafts without the labor of retyping.) Make the revision process an essential part of your attitude toward writing. In a first draft you will usually set down the material you need to shape and perfect. Think of that first draft as a rough-cut piece of wood that must be sanded with finer and finer grades of sandpaper.

7. Leave some time between drafts. We tend to know what we mean when we've just thought it and (supposedly) pinned the idea down in writing. Some distance allows us to discover defects. Give yourself at least a day away from a draft before revising. We know that under a deadline such as a due assignment you may not have the luxury. The solution: start earlier. After all, how can you "*re*-vision" if you haven't first stopped looking at something?

8. After your draft feels ready for a short walk in public, take the risk (for the benefit) of requesting feedback. Group situations are designed for that purpose. As we've mentioned already, you have to be ready to assess feedback and to use it for improving your text. Be aware, however, that it is easier to please your parent or spouse than it is to please an independent audience such as an editor. Seek frank but unbiased feedback.

The most important perspective for any writer is to set high standards and to be ready for disappointment. As coaches say about exercise, "No pain, no gain." We are not suggesting that writing is a form of punishment, but it is a constant struggle. And, just as athletes can find great pleasure in preparing for the game, you can find as many pleasures in the process of writing as in the results. If only results—the winning or losing—matter to you, you can find success in something as insignificant as betting on the toss of a coin.

Something essential to you must be at the heart of the endeavor for you to invest so much effort in, let us say, hours of exercise for one minute on a balance beam. As we have said previously, there must be satisfactions in the exercise itself—the doing. What we do as writers is practice, plan, and engage in the intricate pressures of choosing well, tearing apart, rediscovering, rebuilding—in short, recognizing that literary works *become*. And when they've become successful, we give pleasure to others.

*"Asking a writer what he thinks about criticism is
like asking a lamppost what it feels about dogs."*

John Osborne

A WORD ABOUT INTENTIONS

Eudora Welty said, "It was not my intention—it never was—to invent a charac-ter who should speak for me, the author, the person. A character is in a story to fill a role there, and the character's life is defined by that surrounded—indeed is created by his own story" (from *One Writer's Beginnings*, Harvard University Press, 1984). The implication of Welty's statement is that her writing isn't a disguise for something she wishes to hide in her fiction, a kind of sugarcoating for what she would like us to swallow about morality, politics, or the ultimate purposes and significance of almost anything. Although any character in a play or story, any speaker in a poem, is a partial revelation of the writer, the inten-tion to reveal one's self or sell one's views is not a necessary or useful approach to the art.

When you write honestly, you can't help but reveal yourself. Your world-view is on display because it is the lens through which you look at experience, choose words, plots, characters, images, and settings. The conscious pressure of trying to make a point—of sending a message—can block the flow and distort the final shape of any literary work. An artwork, when it goes well, has a life of its own, its own demands. Sometimes *it* has something to say, and you need to let the writing process make such discoveries. (Allegories, of course, do begin intentionally but the great ones, like *Pilgrim's Progress* or *Animal Farm*, quickly begin to escape the message so that the characters live.)

To quote Welty again, "If somewhere in its course your work seems to have come into a life of its own, and you can stand back from it and leave it be, you are looking then at your own subject—I feel."

Aside from thematic or didactic intentions, we often find ourselves highly motivated by aesthetic ones—we want to put the craft on display. We act like the tennis player who falls down after every difficult shot to punctuate its diffi-culty. "Look how clever I am" or "look how hard I am trying," such an atti-tude appears to say. However, no one enjoys reading for long a collection of skill exhibitions—not even creative writing teachers. Writing that only calls at-tention to the author's virtuosity is rarely successful.

Nor should you approach your work as if preparing a treasure hunt. Don't put yourself in the position of having to explain that you have purposely buried a hidden meaning for the reader to dig out. Writing is not like a jigsaw puzzle that the reader puts together after searching out the missing pieces. Of course, the ideas or characters or events may be so complex that complex forms are the only way to show them, as in Faulkner or T. S. Eliot. But the purpose of complex presentation is not to force the reader to dig out but rather the only way the writer can dig in.

While you write, themes will emerge as you struggle with language, form, and characters. Though it is convenient to begin with an idea, most often a character, situation, image, or even a word that sticks in the mind is the typical and most useful starting place. Trust the writing process and the reader. Don't ask, "How am I going to get across that our struggles in Iraq or Afghanistan are caused by our economic interests (or foolishness or commitment to ideals)?" Ask, "What would my characters do next?" "How do they feel about the situation in which they have been thrust?" "What words will best connect with the words I have just put down?" "How do I make this dialogue a struggle between characters, not a lecture?" Only in the late stages of revision, when a work has announced its purpose— *its* intention—can we allow ourselves some calculating decisions about the emerging ideas, and then only to be true to the work we have come to understand. If the process sounds mysterious to you, it is.

Does trust in the process mean that writers proceed blindly ignorant about where they are going? Sometimes yes and sometimes no. That's not the issue. Even a writer who starts with a detailed plan needs to be open and flexible. A writer's intentions are not what finally matter to the reader, and holding on to intentions or outlines too fiercely or justifying a work in terms of intentions is a more acute case of nearsightedness than writing without a clear direction.

In spite of what we have just said, we are not partisans of the idea that art is an end in itself. At bottom, literature means and is about what it means to be human. What Cynthia Ozick calls "a corona of moral purpose" (in "Innovation and Redemption: What Literature Means," *Art and Ardor,* 1983) surrounds every significant work of literary art.

This moral purpose is different, however, from saying that literature must be directly applicable, like directions for building bookshelves or a sermon. We each have our own way of knowing that literature affirms our ability to choose. In writing, we are choosing—asserting our freedom and capacity for growth and change. When we do this for ourselves, we do this for others as well: We do it for everyone. This, as Ozick points out, is the essential, implicit moral of creative acts. It is inherent; the rest is skill.

Good luck and remember that everything on the page sends a message.

"If there's a book you really want to read, but it hasn't been written yet, then you must write it."

Toni Morrison

2

JOURNAL/RESEARCH/INVENTION

"I am enamoured of my journal."

Sir Walter Scott

 ### WHY KEEP A JOURNAL?

As you've probably already noticed, we use many sports metaphors and analogies in this book. This strategy is not merely stylistic; it is also thematic. We truly believe that writing (some might say all art) satisfies a basic human impulse—the need to play.

This chapter is about ways that writers prepare for playing the game well. What worked for them will work for you.

Almost all writers keep a journal and almost all do research (broadly considered). These everyday tasks have changed dramatically because of computers and the Internet. The underlying reasons for doing the work, however, have not changed. In the first section of the chapter, we discuss the hows and whys of journal keeping and, in the second, the role of research in preparing to write. Both are in the service of the writer's invention, the final section.

 ## KEEPING JOURNALS

Many writers keep several different journals or notebooks:

> A *working journal* in which they practice writing and work out parts or whole drafts of a poem, story, essay, or play.
>
> A *journal of ideas* for future writing or a record of work in progress.
>
> A *commonplace book* in which they jot down quotations from their reading, along with their reactions, as models or for inspiration. With computer programs, these may include downloads from the Internet, photographs...anything.

A single journal can serve all of these purposes. (Computer journal programs now allow a writer to combine all these activities along with downloads from research. We'll say something later about the flexibility inherent in the technology.)

What follows is an excerpt from a real journal that contains aspects of all three journal activities. The Greek poet George Seferis is reading to get himself started on his writing; he is reacting to his experience; he is free-associating; and, finally, he is starting to develop a poem.

> Tuesday Morning, October 8, 1946
>
> I have been working on Cavafy again since last Saturday afternoon. I am reading articles about the poet written in the past and more recently. They bore me. Too much "literature," too much padding in all of them; very few noteworthy observations. I don't yet know if I'm in Cavafy's ambience. A thought put aside for the moment: *I am trying to return to the habit of working* [italics added].
>
> I'll read every morning—I started yesterday—about a hundred lines of the *Iliad*.
>
> Yesterday and today were superb days, too much for me; they distract me; I feel terribly lost. As in a ruined house, I have to put many things in order. I don't know if I'll ever be able to reconstruct it.
>
> After swimming: the light is such that it absorbs you as blotter does ink; it absorbs the personality.
>
> > Days are stones. Flintstones
> > that accidentally found each other and made two or three sparks,

> stones on the threshing floor, struck by horseshoes,
>   and crushing many people.
> pebbles in the water with ephemeral rings,
> wet and multicolored little stones at the seashore,
> or lekythoi, gravestones that sometimes stop the passerby
> or bas-reliefs with the rider who went far out to sea
> or Marsyas or Priapus, groups of phallus-bearers.
> Days are stones; they crumble one on top of the other.
>
> from *A Poet's Journal*

The final entry appears to be the conclusion of a mind voyage Safaris took on paper.

Journal keeping can get even more elaborate. Some writers keep separate journals for all aspects of their work: drafts, exercises, dreams, ideas, quotations, newspaper clippings, and so on. We even know one writer who keeps a separate journal for submissions to publications and payments for manuscripts. Most of us are hardly so organized (or need to be), and so we recommend much less elaborate journal keeping for you. Of course, as you would suspect, the flexibility of computer programs allows you to do all these tasks without a multitude of physical journals, as well as allowing you to do useful internal searches.

Whether you keep your journal on your computer or on paper, the point is to keep at it. Writing needs to be a regular part of your life. Many would-be writers hope that an occasional stab at a narrative in any genre when the mood strikes them will produce significant results. That attitude is something like expecting to play a par round of golf by playing only once a month.

Let us put the matter less kindly. You should take an armchair writer about as seriously as you take an armchair athlete. Writers write; posers talk about writing. The journal is one place for you to be a writer.

"You fail only if you stop writing."

Ray Bradbury

 ## Your Journal

Today, buy yourself a computer program designed for journaling, a physical journal, or both. Note that you also can download freeware on which to keep your journal or use your word processing program. We suggest no particular program both because each one has features that may appeal to you and because new computer and Internet programs are being devised even as we write this. Electronic tools for jotting ideas down on the fly are available on hand-helds, or your cell phones or some other form of technological wizardry. You can even send yourself a text message or photo to record an idea or event that might be the source for a poem, story, essay, or play. If you need a real audience, write someone e-mails and save them as Lee Lawrence did (see pp. 20–22). These days, saving detail is both easier and more complex—easier because of the rich variety of tools; more complex because so much information is now available that selection of what to store can be challenging.

If you want to keep your journal in handwriting, we suggest that you buy either a ruled composition book with a hard cover (approximately 8½ by 11 inches) or, if you want something more portable, a hardcover "record book" (5 by 8 inches) with ruled lines. The idea is to keep your journal in a form that ensures permanence. Avoid loose-leaf notebooks or spiral notebooks from which you can inadvertently rip pages. Tiny flip notebooks don't give you enough room to jot down more than a few words. (Many writers, however, do carry around some kind of small notebook for ideas that come to them in the middle of a workday, a dance, or in their dreams.) If you carry your journal around with you, be sure to write your name, address, and phone number at the beginning along with the statement that, in case of loss, you will reward the returner. On the computer, of course, back up…back up…back up.

Once you have your journal, practice making it part of your daily routine. At first you will probably need a conscious strategy for keeping it up. Pick a time of day that you promise *always* to write. The time you choose will be one that works for you, but it makes sense to choose one in which you are not likely to be interrupted by a phone call or the meter reader. For those who keep journals electronically, you can set your computer to boot up your journal automatically when you turn it on as an invitation to work.

If you can't keep your writer's notebook every day, then set up an appointment with it for at least three times a week. Discipline problems? Find some way to reward yourself for keeping it or to punish yourself when you don't. You may have to modify your behavior to develop the journal-keeping habit, but once you have developed the habit, you will no more think of not writing in your journal than you would think of not brushing your teeth or running your laps.

It won't do simply to greet the blank page with "Hello, dear journal, I've got nothing to write. Goodbye." That's like doing one pushup and believing that you have exercised. You have to give the journal enough time so that you can work up a sweat—twenty to thirty minutes a session minimum, enough to get you beyond simply saying "hello" and into the rhythm of writing. To put it another way: You have to run more than a block to work up a sweat.

Journal keeping has nothing to do with feeling inspired. You write in it because you are or want to be a writer. And even when the goddess Inspiration has deserted you, you continue to write on to prepare yourself for her return.

WHAT TO WRITE IN THE JOURNAL

What you stuff into your journal depends on your way of looking at and react-ing to what you see, learn, and remember. The journal is the writing place in which you have no commitment to anyone but yourself; you write what you want to write. We can, however, offer you some basic principles that can make your journal more useful over the short and long run.

In some writers' journals, you might find:

lists of books to read

drafts of letters

quotations

columns of words

bits of dialogue

dreams

ramblings about events and people

memories

story possibilities

descriptions

lists of intriguing words and phrases

pasted-in articles

downloaded research material (for a journal kept on a computer)
... in short, anything.

Some of this material simply keeps you working as a writer. Some of it is the record of your thoughts, a place to hold and look at your past self at some future time. Some of it will end up in writing meant for other eyes.

John Steinbeck kept a journal in which he blended observations about his daily life with reminders to himself about the ongoing challenges of his work-in-progress, *The Grapes of Wrath*. Here is an excerpt:

> Early start this morning. Can't ever tell. Worked long and slowly yester-day. Don't know whether it was good, but it was a satisfactory way to work and I wish it would be that way every day. I've lost this rushed feeling finally and can get back to the easy method of day by day—which is as it should be. Got the iron gate for an autograph. That is a bargain. Today I shall work slowly and try to get that good feeling again. It must be. Just a little bit every day. A little bit every day. And then it will be through. And the story is coming to me fast now. And it will be fast from now on. Movement fast but the detail slow as always. I seem to be delaying pretty badly today. Half an hour gone already and I don't care because the little details are coming, are getting clearer all the time. So the more I wait, the more of this book will get written.

How about the jail. Today, the preacher and Tom and the raid on the tent and the killing of the preacher. Tom's escape. Kills. Goes back to the camp to hide. Tom—half bitterness, half humane. Escapes in the night. Hunted, hunted. Over the last pages Tom hangs like a spirit around the camp. And in the water brings stolen food. Must get to work now. The thing speeds up.

from Working Days: The Journals of The Grapes of Wrath

Though anything goes in the journal, you do have a responsibility to yourself as a writer. Imagine, for example, that you have written the following journal entries:

> I met a strange man on a train and was he interesting. He told me about his life. He might make an interesting story.

> The mountains in the north of Italy are simply tremendous. So big and with such lovely names.

> April. I really feel low today. It's the lowest I've felt in years. He disappointed me in the worst way.

> Friday the 13th. A good idea for a story about a future world based on an incurable disease. I wonder what would happen?

Suppose today you decide to look back over your old journals because your mind is sluggish and you want some ideas for a story or some precise information about an event in the past that has come up in a poem or personal essay. The old journal entries just cited would hardly trigger images with which to recapture the past, let alone your past feelings. The entries lack alertness, an awareness of the senses, discrimination, contemplation, or imagination. They indicate that you had worked neither at seeing nor at reporting. In fact, precisely when did you write all that?

Compare those journal entries to the ones Lee Lawrence kept in Afghanistan and Iraq while researching the lives of Army chaplains. She also kept her writer's diary as "e-mails to Bill [her husband] which was my form of journaling.... I need a reader in mind and the only person I can think who would want to 'listen' is Bill. So I would write on my laptop and then copy and paste into e-mails when I had access to an Internet connection. Some read more like letters...." Notice that she is already writing for an audience.

 ### JOURNAL EXCERPTS

26/04/07 Mazar-e-Sharif

Hours later, I wade across the camp through the deep gravel (I am getting really really sick of gravel—the army has it everywhere!) to a bunch of B-huts behind the chapel where, I hear, the Croats are hosting a barbecue....

30/03 evening (Bagram)

The room is a windowless cell. The sound of rain and thunder—we had seen clouds illuminate in the distance before turning in and had speculated on whether somewhere someone was letting bombs loose. Turns out it was not the coalition forces but Zeus. Not that any of that light penetrated into my cell so that I slept as though buried until a banging on the door pulled me above ground. It was 10:20 by my watch; 12:20 by everyone else's. Lucky for my ego, Terry [her collaborator] had also slept and he was banging on my door because someone had just banged on his.

April 15, 2007 (Forward Operating Base Salerno)

The base is a giant colorless square—brown dirt, brown buildings, green tents made brownish by dust. Only the chapel sports some color with its fake stained glass windows in blues and reds and greens, the same color as the filters on the flashlights so that, from a distance, these dots of movement are not visible. A cypress tree rises like a dark green flame between my hardened quarters and the women's showers and latrines. I find myself looking for the cypress: it is spot of elegance in an otherwise barren place and, at night, it points straight up to an expanse of blackness out of which, as my eyes adjust, stars appear, pinpricks at first and sparse, then brighter beacons surrounded by a multitude of smaller sparks. The familiarity of the Great Dipper and the surety of the Northern star—anchors.

Bunker Time

Never really told you about my version of the explosion: in the shower and a noise that was loud, sudden and physical, the kind of noise you know is not good not so much because of what you heard, but because of the shift in the air that you felt. Once dressed, I figured I should maybe go outside – I think the building with the showers is hardened but it feels flimsy and somehow being in a place alone is worse than in company. So when I finally figured out that the laughter I was hearing was coming not from a tent but a bunker, I skedaddled. I hadn't been there long when another blast shook us all, and I looked outside the bunker and saw the smoke. Sgt Walker, the guy whose neck is so big the neck protection won't fit around, figured it hit 300 feet away. Someone said, "well the guards in the tower aren't moving, so...." We all looked at the wooden tower and all of sudden saw the two guards, chin tucked down, scamper down the wooden steps. We ran further inside the camp to another bunker where I sat, about the fifth one in, next to a young white guy who was supposed to have been back home in January but got stuck with the stop order. His wife is in the unit that is supposed to replace his here in Salerno. She is trying to transfer out; he's trying to get home. One story out of so very many. I heard Shields (or was it Marks) in a snippet of the Lehrer News Hour say how this war is being fought by just 2 percent of Americans, those in uniform and their families. Being here makes me realize just how true that is and the heavy price they pay in terms of their identity as a parent, as a spouse. And while I think it's fair to say that when you sign up for the military you should expect to have to deploy, it is wrong to be stretching them thin because of poor management and policy. The Air Force is cutting back while the Army is extending deployments—how can this be??

Back in the bunker, he told me about his wife but talk also veered to silliness, laughter being the single best reliever of tension. Another rocket hit, and then as I stared at the closest end of the bunker who should appear but Chaplain Bishop with his broad funny face. He was laughing, fetched us water then, when they were sweeping the area, he headed out to the hospital to check in on the medics. Sgt Walker took his place at the head of the bunker, his bulk filling the opening. He told me later that when he saw the chaplain he knew everything would be fine; that gave him the courage to stand out there. I stayed well inside the bunker, chaplain or no chaplain.... my only regret was that I didn't have my camera.

April 16, 2007

Interviewed two of the chaplains today along with a few soldiers waylayed as we walked about. Then the wind kicked up and the dust blew and we went around chasing dust-ups...by the time the afternoon was over, I felt like I had just given myself a dry shampoo—did you ever use one of those? It was a spray can that jetted a powder onto your scalp and you were supposed to work it through your hair and then brush it out. The result, the can claimed, was to leave your hair clean. What it left it was powdery and dry and your scalp feeling slightly caked. The dust storm did a far better job, thanks probably to the wind that blew the dust through and through absorbing all oils and moisture and leaving you feeling the way a baby's bottom probably feels after a good dusting with talcum.

April 18, 2007

Show time is in an hour, and I find myself sad to leave this barren patch of land. In the same ways that your eyes adjust to the black of night to see more and more of stars, so does your brain start picking out subtle signs of beauty and order amid the brown dust and the gray gravel. By the cypress tree, boots have carved a path through the rough gravel, creating a strip of lighter, smaller stones. By the hospital, rocks delineate a triangle in which a few flowers grow. And if you stand at the end of one of the paths that cuts through the hardened quarters, the plain tan buildings work together *like the angled silhouettes in a De Chirico painting* [italics added].

Well, almost.

These entries served as the basis for more formal pieces that Lawrence published in her blog and the *Christian Science Monitor* and she will use in the documentary which, at this writing, she is preparing. The following is a selection from one piece. Note how she cuts out material, moves it around, adds to it, and dramatizes it.

Even news that directly affected us was sometimes hard to get. Again in Bagram, Air Force personnel at the hospital asked us one day whether we'd heard that the base had come under attack the day before.

Really? Yes, mortars rained down just inside the perimeter for about four hours—or was it six? Accounts varied, and nobody we spoke to could tell fact from rumor because, though we'd all been right there, we hadn't heard or seen a thing.

By contrast, when rockets hit Salerno, a medium-sized FOB (forward operating base) south of Kabul, we all knew it. I'd just spent two days hopping in and out of Black Hawk helicopters, shadowing Air Force Chaplain Gary Linksy as he traveled to seven tiny outposts to say mass. I'd already discovered that the dust, whether whipped up by nature or the whir of rotor blades, acts like those old dry shampoos that absorb the oil in your hair, leaving it technically clean but feeling dull and gritty.

When I got back to Salerno, I headed straight for the shower trailer. I had the place to myself and was all lathered up when I heard the first big boom. It felt like the world had taken a convulsive in–out breath.

People talk about the fight or flight response—my response was freeze and focus. I stood still, water pouring over me. Then my focus narrowed: Rinse off. Get dressed. Gather toiletries. Poke head out of trailer.

I could see the walls of various structures coming in at angles to one another, as deserted and stark as a De Chirico painting. Another boom. Do I leave? Stay put? Someone is speaking over the loudspeaker, but I can't make out the words. Then laughter—guys must be playing cards over in that tent, so how bad can this be? But, wait, that's not a tent. That's a bunker. A bunker. I need to be in that bunker.

The thought propelled my legs, and the next thing I knew I was staring up at a man with an open, kind face and a body so massive the largest size neck armor was too small. I took one look at Sgt. Robert Walker and stuck to him like glue. When the next rocket hit, those of us near the opening of the bunker saw the dust kick up 300 yards away.

"How bad can it be?" one soldier said, "The guys in the guard tower are still there."

Right on cue, the guys in the guard tower charged down the stairs, chins tucked in and backs hunched. I looked at Sergeant Walker. When he headed for a bunker farther inside the FOB, I was right behind him. (About a week later an all-female singing group called Purple Angels performed at the base—and who do you suppose was their designated driver and bodyguard? You know it— Sergeant Walker.)

> We sat in the next bunker for about an hour. A soldier told me all about his wife; a civilian contractor explained bluntly that we were basically defenseless—"If a rocket hits the bunker square on, we're gone." And a jolly-looking fellow brought us bottles of water. (It was my introduction to National Guard Chaplain Kurt Bishop, whose operating room ministry I would later profile for the Monitor.) And here I was clutching toiletries instead of my camera. I consoled myself, thinking that maybe a camera would have stifled conversation – but I now doubt it.

Before we make additional suggestions about journal keeping, it may be worthwhile to say something about the relationship between the journal and the growth of the writer's imagination. The very effort put into keeping a journal over a period of time sharpens both memory and awareness, both within and outside the journal. Because you know you are keeping a journal, you start to become more conscious of your surroundings, more sensitive to the flow of your experience, your thinking, and your reading. You are more aware precisely because you know you are going to write, and as you write, you become more awake to what you need to put down. The cycle is continuous, a whirlpool that sucks you deeper into both the world and yourself—that is, your material as a writer. Put the matter another way: Each entry is a time capsule you have sent to yourself.

When you compare Lee Lawrence's entries with the earlier ones, some principles of journal keeping should be clear:

1. Date each fully and precisely. (Computer journals will do so automatically.)
2. Make your journal entry as specific as you can.
3. Start trying to find the hard nouns and verbs that capture the feel of the situation.
4. If you are being flabby, tell yourself to straighten up. Talk to yourself in your journal. And play with the material. Start thinking about it. Let yourself go.
5. Look for associations in your past or in literature—anything that will help you recapture the emotion and feel of the event at some future time.

All this work in your journal hones skills you will need when you sit down to begin constructing something for an audience.

 ## GETTING STARTED

Open your journaling program or journal.

An effective first entry might be a brief overview of your life. Hit the most memorable points, especially the turning points when, had events or choices been different, you think your life might have been different. Don't try to be complete at this point. Leave yourself material for the entries that will come as you work into the journal-keeping habit. In later sessions start adding:

1. Your likes and dislikes.
2. Detailed sketches of people who are important to you—parents, brothers and sisters, friends and relatives, enemies, and so on. (See Anaïs Nin's sketch of her dance teacher on pp. 28–29.)
3. Memory portraits of homes, rooms, toys.
4. The truth about your weaknesses (it's permissible to write about what you think are your strengths too), fears, and anxieties.

What you are engaged in is self-exploration, the writer's archaeological dig. Even a writer who is writing in a naturalistic tradition filters the world through his or her own mind, a mind shaped by memories and experiences.

Write spontaneously—a suggestion easier to recommend than to follow. Try the technique used in this student passage:

June 5, 2007

One early memory lives in fragments like a torn up photograph, some of it lost for good. What I see now is the steaming black car waiting in the slush and someone helping me climb up and into the back seat, shutting the door, making me its prisoner. Weren't they coming too? They stood together in the snow watching me through the wet streaked window. Clouds of exhaust billowed up between us, and I couldn't see their faces. As the car huffed forward, my mother, pulling her gray coat close, my mittened and booted big sister waving, our white house, the white pickets, the towering spruce, all grew tiny in the frame of the rear window, then disappeared. And suddenly I was tiny too.

Foldup cots all in a row covered half the dark basement of the house I can't remember reaching. Their color matched the uniforms my sister and I had been given by our Uncle Jack, a soldier. He had taken our picture in these little soldier-girl dresses as we saluted his camera, un-smiling. He said we were his brave little WACs. With the others—there must have been others—I followed orders from a faceless woman whose shoes laced like a man's and whose skirt made "pftt pftt" sounds when she moved. It was time to nap, she said, and I should lie on my cot, be quiet, close my eyes and sleep. I closed my eyes. The enemy air smelled awful from a mix of green peas cooking somewhere in the house and the slightly sweet odor of children's little accidents trapped in the cots. At home we sometimes made our house dark, and we had to be quiet. It was a test my mother said, so we could practice being safe from Germans. We would draw the paper shades down, pull the flowered curtains together, dim the lights and whisper until a siren said the test was over. The black half moons painted on the lights of our car were supposed to keep us safe too. I must have wondered if being sent away to the basement and the smells was another kind of test. I wanted to be brave, a good soldier like Uncle Jack. But in that basement I added tears to the reeking cot. I waited for the siren, but I really didn't think it would come.

The writer is trying to recapture the names, feel, smell, sound, color...the moment of that first day in nursery school. Is it a historically precise memory? Probably not. The writer undoubtedly added sensory details, as well as the inset memory of Uncle Jack, to capture that moment, making it meaningful to herself or someone else. The point of the journal, of course, is not necessarily to be exact; it is to write and keep on writing.

●   ●   ●   ●   ●   *EXERCISE*   ●   ●   ●   ●   ●

Put at least one of your early family memories into your journal with all the sensory detail that might have been present. You should try doing it in the present tense. Why is that memory important to you?

———————————●———————————

Spontaneity does not mean sloppiness, and by *sloppiness* we are not referring to handwriting, typos, or abbreviations known only to you (though an unreadable journal entry will be useless for future exploration and to your biographer). Even though you wish to keep the material flowing, try different ways of saying it, look for the precise word, and keep a running commentary to yourself on exact information you will need later to make the journal entry complete.

Your family, with its experiences and stories, is important research material for your journal. It is the stuff out of which you can build completely imagined scenes, even in stories having nothing to do with your family. And it may be the stuff of the narratives you wish to write. Who are the characters in your family tree, what happened to them, and what do they mean to you? Because celebrations, dislocations, relocations, operations, vacations, maturations, and more are the stuff of life, they are the stuff of literature. In your journal, start practicing your re-creation of them: having your first birthday party, moving to a new house, getting your driver's license, realizing that one of your parents had a specific fault, your first awareness of death.

KEEPING UP

What we have suggested up to this point are ways to build the journal-keeping habit through the subjects you know best. In fact, you will probably return again and again to these same subjects as events in your life shake out more memories. However, your life will flow on, and in your journal you will paste more word and actual snapshots of daily events, ideas, character sketches, and pieces of your reading.

Some of you may already have the habit of writing often through participating in such Internet activities as personal Web pages, blogging, file sharing, MySpace, Bebo, Facebook, and—since a book takes time to process—who knows what new "social networking" programs in the offing. Though these activities do keep you writing, they are more akin to publishing; that is, making public. Think of your journals as a private space where you can experiment, put your worst foot forward, be incomplete and hesitant, and more emotionally honest than you might want to be to the world at large.

Here is a sample activity you might do routinely in your journal. From your reading, copy short passages that appeal to you and then analyze the reasons for this appeal. What strikes you in your reading tells you something about yourself as a writer-in-the-making. Be alert to other writers' techniques and comment on them, even imitate and parody them. For example, if Cormac McCarthy is one of your favorites, copy a paragraph that you think is representative of his work and then model a paragraph of your own on his sequence of sentences, saving even the shape of the sentences: introduce new characters, nouns, verbs, and modifiers. Beware, on the other hand, of a writer's weaknesses such as McCarthy's overuse of modifiers.

You might sharpen your skills by following Ben Franklin's practice when he was young. He read articles in the *Tatler* and *Spectator*, put them away, tried to reproduce them as closely as possible, and then compared his version to the original. Such imitation is a way of involving yourself in the world of words and of making your journal a laboratory in which you experiment with your medium—language.

As a writer you will, of course, keep reading, and your reading is always a source for journal keeping, even on those days you feel wiped out, empty of anything to say. It is those days that test your mettle (and mental) as a writer. Keep going.

1. Write a letter in your journal—to your parents (the letter you always should have written), to someone you want to curse out, to an author you admire.
2. Open a dictionary at random and look at a page of words. Jot down a few that interest you because they are strange or suggestive. Play with them.
3. Try to recapture in detail the last moment you felt pleased with yourself.
4. Retell the plot of a book—even one from your childhood.
5. Turn on some music and free-associate: Write the thoughts the music evokes.
6. Try freewriting on the computer with the monitor turned off, allowing yourself to read what you have written only after the writing session is over. After practicing this technique for a while, evaluate the results.

Nothing much may come of all this play except the habit of keeping to your discipline, but that is no small matter. And we know that it is easier to write *discipline* than it is to summon reserves for running that last mile when your legs are leaden. Sometimes you won't; sometimes you will. What separates the writers from the pretenders is that most times the writers keep going.

> *" I never travel without my diary. One should always*
> *have something sensational to read in the train."*

> Gwendolyn in Oscar Wilde's
> *The Importance of Being Ernest*

 ## WHAT WILL YOU DO WITH IT ALL?

In most of your journal writing, you will practice your craft, discover yourself, and store flour for future baking. Some people, however, fall so in love with journal keeping itself that it becomes the major part of their writing, as it did with Anaïs Nin, who is mostly known for her published diary. Study the selection from the following extended journal entry:

October, 1933

The death of Antonio Francisco Miralles in a hotel room, alone, of asthma. Miralles, my Spanish dancing teacher....

I was the favorite.

He was like a gentle Svengali, and by his eyes, his voice, his hands, he had the power to make me dance as well as by his ordinary lessons. He ruled my body with a magnetic rule, master of my dancing.

One day he waited for me at the door, neat and trim. "Will you come and sit at the café with me?"

I followed him. Not far from there was the Place Clichy, always animated, but more so now, as the site of a permanent fair. The merry-go-rounds were turning swiftly. The gypsies were reading fortunes in little booths hung with Arabian rugs. Workmen were shooting clay pigeons and winning cut glass for their wives. The prostitutes were enjoying their loitering, and the men were watching them.

My dancing teacher was saying to me: "Anaïs, I am a simple man. My parents were shoemakers in a little village in the south of Spain. I was put to work in an iron factory where I handled heavy things and was on the way to becoming deformed by big muscles. But during my lunch hour, I danced. I wanted to be a dancer and I practiced every day, every night. At night I went to the gypsies' caverns, and learned from them. I began to dance in cabarets. And today, look!" He took out a cigarette case engraved with the names of all the famous Spanish dancers. "Today I have been the partner of all these women. If you would come with me, we could be happy. I am a simple man, but we could dance in all the cities of Europe. I am no longer young but I have a lot of dancing in me yet. We could be happy."

The merry-go-round turned and sang, and I imagined myself embarking on a dancing career with Miralles, dancing, which was so much like flying, from city to city, receiving bouquets, praise in newspapers, with joyous music at the center always, pleasure as colorful as the Spanish dresses, all red, orange, black and gold, gold and purple, and red and white.

Imagining…like amnesia. Forgetting who I was, and where I was, and why I could not do it. Not knowing how to answer so I would not hurt him, I said, "I am not strong enough."

"That's what I thought when I first saw you. I thought you couldn't take the discipline of a dancer's life. But it isn't so. You look fragile and all that, but you're healthy. I can tell healthy women by their skin. Yours is shining and clear. No, I don't think you have the strength of a horse, you're what we call a *petite nature*. But you have energy and guts. And we'll take it easy on the road."

Many afternoons, after hard work, we sat at this little café and imagined what a dancer's life might be.

from *The Diary of Anaïs Nin*, 1931–1934

This entry is much more than a recording of the day's events. Nin's impulse is to fashion material as she recalls it, a sure sign of someone who is already practicing the art of storytelling. Because this entry was written five years after Nin gave up dancing, the dialogue must have been created. She is *telling a story* based on her memories as they well up. We know from studying her writing practice that her published diaries are not spontaneous outpourings but rather carefully rewritten and edited.

Your journal, on the other hand, is most likely going to be a resource for the writing that you hope will be published or produced. Much of the time, of course, few entries transfer exactly from the journal into your public writing. Read and compare the following entry from Hawthorne's journal with the following passage that appears in his *The Blithedale Romance*:

In a bar-room, a large oval basin let into the counter, with a brass tube rising from the centre, out of which gushes continually a miniature fountain, and descends in a soft, gentle, never ceasing rain into the basin, where swim a company of gold fishes. Some of them gleam brightly in their golden armor; others have a dull white aspect, going through some process of transmutation. One would think that the atmosphere, continually filled with tobacco-smoke, might impregnate the water unpleasantly for the scaly people; but then it is continually flowing

away, and being renewed. And what if some toper should be seized with
the freak of emptying his glass of gin or brandy into the basin? Would
the fishes die, or merely get jolly?

Journal entry for May 16, 1850

The prettiest object in the saloon was a tiny fountain, which threw up its feathery
jet, through the counter, and sparkled down again into an oval basin, or lakelet,
containing several gold-fishes. There was a bed of bright sand, at the bottom,
strewn with coral and rock-work; and the fishes went gleaming about, now turning up the sheen of a golden side, and now vanishing into the shadows of the
water, like the fanciful thoughts that coquet with a poet in his dream. Never
before, I imagine, did a company of water-drinkers remain so entirely uncontam-
inated by the bad example around them; nor could I help wondering that it had
not occurred to any freakish inebriate, to empty a glass of liquor into their lakelet.
What a delightful idea! Who would not be a fish, if he could inhale jollity with the
essential element of his existence.

from The Blithedale Romance (1852)

Notice that the entry marinates for a time before it turns up in the published novel. Some material disappears, such as the tobacco smoke, and some
material is added, such as the detailed description of the sand. Do you notice any
other changes? As with Lee Lawrence's journal, the material in Hawthorne's
journal is the seedling that he nurses into a full passage, pruning and adding as
he needs to. Still, he had a seedling.

In our discussion of Nin's *Diary*, we have already noted the critical and popular acceptance of the diary or journal as a literary form. Its appeal stems from the
sense of intimacy and spontaneity it can convey. In blogs, this sense is heightened
by the immediacy and apparent artlessness. We suspect, however, that the most
read blogs are the result of more careful consideration, like the entries of Nin and
Lawrence which are heightened and embellished with a potential reader in mind.

Ultimately, those who keep their journals, whether on paper or on their
computer, most consistently will find themselves writing better and better. It's
rather like, having practiced the basic chords on the guitar or other instrument,
your jazz improvisations will be more fit for a public.

● ● MORE SUGGESTIONS FOR JOURNAL WORK ● ●

1. After you have been keeping a journal for a while, reread it to see whether
any patterns have begun to develop.

2. Take a journal piece that you have previously written for yourself and revise
it with a reader in mind. How has it changed?

After a time—and we would not say what that time might be—your journal will become a resource not only for passages such as those found in this chapter but also for whole works. Often you will find that ideas or impulses appearing over a period of time in your journal start to form a pattern that sparks or confirms a story, essay, poem, or play. Our space being limited, we cannot give an extended example of such a development in operation. You will simply have to trust that, in time, the effort made on the practice field will pay off in the game.

 ## THE RELATIONSHIP BETWEEN INVENTION AND RESEARCH

> *" Time spent researching varies from book to book. Some novels require months, even years of research, others very little. I try to do most of my research before I begin but inevitably questions emerge during the writing."*
>
> Jonathan Kellerman

The root meaning of *invent* is "to come upon" or "to find." In this sense, it is related to *discover*. The origin of the word tells us that what we are after already exists, though perhaps only somewhere inside the writer. The meaning also suggests a seemingly paradoxical relationship between invention and research. Many of the masterpieces of our literary culture, the "great originals" of our most individualistic writers, are the result of voluminous research. Melville's *Moby Dick* is such a work. Critics have discovered the many sources on whales and whaling that Melville used to help him create this vast, imagined world. His reliance on research, however, does not diminish Melville's achievement. In fact, in some ways the marvel of what he accomplished is only enhanced by the discovery of his methods, including his dependence on facts.

The coastal Newfoundland of Annie Proulx's *The Shipping News* also blends research and invention. Proulx has remarked on the attraction of the region, the ways in which she came to know it as an engaged writer–researcher, and the issues that her field work raised:

Rarely have I been so strongly moved by geography as I was during that first journey up the Great Northern Peninsula. The harsh climate, the grim history, the hard lives and the generous, warm characters of the outport fisherman and their families interested me deeply. Yet I could also see contemporary civilization rushing in on the island after its centuries of isolation and the idea for *The Shipping News* began to form. *Over the next few years I made nine trips to*

Newfoundland, watching, observing, taking notes, listening [italics added]. I am keenly interested in situations of change, both personal and social, and in this book I wanted to show characters teetering along the highwires of their lives yet managing to keep their balance, lives placed against a background of incomprehensible and massive social change.

In the introduction to her novel *Passenger to Frankfurt,* Agatha Christie has some advice for writers that is worth repeating here. She raises the novice's question: "How shall you get full information [for people, places, and events to give your work verisimilitude] apart from the evidence of your own eyes and ears? The answer," Christie maintains, "is frighteningly simple":

It is what the press brings to you every day, served up in your morning paper under the general heading of News. Collect it from the front page. What is going on in the world today? What is everyone saying, thinking, doing? Hold up a mirror to 1970 [when Christie's book was published in England].

Look at that front page every day for a month, make notes, consider and classify.
Every day there is a killing.
A girl is strangled.
Elderly woman attacked and robbed of her meager savings.
Young men or boys—attacking or attacked.
Buildings and telephone kiosks smashed and gutted.
Drug smuggling.
Robbery and assault.
Children missing and children's murdered bodies found not far from their homes.
Can this be England? Is England *really* like this? One feels—no—not yet, *but it could be*.
And yet one knows—of one's own knowledge—how much goodness there is in this world of ours—the kindnesses done, the goodness of the heart, the acts of compassion, the kindness of neighbor to neighbor, the helpful actions of girls and boys. Then why this fantastic atmosphere of daily news—of things that happen—that are actual *facts*? To write a story in this year...you must come to terms with your background. If the background is fantastic, then the story must accept its background.

Christie's point is that we must do all we can to feel the pulse of the world around us, to be engaged, to look outward as well as inward, and to make our personal sense out of the cascade of facts that rushes past, selecting what we need for our work.

Agatha Christie's imagination and inventiveness were remarkable, but her writing comes alive because she created a world that her readers and characters can live in together. Like most successful writers, she knew the value of research—of finding the facts that she needed to stimulate her imagination and to weave into the fabric of her work.

Take her advice and make one of your journal practices the kind of reading you do in your newspaper, blogs, or the home pages of major research engines like Yahoo or Google. Scan the articles every day for a month, make notes, consider, and classify. You'll find that imagination and facts are inseparable, that invention and research are parts of the same process.

Headlines bring us in touch not only with what is going on in the world but also with stuff for the imagination. Would any writer ignore the following headline and news story?

A Gate-Crasher's Change of Heart

BY ALLISON KLEIN
Washington Post Staff Writer
Friday, July 13, 2007; B01

A grand feast of marinated steaks and jumbo shrimp was winding down, and a group of friends was sitting on the back patio of a Capitol Hill home, sipping red wine. Suddenly, a hooded man slid in through an open gate and put the barrel of a handgun to the head of a 14-year-old guest.

"Give me your money, or I'll start shooting," he demanded, according to D.C. police and witness accounts.

The five other guests, including the girl's parents, froze—and then one spoke.

"We were just finishing dinner," Cristina "Cha Cha" Rowan, 43, blurted out. "Why don't you have a glass of wine with us?"

The intruder took a sip of their Chateau Malescot St-Exupéry and said, "Damn, that's good wine."

The girl's father, Michael Rabdau, 51, who described the harrowing evening in an interview, told the intruder, described as being in his 20s, to take the whole glass. Rowan offered him the bottle. The would-be robber, his hood now down, took another sip and had a bite of Camembert cheese that was on the table.

Then he tucked the gun into the pocket of his nylon sweatpants.

"I think I may have come to the wrong house," he said, looking around the patio of the home in the 1300 block of Constitution Avenue NE.

"I'm sorry," he told the group. "Can I get a hug?"

Rowan, who lives in Falls Church and works part time at her children's school, stood up and wrapped her arms around him. Then it was Rabdau's turn. Then his wife's. The other two guests complied.

"That's really good wine," the man said, taking another sip. He had a final request: "Can we have a group hug?"

The five adults surrounded him, arms out.

With that, the man walked out with a crystal wine glass in hand, filled with Chateau Malescot. No one was hurt, and nothing was stolen.

The homeowner, Xavier Cervera, 45, had gone out to walk his dog at the end of the party and missed the incident, which happened about midnight June 16. Police classified the case as strange but true and said they had not located a suspect.

"We believe it is a true robbery," said Cmdr. Diane Groomes, who is in charge of patrols in the Capitol Hill area. But it's one-of-a-kind, she said, adding, "I've never heard of a robber joining a party and then walking out to the sunset."

The hug, she said, was especially unusual. "They should have squeezed him and held onto him for us," she said.

Rabdau said he hasn't been able to figure out what happened.

"I was definitely expecting there would be some kind of casualty," Rabdau said this week. "He was very aggressive at first; then it turned into a love fest. I don't know what it was."

Rabdau, a federal government worker who lives in Anne Arundel County with his family and lived on Capitol Hill with his wife in the 1980s, said that the episode lasted about 10 minutes but seemed like an hour. He believes the guests were spared because they kept a positive attitude during the exchange.

"There was this degree of disbelief and terror at the same time," Rabdau said. "Then it miraculously just changed. His whole emotional tone turned— like, we're one big happy family now. I thought: Was it the wine? Was it the cheese?"

After the intruder left, the guests walked inside the house, locked the door and stared at each other. They didn't say a word. Rabdau dialed 911. Police arrived quickly and took a report. They also dusted for fingerprints—so far, to no avail.

In the alley behind the home, investigators found the intruder's empty crystal wine glass on the ground, unbroken.

As Agatha Christie insisted, such reports from the newspapers are among the great sources for the ongoing research that a writer needs to do even without a specific project in mind. Of course, when you do have a project under way, relevant items will leap out at you once you're in the habit of being on the alert for anything you can use.

●   ●   ●   ●   ●   *EXERCISE*   ●   ●   ●   ●   ●

In your journal, sketch a story, play, or poem that you might make from the newspaper report. What do you make of the final line in the preceding report?

SEARCHING AND IMAGINING

New information is liberating and stimulating, especially for the writer whose imagination can take a few fresh facts and combine them in a way that gives them new meaning. On a more sophisticated level, many writers have created their most important work out of intense, prolonged periods of study. Gary Snyder has combined his formal Zen training and his explorations of American Indian culture into highly personal poems. Writers who do a great deal of translation, like Robert Bly, are in fact "researching" into language itself and into the sensibilities of writers whose poems grow out of another culture.

Through research all writers establish an authentic sense of place and time in their narratives. How did people dress in 1944? What were hairstyles like? What songs were popular? When did ragged jeans become a fashion statement? What were new parents in Southern California naming their children? What is a likely Parisian neighborhood for an American cultural attaché to live in today? How can one effectively suggest this place? How would this person get to work? To the theater? What do the Japanese call a wrench? How does a film-maker organize a shoot on location? How much annual rainfall is there in the Iraqi desert? It opens the mind to look for what was going on the year you or your parents or grandparents were born. Once discovering this information was a laborious task; now most of the information can be gleaned from the Internet while the writer is sitting anywhere.

You find answers to these questions, of course, on the Internet, from interviews, in libraries, and from your own direct experience. The interaction between research and invention is twofold: (1) You search because you need facts to fill your imagined world; and (2) Facts themselves, whether sought or randomly discovered, stimulate your imagination. Moreover, factual accuracy contributes to **verisimilitude,** the sense the reader receives that your work reflects a real world, even when it does not (see pp. 225–228).

●   ●   ●   ●   ●   *EXERCISE*   ●   ●   ●   ●   ●

Imagine that you have written in your journal the following idea for a story about a relationship in difficulty:

Insert scene for Gordon to be waiting for Denise to come home after their fight. Gordon decides to make her favorite meal as a peace offering.

Now is the moment to write the scene in which we follow Gordon preparing the meal. Denise is mad about spinach salad with shallot dressing, Mejillones a la Gallega, and chocolate mousse for dessert. You need to find the ingredients and the recipes. Also Gordon decides to set the table with their most elegant and expensive table linens, silverware, plates, and glasses. While Gordon works, have him interact with the process and be thinking about their argument. You probably will need to do some research on the Internet or in a library or cookbook to find the recipes and the names of the items he is using for the elegant table settings. You can pick the wine.

What's important for a writer who is searching for a good path to follow is simply to get started. Hard facts get the creative juices flowing. You can research your way into a creative effort that will give you satisfaction and confidence in your ability to break through the block next time. Perhaps *research* is too academic a word; you are not writing a term paper. *Search* is the main issue here.

Various sources must have nourished the poems of Adrien Stoutenburg, a writer whose works are filled with information about nature and history. Here is a brief excerpt from her sequence poem "A Short History of the Fur Trade":

> In summer, even chiefs went bare,
> though seldom without the pointed jewels
> of claws strung into necklaces,
> of clacking halos of dead teeth
> strung through their black and dancing hair.
> Beaten hides of bison kept out the cold,
> and their swift horns, headgear for warriors,
> blazed like new moons turned into bone,
> or served as flagons for an antelope's blood,
> while the cosmetic bear, crowded with fat,
> supplied his oozing brilliantine
> to blaze on scalps and in a stone lamp's
> rancid flame.
>
> from *Land of Superior Mirages*

Of course, Stoutenburg's poem is no mere listing of facts. She has transformed her material into a highly personal, emotional statement. Her originality is in her selection of material, the freshness of her imagery, the intense charge of her language. Nevertheless, a passage like the one just quoted is rooted in facts that the author had to master about the fur trade and American Indian culture.

Audiences may be scarcely conscious that something they are reading or seeing is filled with material discovered through research and used either to generate ideas or provide the dense detail that makes for an effective narrative—or both. It is best that, as they are participating in the narrative, they respond to the underpinning facts and make the work come alive.

● ● ● ● ●   *EXERCISES*   ● ● ● ● ●

The following exercises are meant to shake your imagination awake. Use them as practice for your journal. However, do not be taken aback if you find yourself in the throes of creating something that you want to keep working on because it has acquired a life of its own.

1. Imagine that something you are working on requires meteorological information. You need to describe the approach of a hurricane, or you want to use increasing wind velocities metaphorically to address an emotion—a rage—building in one of your characters. The scale that Sir Francis Beaufort devised—a "found poem" in itself—is just what you need. Reproductions of this scale are found in most dictionaries and on the Internet (www.spc.noaa.gov/faq/tornado/beaufort.html.).

Now go ahead and build a descriptive paragraph or a short poem out of this "research" material. You might do a dramatic beat in which one character knows this information and uses it to frighten other characters.

2. The material you have researched for one purpose can jostle your imagination in other ways. For example, you might try to make your own version of such a scale. How about a scale that rates men's clothing styles by the effect they have on women? How about a scale that measures the effects of different kinds of speakers (or jokes) on listeners? Be true to the terse, efficient nature of the *Beaufort scale*. Keep your language similarly flat and objective.

3. Gather a few provocative human interest stories from the Internet or a newspaper. Building on the facts, develop a story, play sketch, or draft for a poem. Following is an ad from the newspaper that is almost a found poem or the start of a novel. Can you build a story or short play from this list or parts of it?

> Sale cheap: 4 cane bottom chairs. $75 total. Need work. One-caret diamond ring. Make offer. Itek Quadritek 1201 2 disc drive, RS232, good cond. Bushwacker, Sears, $70. BMX boy's bike, $40. Rocker, contemporary ladder back, $30.

4. Place a character you know within a well-known painting or photograph. Describe the character's situation from a first-person perspective and then in the third person. Try Da Vinci's *The Last Supper* or Renoir's *The Boating Party*. You can find these paintings in an art book or on the Internet. See Billy Collin's "The Brooklyn Museum of Art," p. 151.

5. Do some research on the tools necessary to perform certain specialized tasks: to shoe a horse, build a model plane, tune a car, hook a rug, cut a diamond. Now develop a story sketch, an essay, or a poem that enlivens the old expression "a poor workman always blames his tools." For an example on how you can weave such information into the plot of a narrative, look at Joyce Carol Oates's *Procedure* on pp. 339–345.

◀━━▶ A WORD ABOUT RESOURCES

Most of your library and Internet research will be in the service of creative work you are already engaged in. In creative nonfiction, however, you will be held more accountable for accurate details on dates, names, figures, geography, and so forth. For this, you need to be sure that you are going to the best possible sources. The Internet is not always one. Wikipedia, for example, is less accurate than the *Encyclopædia Britannica.* Also, sometimes it is easier to track useful books and periodicals in a library, especially if it has an open stack system. Whichever you are using at the moment, keep several things in mind. One, you may go back to sources and need to record where you found information. That is easy on the Internet because you can bookmark sites you visit. Two, the number of sources in either libraries or on the Internet seems almost infinite. Beware the beguiling pleasures of research, especially because your search will not be in the service of scholarship but in the service of your creations. A useful strategy is to start writing when you have completed 50 percent of your research. While writing you will also realize what other information you need.

SUMMARY

The journal, invention, and research go hand-in-hand in writing, just as they do in other creative processes. No scientist ever made a major breakthrough without gathering information and exploring various approaches to the problem at hand and keeping notes and records. The original thinker in any field is the person who keeps at least one foot on the ground.

> *"For me the research that underlies the writing is the best part of the scribbling game. On jumbly shelves in my house I can find directions for replacing a broken pipe stem, a history of corn cribs, a booklet of Spam recipes, a 1925 copy of* Animal Heroes of the Great War *(mostly dogs but some camels); dictionaries of slang,*

dialect and regional English... This digging involves more than books. I need to know which mushrooms smell like maraschino cherries and which like dead rats, to note that a magpie in flight briefly resembles a wooden spoon, to recognize vertically trapped suppressed lee-wave clouds; so much of this research is concerned with four dimensional observation and notation."

Annie Proulx

CHAPTER 3

POINT OF VIEW

> *"Every human being has hundreds of separate people living under his skin. The talent of a writer is his ability to give them their separate names, identities, personalities and have them relate to other characters living with him."*
>
> Mel Brooks

 WHAT IS IT?

We are fated—some might say "doomed"—to experience, observe, and understand everything from a *point of view,* a metaphor for having a mental attitude or opinion. We say: "That's how he sees it" or "That's your story." It is no wonder, then, that writers share with readers the common definitions of the metaphor: We, too, always look at something from one viewpoint, and, as a consequence, our reactions must be different from someone else's, if only by a millimeter.

Because writers share the common fate, they are intensely aware of its power and can manipulate it for effects in their work. A point of view or points of view is part of the common genome of all writing. When Mark Twain had a naïve twelve-year-old narrate the events in *Huckleberry Finn,* he made a fateful decision. When Barbara Kingsolver chose to have four different daughters of a missionary and their mother tell of their African experiences in *The Poisonwood Bible,* she made a fateful decision. In these novels—one told by a naïve boy and other told by women of various ages—the writers are limited to narrating aspects of the story, and so the reader can only see those aspects. Though the writers might choose to change the point of view, they would be limited by their new position.

As for readers, they expect everything from a poem to a play to have one, for characters to have one, for narrators to have one, and for the writer to have one, even when it is difficult to make out. A completely neutral writer is an oxymoron.

Because writers also expect that a reader will bring a point of view to the work, they make a host of decisions. Think of the fatefulness of Allen Ginsberg's decision to tell *Howl* as if he were a latter day Walt Whitman or Polonius's belief that Hamlet suffers from lovesickness.

In life and in art, one may move from one viewpoint to another. A house that looks good to us from a distance, we see, on close inspection, actually needs a new roof, glass in the windows, and paint. Our changed view may change our feelings or judgment about whether or not to buy it. The Realtor, even if she sees the flaws, will probably "see" the house quite differently: "It's a steal," she says. It looks different to different people viewing it from what may seem to be the same perspective: a painting contractor, a ten-year-old who has lived there since birth, a neighbor who doesn't like the present owners, a banker who holds the overdue mortgage.

In sum, the way writers manipulate point of view shapes their writing and their audience's experience of the work.

 ## WHO WILL DO THE TELLING?

We began this book with a point of view. That point of view involves both decisions we made before we began writing and decisions we made, consciously or unconsciously, as we were writing and revising. Though the aims of this book are different from the aims of a story, poem, or play, the essential point-of-view question is the same: Who is going to do the telling? As you will see, deciding who "who" will be is not merely a matter of deciding whether the speaker will be first, second, or third person and whether the "voice" will be an omniscient one, a limited one, the voice of someone who has been directly involved, or that of an onlooker (see "The Range of Perspectives" later in this chapter). The narrator that a writer chooses will reflect both his or her viewpoint about the world and the audience. Point of view is, then, partly about how to tell.

In planning, writing, and revising this book, for example, we had to decide whether to pretend we were authorities delivering the gospel from on high about formulas for writing success or, at the other end of the spectrum, whether to act as friends sitting at a table discussing writing processes and problems with a touch of humor. We finally decided to take a position somewhere between authority and collegiality. Our decision about viewpoint derived from what we believed our audience already knew and what it needed to know about writing, about the range of your experience as readers and writers, as well as our thesis that although ideally all matters are open to discussion, some guidelines and an introduction to standard techniques help when you are starting to play the game. In this sense, choosing a point of view is closely related to searching for a tone or style that communicates just where we stand about the writing process. Point of view, considered this way, is a process that is closely connected with *what* to tell, *how much* to tell, and *how* to tell it

When we were shaping what and how we tell, we knew that point of view would determine how you responded. What if we had written: "Point of view is implicated in every decision the writer makes, including diction. Structure your point of view to maximize effects." We suspect that one of your reactions would be to see such a statement as a sign that we were hidebound rule makers directing you to follow a set of rules for achieving success. Since we actually feel that effective writing involves continual decision making and because we do not care for the platform and the bureaucratic, we are more likely to say, "Point of view affects everything you do in your writing, including your choice of words." All we are about is heightening your awareness of point of view and suggesting ways to talk about it.

Let us examine how a complex point of view functions in Shelley's "Ozymandias." After you read the **sonnet,** go back over it and try to isolate the various points of view it incorporates. Make a list outlining (1) whose mind is being reflected and (2) what attitude is revealed in each case. Then read our commentary.

> I met a traveller from an antique land
> Who said: Two vast and trunkless legs of stone
> Stand in the desert... Near them, on the sand,
> Half sunk, a shattered visage lies, whose frown,
> And wrinkled lip, and sneer of cold command,
> Tell that its sculptor well those passions read
> Which yet survive, stamped on these lifeless things,
> The hand that mocked them, and the heart that fed;
> And on the pedestal these words appear:
> 'My name is Ozymandias, king of kings:
> Look on my works, ye Mighty, and despair!'
> Nothing beside remains. Round the decay
> Of that colossal wreck, boundless and bare
> The lone and level sands stretch far away.

1817

Immediately, we are told that the "narrator" or "speaker" heard a story. As readers, we recognize the first person point of view. But that's only the beginning of point-of-view complications. The remainder of the poem is the speaker's report of the traveler's experience.

Let us construct a fiction of what happened in the writing process that may have led to his decision about point of view:

1. Shelley hated tyrants and believed that the poet's task was to challenge tyranny in preparation for the creation of more perfect societies. Let's not worry about how he came to this position.

2. In a book, in a dream, from a friend—somehow—an image came to Shelley of a tyrant whose broken statue stands in a desert. He jots the image down in his journal. Maybe he launches into the poem immediately. Maybe he writes a first draft in his journal and, coming across it years later, is moved to complete it. No matter.

3. At some point, Shelley had to decide who would tell the story. The most obvious person is himself, or, rather, the voice he creates to tell the story of Ozymandias's statue. Shelley could have cast the traveler as the persona and saved the extra step of narrating through someone who encountered the traveler. Perhaps Shelley feared that his message would be discounted by readers who would identify such a speaker with the poet, who was known to hate tyrants. Locating the story in another's experience can be a way of increasing the reader's readiness to accept it. At the same time, Shelley's surrogate hears the tale and passes it on to us, and if we know Shelley's attitude (point of view) toward tyrants, we catch his intention. The poem is not, finally, addressing the haughtiness and transient stature of Ozymandias, but of all tyrants—especially those of Shelley's own day. (We might note that in any successful revolution one of the first acts is to topple the tyrant's statue.)

4. Looking further, we can see that the poem contains no less than four points of view: (1) what Ozymandias thought of himself (the inscription still visible on the pedestal); (2) what the sculptor thought of Ozymandias (through capturing his inner nature in stone); (3) what the traveler records of his own experience; and (4) what the persona retells upon hearing the traveler's story. At some point, Shelley found that this layered perspective projected most effectively his feeling about tyranny. The character of Ozymandias—of tyranny—becomes a shared understanding of sculptor, traveler, conveyor–poet, and reader. Only the king himself is left out, his haughty words—actually blasphemous words—shown to be absurd.

Our speculations tell something about how point of view drives the narrative. Many of these decisions you will have to make as you discover the needs of your work; nevertheless, you will save yourself a good deal of grief if you start working them out before you start putting words down. We know one writer who plunged into a novel told in the first person and on page 110 found out that the narrator had to die for his plot to work. The writer then had to figure out how a dead person could be talking and who was going to tell the rest of the novel. Could he rewrite all 110 pages with a deadline just two months off? Not to leave you wondering, the novelist invented a second narrator who found the dead narrator's tape recording of the first half of the novel and then finishes the story in his first person voice. Such a solution is mechanical and calls attention to itself.

Now that you've had a chance to think about point of view for a while, do the following exercise in your journal.

●   ●   ●   ●   ●   *EXERCISE*   ●   ●   ●   ●   ●

Compose a description that shows a different attitude toward Ozymandias. Try the point of view of an archaeologist or a painter or a child.

> *" Style is the perfection of point of view."*
>
>   Richard Eberhart

As we said earlier, the point of view you choose affects many other aspects of writing. Because point of view touches on attitude and personality, it can affect the words that you use and even the sentence patterns with which you string them together. Examine the following passages and jot down what you think about each narrator. We have commented at the end.

1. In the fall the war was always there, but we did not go to it any more. It was cold in the fall in Milan and the dark came very early. Then the electric lights came on, and it was pleasant along the streets looking in the windows.

    from Ernest Hemingway, "In Another Country"

2. There was music from my neighbor's house through the summer nights. In his blue gardens men and girls came and went like moths among the whisperings and the champagne and the stars. At high tide in the afternoon I watched his guests diving from the tower of his raft, or taking the sun on the hot sand of his beach while his two motorboats slit the waters of the Sound, drawing aquaplanes over cataracts of foam.

    from F. Scott Fitzgerald, *The Great Gatsby*

3. Joseph, who whilst he was speaking had continued in one attitude, with his head reclining on one side, and his eyes cast on the ground, no sooner perceived, on looking up, the position of Adams, who was stretched on his

back, and snored louder than the usual braying of the animal with long ears, then he turned towards Fanny, and, taking her by the hand began a dalliance, which, though consistent with the purest innocence and decency, neither he would have attempted nor she permitted before any witness.

from Henry Fielding, *Joseph Andrews*

4. I went along up the bank with one eye out for pap and 'tother one out for what the rise might fetch along. Well, all at once, here comes a canoe; just a beauty, too, about thirteen or fourteen foot long, riding high like a duck. I shot head first off the bank, like a frog, clothes and all on, and struck out for the canoe. I just expected there'd be somebody laying down in it, because people often done that to fool folks, and when a chap had pulled a skiff out most to it they'd raise up and laughed at him. But it warn't so this time.

from Mark Twain, *Huckleberry Finn*

5. This is just a kid with a local yearning but he is part of an assembling crowd, anonymous thousands off the buses and trains, people in narrow columns tramping over the swing bridge above the river, and even if they are not a migration or a revolution, some vast shaking of the soul, they bring with them the body heat of a great city and their own small reveries and desperations, the unseen something that haunts the day—men in fedoras and sailors on shore leave, the stray tumble of their thoughts, going to a game.

from Don DeLillo, *Underworld*

6. I am an invisible man. No, I am not a spook like those who haunted Edgar Allan Poe; nor am I one of your Hollywood-movie ectoplasms. I am a man of substance, of flesh and bone, fiber and liquids—and I might even be said to possess a mind. I am invisible, understand, simply because people refuse to see me. Like the bodiless heads you see sometimes in circus sideshows, it is as though I have been surrounded by mirrors of hard, distorting glass. When they approach me they see only my surrounding, themselves, or figments of their imagination—indeed, everything and anything except me.

From Ralph Ellison, *Invisible Man*

Our reactions were: (1) Understated, matter of fact, direct—as if told at a bar. A person whose emotions are masked. (2) A wistful fellow with a romantic imagination. Slightly adolescent, but polished too. (3) An entertainer, self-conscious effect-maker. He revels in his circumlocutions and false delicacies. An ironist. (4) An unlettered youngster; impetuous, observant, worldly wise.

(5) Aware of detail and slightly superior to the scene he describes. He sounds a bit like a travelogue announcer. (6) Angry and superior at the same time—as if the reader is an enemy who needs to be educated.

THE DECISION AND ITS CONSEQUENCES

Since the writer knows that readers hear and respond to the narrative only through the narrator's voice, consciously or unconsciously the writer has the following decisions to make. He or she must

1. choose a narrator, usually first or third person (see pp. 48–50),
2. decide what the narrator's attitude will be, and
3. decide how the reader should respond to the narrator and how to make the narrator create that response.

Point of view is a triangle in prose and poetic narratives (drama is another matter). On one side is the sum of all seen from a particular angle. On the other side is the sum of all the characteristics of the persona the writer has chosen. And on the third side is the voice or the sum of the words through which the other two sides are expressed. For example, in the Mark Twain example earlier, to express his vision of a hypocritical and often corrupt society, Twain created Huck Finn, who sees the world naively (as Twain surely does not) and speaks the story in the language appropriate to his naiveté.

Let us further explore the decisions involved in choosing the angle.

Think of a baseball game. Nine players are on the field. A batter is at the plate. Perhaps there are one or more base runners. Umpires are at their positions. So are coaches. Each manager is in a dugout along with his coaches and the other players—some players are out in the bullpen. Ball and bat girls and boys are doing their jobs. Fans are in the stands, along with vendors of snacks, drinks, and souvenirs. Security guards patrol the area. In the press box, sports journalists are hard at work. Mini-studios hold members of the radio and television broadcast crews.

Think of all the people who are involved in the scene, all the potential stories. But perhaps there is just one story to tell: the simple story of the game. Who should tell it?

As soon as we attempt to answer this question, we see that there is an intimate connection between the telling and what is told. The shortstop's story can never be the same as the ball girl's or the visiting manager's. Which story holds the truth? Which truth? The decision about who tells the story (even if the "story" is about someone's feelings as expressed in a poem) makes the story take on certain contours. No convincing narrator is totally objective, and the subjective perceptions and needs of the storyteller make the story come out the way it does.

Umpires are neutral, or are supposed to be, but the umpire's story is about calling the game, not playing in it. A journalist may not favor either team, yet his love for the game itself—or for his job, or his wife, or his lunch—can affect how he reports what he sees. And his story is, at bottom, about reporting.

By this time, the point about point of view should be clear. Decisions regarding point of view involve as many combinations and possibilities as a baseball game. Like many other concerns, it has endless reverberations.

● ● ● ● ●   *EXERCISE*   ● ● ● ● ●

Choose a place—perhaps your workplace or a dorm—and describe it from different physical and psychological vantage points. (For example, how might a French chef see a McDonald's?)

———————————●———————————

As we have seen, the term *point of view* covers a wide range of results that come from a writer's decisions. Deciding to tell a story in the first or third person is merely the first decision. The usefulness of the information readers receive depends upon how the writer filters the material through a narrator's consciousness and what coloring that consciousness gives to the information. For example, we get the information about what has happened in Emily Brontë's *Wuthering Heights* from Lockwood as reported to him by Nelly Dean, and much of her information is secondhand. In Daniel Defoe's *Moll Flanders,* we learn all that happens from Moll, but the whole experience happens to her directly and is her autobiography. Though both novels are written in the first person, there are far more differences than similarities. In F. Scott Fitzgerald's *The Great Gatsby,* a character who is not at the center of the action tells the story; in Camus's *The Plague* we receive, without knowing it until near the end, all of our information from a first-person narrator who hides his identity and presents the story clinically. In T.S. Eliot's "The Love Song of J. Alfred Prufrock," we are always in the presence of Prufrock who speaks to the reader but not aloud. In Arthur Miller's play *View from a Bridge,* the lawyer speaks to the audience as a direct participant and an explicator of the action much as a Greek chorus does of *Antigone* or *Oedipus*. In Dorothy Canfield Fisher's "Sex Education," printed at the end of this chapter, not only are there two narrative points of view, but the events are seen from different angles created by time. The possibilities of point of view are infinite.

THE RANGE OF PERSPECTIVES

Third Person

The third-person narrator speaks as an onlooker or reporter rather than as a participant. The degree to which the narrator has access to external and internal information and the degree to which the narrator is allowed to express judgments about that information determine the narrative stance. Within the broad third-person category, the narrator has three options:

Full Omniscience. The fully omniscient narrator may access the minds, feelings, and dreams of all the characters in the work as well as set the scene and describe the action in any number of places. Thus, the author, through the narrator, can shift focus along the way, giving the reader a variety of perspectives. Omniscient narrators also may shift back and forth between subjective and objective approaches, sometimes becoming engaged in explaining, interpreting, assessing, and moralizing on the events and characters. The narrator may at times comment extensively, as Fielding and Dickens do. Or, since the narrator may be in many minds, the author can deliver a variety of points of view about an event as in William Faulker's *Light in August*. When no one character has the total picture, the reader is forced to put together the sequence and relationships among the events.

The absence of any limitation on the narrator's information (and presence) can create havoc for an inexperienced writer. The tendency is to lose focus, to bully the reader, and to subjugate the story and characters to thematic concerns that may crush the story and characters under a ton of argument and commentary. On the other hand, the omniscient narrator can exploit the very idea of point of view to tell a story of great complexity and sweep.

Limited Omniscience. The limited omniscient narrator stands behind the shoulder of one character, usually the major character, and conveys to the reader only what that character experiences, knows, and feels. Other characters are treated objectively: What they say and do is recorded. However, what the central character thinks about them is an important ingredient. Sometimes, on top of this limited omniscience, the narrator is permitted knowledge or conjecture beyond what the central character knows so the reader can gain perspective on that character, get outside of the main character's head. Most successful stories and novels use some variation of the limited omniscient point of view, as in John Updike's *Rabbit Run* in which we see all the events through Rabbit Angstrom's consciousness.

Objective Limited. The objective limited point of view is most like that of the dramatist. Setting, action, and dialogue are the only tools the author allows the narrator. Readers are given no direct access to the minds of the characters and are left to form judgments on their own on the basis of what the characters say and do. This perspective is as difficult, in its own way, as unlimited omniscience. In a play such as "Procedure" (see Chapter 14), Joyce Carol Oates puts us in contact directly with the characters so that their different points of view are acted out rather than stated.

First Person

In first-person point of view, the narrator is one of the characters in the narrative, either a witness to the events or a participant. The narrator's relationship to the events and to the other characters determines what can be convincingly revealed. The first-person narrator does not have access to the minds of others (unless the narrator is a psychiatrist revealing professionally gained knowledge— a cute trick). At every moment of the story's progress, the first-person narrator is being characterized by the way he or she thinks and speaks. An interesting example occurs in "Flowers for Algernon" in which the narrator goes from simplemindedness to great intelligence and back again. The very language he uses also changes from simple to complex to simple again.

Central Character. When the first-person narrator is the central character, the fiction borrows the appeal of autobiography. The author has to be careful to restrain this kind of narrator. It is easy to sacrifice the development of the story to the narrator's ego. Often first-person narration is an exploration of how memory works and how a person comes to understand, with the passage of time, the meaning of events that happened years earlier. Ralph Ellison's *Invisible Man* is a powerful example of this technique.

Minor Character/Witness. "I was there" can be almost as compelling as "It happened to me." This kind of narrator has to be a true personality, not merely a convenient reporter of events. The reader must be able to weigh the degree of emotional interest—bias—of this narrator as well as of the central character narrator. Nick Carroway relates the events in *The Great Gatsby* because Fitzgerald's point of view is that Nick is the one who learns from the events even if he is not the central character. In Alice McDermott's *Charming Billy,* we don't even realize that the narration is a first person until page 3 and, even then, the storyteller remains in the background until the end of the novel.

In the hands of an unsubtle writer, the first person may be simply a way of framing the story because the first person appears easier. In such cases the "I" is simply a set of eyes and ears without real involvement in the action. We can't recommend this device as a general practice since it can be rather clunky and the author might as well use an omniscient narrator. You want the first person involved in some way, as is Arthur Conan Doyle's Dr. Watson, who tells about

Sherlock Holmes, has opinions about and reactions to the mystery, and also is involved in events.

The possibilities and effects of point of view are so various that we could hardly illustrate and discuss them in a book twice the size of this one. The aim here is to suggest the limitations and consequences so that you will be aware of them at all moments in your planning and drafting.

●   ●   ●   ●   ●   *EXERCISES*   ●   ●   ●   ●   ●

1. Describe an object

    a. as if you secretly desired it;
    b. as if you were trying to, but could not quite, conceal your contempt for it;
    c. as if you had never seen anything like it before (you are from Alpha Centauri);
    d. as a child of ten might describe it; and
    e. as your roommate, mother, father, sister, or brother might describe it.

2. Write a blog for the big bad wolf in "Little Red Riding Hood" or the witch in "Hanzel and Gretel" justifying their behavior.

In each of the sections dedicated to different genre, we will touch again on point of view. Here we present a story that illustrates how a writer can manipulate the effects. As you read it, jot down your changing point of view. We will follow the story with our own explorations of Dorothy Canfield Fisher's technique.

Sex Education

It was three times—but at interval of many years—that I heard my Aunt Minnie tell about an experience of her girlhood that had made a never-to-be-forgotten impression on her. The first time she was in her thirties, still young. But she had then been married for ten years, so that to my group of friends, all in the early teens, she seemed quite of another generation.

The day she told us the story, we had been idling on one end of her porch as we made casual plans for a picnic supper in the woods. Darning stockings at the other end, she paid no attention to us until one of the girls said, "Let's take blankets and sleep out there. It'd be fun"

"No," Aunt Minnie broke in sharply, "you mustn't do that."

"Oh, for goodness sakes, why not!" said one of the young girls, rebelliously. "The boys are always doing it. Why can't we, just once?"

Aunt Minnie laid down her sewing. "Come here, girls," she said, "I want you should hear something that happened to me when I was your age."

Her voice had a special quality which, perhaps, young people of today would not recognize. But we did. We knew from experience that it was the dark voice grown-ups used when they were going to say something about sex.

Yet at first what she had to say was like any dull family anecdote. She had been ill when she was fifteen; and afterwards she was run down, thin, with no appetite. Her folks thought a change of air would do her good, and sent her from Vermont out to Ohio—or was it Illinois? I don't remember. Anyway, one of those places where the corn grows high. Her mother's Cousin Ella lives there, keeping house for her son-in-law.

The son-in-law was the minister of the village church. His wife had died some years before, leaving a young widower with two little girls and a baby boy. He had been a normally personable man then, but the next summer, on the Fourth of July, when he was trying to set off some fireworks to amuse his children, an imperfectly manufactured rocket had burst in his face. The explosion had left one side of his face badly scarred. Aunt Minnie made us see it, as she still saw it, in horrid detail—the stiffened, scarlet scar-tissue distorting one cheek, the lower lip turned out so far in one corner that the moist red mucous-membrane lining always showed, one lower eyelid hanging loose, and watering.

After the accident, his face had been a long time healing. It was then that his wife's elderly mother had gone to keep house and take care of the children. When he was well enough to be about again, he found his position as pastor of the little church waiting for him. The farmers and village people in his congregation, moved by his misfortune, by his faithful service and by his unblemished character, said they would rather have Mr. Fairchild, even with his scarred face, than any other minister. He was a good preacher, Aunt Minnie told us, "and the way he prayed was kind of exciting. I'd never known a preacher, not to live in the same house with him, before. And when he was in the pulpit, with everybody looking up at him, I felt the way his children did, kind of proud to think we had just eaten breakfast at the same table. I liked to call him 'Cousin Malcolm' before folks. One side of his face was all right, anyhow. You could see from that that he *had* been a good-looking man. In fact, probably one of those ministers that all the women—" Aunt Minnie paused, drew her lips together, and looked at us uncertainly.

Then she went back to the story as it happened—as it happened that first time I heard her tell it. "I thought he was a saint. Everybody out there did. That was all *they* knew. Of course, it made a person sick to look at that awful scar—the drooling corner of his mouth was the worst. He tried to keep that side of his face turned away from folks. But you always knew it was there. That was what kept him from marrying again, so Cousin Ella said. I heard her say lots of times that he knew no woman would touch any man who looked the way that he did, not with a ten-foot pole.

"Well, the change of air did do me good. I got my appetite back, and ate a lot and played outdoors a lot with my cousins. They were younger than I (I had my sixteenth birthday there but I still liked to play games. I got taller and laid on some weight. Cousin Ella used to say I grew as fast as the corn did. Their house stood at the edge of the village. Beyond it was one of those big cornfields they have out West. At the time when I first got there, the stalks were only up to a person's knee. You could see over their tops. But it grew like lightning, and before long, it was the way thick woods are here, way over your head, the stalks growing so close together it was dark under them.

"Cousin Ella told us youngsters that it was lots worse for getting lost in than woods, because there weren't any landmarks in it. One spot in a cornfield looked just like any other... 'You children keep out of it,' she used to tell us almost everyday '*especially you girls*.' It's no place for a decent girl. You could easy get so far from the house nobody could hear you if you hollered. There are plenty of men in this town that wouldn't like anything better than—she never said what.

"In spite of what she said, my little cousins and I had figured out that if we went across one corner of the field it would be a short-cut to the village, and sometimes without letting on to Cousin Ella, we'd go that way. After the corn got really tall, the farmer stopped cultivating, and we soon beat down a path in the loose dirt. The minute you were inside the field it was dark. You felt as if you were miles from anywhere. It sort of scared you. But in no time the path turned and brought you out on the far end of Main Street. Your breath was coming fast, maybe, but that was what made you like to do it.

"One day I missed the turn. Maybe I didn't keep my mind on it. Maybe it rained and blurred the tramped-down look of the path. I don't know what. All of a sudden, I knew I was lost. And the minute I knew that, I began to run, just as hard as I could run. I couldn't help it, any more than you can help snatching your hand off a hot stove. I didn't know what I was scared of, I didn't even know I *was* running, till my heart was pounding so hard I had to stop.

"The minute I stood still, I could her Cousin Ella saying, 'There are plenty of men in this town that wouldn't like anything better than—' I didn't know, not really, what she meant. But I knew she meant something horrible. I opened my mouth to scream. But I put both hands over my mouth to keep the scream in. If I made any noise, one of those men would hear me. I thought I heard one just behind me, and whirled around, the other way, and I spun around so fast I almost fell over. I stuffed my hands hard up against my mouth. And then—I couldn't help it—I ran again—but my legs were shaking so I soon had to stop. There I stood, scared to move for fear of rustling the corn and letting the men know where I was. My hair had come down, all over my face. I kept pushing it back and looking around, quick, to make sure one of the men hadn't found out where I was. Then I thought I saw a man coming towards me and I ran away from him—and fell down, and burst some of the buttons off my dress, and was sick to my stomach—and thought I heard a man close to me and got up and staggered around, knocking into the corn because I couldn't even see where I was going.

"And then, off to one side, I saw Cousin Malcolm. Not a man—. The minister. He was standing still, one hand up to his face, thinking. He hadn't heard me.

"I was so *terrible* glad to see him, instead of one of those men. I ran as fast as I could and just flung myself on him to make myself feel how safe I was." ...

Aunt Minnie had become strangely agitated. Her hands were shaking, her face was crimson. She frightened us. We could not look away from her. As we waited for her to go on, I felt little spasms twitch at the muscles inside my body.—"And what do you think that *saint,* that holy minister of the Gospel did to an innocent child who clung to him for safety? The most terrible look came into his eyes—you girls are too young to know what he looked like. But once you're married, you'll find out. He grabbed hold of me—that dreadful face of his was *right on mine*—and began clawing the clothes off my back."

She stopped for a moment, panting. We were too frightened to speak. She went on: "He had torn my dress right down to the waist before I—then I *did* scream—all I could—a pulled away from him so hard I almost fell down, and ran and all of a sudden I came out of the corn, right in the backyard of the Fairchild house. The children were staring at the corn, and Cousin Ella ran out of the kitchen door. They had heard the screaming. Cousin Ella shrieked out, 'What is it? What has happened? Did a man scare you?' And I said, 'Yes, yes, yes, a man—I ran—!' And then I fainted away. I must have. The next thing I knew I was on the sofa in the living-room and Cousin Ella was slapping my face with a wet towel."

She had to wet her lips with her tongue before she could go on. Her face was gray now. "There! That's the kind of things girls' folks ought to tell them about—so they'll know what men are like."

She finished her story as if she were dismissing us. We wanted to go away, but were too horrified to stir. Finally, one of the youngest girls asked in a low trembling voice "Aunt Minnie, did you tell on him?"

"No, I was ashamed to," she said briefly. "They sent me home the next day, anyhow. Nobody ever said a word to me about it. And I never either. 'Till now." ...

By what gets printed in some of the modern child-psychology books, you would think that girls to whom such a story had been told would never develop normally. Yet, as far as I can remember what happened to the girls in the group, they all grew up about like anybody. Most of us married, some happily, some not so well. We kept house. We learned more or less—how to live with our husband; we had children and struggled to bring them up right—we went forward into life just as if we had never been warned not to.

Perhaps, young as we were that day, we had already had enough experience of life so that we were not quite blank paper for Aunt Minnie's frightening story. Whether we thought of it then or not, we couldn't have failed to see that at this very time Aunt Minnie had been married for ten years or more, comfortably and well married, too. Against what she tried by that story to brand into our minds, stood the cheerful homelife in that house, the good-natured, and hard-working husband, and the children—the three rough-and-tumble, nice little boys, so adored by their parents, and the sweet girl baby who died, of whom they could never speak without tears. It was the actual contact with adult life that probably kept generation after generation of girls from being scared by tales like Aunt Minnie's into a neurotic horror of living. . . .

Of course, since Aunt Minnie was so much older than we, her boys grew up to be adolescents and young men while our children were still little enough so that our worry over them were nothing more serious than whooping cough and trying to get them to make their own beds. Two of our aunt's three boys followed, without losing their footing, the narrow path which leads across adolescence into normal adult life. But the middle one, Jake, repeatedly fell off into the morass. "Girl trouble," as the succinct family phrase put it. He was one of those boys who have "charm," whatever we mean by that, and he was always being snatched at by girls who would be "all wrong" for him to marry. And once, at nineteen, he ran away from home, whether with one of these girls or not we never heard, for through all her ups and downs with this son, Aunt Minnie tried fiercely to protect him from scandal that might cloud his later life.

Her husband had to stay on his job to earn the family living. She was the one who went to find Jake. When it was gossiped around that Jake was in "bad company" his mother drew some money from the family savings-bank account, and silent, white-cheeked, took the train to the city where rumor said he had gone.

Some weeks later he came back with her. With no girl. She had cleared him of that entanglement. As of others, which followed, later. Her troubles seemed over when, at a "suitable" age, he fell in love with a "suitable" girl, married her and took her to live in our shire town, sixteen miles away where he had a good position. Jake was always bright enough.

Sometimes, idly, people speculated as to what Aunt Minnie had seen that time she went after her runaway son, wondering where her search for him had taken her—very queer places for Aunt Minnie to be in, we imagined. And how could such an ignorant home-keeping woman ever have known what to say to an errant willful boy to set him straight?

Well, of course, we reflected, watching her later struggle with Jake's erratic ways, she certainly could not have remained ignorant, after seeing over and over what she probably had; after talking with Jake about the things which, a good many times, must have come up with desperate openness between them.

She kept her own counsel. We never knew anything definite about the facts of those experiences of hers. But one day she told a group of us—all then married women—something which gave us a notion about what she had learned from them....

We were hastily making a layette for a not especially welcome baby in a poor family. In those days, our town had no such thing as a district-nursing service. Aunt Minnie, a vigorous woman of fifty-five, had come in to help. As we sewed, we talked, of course; and because our daughters were near or in their teens, we were comparing notes about the bewildering responsibility of bringing up our girls.

After a while, Aunt Minnie remarked: "Well, I hope you teach your girls some *sense*. From what I read, I know you're great on telling them 'the facts,' facts we never heard when we were girls. Like as not, some facts I don't know, now. But knowing the facts isn't going to do them any more good than *not* knowing the facts ever did, unless they have some sense taught them, too."

"What do you mean, Aunt Minnie?" one of us asked her uncertainly.

She reflected, threading a needle: "Well, I don't know but what the best way to tell you what I mean, is to tell you about something that happened to me, forty years ago. I've never said anything about it before. But I've thought about it a good deal. Maybe—"

She had hardly begun when I recognized the story—her visit to her Cousin Ella's mid-western home, the widower with his scarred face and saintly reputation and, very vividly, her getting lost in the great cornfield. I knew every word she was going to say—to the very end, I thought.

But no, I did not. Not at all.

She broke off, suddenly to explain with impatience: "Wasn't I the big ninny? But not so big a ninny as that old cousin of mine. I could wring her neck for getting me in such a state. Only she didn't know any better, herself. That was the way they brought young people up in those days, scaring them out of their wits about the awfulness of getting lost, but not telling them a thing about how *not* to get lost. Or how to act, if they did.

"If I had had the sense I was born with, I'd have known that running legs off in a zigzag was the worst thing I could do. I couldn't have been more than a few feet from the path when I noticed I wasn't on it. My tracks in the loose ploughed dirt must have been perfectly plain. If I'd h' stood still and collected my wits, I could have looked down to see which way my footsteps went and just walked back over them to the path and gone on about my business.

"Now I ask you, if I'd been told how to do that, wouldn't it have been a better protection for me—if protection was what my cousin thought she wanted to give me—than to scare me so at the idea of being lost that I turned deaf-dumb-and-blind when I thought I was?

"And anyhow that patch of corn wasn't as big as she let on. And she knew it wasn't. It was no more than a big field in a farming country. I was a well-grown girl of sixteen, as tall as I am now. If I couldn't have found the path, I could have just walked along one line of cornstalks—*straight*—and I'd have come out somewhere in ten minutes. Fifteen at the most. Maybe not just where I wanted to go. But all right, safe, where decent folks were living."

She paused, as if she had finished. But at the inquiring blankness in our faces, she went on: "Well now, why isn't teaching girls—and boys, too, for the Lord's sake don't forget they need it as much as the girls—about this man-and-woman business, something like that? If you give them the idea—no matter whether it's *as* you tell them the facts, or as you *don't* tell them the facts, that it is such a terrible scary thing that if they take a step into it, something's likely to happen to them so awful that you're ashamed to tell them what—well, they'll lose their heads and run around like crazy things, first time they take one step away from the path.

"For they'll be trying out the paths, all right. You can't keep them from it. And a good thing, too. How else are they going to find out what it's like. Boys' and girls' going together is a path across one corner of growing up. And when they go together, they're likely to get off the path some. Seems to me, its up to their folks to bring them up so, when they do, they don't start screaming and running circles, but stand still, right where they are, and get their breath and figure out how to get back.

"And, anyhow, you don't tell 'em the truth about sex" (I was astonished to hear her use the actual word, tabu to woman of her generation) "if they get the idea from you that it's all there is to living. It's not. If you don't get to where you want to go in it, where there's a lot of landscape all around it a person can have a good time in.

D'you know, I believe one thing that gives girls and boys the wrong idea is they way folks *look*! My old cousin's face, I can see her now, it was as red as a rooster's comb when she was telling me about men in that cornfield. I believe now kind of *liked* to talk about it."

(Oh, Aunt Minnie—and yours! I thought.)

Someone asked, "But how *did* you get out, Aunt Minnie?"

She shook her head, laid down her sewing. "More foolishness. The minister my mother's cousin was keeping house for—her son-in-law—I caught sight of him, down along one of the aisles of cornstalks, looking down at the ground, thinking, the way he often did. And I was so glad to see him I rushed right up to him, and flung my arms around his neck and hugged him. He hadn't heard me coming. He gave a great start, put one arm around me and turned his face full towards me—I suppose for just a second he had forgotten how awful one side of it was. His expression, his eyes—well, you're all married women, you know how he looked, the way any able-bodied man thirty-six-or-seven, who'd been married and begotten children, would look—for a minute, anyhow, if a full-blooded girl of sixteen, who ought to have known better, flung herself at him without any warning, her hair tumbling down, her dress half-unbuttoned, and hugged him with all her might.

I was what they called innocent in those days. That is, I knew just as little about what men are like as my folks could manage I should. But I was old enough to know all right what that look meant. And it gave me a start. But, of course, the real thing of it was that dreadful scar of his, so close to my face—that wet corner of his mouth, his eye drawn down with the red inside of the lower eyelid showing—

"It turned me so sick, I pulled away with all my might, so fast that I ripped one sleeve nearly loose, and let out a screech like a wildcat. And ran. Did I run! And in a minute, I was through the corn and had come out in the backyard of the house. I hadn't been more than a few feet from it, probably, any of the time. And then I fainted away. Girls were always fainting away; it was the way our corset-strings were pulled tight, I suppose, and then—oh, a lot of fuss."

"But anyhow," she finished, picking up her work and going on, setting neat, firm stitches with steady hands, "there's one thing, I never told anybody it was Cousin Malcolm I had met in the cornfield. I told my old cousin that 'a man had scared me.' And nobody said anything more about it to me, not ever. That was they way they did in those days. They thought if they didn't let on about something, maybe it wouldn't have happened. I was send back to Vermont right away, and Cousin Malcolm went on being minister of that church.

"I've always been," said Aunt Minnie moderately, "kind of proud that I didn't go and ruin a man's life for just one second's slip-up. If you could have called it that. For it *would* have ruined him. You know how hard as stone people are about other folks' let-downs. If I'd have told, not one person in that town would have had any charity. Not one would have tried to understand. One slip, *once,* and they'd have pushed him down in the mud. If I had told, I'd have felt pretty bad about it later—when I came to have more sense. But I declare, I can't see how I came to have the decency, dumb as I was then, to know that it wouldn't be fair."...

It was not long after this talk that Aunt Minnie's elderly husband died, mourned by her, by all of us. She lived alone then. It was peaceful October weather for her, in which she kept a firm roundness of face and figure as quiet-living countrywomen often do, on into her late sixties.

But then Jake, the boy who had girl trouble, had wife trouble. We heard he had taken to running after a young girl, or was it that she was running after him? It was something serious. For his nice wife left him and came back with the children to live with her mother in our town. Poor Aunt Minnie used to go to see her for long talks which made them both cry. And she went to keep house for Jake, for months at a time.

She grew old, during those years. When finally she (or something) managed to get the marriage mended so that Jake's wife relented and went back to live with him, there was no trace left of her pleasant brisk freshness. She was stooped and slow-footed and shrunken. We, her kinspeople, although we would have given our lives for any one of our own children wonder whether Jake was worth what it had cost his mother to—well, steady him, or reform him. Or perhaps just understand him. Whatever it took.

She came of a long-lived family and was able to go on keeping house for herself well into her eighties. Of course, we and the other neighbors stepped in often to make sure she was all right. Mostly, during those brief calls, the talk turned on nothing more vital than her geraniums. But one mid-winter afternoon, sitting with her in front of her cozy stove, I chanced to speak in rather hasty blame of someone who had, I thought, acted badly. To my surprise this brought from her the story about the cornfield which she had evidently quite forgotten telling me, twice before.

This time she told it almost dreamily, swaying to and fro in her rocking-chair, her eyes fixed on the long slope of snow outside her window. When she came to the encounter with the minister she said, looking from the distance and back into my eyes: "I know now that I had been, all along, kind of *interested* in him, the way any girl as old as I was would be in any youngish man living in the same house with her. And a minister, too. They have to have the gift of gab so much more than most men, women get to thinking they are more alive than men who can't talk so well. I *thought* the reason I threw my arms around him was because I had been so scared. And I certainly had been scared, by my old cousin's horrible talk about the cornfield being full of men waiting to grab girls. But that wasn't all the reason I flung myself at Malcolm Fairchild and hugged him. I know that now. Why in the world shouldn't I have been taught *some* notion of it then? 'Twould do girls good to know that they are just like everybody else—human nature *and* sex, all mixed up together. I didn't have to hug him. I wouldn't if he'd been dirty or fat and old, or chewed tobacco."

I stirred in my chair, ready to say, "But it's not so simple as all that to tell girls—" and she hastily answered my unspoken protest. "I know, I know, most of it can't be put into words. There just aren't any words to say something that's so both-ways-at-once all the times as this man-and-woman business. But look here, you know as well as I do that there are lots more ways than in words to teach young folks what you want 'em to know."

The old woman stopped her swaying rocker to peer far back into the past with honest eyes. "What was in my mind back there in the cornfield—partly, anyhow—was what had been there all the time I was living in the same house with Cousin Malcolm—that he had long straight legs, and broad shoulders, and lots of curly brown hair, and was nice and flat in front, and that one side of his face was good-looking. But most of all that he and I were really alone, for the first time, without anybody to see us.

"I suppose, if it hadn't been for that dreadful scar, he'd have drawn me up, tight, and—most any man would—kissed me. I know how I must have looked, all red and hot and my hair down and my dress torn open. And, used as he was to big cornfields, he probably never dreamed that the reason I looked that way was because I was scared to be by myself in one. He may have thought—you know what he may have thought.

"Well—if his face had been like anybody's, when he looked at me the way he did, the way a man does look at a woman he wants to have, it would have scared me—some. I'd have cried, maybe. And probably he'd have kissed me again. You know how such things go. I might have come out of the cornfield halfway engaged to marry him. Why not? I was old enough, as people thought then. That would have been Nature. That was probably what he thought of, in that first instance.

"But what did I do? I had one look at his poor horrible face and started back as though I'd stepped on a snake. And screamed and ran.

"What do you suppose *he* felt, left there in the corn? He must have been sure that I would tell everybody he had attacked me. He probably thought that when he came out and went back to the village he'd already be in disgrace and put out of the pulpit.

"But the worst must have been to find out, so rough, so plain from the way I acted—as if somebody had hit with an ax—the way he would look to any woman he might try to get close to."

"That must have been—" she drew a long breath—"well, pretty hard on him."

After a silence, she murmured pityingly, "Poor man!"

Some of the thematic elements and story telling techniques in "Sex Education" are a bit old-fashioned. Except for certain pockets of tradition, we don't get quite as worked up these days as they did in 1946 when sex education in schools was still a hot issue and most young people were left to pick up any specific knowledge of sex in the streets or from furtive and brief talks with parents. The other elements still have resonance; young people do behave intensely during puberty and, with new experiences and maturity, perceptions do change.

Like "Ozymandias," the story has an observing narrator, the niece, who listens to Aunt Minnie's changing point of view about the incident in the corn field. The niece also represents a generation that was beginning to modify its attitudes about the proper behavior of women. She and her friends want to do what the boys do—camp in the woods. The more objective first-person narrator also allows the author to present the stories as discreet units because the niece can provide the bridges. If the narrator were Aunt Minnie, she would have to be aware right at the beginning that her point of view had changed and we'd lose the humor and pathos.

In a way, point of view itself is the dramatic subject: not only does Aunt Minnie's point of view about the incident change, but also the niece's point of view toward Aunt Minnie changes. We understand implicitly that time has been a factor; even more important, some experiences happened with Aunt Minnie's son that deepened her understanding of the need for better education about sex and particularly about the sexual energies released during puberty. Ironically, the "sex education" comes too late for Aunt Minnie and the sad implication is that she feels she has missed out on an opportunity.

You probably noticed other examples of point of view. Aunt Minnie's parents send her to Ohio because they think she has been ill and is run down; we realize that she is run down because she is in the throes of puberty. Cousin Malcolm is handsome seen from one angle and frightening seen from another. This fact underlies Aunt Minnie's ambivalence toward him and is an emblem of the attitudes about sex. From the niece's point of view, Aunt Minnie had a "comfortable" marriage; clearly, however, Aunt Minnie looks back at Cousin Malcolm as the lost romantic love. Aunt Minnie's point of view not only changes through time, but as the last few paragraphs show, she realizes that there are other points of view.

● ● ● ● ● *EXERCISE* ● ● ● ● ●

Write the incident from Cousin Malcolm's or Cousin Ella's point of view. You will have to think about how they looked at the sixteen-year old Cousin Minnie.

———————————●———————————

We can't resist giving you one more instance of point of view as the controlling element in a piece. The following poem by John Godfrey Saxe is a variation of a classic parable about the limits of man's understanding.

The Blind Men and the Elephant

It was six men of Indostan, to learning much inclined,
who went to see the elephant (Though all of them were blind),
that each by observation, might satisfy his mind.

The first approached the elephant, and, happening to fall,
against his broad and sturdy side, at once began to bawl:
"God bless me! but the elephant, is nothing but a wall!"

The second feeling of the tusk, cried: "Ho! what have we here,
so very round and smooth and sharp? To me tis mighty clear,
this wonder of an elephant, is very like a spear!"

The third approached the animal, and, happening to take,
the squirming trunk within his hands, "I see," quoth he,
"the elephant is very like a snake!"

The fourth reached out his eager hand, and felt about the knee:
"What most this wondrous beast is like, is mighty plain," quoth he;
"Tis clear enough the elephant is very like a tree."

The fifth, who chanced to touch the ear, said; "E'en the blindest man
can tell what this resembles most; Deny the fact who can,
This marvel of an elephant, is very like a fan!"

The sixth no sooner had begun, about the beast to grope,
than, seizing on the swinging tail, that fell within his scope,
"I see," quoth he, "the elephant is very like a rope!"

And so these men of Indostan, disputed loud and long,
each in his own opinion, exceeding stiff and strong,
Though each was partly in the right, and all were in the wrong!

So, oft in theologic wars, the disputants, I ween,
tread on in utter ignorance, of what each other mean,
and prate about the elephant, not one of them has seen!

● ● ● ● ● *EXERCISE* ● ● ● ● ●

Do an Internet search on the poem and find the other variations of the parable.
Try your hand at writing a new version about the limitations of point of view.
For example, a later adaptation of the parable goes like this:

> Three blind elephants put their feet on a man. The first one says:
> "A man is flat." The second one says: "A man is very flat." The third
> one says: "A man is exceedingly flat."

———————————◆———————————

As you continue experimenting with point of view, you will become more
and more aware of its ramifications. Selecting the appropriate narrator for a
story, poem, or even an essay has a lot to do with the shape of the work. The
choice determines what information, in what order, with what coloring, reaches
the reader and how the reader will respond to those elements. Once you have
made—or remade—this fundamental decision, you are destined to follow out
its logical consequences for the reader.

> *"Anecdotes don't make good stories. Generally I dig*
> *down underneath them so far that the story that finally*
> *comes out is not what people thought their anecdotes*
> *were about."*
>
> Alice Munro

CHAPTER 4

LANGUAGE IS YOUR MEDIUM

"The ill and unfit choice of words wonderfully obstructs the understanding."

Francis Bacon

 THERE IS NO SUCH THING AS A SYNONYM

Words and sentences are the writer's nuts and bolts, nails, screws, and bricks. Just as cabinetmakers develop an acute sense of the limits and purposes of materials—the strengths, lengths, thicknesses, and infinite properties of bolts, glues, and woods in combination—so do writers develop a heightened awareness of the infinite properties of words.

A cabinetmaker knows that you don't use a tenpenny nail when you need a brad, or a hacksaw when you need a coping saw. The writer must learn to make analogous judgments: when to use an adjective and when not, when to use a Latinate word, a complex sentence, a nickname, a noun instead of a pronoun, a quiet word rather than a noisy one. Your first job as a writer is to master the medium of your trade—language itself. Achieving mastery is not easy.

You should already be using your journal to exercise your awareness of how words function in particular circumstances. However, just as painters are aware of colors whenever they open their eyes, just as composers are alert to sounds at all times, so too writers are always on a busman's holiday, listening to how people use words and, in their reading, testing the choices of other writers.

Our purposes in this chapter are (1) to get you thinking about ways to hone your word sense, (2) to introduce the complex decision making that goes into finding the right words to nail your meaning to the reader's mind, and (3) to alter some mistaken notions you may have about effective word choice (diction).

We offer one basic principle:

For a writer, there is no such thing as a synonym.

This principle may come as a surprise if you have spent years doing synonym exercises in English classes or if you have been repeatedly warned against repeating a word and told to replace a word with a synonym. Teachers give such exercises and warnings in the name of vocabulary building. Or they have the notion that repetition is, somehow, almost a grammatical error and confuse it with its wicked cousin . . . redundancy. The writer's ideal, however, is to find the exact word or phrase for the job. We assume there is always a best choice. For a *best* choice, there is no substitute. What word can you substitute for *rose* and mean *rose* with all of its associations?

It is important to grasp how words that appear to refer to the same object or idea on the surface actually differ. For example, *home, house, residence, dwelling* and *domicile* refer to the place where someone lives. Given that you can use only one of the words in a particular circumstance, you must choose the one that not only will have the correct **denotation** but also will carry the **connotation** you desire. "He was eager to be finally going to his domicile" just doesn't feel right for a context in which the writer imagines his character's emotions on returning to his house. But it might be effective if a stuffy character is saying to another character whom he is trying to impress: "The rooms in my domicile are all furnished with Persian carpets." Or, one can envision a poet playing with the idea that *domicile* derives from that Latin word for *house*.

The criteria for choosing are easy to enumerate, less easy to apply. Your choice must always be

1. accurate
2. precise
3. concrete (unless an abstract term is clearly necessary)
4. appropriate
5. idiomatic

As you can see, these criteria for word choice are the same for "creative" writing as they are for "ordinary" writing (reports, analyses, instructions). One of the bits of misinformation that hampers beginners is the idea that they must use a special language. Actually, what they must do is learn as well as they can the only language we have. Creativity is not measured by the difficulty or sophistication of your words. Nor is it a sign of creativity to foil the reader's expectation at every turn by choosing words for their puzzle quotient. Finally, creativity does not license the misuse of language. Only a responsible, caring attitude toward language leads to effective writing of any kind.

For the following passage, fill in the blank with one of these alternatives—*diaphanous, see-through,* or *transparent.*

> After she dismissed her ladies-in-waiting, the queen snuffed all but one of the candles. She slipped off the heavy flannel nightgown and put on a _____ gown before opening the secret door that led to the tower where Tristram waited.

Which criteria governed your choice? Most writers would choose *diaphanous* because it feels right for a queen and for the world of secret doors and towers and assignations. The word from the Greek words for *through* plus *show* is accurate in that it literally means what the writer intends it to mean. It is precise in that the range of meaning is limited. It is as concrete as something filmy can be— that is, it conveys an image. Most important here, the choice is appropriate in the context: *Diaphanous* carries with it the sense of delicacy and romance that suits the queen's seductive intent. *See-through* sounds crass, and *transparent* sounds almost scientific ("having the property of transmitting rays of light through its substance"). Is *diaphanous* in this context idiomatic? Although it isn't the kind of word we are likely to use when ordering lingerie at Victoria's Secret, it is consistent with a special style—the conventional idiom for historical romance writing.

What a word connotes, either alone or in a particular context, may differ slightly from person to person, depending upon one's experiences with life and language. There are no rules except to be sensitive to choosing the most telling words for the context. Since connotations are in the ear of the listener, the point is to be aware of all the fine adjustments that you may need to make when revising.

●   ●   ●   ●   ●   *EXERCISES*   ●   ●   ●   ●   ●

1. Write a short scene in which *home* is the most appropriate word for the emotional state a character has when thinking about where she was brought up. Now try substituting *residence* or *house.* Is there any change in tone? In what context might *residence* and *house* carry the desired denotation?

2. Write a brief scene for each word in these triplets:

   a. eat/dine/consume
   b. hate/detest/loath

   c. sexpot/seductress/temptress
   d. teacher/mentor/professor
   e. frugal/cheap/economical
   f. book/volume/tome

One way of sharpening your language skills is to practice and then evaluate word substitutions while you are reading already published works. When you write, however, we recommend a sparing and careful use of your printed or computer thesaurus. A word chosen from a list simply because it is on the list is not likely to be an effective choice. The thesaurus can be a good memory jogger; it can provide you with a range of possibilities from which to make choices, particularly when you know there is a better word and just can't bring it to mind.

For choosing the best word when you are in doubt, you may find it useful to know its history. It is simple to search the Internet for both definitions and a description of sources. You may even shake loose new ideas for writing the passage you are working on. (If you can afford one, buy the *Oxford English Dictionary* or its software version, both of which contain extensive descriptions of a word's history and use.)

Our statement that "for the writer, there is no such thing as a synonym" requires one modification. Pronouns point to other words and phrases and so, in a way, they act as synonyms. Assuming that the reference is clear, pronouns can provide variety for the eye, since *he* stands for *George* and *it* stands for *balloon*. (See "Excessive Variation" pp. 77–78.)

CHOOSING WELL

> " *The most valuable of all talents is that
> of never using two words when one will do.* "
>
> Thomas Jefferson

Now let's examine the criteria listed earlier in more detail.

Accuracy

When a word choice is accurate, it is free from error. It is "correct" in the sense that its accepted meaning is the meaning the author intends. Unless a word choice is accurate, it has no chance of being effective. Here are some examples of inaccuracy in diction from the work of beginners:

1. Landing a thumb on the sheet resonated through her ears, then forefinger, middle finger, the ring, and the pinky, each alighting as gingerly as Armstrong's first *tenuous* steps on the moon, Bea secured a fistful of bloody sheet. [The writer has confused *tenuous* with *tentative*. Given the context "resonated through her ears" is too loud.]

2. I went through the muggy July day as if I were in a trance, *immune* to the outside world and locked up inside my body. [The action suggests that *impervious* or *untouched by* would be a more accurate. Incidentally, *body* probably should be *mind*.]

3. Brad had won far *lesser* awards than his father who had twenty medals. [The writer has confused *fewer* and *lesser*. Unintentionally, the writer has addressed the significance of the awards rather than the number of them.]

4. Though a conventional lady now, in the 20s, her grandmother was a *flopper*. [The word is *flapper*, and *flopper* may create unintended suggestions and laughter. The reader has no way of knowing if the word comes from ignorance or mistyping.]

5. I tried to light the half-smoked Camel, but my fingers were shaking and I lit it twice. Finally, the *stogie* ignited. [A *stogie* refers to a cigar, not a cigarette.]

Among the regrettable results of such inaccurate diction is that the writer may (1) confuse the reader; (2) stop the reader who will mentally correct an error but who will be annoyed and may lose respect for the writing; or (3) provoke laughter when the writer wanted to cause a different reaction. Two ways to avoid the problems in the preceding examples are to steer clear of using any word that you haven't seen or heard in context and to proofread carefully and often. Knowing what the words point to is essential for clarity.

Precision

The connotation and denotation of words have greater and lesser ranges. It is just as accurate to call Mr. Williams the *spouse* of Mrs. Williams as it is to call him her *husband*. However, while *husband* is the more sharply defined term and thus the more precise, some occasions will dictate *spouse* as the better choice. *Spouse* (from the Latin "sponsus," a betrothed man) is precise in a legal context but not in other contexts. Here are some examples of damaging imprecision:

1. The small town *loomed* in the distance. [In the broad sense, *loomed* is accurate; however, its normal and expected usage has to do with figures, states, or images of impending doom or magnitude. A "small town" would be far less likely to loom than a mountain.]

2. The microwave timer buzzed and the smokey aroma of cooking meat penetrated her consciousness causing her stomach to lurch. [Many problems

here. *Aroma* is accurate but not precise because we associate *aroma* with a pleasant smell, not one that turns your stomach. Is the ready-made phrase "penetrated her consciousness" accurate? precise? concrete? appropriate? idiomatic? In the context, do we need to be told that the meat is "cooking"?]

3. The airline crash dominated the headlines: "Thirty dead, sixty-eight *wounded.*" [We would expect *injured* in such a situation, even if the people have suffered wounds. As worded, the passage suggests a battlefield statistic rather than an accident.]

4. The club was *quite nice.* It *clearly* catered to an upper-class, upwardly mobile clientele. It was filled with twenty- and thirty-year-olds who had skipped lunch for the *healthy* pursuit of fitness. [In addition to using the weasel-word *quite* and the nonword *nice*, this writer has shoved in the unnecessary word *clearly* and the self-evident word *healthy*. When words are meaningless or useless, your diction is not precise. Being *pre*cise and being *con*cise are often two sides of the same coin.]

5. He clutched a long wooden staff with ornate carvings *inscribed* on it. [The probable redundancy and definite wordiness causes imprecision and fuzziness. How about ending after "carvings"? How about "...staff ornately carved" or "with ornate inscriptions"? At any rate, the carvings wouldn't be inscribed, the designs or figures—wreaths, snakes, legends—would be.]

The search for preciseness is not simply a matter of choosing words. Choosing words in the appropriate context is a factor. The following description is, from one point of view, not precise:

> Harriet realized that Don had gone without saying goodbye. His empty coffee cup with the picture of black and white cows on it sat beside the business section of the *Times*.

Of course, "black and white cows" have a precise name—Holsteins. Let's say, however, that the writer wants the reader to realize that to Harriet a cow is a cow is a cow. They all give milk. How can the writer communicate that it is Harriet who is being imprecise, not he?

> Harriet realized that Don had gone without saying goodbye. His empty coffee cup with the picture of black and white cows on it sat beside the business section of the *Times*. She could hear Don yelling: "How many times have I got to tell you that they are . . . " What was the word? Holsters? Something like that.

Now we have a more precise picture of Harriet's mind because the writer has let the reader know that her imprecision may be a bone of contention with her husband. The elegant solution to imprecision dramatizes and characterizes.

Imprecise diction leaves the reader with a foggy notion of the actions, things, or emotions that the writer wants to evoke. Like a hastily taken snapshot with a cheap camera, the narrative is unfocused.

Concreteness

Concrete diction is usually preferred over abstract or general diction. Concrete diction evokes images, bits of sensory experience. (See the "Imagery" section in Chapter 5, "The Elements of Poetry.") Compare the impact of these three statements:

> John exhibited emotional hostility.
> John was angry.
> John fumed.

The first is formal and abstract, though perhaps appropriate for a psychological case study. The second is abstract, but at least it is clear and direct. The third is concrete: It gives us, by way of metaphor, a vivid picture that conveys the meaning more forcefully, more economically, and more memorably than the other two. *Fumed* suggests the release of dangerous gases.

We are not saying that abstract language must be eliminated from all writing. Writers need words that point to concepts and categories as well as those that refer directly to sensory experience. However, it is always dangerous to depend too much on words that *tell* rather than *show*—to depend on words that may point well enough but do not tickle the imagination. As they struggle with their craft, writers learn the fine balance between abstract and concrete formulations. However, as a rule of thumb we suggest that *when in doubt, make it concrete.*

(**Figurative language,** discussed later in this chapter, often expresses the abstract in concrete terms.)

Concreteness is relative. Even terms that are not abstract can become more concrete by becoming more specific. In the sentences that follow, the italicized general terms are followed by more precise alternatives in parentheses:

1. The *girl* (child, toddler, daughter, princess, Alice) *cried* (wailed, sobbed, whimpered).
2. *He* (the student, Edgar) *got* (asked for, ordered, bought, demanded) *food* (Italian food, a pizza, a pepperoni pizza).
3. Edgar also ordered a *drink* (beer, Sprite, Guinness).

Though a good deal of the writer's search for the concrete occurs in revision, as you write more you will acquire the habit of mind that recognizes abstract diction as the work unfolds.

● ● ● ● ●   *EXERCISES*   ● ● ● ● ●

Revise the following for greater concreteness:

1. The man walked slowly down the street.

2. An emotional condition was manifest in her appearance.

3. The building seemed quite imposing.

4. Jane put on her clothes and ate some tasteless food.

————————————●————————————

The general principle for achieving concreteness is that you call things by the most specific name you can and you describe actions with the most specific verbs you can, leaving minimal work to be done by modifiers. For today's reader, product names also create a firm sense of time and place and are useful for creating **verisimilitude** (see pp. 225–228). Of course, to be concrete you must either be observant or research enough to appear so. We all know that a forest is made of trees, but few of us are in the habit of thinking about the names of the trees and what our response may be to those names. Beware, however, that the name of the tree also needs to be precise. An acacia, despite is lovely sound, is not one under which American lovers might rest after a long hike in Yellowstone National Park. It's an African savannah tree.

Appropriateness

When you choose your words, you have to please two masters. First, you need to consider how appropriate your diction may be for your particular audience. Second, you have to consider how appropriate your diction may be for your genre, your character (see Chapter 3, "Point of View," pp. 41–44), and the set of circumstances, including the overall language context within which your decisions take place. Compare the diction in the following three sentences:

> The patient manifests the delusion that his *siblings* are poisoning his food. [psychiatric case history]
> Henry called in the private eye because he thought his *brother and sister* were putting curare in his pasta. [fiction narration]
> "I tell ya Doc, my *siblings* is out to get me." [speech of an uneducated person who wishes to impress.]

Since you are part of an audience yourself, and since you will probably write for people like yourself, you already have a sense of what diction is inappropriate because it will offend. You don't use street language in a poem for a religious periodical. Similarly, common sense will lead you to consider the age, experience, and knowledge of the audience you wish to address. If you have any doubts about the diction appropriate for an audience, study the kinds of writing your intended audience already reads.

Here is an example of the problem in choosing appropriate diction for audience and character. Let us say you are writing for eight- to twelve-year-olds:

> Tom arranged with Becky for a rendezvous at her house.

Your editor self (or an outside editor) tells you that your audience is not likely to know what *rendezvous* means, and you know how looking up a word interrupts the flow of your own reading. So you agree to do the dictionary work for your young reader:

> Tom arranged with Becky for a rendezvous (a meeting) at her house.

Oops! You realize this solution won't do because the new version reads like an essay. You try some substitutions:

> a. Tom arranged with Becky for a meeting at her house.
> b. Tom made an agreement with Becky to present himself at her house.

The (b) revision sounds like something corporate lawyers might say. The (a) attempt is easily accessible, but the romantic overtones of *rendezvous* and your sense of Tom's show-off character (*he* might use such a word) are lost. And, though the thesaurus might tempt you with a word like *assignation,* this temptation would have to be resisted on grounds already mentioned.

> Tom told Becky that he'd be at her house that evening.

Too bland.

What about turning the problem with *rendezvous* into the solution? Suppose Tom does know the word but neither the reader nor Becky does.

> "Let's rendezvous at your house," Tom said.
>
> "I don't think my parents would like that and I'm sure I wouldn't either," said Becky, tossing her head.
>
> "We meet at your house all the time."
>
> "Oh, is that all?"

In this case, a bit of inventiveness allowed you to teach a new word and to show Tom's character.

The words that reach your audience must convey more than surface information; they must fit many purposes simultaneously. Consider the following passage:

> The death of a famous actress is the signal, as a rule, for a great deal of maudlin excitement. The world that knew her rushes up on that last stage where she lies with her eyes sincerely closed and joins, as it were, in her death scene, posturing and poetizing around her bier like a pack of amateur mummers. For a few days everyone who knew her is a road company Mark Antony burying her with bad oratory. The stage is a respectable and important institution, what with its enormous real estate holdings, but we still patronize an actress, particularly a dead one.
>
> from Ben Hecht, "Actor's Blood"

The narrator of this passage is not simply reporting the fact of someone's death. We can tell that the narrator is familiar with the world of acting ("scene," "mummers," "road company," "Mark Antony"). Moreover, the writer has chosen words to reveal a contemptuous or ironic attitude about Hollywood.

●   ●   ●   ●   ●   *EXERCISES*   ●   ●   ●   ●   ●

1. In the preceding passage by Hecht, locate and describe the word choices that reveal the narrator's attitude. Consider accuracy, precision, concreteness, and especially appropriateness.

2. Answer the questions that follow this passage, which is intended for a historical novel about fifteenth-century England:

> With sword or lance or any kind of sidearm Alex was a deadly practitioner. As a hand-to-hand blood spiller he was second to none. He knew a thousand songs, most of them dirty. He was a royster, a rogue, a ruffian, a fornicator, and a basterlycullion, but otherwise and in all other respects the best man in the world.

   a. Is the overall impact of this passage aided or hindered by words we might have difficulty understanding?
   b. Which words contribute to the historical flavoring?
   c. Given your understanding of the writer's purpose, do any of the word choices misfire? Why? What changes do you suggest?

3. Here is a passage from a story intended to be a naturalistic look at a contemporary problem. Can you find language in it that is more properly associated with escapist romance fiction? What is the consequence of this diction clash? (Regina is considering artificial insemination.)

Regina nodded, mute, hugging the sheet around her neck. She wanted to ask him what her chances were, whether he thought it would work, how many babies were conceived this way. But part of her was tired of statistics and percentages, and the other part of her was just tired. So she pushed her fears down into a deep, secret place in her heart and forced a "brave girl" smile.

———————●———————

In a given context, any word or word combination can be appropriate. The writer's job requires an understanding of all the ways in which word choices can be appropriate or inappropriate in particular cases.

Idiomatic Usage

An **idiom** is a word combination whose meaning cannot be logically derived from its combined parts. When we say "the kettle is boiling," we are speaking idiomatically (and probably putting words together in an untranslatable way). After all, the kettle is *not* boiling, the water is. When you "blow an assignment," you don't literally puff air at it. We can hardly communicate without using idioms; they are the soul of language. However, when we write, we often confuse idiomatic expressions with trite expressions and have been frightened away from using natural English idioms. While it is true that triteness is to be avoided, the rich idiomatic resources of our language should be employed whenever they are appropriate—and they almost always are appropriate.

The following sentences contain trite expressions that obscure what is meant beneath lifeless similes or metaphors:

1. He was *as handsome as a prince.*
2. She had a *devilish twinkle* in her eyes which, at times, would *flash with anger.*
3. Their marriage started out *all lovey-dovey.*
4. Whenever they went out for pizza, they would *travel down memory lane,* recalling the *long lost images of their youths.*

The following contain serviceable idioms because they appear to be part of natural speech:

1. Despite Elliot's good looks, Buffy could not *work up* any interest in him.
2. Elliot *ducked out* the back door rather than *face up to* Buffy's anger.
3. Elliot *daydreamed* about Buffy so much that he forgot to take class notes.

The advantage of such words and phrases as *work up* instead of *show* or *ducked out* instead of *left by* is that they create a sense of the character's action rather than the writer's telling. Trite expressions, on the other hand, signal their tiredness to an alert reader who will sense that the writer has *plugged in* the first available *off-the-rack* phrase to arrive quickly at *the bottom line.* These are constructions whose impact has been worn away through overuse. Of course, what might be trite in one circumstance can actually accomplish the writer's purpose in another:

> Priscilla had always thought Jeffrey *as handsome as a prince*—in fact, a character in the romances she read by the hour.

In this example, the author used the trite expression to characterize Priscilla's way of thinking as trite.

Generally speaking, then, you want to avoid the trite, but *not at the expense of the natural.* Examine these alternative passages:

1. In spite of the statistical probability that the situation would eventuate negatively, and half-wondering if she wanted it to, she perpetrated a fraudulent optimism upon herself and aimed her countenance in the direction of the inevitable harsh resolution.
2. Hoping against hope, she faced the music.

Neither of these renderings is effective. However, the first is so clotted, tortured, and unnatural that, if we had to choose, we'd select the trite yet smooth and spontaneous movement of the second.

In brief, you will usually want to work at a natural, idiomatic diction that captures the quality of friendly rather than academic or professional talk. There are exceptions, of course. Writers of historical fiction might use a more formal or archaic diction to suggest a previous age.

● ● ● ● ●   *EXERCISES*   ● ● ● ● ●

1. Match the phrase in the left column with the idiomatic form on the right:

withdraw his assertion	bank on
expect to receive	tune in
adopt a different attitude	pay off
redeem a loan or note	back down
adjust for sharper reception	change one's tune

2. Write two short scenes, the first using any three items from column A and the next using the parallel items from column B. Now examine the differences.

A	B
accept an offer	→ bite at
look for an implied meaning	→ read between the lines
extort all one's money	→ bleed white
disclaim further responsibility	→ wash one's hands of
spent money foolishly	→ blew
stop operating	→ crash
malfunction	→ break down
bring into custody	→ bust
eat greedily	→ wolf down

We encourage you to use idioms rather than to go out of your way to avoid them and end up with stuffy or overwritten prose. Here are some guidelines:

1. Prefer a common idiom to eccentric diction: Buffy felt that he had *no call* to *jump down her throat* simply because she forgot the mustard.
2. Prefer nothing to trite diction: He was handsome (*not* "as handsome as a prince"). Buffy felt a mess (*not* "as if she had been through a meat grinder").
3. Prefer something you may think is trite to a forced expression: When they walked by without saying hello, Buffy felt that she had been given the cold shoulder (*not* "as chilled as a lobster in a freezer").

 ## SOME DICTION PROBLEMS

> *"Proper words in proper places make the true definition of style."*
>
> Jonathan Swift

Many novice writers have the mistaken notion that they should "write writing." That is, they believe effective writing consists of verbal prestidigitation and pyrotechnics. They believe that the words need not be chosen for specific tasks but rather that the words chosen need to sound important and weighty. Some beginners were actually taught to worship words for words' sake; some simply pile words upon words as a substitute for thinking. The result of believing in this false god is twofold: (1) The writing becomes padded and/or inflated; and (2) problems in effective word choice are actually disguised. But even before that happens, the false god leads the writer to put enormous efforts into the wrong type of work: the work of impressing rather than sharing with the reader.

We might have discussed the various guises in which padded and inflated diction choices appear under one or another of our major headings: accuracy, precision, concreteness, appropriateness, and idiomatic. However, the following strivings after quick effects appear often enough to merit separate attention. They are not positive criteria for emulation but negative habits to be avoided.

Overwriting

Many of the problems discussed elsewhere in this section also fit into the **overwriting** category. You overwrite when you puff up your language without adding meaning or impact, as in the following example from the beginning of a story:

> It's funny how certain things, the biggest moments and the smallest *passing thoughts alike, how they* can *both* become your sweetest memories later on. And, *years later,* when the places and the people who gave you these tender times are gone, their memories become *starbright* highlight colors for the tapestry of your life.

The problems in this passage cannot be solved only by removing the obvious overwriting we placed in italics. Taking out such overblown adjectives as *starbright* is only the first step. One still needs to deal with the padding sewn tightly to the rather obvious, even silly, thought that both big and little events can become pleasant memories. This type of overwriting can disguise shallow thinking even from the writer. (Of course, the passage might work if it revealed a rather foolish character's habitual style.)

One type of overwriting grows from a virtue—the virtue of presenting concrete detail for the reader. This virtue becomes a problem when the writer becomes too ambitious and present too many details to absorb.

> As he entered the kitchen, Edward glanced at a double-sided stainless steel sink made by Cleanware overflowing with a dirty pasta pot to which was attached a two-inch string of spaghetti, a small four-inch frying pan loaded with bacon grease, and a Limoge plate made in 1876 on which was a disgusting mix of Johnson steak sauce and fresh cut green beans. His eyes glittered as he smiled ferociously as he thought of what he would say to his roommate.

It is unlikely that concreteness of this sort is doing useful work in the poem, story, or play. Is Edward really taking all the mess in with a "glance"? Since there is no reason in the story to give us all this detail, the elaboration becomes a distraction and feels inauthentic. Unless you are writing a comedy, readers will either laugh or skip the description—or even close the book. Perhaps a corrolary principle to the general principle for achieving concreteness is "no more than just enough." (Incidentally, do eyes "glitter" and can smiles be "ferocious"?)

Overmodification

Overmodification also comes from the admirable attempt to be concrete. However, the piling up of adjectives, adverbs, and prepositional phrases is a signal that something is wrong and that the writer has done the wrong kind of work. Often the muscle of sentence structure and meaning gets covered over by the modifying fat. Adverbs and adjectives create concrete images only when they specify a class for which no concrete word exists. For example, if you need to describe the "*red* walls" in your character's room, you'd be hard put to find a single word that will do the job. In the following cases, the modifications are unnecessary because their meaning overlaps the meaning of the modified word.

> A faded *woven tapestry* hung from the *lintel of the door*. [Most tapestries are woven; *lintel* is the part of the door from which one would hang something as large as a tapestry.]
>
> Her lungs felt as if someone had stabbed her *with a knife*. [Here a trite simile is automatically continued to its predictable end. Without the unnecessary final phrase, the expression is sharper.]

Notice that this type of modification is really redundancy.

Some modifying fat simply muddies the work. Read the following passage with and without the words we have struck through.

> "A sad saint is not a saint," she often said, one of her many expressions from a ~~seemingly~~ endless tape. These quotes poured out from her with force or tenderness as the situation demanded. In a less energetic person, remarks such as these would bore, but Bridget's desire to serve gave her ~~ebullient~~ Christian advice a distinctive ~~palatable~~ flavor.

Having removed some of the clutter, the passage is ready for even further editing since the idea of "Christian advice" being made "palatable" requires its own sentence. A useful principle for any writer is to avoid adjectives and adverbs unless the modification is absolutely necessary to present an exact picture. In addition, it is good practice to avoid squeezing into one sentence ideas that may require room to breath on their own.

Another type of overmodification occurs when you use such intensifiers as *very, seem, definitely, kind of,* and *certainly*. They are often called weasel words. The problem is that "very red walls" does not help the reader see "bloodred walls." And one person's *very* may be another person's *kind of*. The weasel word *seemed* leads the reader to falsely expect another reality will shortly be described: "George *definitely seemed* ready to ask for her hand in marriage and got down on his knee to do just that." If George only seemed ready, then we would expect he's on his knees to pick something up. After a time, such word choices lead a reader to doubt whether the writer has a clear picture of the situation about which she is writing.

Saying It Twice

Redundancy is a common problem and has many causes, some of which we have already addressed. In the example that follows, the writer refused to pay attention to what his words were saying, or were supposed to say:

> Gradually he was able to force himself to stay in his chair when a lady came through the door—although he knew in his heart he was acting like a *worthless* cad. (Notice that the adjective leads to redundancy since "worthless" is contained in "cad.")

> With a thump, the dead girl's first, then second arm dropped like leaded, heavy steel. [The pile up of words to describe the event is not only overkill, so to speak; it becomes visually incomprehensible since "leaded steel" appears to be nonsensical. Is there such a thing as "light" steel?]

When something is clearly redundant, the reader is likely to stop and try to figure out why the duplication has occurred. In most cases, stopping readers is not a good idea. Too many stops and they are likely to take another road. Keep in mind that redundancy is the Darth Vader of repetition, the father who represents evil writing. However, repetition can be the good brother if it is in the service of clarity or rhetorical force.

Excessive Variation

The problem of excessive variation used to go by the name of "elegant variation," which is actually inelegance. Simply searching for a way to avoid repeating key words and phrases often creates absurd expression. While repetition can become deadly, often the means taken to avoid it creates even worse problems. In the following passage, the student writer seems to be driven by a misguided but honest desire to avoid repeating his key noun:

> As Jim entered the turn, the *motorcycle* seemed to sink into the ground. He could feel the shocks being compressed as the force of the turn pushed him and his *machine* to a lower center of gravity. As he leaned into the turn, he stuck out his knee for balance. It was hard to remain in control, but Jim calmly, smoothly, lifted his head, twisted the *vehicle* upright, and pulled back with his right wrist. Instantly, the *bike* shot forward, its front wheel once again coming off the ground. Already entering the next turn,

Jim shifted his weight forward and braked hard. Slowing to 100 miles per hour, he leaned the *Kawasaki* once more over to the left. Passing by the pits, he could see David and Georgetti keeping track of his time on the *cycle* while Rhonda displayed it on the leader board for him to see. At the end of the first session, Jim pulled his *trusty mount* back into the pit.

The result is a scattered effect, as well as some uncertainty about whether the writer is always referring to the same thing. Most of all, the reader becomes aware of the writer's struggle to avoid repetition rather than reading through the words to the action.

Latinate Diction

Linking up a series of polysyllabic words from Latin roots makes your writing appear self-consciously learned and unpleasantly pretentious. It also slows the reader down, as the following sentence illustrates:

Jane held to her assertion despite Bill's remonstrance to the contrary. [Can you put this into plain English?]

For most readers, any work in which the writing is heavily Latinate appears to smack of the academic, legal, or bureacratic. For that kind of writing, few people settle into their armchairs with expectations of an enjoyable or emotionally meaningful read.

Archaic Diction

The troublesome habit of archaic diction usually springs from a misguided notion about how to sound "literary" or "poetic." We no longer believe that such words or expressions as *yore, thee, o'er,* or *finny prey* (for *fish*) confer a poetic or dignified quality to writing. In fact, the convention of our day is that effective writing demands the words and rhythms of everyday speech. "Alas! The computer sent him ill tidings about the memory on his disk." *Alas* and *ill tidings* sound like attempts to impose emotions rather than create them. As well, they sound silly in any context that is not meant to be humorous.

Sonic Boom

Sometimes intentionally, sometimes not, a writer allows the sounds to drown out meaning by calling too much attention to themselves, as the following case demonstrates:

The blustery day threatened to batter the delicate blossoms that had drawn *gaggles* of *gawking* tourists to the nation's capital. [One might argue that the alliteration on *b* has a positive effect, but certainly the italicized words make too much noise and pull the reader away from the sense.]

Like archaic diction, such writing is most often an attempt to dress up the work in order to impress the reader.

Passives and Operators

After years of writing academic essays or job related reports, beginning writers often pick up the habit of constructing sentences containing **weak passives** and **operators** under the mistaken notion that they are more professional sounding. Either evil twin would be a stylistic problem in any kind of writing. In creative writing they are deadly. Look at the following from a story about an old man entering senility. Early in the story, the author tells us something about the man's background:

> Arthur's fine clothes were abandoned by him one by one as he gradu-ally traded the life of a young buck for his first real home. Years later when his daughter finally made the decision to ask him why he had given up studying law to pay an extended visit to his sister Ruth, the only answer she got was: "The law's pretty dry."

In the first sentence, Arthur the actor recedes into the background; rather than abandoning his clothes, he is the passive receiver of the action. In the second sentence, Ruth's action is to "make a decision" rather than decide. The word *make* (an operator) controls the sentence. This type of expression has three problems: (1) Readers have to look around for the actor and the true action, (2) thereby slowing them down and (3) injecting more words (eight) into the example for the reader to trudge through. Look at a rewrite to increase the vigor of the sentences:

> As he gradually traded the life of a young buck for his first real home, one by one Arthur abandoned his fine clothes. Years later, when his daughter finally decided to ask why he gave up studying law to pay an extended visit to his sister Ruth, the only answer he gave was: "The law's pretty dry."

The piling up of sentences filled with passive constructions and operators not only slows the reader but also sounds stuffy. In short, such writing does not appear like storytelling. If you tend to write in such a voice, a useful tech-nique for fixing the problem is to circle all verbs during your first revision and removing the offending structures mercilessly. (Fortunately, your computer grammar checker will pick up many passive constructions even if it misses the operators.)

If, as we have suggested, successful writing comes from editing and rewriting, then every good writer must become a word detective, hunting down the criminal elements in early drafts and taking them out of circulation.

Breaking bad habits is only part of the job. A writer also must develop the habit of using effective diction that is accurate, precise, concrete, appropriate, and idiomatic. A writer must understand what it means to live without the comfort of synonyms.

A useful technique for training yourself to look on adjectives and adverbs with a cold eye is to circle each during one stage of editing. Then look to see if you need the modifier. This strategy also will force you to look more closely at the nouns and verbs to check whether they are flabby.

● ● ● ● ●   *EXERCISES*   ● ● ● ● ●

Locate and describe the diction problems in the following passages; then write improvements.

1. The sudden shriek startled everyone. It was followed by a long hysterical wail, which was rapidly coming in their direction. Still screaming, Koz burst into the kitchen and leapt onto the chair.

2. Arthur, crisply dressed in a white linen suit, made a few disdainful comments about the inadequacies of the larder, before permitting Beatrice to mollify him with a bowl of porridge. Marsha burst into this quiet nest of domesticity with the sneer of an I.R.S. auditor surprising citizens guilty of a different sort of fiction. Today, she chose to adorn her perfect body with a translucent beach robe over the tiniest bikini, both in a matching flowered print.

3. Her first drag sent her into a fit of coughing. Her lungs felt as if someone had stabbed her with a knife. Hunger ate at her stomach.

4. She had never mentioned the incident to anyone, not even Mark, and tried to avoid Cooper whenever possible. If only she'd come up with a clever, gentle put-down, she thought, she could have curtailed the problem without this awkwardness between them. As it was, she spoke to him from a cool distance. [The incident is an attempted rape.]

5. Just as they began to move out of the driveway, the police car drove in front suddenly and blocked their car. If Sybil hadn't dissuaded him from leaving earlier, they would have escaped.

6. The white tiled kitchen is medicinal in the blinding fluorescent lights. The rows of looming metal shelving units house an array of worn and dented industrial aluminum items of various sizes

7. The first thing that Jeff noticed when he was walking into the room was the smell of evergreen. He made an effort to ignore it.

8. I couldn't lose this chance. Not when I was getting nearer to finding the murderer. Maybe this call would give me the clue that was keeping me from solving the case.

9. With a cold gleam in her eye, the bat was swung by Katherine again and struck him hard in the ribs and across the stomach. An audible gasp of air escaped from the man's bloodied lips.

10. I looked at my father dozing in his favorite chair nearest the huge elm tree that afforded him a modicum of relief from the summer's heat.

11. The chance that he might lose her caused him evident stress, and to help the situation, she lowered some of her defenses and began to open up.

12. Paul pulled off the road. A jeep lay below them on the bank of a river, resupinate, front facing up the steep bank towards them.

13. The downstairs was our main play area. The main attraction was a 3 foot tall by 4 foot wide, black, wooden toy box. It was before child-safe hinges and it took two of us to get a toy out it.

> *" For your born writer, nothing is so healing as the*
> *realization that he has come upon the right word."*
>
> Catherine Drinker Bowen

 ## FIGURES OF SPEECH

Writers achieve economy and vividness through figures of speech, those complex ways of perceiving and phrasing feelings and comparisons and contrasts. At bottom, metaphors, similes, and other figures of speech are not special literary devices; they are the ways in which our minds try to understand and communicate our experience. "I could eat a horse" may lack freshness but at least it is an attempt to describe the fact that "I am hungry enough to eat a big animal." Everyday language is filled with these constructions. When we speak of "the head of a pin," "the teeth of a gear," or "a computer freezing up," we are speaking figuratively. To call someone "gutless" is not to make a literal statement but a figurative one about a lack of courage. Colloquial expressions like "get off my back" attest to the figurative habits of mind that generate new ways of communicating our ideas and feelings.

Some of the most successful figures eventually turn into idioms or clichés—metaphors that have either lost their imaginative punch or are so much a part of the language that we have lost our sense of their origin. Let's explore a few of these.

Who first came up with the expression "surf the net" for seeking information on the internet? (Surely he or she came from California.) Does the image of riding a surfboard come to mind when the expression is used? Do we any longer enjoy the particular areas of overlap between two relatively unlike things—the back and forth movement on a wave and the search for a site that might interest us? Once we stop seeing that connection, the metaphor is dead and may have become a cliché, an expression to be avoided unless selected for special, limited purposes (to make fun of it, for instance) or an idiom that feels so natural we don't think about it as an analogy.

In Linda Pastan's poem, "Death Is Intended," the expression "quit while you're ahead" is reenergized by its context:

Death Is Intended

On Feb. 6, 67-year-old Guy Waterman—naturalist, outdoorsman, devoted husband...decided to climb a New Hamshire mountain, lie down on the cold stones and die overnight of exposure. "Death is intended" he wrote.

New York Times Book Review

...the melancholy beauty of giving it all up.

Robert Hass

Isn't that what Eskimos did when they were old,
dragged themselves through a wilderness
of ice and up some mountain?
Then they could fall asleep forever,
their dark eyes speckled with falling snow—
not suicide exactly, but the opening
of a door so death could enter.
"Quit while you're ahead," my father told me
as I was feeding quarters into slot machines.
and that's what Waterman did, he quit
before infirmity could catch him, or other afflictions
whose breath he could already smell.
But I wanted more: a waterfall of coins
spilt on my lap, the raw electric charge
of money. I came away with nothing;
but I still want more, if only more chapters
in the family book I'm part of: I want
to read all the unfolding stories—each child
a mystery only time can solve.

Was it bravery or cowardice, what Waterman did,
or are those simply two sides of a coin,
like the coin some casual God might flip,
deciding who would live or die that day?

I'd rather flip the coin myself, but not at 67.
And not quite yet, I tell myself at 70, as spring
streams in over our suburban hills, enflaming
even the white New Hampshire mountains.

Pastan restores the original sense of the expression and attaches it to the idea of suicide as an alternative to the deterioration of age. To live or die becomes two sides of a coin one flips; you control your fate or the law of averages controls it.

Pastan's poem demonstrates that we don't have to avoid every expression we recognize as a dead metaphor. In fact, we can't. One wouldn't think twice about saying, "After the leader worked his way over the log that bridged the chasm, the others *followed suit*." Though we would no longer stop to enjoy the buried picture of cardplayers playing out the same suit that the previous player led, we know what the phrase means: It seems like a literal statement to us now and not a figurative one. As we said earlier, many of these formulations are simply available idiomatic expressions that work far better than outlandish alternatives that some writers invent to avoid sounding trite.

Figurative expressions are literal lies. In the equation of **metaphor,** two unlike things (events, traits, or objects) are asserted to be identical: A = B. "The moon is a ghostly galleon tossed up on silvery seas." Well, the moon is no such thing, but claiming that it is—discovering an area of overlap between the way this particular moon looked and the appearance of a certain ship under certain circumstances—allows the writer to tell us much about the way things felt, not just the way they looked.

Direct statements of identity, "X is Y," are not the only constructions that release metaphor. The ways in which parts of speech unexpectedly relate can release subdued metaphors. The passage "Each footstep puffed a plume of dust" contains two metaphors. In the second, we are asked to see a relationship between the particular shape the dust took and a plume or feather. Of course, dust and feathers often go together, but not in this way. To give a footstep breath with which to puff likens that action to animal or even human behavior—**personification.** We all learned that by sixth grade.

Examine the passage from "Ants," the witty poem by Vicki Hudspith that follows. It is an extended simile linking ants with us.

Ants are not fond of margarine. Like us they prefer
Butter. They do not have cholesterol problems
Because as yet they do not own TVs. For centuries
They have toiled in order that they might be able to
Take a night off and watch the Northern Lights which
Are their version of canned laughter. They hate picnics
But feel compelled by folklore to attend them
Or at minimum do a drive by chicken leg grab. Their
Queen is a pain in the ass. They don't love her but
Without her they would be common, so they serve her.
She is an insatiable nymphomaniac but they don't

> Hold that against her trying instead to stay busy with work.
> Forgotten ancient languages have been genetically
> Imprinted in them at birth and they say things they
> Don't understand. Like us they often make bad marriages....
>
> from *Mudfish*

The comparison and contrast is, of course, partly tongue-in-cheek. Hudspith says of the poem, "[Ants] are much like us, it seems: they work too hard, don't understand why they do what they do, and like music they look ridiculous dancing to!" She is not the first, of course, to use the simile, but the way she extends it is fresh. She takes two unlike things, finds the linking aspect, and exploits the figure of speech to the hilt. (Oops!)

In the preceding examples, a literal fabrication makes something not only vivid but fresher and clearer as well. Though it seems paradoxical, effective figures of speech do just that—lie to make things clear. Without this heightened clarity, figurative language is no better than muddy language of any kind. The writer of the following sentence probably felt proud of the way in which he made an abstraction concrete—one of the goals of much figurative expression: "Time is like a trail cut through the woods that we crawl down with our noses in the dirt." What can anyone learn about time or about human nature here? Nothing. What has gone wrong? For one thing, the writer has lost sight of his original intention. The simile, which begins with an attempt to characterize time through images of distance and motion, abruptly shifts to concerns that have no clear relevance to time. However, if the time under discussion was the time spent humbling ourselves before authority, the extended simile just might work.

As with any tool, you use similes and other figures of speech delicately. The following poem is the response to a workshop exercise and is constructed almost entirely out of similes. What is the effect of each one? Of the entire catalog?

Anatomy of Melancholy

The blue tears stain my cheeks Like a leaky fountain pen
Spurting its juice on white paper, Like a ripe blueberry
Bursting upon a milk-white tablecloth.
A droopy head hangs low Like the daisies knocked down by
Blowing gusts of wind, Like the signpost ran into
By the drunk kid in the red Corvette.
The thin lips pressed to viseful grip,
Like a sad clown's inverted grin
Stamped on white facepaint, Like the crescent moon hanging
Upside down in the darkening sky.
A saggy flesh drapes the frame
Like the Auschwitz inhabitants doomed
To the fuming chloride showers, Like the jowls of the bulldog
Standing guard at the house next door.

While many of the expressions are successful, the parts are not subordinated to the whole. After a while, the reader ceases to be in touch with what the poem is about; the piling up of similes becomes an end in itself rather than the means to an end.

One more point about similes: They are not simply comparisons using *like* or *as*. The sentence "Jane looks like her sister" is a literal comparison (it is actually true) rather than a figurative one. Remember, it is the discovery of an area of likeness or overlap between two essentially different things that is the basis for a figurative expression.

● ● ● ● ●   *EXERCISES*   ● ● ● ● ●

1. Expand three of the following statements: first with a literal comparison, next with a metaphor or simile, last with an **analogy**—the resemblance in a number of particulars of two things otherwise unlike as in Hudspith's poem "Ants." In doing this exercise, don't worry about saving all the words from the statement. The goal is vivid communication that is both clear and suggestive.

Example: My Ford Escape takes off rapidly.

Literal comparison: My hybrid Ford Escape accelerates just like your Toyota Prius.

Figure of speech: My Ford Escape takes off like a bullet.

Analogy: My Escape reminds me of a well-trained long distance runner. Like him, it has no extra weight to slow it down and can go almost forever because it conserves energy. Just like a well-conditioned athlete, I expect it to last a long time.

(You might notice that the name *hybrid* car is an analogy from botany in which scientists make a new plant from combining two or more old ones. And that use of *hybrid* is an analogy built from the Latin for combining words from different languages. You can't escape the operations of metaphor.)

a. A Swiss knife is a handy tool.
b. My dog is very affectionate.
c. The exam was difficult.
d. Lisa has a lovely complexion.
e. When I came home, my parents were up waiting for me.

2. Complete the following sentences, using or creating vivid figurative expressions:

a. When he smiled, . . .
b. The sun . . . through the trees and . . . whatever it touched.

    c. When I heard the tailpipe clatter on the road, . . .
    d. They shook hands carefully, like . . .
    e. Her computer skills were as professional as . . .

3. To develop your sense of figurative language, choose one of the works in this book and track every use of metaphor or simile. Be alert: Sometimes metaphors are buried deeply. For example, *grow* comes from *green*. When something is green, it is growing. Check the history of a few words to see if you can find the source of the buried metaphor.

Though we have been giving examples from poetry, figurative language is part of all writing. Indeed, as we have pointed out already, it is a natural way of talking and thinking. When a teenagers says, "I'll meet you if I can get a *set of wheels,*" he is using the part for the whole, a figure of speech called **synecdoche.** When you talk about your *desktop,* meaning your computer, you have referred to the place on which it sits. This figure of speech is called **metonymy.** (See Chapter 5, p. 130, for an example from Dylan Thomas.) Such figures of speech are part of the writer's toolbox, but problems emerge when the figures go berserk.

Metaphors and similes can be so farfetched, so forced, that readers will either tune out or be so dazzled by the writer's ingenuity that they will miss the point. Often, the problem is that elements in the metaphor are in conflict with one another. We call such a construction a **mixed metaphor.** The writer who puts down "My spirit, like my blood, slowly drips from my body, white feathers now turned crimson" has lost hold of effective figurative logic. It would seem that the spirit is being likened to white feathers, but it is also likened to blood. Once it is blood, it can't drip on itself, turning itself crimson; it must have been crimson to begin with. Such a mishmash gives a reader a headache or a laugh when the writer wants a tear: "After she told him that they were finished, he found himself sweating like a bullet." Mixed metaphors often come from overwriting, the irritable search after originality, or allowing needless complexity and elaboration to ruin a workable insight.

When we use images suggestively, they turn out to be more than descriptive. They may involve the sort of figurative comparisons discussed earlier in which one term is equated or related to another in a special way. Sometimes images generate associations in which the second term is not named but still understood. When an image represents something other than or beyond itself, it is being used as a **symbol.**

Many symbols are conventional: Their meanings are shared by a community or culture. The American flag is one such symbol; the cross is another. Traditionally, the color white is a symbol of purity, red of passion, purple of royalty. No one can refer to a snake or serpent without suggesting the meanings developed in the story of Adam and Eve. We use symbols of this sort all the time, often without even thinking about them.

In our own writing, we can also generate meanings in a particular work through local symbols. For example, in the following poem by A. E. Housman, "London" suggests all that is opposed to gentleness, innocence, and inexperience. It becomes a symbol for a worldly toughness and a worldly style.

> From the wash the laundress sends
> My collars home with ravelled ends;
> I must fit, now these are frayed,
> My neck with new ones, London-made.
> Homespun collars, homespun hearts,
> Wear to rags in foreign parts.
> Mine at least's as good as done,
> And I must get a London one.

Often there is little distance between symbolism and synecdoche or metonymy. You could say here that "collars" symbolizes all of the person's clothing, style, and way of life. If you think the reference is only on the concrete level, you might say that "collars" is the part that stands for all of the speaker's garments (synecdoche). Housman's reference to "hearts" is the conventional one in which the organ represents the center of emotion.

When a writer happens upon a stunning way of describing something that condenses a good deal of meaning into a small compass, the reader sees the world as one might see a painting. It is impossible to express F. Scott Fitzgerald's final sentence in *The Great Gatsby* in any other way than he did: "So we beat on, boats against the current, born ceaselessly back into the past." One could rephrase the sentence and say that "we continually struggle to change our lives but do so without effect because we are doomed to repeat the errors of the past." After the champagne of Fitzgerald, however, the translation is flat beer. Exact expressions that allow the reader to share a thought or picture are one of the pleasures of literature, and when they are exact, we are hard put to say them in any other way.

 STYLE

> " *Words have weight, sound and appearance; it is only*
> *by considering these that you can write a sentence*
> *that is good to look at and good to listen to.* "
>
> Somerset Maugham

Consider what judgments you might make about the writer of each of the following four passages, all of which are based on the same information:

1. Also passed by Congress in this session was legislation which prohibits the expenditure of appropriated funds to influence the awarding of federal grants, contracts, and loans, and requires that an applicant for a federal grant, contract, or loan disclose any payments made with nonappropriated funds that would have been prohibited if made with appropriated funds.

2. The new law that Congress passed states that you can't use money from one government grant, contract, or loan to get another one. Also, the law requires you to disclose any money you spend to get government money.

3. What's the world coming to? Now Congress has passed a law that stops self-respecting lobbyists and gun-makers from using money from one government dole to wheedle another government dole. And, get this, even if you use your own money to lobby for some government largess, you have to tell about it. There go the general's free tickets for Redskins' games.

4. The work was going slowly and badly. Bill had assigned me the Herculean chore of turning dark bureaucratic prose into instructions for the contract men (and sometimes, but not too often, women), delivery date of said instructions yesterday but five o'clock today would do. The screen was filled with so many drafts that I thought I might blow out the computer's brain. My instinct was simply to say: "Don't do bad things with government money." Then I added: "Like using it to get the next contract." That wasn't going to fly. The Congressional bill wasn't quite that simple. I took two aspirin to comfort my headache, due only partly to the argument with JoAnn the night before. Perhaps the easiest approach was to make a list of all the possible ways our contract people could violate the law and put "thou shalt not" at the beginning.

You will have little difficulty in describing these styles—cool legalese, abstract reportorial, sarcastic editorial, tough guy narration—and understanding them as versions of formal, informal, and colloquial style. These large categories are part of our reading glasses, the lenses through which we see the work. When we know the style, we already know something about what we are going to read, and that makes us more comfortable. Usually we recognize the style in the first few sentences or paragraphs; sometimes the style floats us on like a river or sometimes makes us decide not to read one word further.

Decisions about diction are primary ingredients in the creation of style. Earlier in this chapter, we reviewed the fundamental considerations that lead to effective word choice. A writer's work is made even more effective through the consistent use of a vocabulary chosen to achieve specific ends. The style of a literary work is part of the reader's experience—the dress of its content. And the dress must be tailored to fit. Not only must it fit the body of the content, it must also be appropriate to the occasion. No sweat suits at a black tie affair.

The range of writing styles is infinite. The following is a spectrum of the alternatives based on diction:

- The diction may be modifier-heavy—or eliminate modifiers altogether.
- It may tend to be polysyllabic—or monosyllabic.
- It may be formal—or slangy.
- It may be connotatively rich—or spare.
- The figurative language may be lavish—or sparse.

Important as it is, diction is only one element of style. Other elements include sentence shapes and lengths; clause relationships; attention to the sounds and rhythms of language; and the projection of wit or humor (through puns or surprising juxtapositions). Many writers and critics associate style with voice, the verbal characteristics by which an author's or narrator's personality is expressed. Most readers of fiction could immediately recognize the following selection as Ernest Hemingway's distinctive style:

> The taxi went up the hill, passed the lighted square, then on into the dark, still climbing, then leveled out onto a dark street behind St. Etienne du Mont, went smoothly down the asphalt, passed the trees and the standing bus at the Place de la Contrescarpe, then turned onto the cobbles of the Rue Mouffetard. There were lighted bars and late open shops on each side of the street. We were sitting apart and we jolted close together going down the old street. Brett's hat was off. Her head was back. I saw her face in the lights from the open shops, then it was dark, then I saw her face clearly as we came out on the Avenue des Gobelins. The street was torn up and men were working on the cartracks by the light of acetylene flares. Brett's face was white and the long line of her neck showed in the bright light of the flares. The street was dark again and I kissed her. Our lips were tight together and then she turned away and pressed against the corner of the seat, as far away as she could get. Her head was down.
> "Don't touch me," she said. "Please don't touch me."
> "What's the matter?"
>
> from *The Sun Also Rises*

Typically in a Hemingway story, the reporting of the character's emotion is kept well in check, though we are aware that deep feelings are present. Hemingway creates some of the affectless reporting through terse sentences. Even the long opening sentence appears clipped because of the repetition of *then*. The sentences are like a film, frame after frame coalescing into a scene. Strangely, the segments of the sentences coordinated with "*and*" (some say that Hemingway even overuses this construction) do not appear joined. Actions are run together, without a logical connection. Drop the "ands" and the picture is the same even though we lose the rhythm. Providing coherent links would radically change our impression and eliminate the detached tone, as in the following reworking:

Her head was back and I could see her face in the lights from the open shops. When we passed the shops, it was dark again. Then I could see it again when we came to the lighted Avenue des Gobelins.

Another typical element in Hemingway's style is the small number of his adjectives and adverbs. He doesn't say "kissed her passionately." Their lips were "tight together," communicates something tamer and limited. What's up? Once you realize that Jake Barnes and Brett cannot make physical love, the mechanical nature of "pressed" is clear. You will also notice that the verbs tend to be monosyllabic—"went," "were," "saw," "turned," and "pressed." All these elements add up to a style in which the effects are flattened. It suits the sense of purposelessness that fills this novel about the Lost Generation. However, handled carelessly, this spare style can be like bread without butter.

Writers may choose a more lavish manner than Hemingway's, if the subjects and emotions they tackle call for such a style. In the following passage from Stanley Elkin's *The MacGuffin*, the third person narrator presents the way the hero thinks in sentences like this one:

And Druff, who at his time of life—it was at *least* past late middle age in his head and even later than that in the cut of his cloth, his chest caving behind his shirts, emptying out, and his torso sinking, lowering into trousers rising like a tide and lapping about him like waves—hard by, as he was, the thin headwaters of the elderly—and was the first to admit the outrageousness of his surmise and discount the chinks in his argument, discounted his vulnerabilities anyway and suddenly knew the man, his driver, the chauffeur Dick, was some kind of spy.

The complex sentence—with its zigs and zags before it comes to a precise piece of information—exactly fits the way that Druff's mind is working as well as how inclined Stanley Elkin is to see the world in complex ways. It may not be everyone's cup of style, but it serves both his purpose and the reading habits of his audience.

A unique style readily identifiable as distinctly yours is hard to come by. Ernest Hemingway, Allen Ginsberg, Tom Wolfe, Emily Dickenson, and a host of other writers with striking styles had models that they knew and imitated. We would not recommend trying to search for a totally unique style just for the sake of being unique. Rather, search for and imitate the style or styles that fit you and the work at hand. Eventually, the borrowing will turn into possession.

●   ●   ●   ●   ●   *EXERCISE*   ●   ●   ●   ●   ●

Consider something you intend to write (or have already written); then choose a passage from another writer, study the style, and apply the techniques you have observed to writing your piece.

" Style is not something applied. It is something that permeates. It is of the nature of that in which it is found, whether the poem, the manner of a god, the bearing of a man. It is not a dress."

Wallace Stevens

 EVOKING STYLES

In the service of their narratives, writers often evoke styles used in other contexts. The intent is to bring to mind the outward appearance of a form normally found in another framework. For example, in *Harry Potter and the Sorcerer's Stone,* J. K. Rowling uses several devices that allow the reader to swallow (with a smile) this absurd biographical entry that gives Harry Potter information he needs to know:

ALBUS DUMBLEDORE

Currently Headmaster of Hogwarts

Considered by many the greatest wizard of modern times, Dumbledore is particularly famous for his defeat of the dark wizard Grindelwald in 1945, for the discovery of the twelve uses of dragon's blood and his work on alchemy with his partner, Nicolas Flamel. Professor Dumbledore enjoys chamber music and tenpin bowling. [p. 194 of the paperback]

Early in the novel, Rowling establishes that each packet of a children's candy called Chocolate Frogs contains a card of a famous figure from the history of wizardry. Three elements attach the strange fictive world to our mundane world: candy, chocolate, and collectable cards of some admired figure (a baseball player, for example). The brief biography on Dumbledore's card imitates the style of such entries: Not only do figures have their public significance, but they also have their private hobbies and lives. Typically the biographies are sketchy, mention what the person is famous for, and conclude with a personal element. In this way Rowling communicates information that Harry Potter and so the reader need to know, but also she creates verisimilitude in her imaginary world by alluding to a real world form and style. She relies on the style to tell us about the content.

In the following passage, the writer attaches a fairy tale style to a story meant to take place in the modern world:

Once upon a time there was a poor unmarried mother who lived in a shelter with her three-year-old daughter. The little girl had beautiful curly auburn hair and big green eyes. People used to tell her mother that she certainly was a pretty child. The mother was pleased to hear it. One day when the mother was out with her little girl seeking a job she met a man.

The style the writer has chosen is signaled by the word choice and the rhythm of the first sentence as well as by brief sentences suitable for a child (even if, as in this case, the writer intends the story for adults). The writer wants to draw our attention to the fairy tale quality because her story will allude to elements in a well-known fairy tale placed in a homeless shelter.

In the sense that we have been discussing it here, style is closely related to form. In every genre, writers use natural style-forms for a myriad of purposes. A poet might use the style of a letter or list to help shape an idea or emotion (see Chapter 7 for examples). A dramatist might characterize someone by making him sound like a manual on how to win friends and influence people, as Arthur Miller does with Willy Loman in parts of *Death of a Salesman*.

Writers may, of course, evoke a style that they think advances their purposes but that, in fact, works against them, as in the following example:

Harken O Life to profound elocution
Blazoned in Starlight for thee to behold.
Grand vision of Spirit before evolution
Proclaiming thy destiny yet to unfold.

From out of the nothing transposed to potential
My unspoken purpose delayed revelation
Awaiting the pattern of matter's essential
Vitality wakened to free animation.

This style is intended to evoke the dignity of the Bible or of such poets as John Milton and William Blake. However, for a variety of reasons, it does not create in the reader a sense of reverence, as the author undoubtedly intended. One is hard put to think of a god as speaking in rhymed couplets in a beat we associate with light-hearted poems such as "The Night Before Christmas." Choosing *elocution* for the divine word is hardly appropriate; it conjures up an image of someone who is speaking at a debate tournament. There is no way to modify this verse without finding a contemporary style more appropriate to the view of the universe as formed by the natural forces of evolution.

Except as a tour de force it is wisest to avoid the diction, sentence structure, and narrative pace of George Eliot for a short-short story that involves the hero writing a love rap. The principle is this: You can't avoid having readers see another style in your writing, but if you don't want to lose them, you had better select a style that is useful for expressing your content and narrative.

INCOMPATIBLE STYLES

Writers who have been working in other forms frequently are unaware that they are bringing to their narratives a style that is not suitable for the purpose. Because they have successfully written papers, reports, or other documents for school or work, they may find it difficult to switch gears, and so, in a genre intended to evoke emotion, the reader hears echoes of the academic, legal, or bureaucratic voice. It is easier to illustrate this problem than to describe it abstractly.

The following passage is from a story intended as an exploration of how the character deals with the death of her husband:

> Rita reported her unhappiness about the death of her husband. Years as a military wife has imbued her with an acceptance of change. She had moved constantly and found herself quick to adjust. Now, however, she has an intrinsic need to work as well as a financial need. She feels the "intrinsic" fails to fulfill the psychological need. She feels her job is unrewarding in either aspect.

The word choices and sentence structure here remind one of a cool and distant social worker's report about a client. The writer has sent the wrong signals. A simple revision can change the style so that readers will immediately feel that they are entering a story:

> Rita felt depressed even though she was used to change. A woman who married a soldier had to learn how to survive the constant moving about from base to base, from north to south. That constant uprooting she accepted. But when Ed was killed in Iraq, she found that she would have to work. Work both for the money and to busy her mind. Her job as a manager at Ben and Jerry's failed miserably to give her much of the first or any of the second.

The revision allows the reader to know what Rita's "intrinsic need" was and why she had it. Rita "feels" rather than a narrator "reports," and the style is active. Of course, the writer might have placed the original version into the mouth of a social worker to characterize him as cold and professional.

In the following passage we do feel that the writer is telling us a story, but the style feels flat and mechanical:

> When she saw the figure she braked, skidding around a little bit, out of instinct or compassion. At first she felt good that she could be helping out someone on a night like this, but then thoughts started flashing across her mind and horror broke out.

Even though we accept this passage as part of a story and not a newspaper report, it sounds like a digest of the event. Too many actions are piled into the sentences and too much of the action and thought is hidden in subordinate clauses or vaguely expressed. Rather than readers entering the moment, they are distanced by the summaries and imprecise diction. A forward-moving revision might go as follows:

> She saw the figure by the side of the road. She braked so hard the car fishtailed. Finally it stopped halfway onto the shoulder. Had she stopped because she felt sorry for the man standing in the downpour? Why did she always want to help out? But when the car had come to a standstill, she realized that picking up a stranger at night was dangerous and she felt dismay replace pity. How she could have been so unthinking, so stupid?

Notice that rather than have the narrator report the actions and feeling, the revision brings the point of view closer to the character's response in the moment. The action is told in brief, punchy sentences that lengthen when we enter her thoughts, and the diction is simpler. The reader feels in the presence of a story rather than a report.

Sometimes beginning writers will use a style appropriate to other forms, like the travel article or advertising. Sometimes they will use a style appropriate to another sub-genre—a romance style in a tough-guy detective story. Unfortunately, readers are more likely to forgive you a distasteful idea or a mixed metaphor than they are to forgive you for sounding like something they didn't expect when they picked up the magazine or book and started reading.

●　●　●　●　●　　*EXERCISES*　　●　●　●　●　●

1. Edit any of the following passages to fit the audience proposed.

This is the beginning of a detective story written for a general audience. [Consider that the style evokes a real estate sales pitch.]

> I spoke into the box, explaining that I was the investigator from the agency Mr. Delamour had called. The box spoke back in a soft but clear velvet tone. "Good morning. Please pull around to the front door, Mr. Hardner."
> Through the Italian brick and iron gate winding around groomed shrubbery was a modestly sized mansion of the same Italian flavor and extravagance. Green lawns bordered with mulched flowerbeds which bordered with the extremely black driveway. The pieces of shrubbery scattered across the lawn had all been clipped into garish sculptures of nude women in surrealistic frolic.
> There was also a fountain next to the side walk of a nude female spilling water out of a jar. This was not as accosting as a large black dog galloping up to me who was undoubtedly named Duke or King. Being

a P.I., I had these problems frequently, so when he came up to sniff my crotch or bite me I grabbed the back of his neck and undramatically kneed him in the throat. He didn't bother me again.

I rang the doorbell and stared into the black windows on the black door. After the three-tone bong the door opened and the velvet voice in a satin blue outfit greeted me.

2. This is a portion of a short story intended for a sophisticated audience that reads literary magazines and the *New Yorker*. [Consider both the romance tone and the real estate pitch.]

> This woman was beautiful—I could not deny myself the pleasurable task of mentally noting this creamy face from a magazine resting on a loosely wrapped body of perfect proportions. I pulled out my notepad.
>
> "You can call me Lana. Ah, would you care for anything to drink?"
>
> "No thank you, ah well actually I'm a bit thirsty; a glass of ice water would be great."
>
> She left the front hall and I proceeded to take note of everything in this first room. Cream walls, stairway up, brown and beige tile floor, generous mirrors, and a dark stained desk stand with erotically twisting carved legs. The real legs came back into the foyer.
>
> "Here you go."

3. Reread "Sex Education" (Chapter 3, pp. 50–59) and see if you can find stylistic features that evoke regional culture. Create a narrative that echoes aspects of a region or culture.

 ## A STYLE CHECKLIST

The following checklist is partly an abstract of other sections in this chapter. We invite you to copy it. Put it by your keyboard and review it often.

1. If you find yourself struggling for an image or a phrase, stop writing. Close your eyes and look at the subject again. What did you see? Show *that* to your reader.

2. Flee the category, the summary. Return to what you saw—even in your mind's eye. "She felt good" doesn't create a picture.

3. Name the things and actions with hard nouns and verbs.

4. If you are pleased by your own cleverness in your choice of a word or image, probably you should delete the phrase. When it doubt, take it out.

5. When you finish your first draft, pretend you are an editor suggesting that 20 percent of what the writer has submitted must be deleted. Find the 20 percent in your piece and cut it.

6. Keep your sentences active and friendly. Passive voice hardly ever; operators never.

7. Learn the style conventions and expectation of your audience—no matter how foolish. Even if you have to use them, be conscious that you are using them. Awareness is the antidote to style rot. We're thinking here, for example, about the particular style that romances once demanded, a style filled with adjectives and adverbs to create breathlessness.

8. Don't *try* to impress your reader with stylistic fireworks. Pyrotechnics draw attention away from content.

9. Pay no attention to rules that lead to unclear writing or writing not suitable for your purposes. "After he left the room, Eleanor was the first person to whom he spoke." That passage is grammatically correct but not suitable for narration. "Eleanor was the first person he spoke to."

> *" Nothing is more satisfying than to write a good sentence. It is no fun to write lumpishly, dully, in prose the reader must plod through like wet sand."*
>
> Barbara Tuckman

SUMMARY

Since personal style is the result of a host of conscious and unconscious choices in everything from dress to speech, we might conclude that a writer (or artist) doesn't have to worry about style since, no matter what you do, your writing will have style. And that is, as a matter of fact, a correct conclusion. But having a *style* and having a *useful style* for your purposes and audience are not necessarily the same thing.

Beyond discovering and honing your basic style, you need to develop an ability to invent styles for specific projects and purposes. If you use Latinate diction combined with long, highly subordinated sentences, your style might sound like that of a professional or bureaucrat who is trying to communicate laws, ideas, abstractions, or summations. Use simpler words and shorter sentences for a style that appears to be a simple reporting of actions and thoughts. Use many adjectives and adverbs, and you give the impression of being ornate (lavish, gushy, generous). Avoid adjectives, and your style becomes plain (curt, Spartan, stingy). Similes and metaphors, like decorative rocks in the lawnmower's path, can slow the pace of your prose. Short sentences speed it up.

None of these generalizations are always true. Some philosophers express quite complex ideas in relatively simple, jargon-free sentences. Some prose that is filled with adjectives moves rapidly.

Experiment with a variety of styles and consciously imitate writers you admire as part of your writing apprenticeship. And read diligently, with an eye to discovering the relationships between stylistic choices and their effects on readers.

> " *The essence of a sound style is that it cannot be reduced to rules—that it is a living and breathing thing with something of the devilish in it—that it fits its proprietor tightly yet ever so loosely, as his skin fits him. It is, in fact, quite as seriously an integral part of him as that skin is…. In brief, a style is always the outward and visible symbol of a man, and cannot be anything else.* "
>
> H.L. Mencken

PART TWO

THE CONCERNS
OF THE POET

MODEL POETRY SUBMISSION

Philip K. Jason
32821 Valewood Drive
Tampa, Florida 34911
(242) 788-4582
pkjason@usna.com

Meeting the Day

His hands are fish that dart
to the center of ripples
at the surface of his name;
his neck is a knotted trunk
that shoots from a mulch of collar;
his arteries surge with coffee.
He moves to the garbage truck's moan
and counts out busfare in his pocket's dark.
Today, he is going to be on time.
He pulls on his tie
and his eyes become paired skaters
that veer through the red creases of dawn.

CHAPTER 5

THE ELEMENTS OF POETRY

> *"One demands two things of a poem. Firstly, it must be a well-made verbal object that does honor to the language in which it is written. Secondly, it must say something significant about a reality common to us all, but perceived from a unique perspective. What the poet says has never been said before, but, once he has said it, his readers recognize its validity for themselves."*
>
> W. H. Auden

 OVERVIEW

Like other writers, poets tell stories, create characters, and formulate ideas, but these activities do not give poetry its special distinction. Although no writer is unconscious of the impact of words as containers of information, poets attend most to the power of linking sound and sense.

Poetry usually looks different from other kinds of writing. We recognize a poem by its ragged right-hand margin and its relatively narrow blocks or columns of type. The right margin is uneven because where and how lines end is a defining element in poetry. All writers compose in sentences and paragraphs, but poets have this other unit—the line. According to William Matthews, "the line in prose is like a fishing line, cast out as far as it will go, straightforward. And the line in verse goes out from the margin, turns back, goes out again, etc. Thus poetry is often linked to dance. The serpentine line of verse goes more down the page than across it." In the following poem, William Carlos Williams takes advantage of the line to write a poem about the dance.

The Dance

In Brueghel's great picture, The Kermess,
the dancers go round, they go round and
around, the squeal and the blare and the
tweedle of bagpipes, a bugle and fiddles
tipping their bellies (round as the thick-
sided glasses whose wash they impound)
their hips and their bellies off balance
to turn them. Kicking and rolling
about the Fair Grounds, swinging their butts, those
shanks must be sound to bear up under such
rollicking measures, prance as they dance
in Brueghel's great picture, The Kermess.

If you read the poem aloud, you can hear how the break of the lines forces you to replicate the wild beat of the music to which the dancers are responding. (To see what quality of the painting William's is trying to capture, you might take a look at it in an art book or on the Internet at www.mala.bc.ca/~lanes/english/kermess.htm.)

Poetry has other distinguishing characteristics. It is the form that most intensely conveys emotion. In fact, poetry is often called the language of emotion. Poets put a high premium on language loaded with sensory materials (images) in order to recreate emotions in us as we read. Poetry stirs us through its mysterious economy that communicates more than the words would seem to allow.

Because of these special demands, writing poetry can be frustrating and yet fun, particularly when we hit on just the right way to say so much and to say it so well and with so much resonance. Our tools are so various and interdependent that it is difficult to make everything work in harmony to create harmony. Nevertheless, as in any other endeavor, practice coupled with knowledge and determination will carry any writer a long way toward success. It's important not to expect to arrive at your destination all at once.

In this chapter we invite you to explore the many possibilities, demands, and satisfactions of writing poetry. Even if you are inclined to write in other genres, practicing poetry is a useful discipline for all writing because it focuses your attention on the sound and rhythms in language.

We begin with a basic introduction to poetry's conventions. Since these conventions are fairly specialized and jargon-filled, some of you will find our review demanding. Though you may already have engaged the material in high school or college, stay with us. You wouldn't want to whittle without some wood and a sharp knife. In Chapter 6, we suggest some exercises that will keep you busy creating poems. In Chapter 7, we review key problems for beginners and illustrate the process of revision.

 ## THE LINE

> *"...There is at our disposal no tool of the poetic craft more important, none that yield more subtle and precise effects, than the line-break if it is properly understood."*
>
> Denise Levertov

At the very outset, the shape on the printed page announces to the eye that the work is a poem. Consider these lines from "Fog Township," a free-verse poem by Brendan Galvin:

> It's that delicate time
> when things could spill
> any way, when fog
> rides into the hollows,
> making bays, and Cathedral
> and Round Hills are
> high islands. Brooks
> have already churned back
> into their beds to trickle
> their own placid names
> again, and cloud shadows
> have drawn across
> the landscape's lightest
> movements. Now I begin
> to hear something trying
> to come through, a message
> tapped on twigs out there:

Galvin has chosen relatively short lines to project both his descriptions of a place and his reactions to that place. The flow of images, and the short but regularly run-on lines (lines ending without punctuation) keep us moving from one unit to the next. No set number of syllables or stresses are repeated—just a limited range that the reader's eye and ear get used to.

Consider these versions we created of Galvin's first sentence:

1. It's that delicate time when things could spill
   any way,
   when fog rides into the hollows, making
   bays,
   and Cathedral and Round Hills are high
   islands.

2. It's that delicate time when things
   could spill any way, when fog rides
   into the hollows, making bays,
   and Cathedral and Round Hills
   are high islands.

3. It's that delicate
   time when things
   could spill any
   way, when fog rides
   into the hollows,
   making bays,
   and Cathedral and Round Hills are high islands.

Although the language of the poem does not change, our experience does. One reason for this change is that the differing line lengths convey different pieces of the developing message; that is, in each case the rate at which we absorb the words and the ways in which the words connect differ because the white space around each line acts as a temporary frame. As we read aloud or silently, we add frame to frame, often overriding or suspending the logic of the **syntax**. Decisions about lines and line break become decisions about the poem as an experience or a sequence of experiences.

As you can see, line length and line break are devices that control emphasis. For example, isolating "making bays" in variation 3 emphasizes that event more than it has in the other variations. Moreover, the contrast between that line and the considerably longer line that follows heightens our awareness of just how short the earlier line is. It also forces us to consider why the last line is so extended. What difference does it make? This is the question we must ask over and over again as alert readers and writers.

Notice, for example, that the last lines of variation 1 and variation 3 are identical but their impact is quite different because the preceding line is of equal length in one case and much shorter in the other. In variation 3, the last line feels heavier and drags. Obviously, the effect—the expressiveness—of a given line length is a function of its context, the environment of other lines that surround it.

But that's not all.

The position of a word on a line influences its emphasis. Generally speaking, what's at the end of a line receives the most emphasis, what's at the beginning secondary emphasis, and the material in the middle receives the least emphasis. This effect may appear contrary to common sense, but when you think of the matter, the end of the line pushes, so to speak, into the white space and so is more isolated. At the beginning of Galvin's poem, "time," "spill," "fog," and "hollows" receive the greatest emphasis. Where Galvin placed them gives the first full syntactical unit (sentence) a different flavor than in our three variations. Galvin's decision to split a line between the words "fog" and "rides" assigns each word relatively equal emphasis. Read the original and the versions aloud again and compare the musical effects of each. Note particularly where Glavin placed "making bays" in a less stressed position, thus emphasizing "Cathedral and round Hill"...the solid land.

● ● ● ● ●   *EXERCISES*   ● ● ● ● ●

Following is the rest of "Fog Township" presented as a paragraph of prose:

> The spring genius of this/foggy township knitting up/cable and chain to bind the acres, among moss stiches laying down her simple seed and fern stich, complicating the landscape a pattern a day: daisy stiches and wild oats, berry knots interspersed with traveling vine and dogwood. Her needles cut from oak tips, click like sparks fired across a gap, and I imagine her crouched on a stump, hair wet, pulling April back together. But for the lethargy that's floating in this fog in nets so fine they can't be seen, I might walk around out there until I meet her, or scare off the jay who's chipping for sustenance along a pine's gray limb.
>
> from *Seals in the Inner Harbor*

1. Reconstruct the line breaks as best you can. Keep in mind the flow Galvin has established in the first part and the emphasis that you think might best serve the meaning and the music. We have started you off by indicating the first two line breaks with a slash (the conventional way of indicating line breaks when the poem is run on). You do the rest. Compare your version with the original that we print at the end of this chapter.

2. Write your own poem about fog or other natural phenomenon and how it makes you feel. Pay special attention to how it alters things. Employ as many different senses as you can. Experiment with line lengths and line break.

By now, we hope one thing is clear: Your lines and line breaks should not be accidental or whimsical. The line is a unit of composition and revision, not an afterthought imposed on a stretch of prose. As a fundamental principle of composition, the line must become a way of thinking and hearing.

◀━━━▶ THE LINE AND METER

Poets don't invent the sounds and accents of the language while in the process of writing poems. These features are inherent in the language itself as everyone speaks and hears it. You have always been halfway to being a poet. **Rhythm,** loosely defined as the recurrence of stressed (accented) syllables, is not a device but a given. Poets pay special attention to this natural dimension of language: heightening it, systematizing it, and using it expressively.

One convention of the poetic line is to identify it with the repetition of a stress that creates rhythm, as in the following: "She *loves* me; she *loves* me *not.*" Knowing how this convention operates is one way to control the power in language. Though this knowledge is not essential—you can certainly begin writing a poem without any consideration of these matters—it is most useful for you to examine the means by which you can create desired effects.

The special terms we use to discuss these physical features of language are our means of sharing observations about how poems work. Think of them as similar to the terms of musical notation such as *clef, staff,* and *bar.*

Traditionally, line length in English poetry is defined by a system of measurement called **meter.** There are three basic conventions of measurement in English poetry: (1) the counting of stressed syllables, (2) the counting of total syllables, and (3) the counting of units comprised of some combination of stressed and unstressed syllables. *Note*: when we say a syllable has *stress,* we mean this relatively; it has more emphasis in natural pronunciation than those that surround it.

The earliest English poetry—*Beowolf,* for example—was based on a line in which only stressed (or accented) syllables were counted no matter what the total number of syllables. It was as if the poets and their audiences heard verbal music only in terms of the stresses and somehow filtered out the unstressed syllables. This poetry was dominated by a four-stress line. The poets repeated initial sounds (**alliteration**) to emphasize syllables. The lines had a strong internal pause (**caesura**) between the second and third stressed syllable:

> They *came* to the *court*yard || *fac*es a-*flame*

We all take this type of poetic measure into our ears early on when we hear nursery rhymes:

> **Baa**, baa, **black** sheep, (4)
> **Have** you any **wool?** (5)
> **Yes** sir, **yes** sir, (4)
> **Three** bags **full**; (3)
> **One** for the **mas**-ter, (5)
> And **one** for the **dame**, (5)
> And **one** for the **lit**-tle boy (7)
> Who **lives** down the **lane**. (5)

This tradition has never vanished, and a good deal of contemporary verse that seems unmeasured is really a version of the accentual line. Poetry whose lines are defined in this way is called **accentual verse.**

Read aloud the following lines from Dave Smith's "Night Fishing for Blues" and you will hear the strong-stress accentual rhythms. (We have added the italics.)

> At Fortress Monroe, Virginia,
> the big-jawed Bluefish, ravenous, *sleek* muscle *slam*ming
> at *rock*, at *pier* legs, *drives* into *Che*sapeake
> *shall*ows, *con*voys *rank* after *rank*,
>   *wheel*ing through *flume* and *flute* of *blood*,   5
>   *some*thing like *hun*ger's *throb hook*ing
> un*til* you *hear* it and *know* them *there*,
>
>   the family.
>   Tonight, not far from where Jefferson Davis
>
> hunched in a harrowing cell, gray eyes quick   10
> as crabs' nubs, I come back over plants
> deep drummed under boots years ago, tufts of hair
>
> *float*ing at my *eyes*, *think*ing it *right* now
>   to *pitch* through *tideturn* and *mud*slur
>   for *fish* with *teeth* like *snapped sa*bers.   15
>
>   from Cumberland Station

There is no fixed line length here; rather, an insistent beat emerges from the piling up of stressed syllables in lines that roughly approximate the traditional four-stress measure. Many lines (3–7, 13–15) reinforce the four-stress pattern—the norm—though the variation from it is pronounced. Lines 5 and 6 illustrate the interplay of sound and stress, not only by alliteration, but through repetition of internal vowel sounds (**assonance**) as well. Note the long "u" sound in "flume" and "flute" and the more subtle short "u" (uh) linking "blood," "something," and "hunger."

●   ●   ●   ●   ●   *EXERCISES*   ●   ●   ●   ●   ●

1. Write a short poem using a four-stress line. In writing accentual verse, pay no attention to the total number of syllables in a line—only the stressed syllables.

2. Develop an accentual stanza using a preset variation. For example, let lines 1 and 4 have three stresses per line, let line 2 have four stresses, and let line 3 have five stresses:

(1)   /   /   /
(2)   /   /   /   /
(3)   /   /   /   /   /
(4)   /   /   /

Repeat your pattern for three stanzas.

In contrast to accentual verse, lines in **syllabic verse** are defined by the total number of syllables without regard to accent. This system is not highly expressive in English poetry or in the poetry of other languages in which the contrast between stressed and unstressed syllables is well-defined, such as Japanese and French. Syllabic verse *has* had its English language partisans who feel that the arbitrary discipline forces decisions that bring surprising results. Marianne Moore's work represents syllabic poetry at its most inventive. Her elaborate stanzaic poems may be analyzed as intricate syllabic patterns. Here are the last three stanzas of "The Fish":

> All
> external
> marks of abuse are present on this
> defiant edifice—
> all the physical features of
>
> ac-
> cident—lack
> of cornice, dynamite grooves, burns, and
> hatchet strokes, these things stand
> out on it; the chasm is
>
> dead.
> Repeated
> evidence has proved that it can live
> on what can not revive
> its youth. The sea grows old in it.
>
> from *Collected Poems*

● ● ● ● ●   *EXERCISES*   ● ● ● ● ●

1. Reline Moore's stanzas. Can you discover any changes in expressiveness?

2. Experiment with a set syllabic line of seven or more syllables. Then try a shorter line. Finally, try a stanza of alternate syllabic line lengths (like Moore's).

> "*Trochee trips from long to short;*
> *From long to long in solemn sort*
> *Slow Spondee stalks, strong foot!, yet ill able*
> *Ever to come up with Dactyl's trisyllable.*

Iambics march from short to long.
With a leap and a bound the swift Anapests throng.
One syllable long, with one short at each side... "

Samuel Taylor Coleridge

When most people think of meter, they think of the system that measures units (*feet*) of stressed and unstressed syllables. This system came into English poetry after the Norman Conquest (1066), perhaps from the mixing of the accentual Anglo-Saxon tradition with the syllabic tradition of the Norman French. We call the poetic system that counts these packages of stressed and unstressed syllables **accentual-syllabic verse**.

Four distinctive units (or feet) are the building blocks for poetry in the accentual-syllabic tradition. Each unit is named by a term borrowed from ancient Greek **prosody**. The dominant unit is the **iamb**, a package that consists of an unstressed syllable followed by a stressed one, as in the word "up*on*." The great majority of poems in accentual-syllabic verse have their lines defined by the iamb. The inverse of the iamb is the **trochee**, in which a stressed syllable is followed by an unstressed syllable, as in the word "*but*ton." The **anapest** is a sort of stretched iamb; it contains two unstressed syllables followed by a stressed syllable , as in the phrase "in the *phrase*." Its inverse is the **dactyl**, an elongated trochee, as in the word "*bat*tery."

Lines dominated by one or another of these feet are named by adjective–noun combinations in which the first term announces the type of foot and the second the number of feet in the line. Thus, we can have iambic, trochaic, anapestic, or dactylic *monometer, dimeter, trimeter, tetrameter, pentameter, hexameter, heptameter,* and so forth. For example, an "anapestic trimeter" is a line of three anapests. Though these terms are sometimes annoying, they are analogous to more familiar constructions from other systems: "dual exhausts," "megabytes," "triple play," and "quintuple bypass," for example.

To discover and indicate the metrical nature of a poem, we employ the process called **scansion**, in which we mark the stressed and unstressed syllables and divide the line, when appropriate, into feet. This technique makes visible what our ears tell us. By carefully scanning—reading, listening, and marking—we find that Andrew Marvell's "Thoughts in a Garden" is cast in iambic tetrameter:

> How vainly men themselves amaze
> To win the palm, the oak, or bays,
> And their incessant labours see
> Crown'd from some single herb or tree,   4
> Whose short and narrow-verged shade

˘   /| ˘ ˘| ˘   /| ˘   /
Does prudently their toils upbraid;

˘   /| ˘   / | ˘   /| ˘   /
While all the flowers and trees do close

˘   / | ˘ /| ˘   ˘| ˘ /
To weave the garlands of repose!   8

If you read the selection aloud and hit the stresses, Marvell's measure is quite regular by the standards of modern practice, but we can see that he was not a slavish metermongerer. The life of metrical poetry is not in the endless reproduction of a pattern, but in the lively interplay of a background beat—the norm—with expressive variation. Marvell's first three lines march briskly along, establishing the pattern. However, the fourth line begins with a variation (or substitution) before settling down once again into the iambic groove. The fifth and seventh lines are again regular, while the sixth and eighth stray from the norm.

You can create variations for emphasis. Notice how the word "crown'd" acquires extra force because of the unexpected change in meter: a trochaic for an iambic foot at the beginning of the line. Another effect of substitution is to change pace. In line 6, the valley (made visible by scansion) of unstressed syllables after the initial iamb quickens that line in relation to those around it.

The unit of two unstressed syllables that we discover in lines 6 and 8 is called the **pyrrhic foot**. This unit is often found in poetry dominated by iambs or another of the four major poetic feet, but it can never in itself be the basis for a line. If you try to write a pyrrhic line, you'll soon discover how the nature of the English language defies you. Try reading the poem aloud without any stresses.

Another foot used only for variation is the **spondee**, a unit of two stressed syllables. The effect of the spondee, or of any piling up of stressed syllables, is to create illusions of deliberateness, weight, slowness, or power—quite the opposite of the effects of a pyrrhic foot. The pyrrhic-spondee combination in the second line of the following passage (also from Marvell's "Garden") illustrates the sharp contrast, pushing against the iambic norm, that lifts the poet's adjective-noun combinations off the page:

˘   /|˘/| ˘ /| ˘   /
Annihilating all that's made

˘ ˘| /   / |˘ ˘|/   /
to a green thought in a green shade.

Keep in mind that the foot is the beat but that the melody comes from many sources—the number of syllables in the words, the syntax, the sound a particular vowel-consonant combination makes, line break, and a host of other factors. The description of the scansion is after the fact rather than a stencil into which poets rub the words.

Here is the opening stanza of Wyatt Prunty's "What Doesn't Go Away." After scanning it for yourself, compare Prunty's contemporary handling of iambic tetrameter with Marvell's:

His heart was like a butterfly
dropped through a vacuum tube,
no air to lift it up again;
each time the fluttering began,
he opened his eyes, first seeing
his family staggered around the bed,
then seeing that he didn't see.
While he died, the nurses wouldn't budge,
blood pressure gone too low, they said.

from *What Women Know, What Men Believe*

Notice how Prunty balances the iambic tetrameter and the colloquial flow of contemporary speech patterns. In the stanzas by both Marvell and Prunty, also observe the role that internal pauses play in breaking up what might otherwise become too mechanical and repetitious. You can vary the meter and where you place the caesura (the pause inside the line) to create energy and pace.

●　　●　　●　　●　　●　　　*EXERCISE*　　　●　　●　　●　　●　　●

Here are some workshop exercises done by Lisa Schenkel, a student in one of our classes. She was asked to write a short passage in strict iambic lines, then to introduce a preponderance of stressed syllables, and then to work it through once again with the metrical balance leaning toward unstressed syllables. Try scanning them. Give yourself the same assignment.

Sunday Evening Matisse

In strict iambic:

Unlike the other nudes, she stands at ease
and watches. Paint in hand, he strokes a breast
with quickness. Black, the lines relax the splash
of pink—her feathered hat. Undaunted
and ready, Barbra breaks her silent stance
and laughs until he puts his paints away.

With piled stresses:

Unlike other nudes, she stands, slouches, smiles
from the door, winks and watches. Black strokes
curve to breasts, pink splashes feather a hat.

Playful, he paints her unposed. Teasing, she flings
pink her hat, spills blue paint slick on tile floors,
slips into the room laughing, and leaves footprints.

With unstressed:

So at ease, she's a bit unlike the other nudes.
She stands with her hands on her hips, as if
impatient for him to finish. Her lips tilt in a
smile as he hurries to capture her. With a dab
of paint he attacks the canvas with a clutter of pink
hat, and black brushstrokes below match her stance.

LINES AND RHYMES

You can control how sharply lines are defined and how regularly that definition is
reinforced. It is easy for readers to respond to a line that ends with punctuation.
They halt and absorb the information. Such a line is called **end-stopped**. A line
that concludes with no such syntactical pause is called **run-on** or **enjambed**. You
can sense the difference by comparing the following passages from Alexander
Pope's "Eloisa to Abelard" and Robert Browning's "My Last Duchess." Read each
passage aloud and jot down your reactions to how each poet handles the line.

Those smiling eyes, attempering every ray,
Shone sweetly lambent with celestial day.
Guiltless I gazed; heaven listened while you sung;
And truths divine came mended from that tongue.
From lips like those what precept failed to move?
Too soon they taught me was no sin to love:
Back thro' the paths of pleasing sense I ran,
Nor wished an angel whom I loved a man.

———————————•———————————

                  Sir, 'twas not
Her husband's presence only, called that spot
Of joy into the Duchess' cheek; perhaps
Fra Pandolf chanced to say, "Her mantle laps
Over my lady's wrist too much," or, "Paint
Must never hope to reproduce the faint
Half-flush that dies along her throat." Such stuff
Was courtesy, she thought, and cause enough
For calling up that spot of joy....

Even though both poets are writing in the same verse form, rhymed
iambic pentameter couplets, each uses the line in a rather extreme and distinctive way. Pope, by ending each line with a pause, reinforces his rhyme

words and creates the feeling of sharply isolated lines and couplets being added one to another. Browning, on the other hand, weakens the impact of the rhyme words, and so we feel that the lines and couplets flow into one another.

Contemporary poets, even poets writing in free verse, follow Browning's model. It allows for tension between metrical regularity and spontaneous human speech. In the following poem by Annie Finch, a poem in **terza rima**, the varied enjambment is a powerful source of energy, one unpredictable element in a predictable pattern of rhyming. Another surprise is the slight variation in line lengths:

Thanksgiving

for Julian

Earth is getting ready to harden and dim
in an unmoving winter. A dry yellow curl
bends the grasses the long year has tufted and brimmed.

The tops start to flatten hushed by the hurl
the wind sends through the trees, and soon they will bow.
Layered on grain, quick-shadowed like pearl,

sky-thick gray clouds anchor down to plow
the black plunging earth. As the furrows grow strange
and dark with their shadows, the morning grows. How

Can a harvest this cold wrinkle open and change?
Laced into earth by their last anxious stalks,
the fields wait. Nothing's there, in the sky's empty range,

but the emptying wind that listens and talks,
or else barely stutters, stumbling by
on its way to bring snow. The day-darkened hawks

slow their long wheeling, up the thin sky,
and then push back downward with shuddering grace
to catch the dry answer this time makes. The high

piled grain, the bleached houses and barns, lean. You place
fourteen dense kernels of looming seed-corn
with care in my left hand. Their saffron-hard trace

of the sun is alive, a long memory torn
from a stalk. So smooth, they call quiet, as loud
as your opened eyes spoke the first day you were born.

from *Eve*

The preceding examples reveal one more fact about the poetic line. **End rhyme** is its most powerful signal. Indeed, end rhyme communicates line length to the ear, and this device can have as much force as the visual signal of the wide white space that follows a line break in print. However, because end rhyme is such a powerful attention getter and one so strongly identified with poetry, beginning writers often overuse it. Beware! The result can be a droning that obscures meaning.

Less emphatic rhyming as well as less predictable line lengths characterises modern verse. In Maxine Kumin's poem, which follows, there are instances of true rhyme on stressed syllables as well as the more subdued echoes of rhymes on unstressed syllables (blister/after) and of matched final consonants (line/on):

Stopped Time in Blue and Yellow

Today the violets turn up blue
in the long grass as ever
a heaven can, the sea-calm color
of promises ballooning into view.
Stems long enough to lace
around your oval wrist,
small petal face
the wash of Waterman's ink,
vigilant cat's eye at the center
yellow as the sluice box where cows drink.

Today under the blue line
that covers your pulse I feel
the small purling sounds
your body makes, going on.
Time squats in the blue-spurred grass
like a yellow blister
and love in the long foreplay of spring
follows skyblue after.

from *Our Ground Time Here Will Be Brief*

●   ●   ●   ●   ●   *QUESTIONS*   ●   ●   ●   ●   ●

1. What principle governs Kumin's line breaks?

2. How do the shortest and longest lines in this poem work expressively?

●   ●   ●   ●   ●   *EXERCISE*   ●   ●   ●   ●   ●

Write a poem about love in which you experiment with various line lengths. Make your shortest line a single word.

THE LINE AND FREE VERSE

Today poets mostly write **free verse**, a term describing a wide variety of practices. In free verse the traditional, quantitatively defined line we find in such poets as Shakespeare, Pope, and Browning is replaced by lines defined far more loosely and subjectively. The poems by Galvin and Kumin that we have already examined are, relatively speaking, "free"—especially if we set them alongside the excerpts from earlier poets. If you read Kumin's poem aloud, you will hear a slight hesitation at many of the line breaks, even when no punctuation occurs. Kumin separates sentence parts in a quite predictable manner, trusting her ear for colloquial speech patterns. One convention of free verse is to break lines at natural, syntactical pauses, whether they are punctuated or not.

In the following excerpt from Margaret Gibson's "Affirmations," line breaks work similarly. However, Gibson sometimes departs from line breaks governed by syntax. Such variations depend more for their effects on what the eye sees than on what the ear hears. This visual focusing is one major device for emphasis in free verse.

> An Eskimo shaman
> will take stone, and with a pebble sit quietly
> for days tracing on stone a circle,
> until snow and mind are one.
> Gazing into the whirl of a knothole   5
> I sit out winter. Someone mutters inside.
> Just one tremor before the walls give me
> another white word for snow
> this wood desk shimmers, as if wind
> had reached wood's spellbound   10
> galaxies and seen
> the pole star
> turning.

from *Long Walks in the Afternoon*

Gibson allows a line break to replace punctutation on occasion, as in lines 5 and 8. Her practice suggests that, for the free verse poet, line breaks serve as a way of visually scoring a feature of the spoken poem.

Another device this passage illustrates is the expressive power of location. Placing "spellbound" at the end of one line and "galaxies" at the beginning of the next emphasizes "spellbound" more. In addition, the hesitation at the line break creates a moment of suspense: We know that the line has ended with an adjective that demands a noun, and when our expectations are fulfilled at the beginning of the next line, our satisfaction comes with extra force. Line breaks, then, are a strategy for creating suspense and surprise—or even for fashioning multiple meanings.

Consider the various ways of reading the following lines:

When she cried
Wolf
Tears down her face
Ran

Is "Wolf" the object of the verb, as in "crying wolf," or is it the subject of the main clause that follows an introductory "when..." clause? Is the first word on the third line a reference to crying or a synonym for "rips"? Many contemporary poets exploit this kind of ambiguity.

When all is going well, every decision a poet makes about the length of lines and where to place the end words and opening words helps the poem communicate. In "Figure Eights" by Siv Cedering, even the white spaces between stanzas are functional. One could almost say that these spaces "mean" something in this reproduction of the experience of skating:

My back toward the circle, I skate,
shift my weight, turn toward the center.

The skill is in the balance, the ability
to choose an edge, and let it cut

its smooth line. The moon is trapped
in the ice. My body flows

across it. The evening's cold. The space
limited. There is not much room

for hesitation. But I have learned a lot
about grace, in my thirty-third year.

I lean into the cutting edge: two circles
interlock, number eight drawn

by a child, a mathematician's
infinity.

from *Letters from the Floating
World: Selected and New Poems*

The stanza breaks at "cut / its smooth line," "flows / across it," and "room / for hesitation" seem to perform what the words describe.

Cedering's decision to shape this poem in unrhymed couplets has other consequences. The most obvious is that the poem's appearance becomes a representation of its content: the paired lines help us "see" the idea of pairing that the skates represented. Such visual communication is another element in much free verse poetry—and even in traditional poetry. Poems on the printed page communicate visually; they have shapes that may or may not correspond to the poem as an experience for the ear.

Though beyond the scope of this book, those of you who want to explore how poems may be shaped like their subjects (**concrete** poetry) can search the Internet for numerous examples.

In much free verse (Gibson's and Cedering's work included), poets break lines between syntactical units and between words that would otherwise seem glued together. These subtle interruptions, as Denise Levertov explains in "Technique and Tune-up," duplicate how "the mind as it feels its way through a thought or an impression often stops with one foot in the air, its antennae waving and its nose waffling" (from *New & Selected Essays,* 1992).

If the experience behind the poem involves how life is fragmented and how one's feelings can undergo abrupt and extreme changes, then a free verse technique in which lines are scattered, syntax is fractured, and margins jump around is, in fact, a prosody that does rise from the poem's occasion. The opening of A. R. Ammons's "Muse" shifts from rising to falling rhythms and helps to produce the feeling of struggle that accompanies the task (our task) of making sense of the fragments:

> From the dark
> fragmentations
> build me up
> into a changed brilliant shape
> realized order,
> mind singing again
> new song, moving into the slow beat and
> disappearing beat
> of perfect resonance:
> how many
> times must I be broken and reassembled!
> Anguish of becoming,
> pain of moulting,
> descent! Before the unending moment of vision:
>
> from *Collected Poems, 1951–1971*

With this rhythm, Ammons moves closer than a metrical poet can to representing the very process of how the mind perceives.

Meter, however, does not altogether vanish in free verse composition, though it is true that metrical expectations and predictability are no longer at work. Metrical passages emerge, consciously or unconsciously, in the poet's work because of the very nature of words and syntax. The impact of a sudden metrical stretch in a free verse poem is akin to the impact of metrical variation in traditional prosody. In the latter, a pattern is temporarily broken as we saw in such poems as Andrew Marvell's "Thoughts in a Garden" (pp. 109–110). In the former, what we will for convenience call a "nonpattern," is broken by the emergence of a metrical stretch. In the broadest sense, the signal sent to the reader is the same: The variation requires extra attention and places special attention on those words, as in Margaret Gibson's "Affirmations," (p. 115). Often, the variation signals change.

Sometimes, as Annie Finch suggests (in *The Ghost of Meter,* 1993), the emergence of meter may signal an attitude toward authority; meter itself represents the old, established way. In her chapter on "Contemporary Free Verse," Finch argues, for example, that the iambic pentameter line closing the following passage in Audre Lorde's "A Litany for Survival" amplifies Lorde's sense of betrayal by authorities. Observe the metrical "lightness" of the second line (mostly unstressed syllables) that precedes the ponderous iambic stomping that follows.

> For by this weapon
> this illusion of some safety to be found
> the heavy-footed hoped to silence us.
>
> from *The Black Unicorn*

Though free verse abandons preset metrical repetition, it does not abandon all types of repetition. The incantatory rhythms of Walt Whitman depend on repetition of grammatical structures, often introduced by repetition of a word, as in this passage from "Respondez":

> Let insanity still have charge of sanity!
> Let books take the places of trees, animals, rivers, clouds!
> Let the daub'd portraits of heroes supersede heroes!
> Let the manhood of man never take steps after itself!

This device, which provides cohesion and continuity, is often combined with lists or catalogs, as in Whitman's "To a Locomotive in Winter" and Allen Ginsberg's "Howl," two poems in which the ghost of meter asserts itself. For more on lists and initial word repetition (called **anaphora**), see the section "List Poems" in Chapter 6, pp. 142–144.

When it is effective, free verse is not the result of spontaneous composition or a disregard for the relationships between means and ends. Like all good writing, effective free verse comes from a mastery of the medium, and especially from considered decisions about how the line, even without a predetermined meter or length, can communicate.

> "*A line is a controller, concentrator of a poem's voice and focus. The line delays, directs the attention, lets it fall on the right thing, the right inflection, phrase or word at the right moment. It is the major domo of the poem.*"
>
> George McWhirter, *Epoc* (Winter, 1980)

● ● ● ● ●   *EXERCISES*   ● ● ● ● ●

1. Compose a free verse poem in which punctuation determines the line breaks.

2. Following Gibson's example (p. 115), write a poem in which decreasing line length is used expressively. Now try another in which line lengths expand.

3. Experiment with line breaks and stanza breaks that separate parts of speech (subject from verb, verb from object, preposition from object, adjective from noun, adverb from verb).

4. Use line break and line placement (see the discussion of the Ammons poem, p. 117) to register one or more of the following experiences: alienation, interrupted sleep, attending to one person or task while remembering another, anger (your computer crashed before you could save your revised poem).

5. Compose a free verse poem in which you occasionally and strategically break out into meter.

LINES IN COMBINATION

Broadly speaking, you can choose one of two major traditions for combining lines into poems: the **stichic** and the **stanzaic** (or **strophic**). In the stichic tradition you write a continuous poem in an unbroken column of type. An example of this tradition is Galvin's "Fog Township." In the stanzaic tradition you write a segmented poem in which white spaces (blank lines) divide the total work into smaller, quasi-independent units as in a ballad.

While in both types we recognize the general look of poetry, we further recognize and are "preset" to respond to a range of more particular typographical designs. The following two-stanza poem by William Wordsworth promises something even before we begin reading it:

A Slumber Did My Spirit Seal

A slumber did my spirit seal;
    I had no human fears:
She seemed a thing that could not feel
    The touch of earthly years.

No motion has she now, no force;
    She neither hears nor sees;
Rolls round in earth's diurnal course,
    With rocks, and stones, and trees.

The visual message of this poem immediately suggests twofoldedness and symmetry: we expect that the shape of the thought or emotion will somehow correspond to the halved whole—and it does. The shift from past tense to present tense is the key to the "before and after" structure. In turn, that structure justifies the decision to cast the material in two *equal* stanzas. The line indentations suggest a further division of each stanza, a division the end rhyme (*ab/ab*) echoes.

Stanzaic poems and poems in **fixed forms** are most effective when some kind of correspondence exists between outer and inner divisions or form. Each of the following Italian sonnets by Jay Rogoff pivots the humor between the eighth and ninth line; when the rhyme scheme changes, the poet takes us from the scene of the crime to the interrogation room:

Murder Mystery 1

Inkstains upon the oriental rug.
Blood mingles with them. Blood today is king.
The lyre lies on the bed strung with one string.
Protruding from her wounds are points stuck snug
as bees' abandoned stingers, which cops unplug.
Only the radio is left to sing.
The floor littered with crow quill pens. "Bring
'em here," says the sergeant with a shrug.

The poet, crammed into his seat with bright
lights blinding, when interrogated, said,
"I don't know what you mean." A lie. The light
was brightened, handcuffs clamped. He stood and read
a poem. Finished, he sobbed, "We used to fight.
I'd never kill her. But I'm glad she's dead."

Murder Mystery 2

Inkstains upon the oriental rug.
The poet at a queer angle. Like a spring
wound round his neck, a strangling catgut string
has popped his eyes. His hands clutch poems and hug
them to his heart. The cops' most violent tug
won't pry them. A pen lies like a torn wing.
From the hall a woman's voice begins to sing.
"Book'er," the sergeant says. "Prints and a mug."

She sat handcuffed. Her robe trailed on the floor.
"What do you know?" "Nothing." "A man is dead."
"A poet," she corrected. "I know no more."
The light was thrown upon her laureled head.
"He did it to himself," she added. "You're
a liar." "No, this is my lyre," she said.

Some poets might emphasize the overall unity of the sonnet; others, like Rogoff, develop material that coincides with the divisions signaled by the rhyme scheme. To put it simply, a mitten tells us one thing about a hand; a glove tells us something else.

Whether writing poems in traditional or free verse structures, the poet chooses or invents groupings to achieve expressive ends. Just as the unequal sections of the Italian sonnet promise a change of scene or direction, so does the diminishing stanza in Theodore Roethke's "The Moment" direct the poem's emotion and meaning:

> We passed the ice of pain,
> And came to a dark ravine,
> And there we sang with the sea:
> The wide, the bleak abyss
> Shifted with our slow kiss.
>
> Space struggled with time;
> The gong of midnight struck
> The naked absolute.
> Sound, silence sang as one.
>
> All flowed: Without, within;
> Body met body, we
> Created what's to be.
>
> What else to say?
> We end in joy.

> from *The Collected Poems*
> *of Theodore Roethke*

The poem's structure—each stanza a line shorter than the one before it— guides our understanding of what's at stake: two people coming together, stripping away both time and space in the process. In their connection or uniting, they are what is left of the world, but they contain it as well.

Will your poem exist primarily in *time,* as a sequence of words, sounds, and rhythms to be heard, or in *space,* as a sequence of signs printed on the page? The work of most contemporary poets hovers somewhere in between, so that reading—finding the essential poem—becomes an act of mediation between what we hear, however silently, and what we see. In addition, you must consider how much the full potency of your work depends on your reader's knowledge of traditions you employ, allude to, or intentionally defy. For example, if you divide your fourteen-line poem into two parts (eight lines and six) to look like a sonnet but do not use rhyme, you must be aware of your assumptions and the demands they place on your readers. You need to gauge the risks you are taking by depending on or ignoring conventions—even the conventions of free verse. Of course, many of the decisions you will make will be revealed as you write, discovering both the sound and sense of your narrative.

The two poems that follow illustrate contrasting assumptions about the essential nature of poetry and about the audience. Karen Swenson's "Time and the Perfume River" is in a fixed form, the **villanelle**, and it gets much of its strength from manipulating the conventions of that form. Consequently, though the poem can reach any reader, it has greater resonance for the reader who is aware of the dynamics of the form and who is familiar with other villanelles. "The Waves," by Mary Oliver, follows only the rules that the poet has discovered for this individual poem. Moreover, Oliver has given special emphasis to the typographical level of the poem, allowing that experience to sit in sharp contrast to sounds, rhythms, and even syntax. Swenson's poem also has a strong typographical impact; the visual shape underscores—or outlines—a musical shape that communicates to the ear. These patterned repetitions of sounds display the poem in time.

Time and the Perfume River

Small Buddhas smile above their blooms
on gilded family altars, glide
along the curves of the Perfume,

that river named before the dooms
of war ripped Hue's old gilded hide
and Buddhas' smiles above the blooms.

The river waves are slapping tunes.
Greens sputtering in a wok provide,
along the curves of the Perfume,

the smoke of incense. Children's spumes
of laughter rock small boats whose guide
is Buddha's smile above his blooms.

Those years death rode the river's flume
his rotting incense justified
along the curves of the Perfume

by leaders' greed for power's boom.
War's drowned now in the river's tide
where Buddhas smile above their blooms
along the curves of the Perfume.

From *The Landlady in Bangkok*

The Waves

The sea
  isn't a place
    but a fact, and
    a mystery

under its green and black
  cobbled coat that never
    stops moving.

When death
happens on land, on some
  hairpin piece of road,
    we crawl past,
      imagining

over and over that moment
of disaster. After the storm
  the other boats didn't
    hesitate—they spun out

from the rickety pier, the men
  bent to the nets or turning
    the weedy winches.
      Surely the sea

is the most beautiful fact
in our universe, but
  you won't find a fisherman
    who will say so;

what they say is,
  See you later.
    Gulls white as angels scream
    as they float in the sun

just off the sterns;
  everything is here
    that you could ever imagine.
    And the bones

of the drowned fisherman
are returned, half a year later,
  in the glittering,
    laden nets.

                From *Dream Work*

● ● ● ● *QUESTIONS AND EXERCISES* ● ● ● ●

1. What elements in Swensen's poem create musical effects.

2. Find and study five or six other villanelles, including Dylan Thomas's "Do Not Go Gentle into That Good Night." Now try a villanelle of your own.

3. Compare and contrast the conventions and effects of the villanelle with those of the English (Shakespearean) sonnet form (see p. 138) and the Italian sonnet (see Rogoff's "Murder Mystery" sequence, p. 120).

4. What is the relationship between (visual) form and content in "The Waves"?

Early in this chapter we asked you to stick with us as we explored the special language and processes of poetry. Keep in mind that these are not formulas. They are ways of talking about what happens and what you want to make happen when you write poetry, especially when you revise it. Making a poem is a process much like throwing a pot on a wheel. You slam a mass of clay on the wheel and draw it up and out, adjust it, work it over and, if you are lucky, you end with a vase. If not, you begin again. Crafting a poem may also take a wide-ranging series of adjustment between the various elements of the sound and the sense.

 IMAGERY

> *"A poem . . . begins as a lump in the throat, a sense of wrong, a homesickness, a lovesickness. . . . It finds the thought and the thought finds the words."*
>
> Robert Frost

Wherever a poem begins, the poet discovers **images**—a piece of language that relates sensory experience—to speak the thought. Though all writers employ **imagery** and the many figures of speech that are built from images, poets *depend* on them. (See the discussions of concreteness and figurative language in Chapter 4.) Because poetry aims at intensity and economy, imagery and figures of speech have special value to the poet. Sensory experience is primary experience: We see, feel, taste, smell, and hear before we think, analyze, choose, and argue. By staying close to imagery, the language of the senses, you can bring your readers close to a fundamental, physical awareness of our world. At the same time, by choosing carefully and by letting associated images coalesce, you can evoke complex states of understanding and feeling.

The image in the title of the following poem gives it a center and circumference.

Briefcase of Sorrow

> *Some writers get into the habit of letting* **of** *name a metaphor without really showing the image to the reader: sea of life, mattress of the soul, river of death . . . or (perhaps the worse) briefcase of sorrow.*
>
> Frances Mayers, *The Discovery of Poetry*

My briefcase of sorrow slumps by the door.
The semester's done. I leave it behind,
all my manilla folders of grief (stacked
and alphabetized, bound with rubber bands
of stretched hope), pens of overachievement,
and pencils of petty angst. At some point,
I suppose I should dump its insides out
on the table, the staple remover
of apocalyse, a few sticky notes
of indecision. Poor briefcase—it can't
ingest them, try as it may, and I should
especially purge the gradebook of mixed
endeavors, the crumbs of last month's sandwich.
Not now. My neighborhood pub calls louder
than some cloying briefcase, strap of pity
wagging as I leave, its two bright buckles
of expectation gleaming for my return
once again, when I will spill its contents,
the paperclips of despair, the Wetnaps
of desire, bring it, light and swinging,
along my side to fill one more time its
compartment of everything and nothing.

Richard Newman from *Borrowed Towns*

On one level we are amused by the image of a personified briefcase as an emblem of the teacher's life. But the image (also an extended metaphor) allows Newman to make us experience more intensely the teaching process (papers, papers, papers to grade), the weariness that an instructor feels at the end of a semester (I need a drink), the students' expectations and hopes, and the knowledge that, like Sisyphus, the process will begin again with the briefcase filling up once more.

Newman says that this poem actually grows from his contrarian character: "If, when I was a student, a writing teacher told me never to write about something (Grandma, poetry, teaching, Oklahoma) or not to write in a certain way (formal, narrative, syllabic), my first instinct was always to go home and break the rule—say, a formal poem about Grandma teaching syllabic poetry in Oklahoma. Now a teacher myself, I often use Frances Mayes's *The Discovery of Poetry*, but the first semester I tried that textbook, we came to the 'Six Danger Signals' section about not using the word *of* to name a metaphor, as in *briefcase of sorrow* and immediately after class I went to my office and wrote the first draft." And so, he combines (1) an emotional reaction to rules, (2) an image of a typical tool of his profession, and (3) further reflection about a typical process for generating a poem.

Observations that discover likenesses are the genesis of many successful poems. Even such rarefied emotional experiences as the sudden sense of absence can be captured by the patient poet who asks, "What is it like?" over and over again. "Gloves," by Jean Nordhaus, is alive with images that finally take us to a place beyond and within.

When all the birds roost
suddenly
the bare tree
bursts into leaf.
plumb, tapered, brown, true
a flock of
weathervanes
nosing into
the wind, they hang
to the branches
like gloves, then
leave suddenly
leaving the branches,
the branches
full of in-
visible hands.

from *A Language of Hands*

You probably noticed how the progression from "leaf" to "leave" to "leaving" echoes the sense of emptiness. The image of the birds filling the tree makes the image of the emptiness possible.

● ● ● ● ●   *EXERCISES*   ● ● ● ● ●

1. How do Newman and Nordhaus use the line to isolate or connect images?

2. Examine other poems in this chapter to see whether line, imagery, or something else function as the primary structural element.

3. Write your own poem by enlarging upon a central image or building a series of associated images.

The interplay between lines and images creates much of the dramatic tension in contemporary poetry. Investigating the possibilities of various line–image units will lead you to an understanding of one more expressive convention. As we said earlier, don't expect immediate results. The first step, however, to internalizing the music and methods of poetry is to constantly read it and, of course, write.

"The Image is more than an idea. It is a vortex or cluster of fused ideas and is endowed with energy."

Ezra Pound

◢◤ SOUND PATTERNS

Now it is time to look more closely into the expressiveness of sounds and sound patterns. Usually in speech and in most prose, the various sounds in our language occur at random. However, the poet can intensify the impact of sounds by repeating them near each other or at regular intervals. As with meter, some feature of language that occurs in a haphazard way when we speak or when we write prose, in poetry is patterned to produce emphasis, cohesiveness, or orderliness. You are already familiar with these terms and effects: alliteration, assonance, dissonance, onomatopoeia, and rhyme.

When Poe, in "The Raven," writes of "this *g*rim, un*g*ainly, *g*hastly, *g*aunt, and ominous bird of yore," he employs alliteration (repetition of initial consonant) on four stressed syllables to underscore his adjectives by linking them sonically. When Shelley, in "Mont Blanc," writes of pines that "in the m*a*ngled soil/Br*a*nchless and sh*a*ttered st*a*nd," he achieves a similar but somewhat quieter effect through assonance (repetition of vowel sound). In both cases, the reader's attention is drawn to words linked by sounds that link the words. *Note:* We are not referring to the spelling of words, since identical sounds are often spelled differently: "stuff"/"enough."

Though mostly we think of poets as creating pleasing sounds, dissonance is a tool that may be quite appropriate in many contexts. When Matthew Arnold writes "who props thou asks in these bad times my soul," the clash of sounds exactly fits his despair about the modern condition. When D.J. Renegade in "Funkiness Manifesto" writes "Rap is urban tongues depicting what the drums be kicking/in syllable knocking rhythm rhyme rocking, syncopated talking" the rough sounds jostle each other much like a jazz shifting of notes and also mimic the jangle of inner-city sounds.

Rhyme is a more complex echoing—a repeated vowel/consonant combination, as in the pair "knock"/"rock." Often, as in the pair "free"/"see," the matching of the final vowel makes up the rhyme. Because rhyme (or "true rhyme") is more emphatic than the other devices, it is customarily used, as we have seen, to signal the ends of lines and to define stanzas. It can, however, occur within a line as in the Renegade quotation. Rhyme sharpens meanings by asking readers to consider the relationships between the words whose sounds mirror one another.

The following lines are the result of an assignment to develop a six-line stanza using true rhyme:

> Early one morning, an Amtrak train
> Rumbles north through the ivory expanse
> Of Maryland landscape. The muffled terrain
> Is sliced by the tracks. Slung like a lance,
> The careless freight, by folly and chance,
> Splatters the snowbank with that human stain.

This first draft exploits the power of rhyme by emphasizing words important enough to carry the extra attention they receive. After leading us to anticipate alternating rhyme (*abab* through line 4), the poet interrupts the pattern with a couplet (lines 4 and 5). This interruption unsettles the reader, who waits for some new resolution of the first pattern. The waiting produces suspense, and then surprise, as the last line delivers the final image with the return of the *a* rhyme.

Although repetition of any sound has the broad effect of calling attention to words, you can achieve more specialized effects when you are sensitive to the nuances of the various sounds. When Poe repeats the harsh gutteral in "The Raven" the effect is quite different from that of Keats's lines from "To August": "Thy hair soft-lifted by the winnowing wing; / Or on a half-reaped furrow sound asleep." In Keats's lines, harsh sounds are almost absent and never prominent.

Although we hesitate to say that sounds *mean* anything, we do feel that they *suggest* meaning. Let's consider consonants first. The following chart shows the range of consonant sounds. The family groupings have to do with how the sounds are pronounced as well as how they strike the ear.

CONSONANT SOUNDS

liquids; *r, l*	"semivowels" along with *w* and *y*, considered the most musical consonants
nasals: *m, n, ng*	firmer, but still "soft"
fricatives: *h, f, v, th, dh, s, z, sh, zh*	produced by vibration or friction, abrasive
plosives: *p, b, k, g, t, d*	produced by blasting open a closed space...can't be prolonged...called "hard" consonants

The following is a student experiment in using sounds. The assignment was to write two short passages of poetry, the first with language that is dominated by softer consonants, and the second emphasizing the plosives.

1. Summer came on slow as a lizard's blink,
    on a flotilla of white wicker chairs and lawn games,
    and all we knew of time was a lurid glow
    in the West-Northwest that we watched from the headland,
    watched it sink seamless into Thursday.

2. Kirk burned for a while on alternate doses
of hard bop and crack. He smoked Kents tit for tat
with the most brutal of the night beasts and
once hocked his axe
for a Palo Alto whore. Even now, dead by the hand
of an outraged husband, he looms over my shoulder
slipping me jacks to cinch a high straight.

● ● ● ● ● *EXERCISES* ● ● ● ● ●

1. In the preceding experiment, which lines or passages seem most success-ful at linking sound and sense? Where would you make improvements? Revise these passages; then go on to do your own experiments with the con-sonant groups. Recite your work aloud. Listen for the similarities among sounds from the same family. Notice how they can almost be mistaken for one another. For example, the word *fish* and the first syllable of *visual* create a near rhyme.

2. Listen and respond to the sounds in the following word pairs. How do the contrasting sounds make you feel? Can you conceive of an instance in which choosing one might better communicate both the sound and the sense of a poem.
   a. pillow / cushion
   b. coast / shore
   c. beast / animal
   d. persist / continue
   e. whiskey / booze

3. Choose one of the poems in this chapter and try substituting apparent synonyms for the nouns or verbs the poet chose. How does your substitution change the sound or the meaning?

———————●———————

For several reasons it's difficult to ascribe specific meaning to the sound of a word. Each person pronounces words differently, stresses different sylla-bles, drags out or shortens consonant/vowel clusters. A word like *moan*, which sounds so mournful as in "the wind moans through the woods" can in other contexts actually appear humorous, as in "she's like the wind through the trees: moan, moan, moan" when said mockingly about a habitual com-plainer. Nonetheless, in context the sound linked to the sense resonates, as in Tennyson's "the immemorial hum of innumerable bees." You can hear the loss in force if you try some word substitution: "the prehistorical sound of count-less bees."

So, we feel that the sounds count but how they count specifically we can't pinpoint. Nevertheless, the poet always seeks for those words and combinations of words that feel right.

Now pronounce each word in the following vowel chart as if you were playing them on the piano or singing them like "do, re, mi." Feel the work your mouth has to do to make the sounds.

bee	high freqency (alto) vowels
bay	
buy	
bit	middle-frequency (tenor vowels)
bet	
bat	
bird	
bud	
bar	low-frequency (bass vowels)
bough	
boy	
bought	
book	
bone	
boot	

This vowel scale groups families by frequency characteristics that can be graphed on an oscilloscope. An interval of high-frequency sounds shows a busy, jagged pattern with many peaks and valleys. Low-frequency vowels, on the other hand, show fewer oscillations over the same interval. Like the consonant families, the vowel families are related by how they are produced. The high-fre-quency vowels are made toward the front of the mouth in a relatively closed space. You can feel a tension in the facial muscles as you pronounce them. The low-frequency vowels begin far back in the mouth, which is open and rounded as these sounds are made.

As with the consonants, repetition of vowels from one or another cate-gory can help give emotional coloring to the passages bonded together by these related sounds. For example, the last stanza of Dylan Thomas's "The Hand That Signed the Paper" gains much of its solemnity from the way in which low-frequency vowel sounds dominate the passage, especially toward the end of lines.

> The five kings count the dead but do not soften
> The crusted wound nor stroke the brow;
> A hand rules pity as a hand rules heaven;
> Hands have no tears to flow.

Conversely, in his elegiac "Do Not Go Gentle into That Good Night," Thomas urges not self-pity or gloom, but active resistance to death; here the strident high-frequency vowels dominate:

> Grave men, near death, who see with blinding sight
> Blind eyes could blaze like meteors and be gay,
> Rage, rage against the dying of the light.

Turn back to the six-line stanza on p. 127. Notice how the strident *a* sound promotes the feeling that the speaker's otherwise flat voice can veil but not hide his anguish.

●   ●   ●   ●   ●   *EXERCISES*   ●   ●   ●   ●   ●

As you have already done with the consonant sounds, explore the effects of piling up vowel sounds from one and then the other side of the spectrum.

1. Write an "aw" poem in which the vowel in words like *call* and *appall* and *thought* is dominant. Notice, again, that spelling is not the key to pronunciation.

2. Write an "ee" poem.

3. Experiment with the ways in which various classes of consonants and vowels work in combination. For example, mix high-frequency vowels and fricative consonants.

4. The following poem is an experiment in sound and meaning that combines different vowels and consonants. Read it aloud. Notice that spelling, the look of the words, does not necessarily produce the same vowel sounds.

> *Vowels*
> loveless vessels
>
> we vow
> solo love
>
> we see
> love solve loss
>
> else we see
> love sow woe
>
> selves we woo
> we lose

losses we levee
we owe

we sell
loose vows

so we love
less well

so low
so level

wolves evolve

Christian Bök

OFF-RHYME

Recently rhyme appears to be coming back into favor, and we see more poems written with rhyme than one might have twenty years ago. Still, contemporary poets tend to favor subdued sound patterns. **Off-rhyme** (also called slant rhyme, near rhyme, and half rhyme) is used more frequently than true rhyme. To discover the possible different effects, experiment with the varying intensities of rhyme. One form of off-rhyme is **consonance**. This is a matching of consonant clusters around changing vowel sounds: "blood / blade," "cut / cat / cot / caught," "dance / dunce." Theodore Roethke's "My Papa's Waltz" combines rhyme with consonance in the first two stanzas (dizzy / easy, pans / countenance) to create a slight discord that fits the subject.

The whiskey on your breath
Could make a small boy dizzy;
But I hung on like death:
Such waltzing was not easy.

We romped until the pans
Slid from the kitchen shelf;
My mother's countenance
Could not unfrown itself.

The hand that held my wrist
Was battered on one knuckle;
At every step you missed
My right ear scraped a buckle.

You beat time on my head
With a palm caked hard by dirt,

Then waltzed me off to bed
Still clinging to your shirt.

In the last two stanzas all the end words rhyme as if the wild dance has becomes less drunken.

● ● ● ● ●   *EXERCISES*   ● ● ● ● ●

Experiment by alternating full rhymes with consonance.

1. Try these end words in your poem: *blend, blonde, blind, bland.*

2. Now use these: *cuff, cough, calf; meat, mat, might, moat.*

Consonance has an eerie richness about it; other types of echoing can be far more subdued. Often the repetition of final consonant sounds, or the pairing of related consonant sounds, serves for rhyme. Listen to the end sounds in the first stanza of Philip Levine's "For Fran":

She packs the flower beds with leaves,
Rags, dampened paper, ties with twine
The lemon tree, but winter carves
Its features on the uprooted stem.

The quiet alternate rhyming of the fricative "vs" pattern and the nasals sets just the degree of containment Levine needs for his gentle homage to his wife. The subdued echoes illustrated by Levine's quatrain are the convention of our time for those who choose to rhyme at all. These modulated echoes can move a sensitive reader (listener). Are they "rhyme"? Well, no and yes. Literally the sounds don't lock together, but in the sense that off-rhyme can serve to make the poem cohere, it serves the same purpose . . . but softly.

● ● ● ● ●   *EXERCISE*   ● ● ● ● ●

Write six lines of alternating rhyme in which the odd-numbered lines end with dental consonants (d, t) and the even-numbered ones end with fricatives (see chart on p. 128).

─────────●─────────

While it is possible to write without a conscious concern for sound or meter, these physical phenomena do their work anyway. In a sense, they just will not be ignored. Any dimension of language to which we choose to pay no heed is ignored at the risk of our sending unintended, ineffective messages. The subterranean effects of sounds and rhythms are part of the "magic" of poetry. To produce magic, one needs knowledge and skill and vigilance.

> *"To me, the greatest pleasure of writing is not what it's about, but the inner music that words make."*
>
> Truman Capote

Our review of the fundamentals is now over. Of course, we have only skimmed the surface of these techniques. Each poet chooses the devices and strategies that solve the problems of each developing poem—but there can be little in the way of informed choice without information. Each poet, as well, must discover, through trial and error as much as by any other means, his or her poetic balance between spontaneous utterance and traditional measures and forms. Each must do what Eavan Boland describes herself doing (in her introductory essay to *The Making of a Poem: A Norton Anthology of Poetic Forms*): "...pushing the music of dailyness against the customary shapes of the centuries."

The conventions of poetry are, finally, the features by which poems are recognized and do their work.

> *"True Ease in Writing comes from Art, not Chance,*
> *As those move easiest who have learn'd to dance,*
> *'Tis not enough no Harshness gives Offence,*
> *The Sound must seem an Eccho to the Sense."*
>
> Alexander Pope

Here is the rest of "Fog Township" against which to check your division of lines (exercise on p. 105):

> the spring genius of this
> foggy township knitting up
> cable and chain to bind
> the acres, among moss stitches
> laying down her simple
> seed and fern stitch,
> complicating the landscape
> a pattern a day: daisy
> stitches and wild oats,
> berry knots interspersed
> with traveling vine
> and dogwood. Her needles

cut from oak tips,
click like sparks fired
across a gap, and I
imagine her crouched on
a stump, hair wet, pulling
April back together.
But for the lethargy that's
floating in this fog
in nets so fine they can't
be seen, I might walk around
out there until I meet her,
or scare off the jay
who's chipping for sustenance
along a pine's gray limb.

from *Seals in the Inner Harbor*

6

PRACTICING POETRY

> *"No one lives in this room*
> *without confronting the whiteness of the wall*
> *behind the poems, planks of books,*
> *photographs of dead heroines.*
> *Without contemplating last and late*
> *the true nature of poetry. The drive*
> *to connect. The dream of a common language."*
>
> Adrienne Rich

Once, to borrow Matthew Arnold's phrase, most people thought that poetry was meant to express only the "best that has been thought and said." The *best* meant high-minded and serious subjects; the grimy events of everyday life were too commonplace to be the subject of a poem. These days writers have a wider view of what constitutes proper poetic subject matter. Picking something to write about is easy so long as your poem is well said and emotionally honest. However, the demands of craft are as stringent as they ever were, and the poet still needs to write something that others will see as a poem.

Sometimes a poem comes to a poet fully dressed. Most often, though, poems are the result of learning how to clothe an emotion or an idea in the form and with the words that will show them off best. As we have said earlier, mastering the craft requires exercising regularly. The poems in this chapter are designed to encourage your practice as well as to hint at the infinite number of subjects and structures you can draw on. It is useful to remember that poems, as other creative works, are built on the bedrock of the forms and subjects of everyday life. So many subjects exist and so many shapes for the subjects that we can only touch on the universe of possible exercises and possible forms.

1. Imitation

We have scrambled the fifteen lines of Susan Astor's poem, "The Poem Queen." The original has five three-line stanzas rhyming *aab*. *Hint:* The first and last lines are in the right place.

> The Poem Queen writes a poem a day,
> To please her when she is alone
> She has more power than they know,
> It will be read.
>
> Some say hers is a magic throne
> Has found a way to burn the snow;
> Her pen is her divining rod;
> Turns gold to lead.
>
> She uses it to handle God,
> In her spare time pauses to pray
> She has a soldier and a drone
> And blossom bread.
>
> That she eats custard made of bone
> Or in her bed.
> And tame the dead.

Reconstruct these lines to reveal the most logical order for the poem. Now turn to the original at the end of this chapter. Answer these questions about it:

a. By what logic are the stanzas ordered?
b. What is the effect of the repeated rhyme sound in the half-size third line of each stanza?
c. What about the short line in itself? What effect does it create?

Write a "character poem" of your own imitating Astor's template. Titles might be "The Prom Queen," "The Car King," "The Duke of Disco," "The Blog Prince," "The Punk Queen."

2. Fixed Forms

You are already familiar with a handful of fixed forms. Sometime in primary or secondary school a teacher asked you to try your hand at a haiku or sonnet.

These forms represent a small portion of those available to you. In fact, in this space we could not even begin to illustrate all the ones that are most frequently used as well as the lesser known forms such as pantoum, ghazal, tanka, and rondeau. You might want to do an Internet search (a useful place to begin would be http://en.wikipedia.org/wiki/Category:Poetic_form) just to see the different forms that poets have used in the past, as well as the ones they are presently inventing or domesticating from another language.

Why work in a fixed form at all? Because, if nothing else, a regular rhyme scheme, rhythm, and/or stanza shape impose a discipline on your word choice as you struggle both to say your say and to shape it. The release of the tension between a preset structure and the impulse for the poem provides an extra measure of satisfaction.

Recast the imitation poem you have just written into the following forms.

Ballad Stanza. This form (a quatrain) rhymes *abxb* or *abab* and alternates iambic tetrameter with iambic trimeter, as in the following examples:

> I saw the new moon late yestreen
> Wi' the auld moon in her arm;
> And if we gang to sea, master,
> I fear we'll come to harm.
>
> "Sir Patrick Spens"

> Water, water, every where,
> And all the boards did shrink ;
> Water, water, every where,
> Nor any drop to drink.
>
> Coleridge, *The Rhyme of the
> Ancient Mariner*

Write four stanzas in the form. Though the ballad stanza can be used for other purposes, it is often associated with the incremental telling of a story, each quatrain containing a bit of additional information. Google either of the sample poems for a more extended model.

Terza Rima. This is a three-line stanza that rhymes *aba bcb cdc* and so forth, the enclosed sound of each stanza becoming the enveloping sound of the next. (See Annie Finch's "Thanksgiving" on p. 113.) Write five stanzas, and stretch the lines out to iambic pentameter. Compare the variations with each other and with your original.

Shakespearean Sonnet. This fourteen line form rhymes *abab cdcd efef gg*. Traditionally, the form has been used to express love—of another, of a country, of God. Write one about yourself.

Blank Verse. Write twelve lines of unrhymed iambic pentameter. This time the poem should be stichic (continuous) rather than divided into sections. Look at Wordsworth for examples.

———————•———————

As well as developing skills and techniques through analysis of other poetry and imitation, to engage the reader, the poet exploits the power of what might be called natural forms—the letter, the notice, the memoir, the list, the recipe, the ritual, the description and the entire toolbox of familiar everyday shapes. (See p. 190 for a discussion of forms used in fiction.)

3. Memory Poem

Try a free verse "memory poem" of your own. Begin with some feeling, image, or event in the present that triggers a flashback to an earlier version of yourself. If you have been keeping your journal for a while, look back through it. Perhaps you can fashion the poem around an action like swimming, running, dancing, or driving a car. Here is a memory poem by Hilary Tham. Compare this treatment of the speaker's father with the prose portrait in "Chinese Medicine" (Chapter 11).

Father

1

It was better than carnival day to see
you, the heroine in the opera, slender
in a gown of sequined silk, diamond
pins in your elaborate wig, your hands
arcing in grace-lineated gestures
as your voice stroked and stretched,
fish glistening upstream
against the roaring of cymbals.
Older, your waist thickened,
you played the hero, strode high
over invisible doorsills, rode unseen horses,
made invisible cities fall
with serpentine ripplings of flags while drums
pounded through my ears and my blood.
Later, you played the saxophone in the band.
I knew you could do anything.

2

My first memory is you, playing
with me and Sister who died.
You sloped a plywood board,
conjured Monte Carlo's Grand Prix
for our little lead cars.

You were commentator and sound effects
and we were squeals and admiration.

3

Those were rain days in our growing season,
and rare. You sowed and followed
the freedom of butterflies, abandoned us
for flights with beautiful women.
Returning for the harvest, you are surprised
there are blackbirds in your ricefield.

from Paper Boats

In the third stanza, you will notice a turn in the point of view that gives the narration its bite. In your poem, you might try to slip in the later memory as a comparison to an earlier one.

4. Formula Poems

The familiar formula (recipe, instructions) can give your poem a focus, a limit, and—if you use some degree of parallel grammatical structure—a basic rhythm. Here is an old recipe for a cocktail called "Golf Links."

1/2 wineglass rye

1/2 wineglass sweet catawba

2 dashes lemon juice

1 teaspoon syrup

2 dashes orange bitters

1 dash angostura bitters

1 dash rum

rinse cocktail glass with Abricotine, strain into same, dash with Appolinaris and dress with fruit.

Allowing our imaginations to take over, we can alter the proportions, ingredients, and procedures in order to provide, let's say, recipes for hate, ambition, or love. How are you feeling right now? Can you think up a recipe for a drink that will reproduce that feeling? It might include a jigger of stars, a Dumpster full of dandelions, a twist of madness, a pinch of turpentine, a teaspoon of powdered California. Get the idea?

Here is a student "recipe poem" that relates two kinds of pleasure:

Jazz Sundae

I love that sultry flavored trumpet
topped with rich, creamy, soothing sax.

Add a dash of drums, and a sprinkle of keyboard.
Then cool to taste.

And here are some other formula ideas: menus (how about one for a restaurant called Blog Café?), 15,000-mile service (on your heart, perhaps), being read your rights (*Mirandized*), a pledge of allegiance, a prayer, loading a new program into your computer, the box score of a baseball game, developing a web page.

A type of formula poem, related to the recipe, gives directions (to go somewhere, to fix something, to assess something). Of course, one kind of process can always be imaginatively transformed into another, gaining strength from the contrast between the familiar formula and the new material it holds. Working with an imaginary map, present directions for getting to forgiveness, ecstasy, indifference, the fountain of youth, inner space, hysteria, or the end of a poem.

Another kind of formula poem involves playing with plot patterns you might use for fiction or drama. Pat Shelley's poem, which follows, is a response to this assignment: *Set the scene; put a person or persons in it; bring in another person or element and make something happen.* Here's the poem:

French Movie

Apricots are falling in the rain;
The new young prunes are growing whiskers;
Two old grandfathers, lost in ruminant thoughts,
Sit among the pails of geraniums
Eating the morning's squash blossoms.

When the old nurse comes out
And leans to pour them a cup of soup
One old grandfather pinches her tit.

from *Bogg* #56

Try a formula poem of your own based on the directions given in italics preceding Pat Shelley's poem.

5. Ritual Poems

Ritual poems are closely related to formula poems but have more to do with behavior patterns outside those of language and literature. The job of a ritual poem is to discover or assess the feeling and meaning latent in such behavior. Because ritual implies order, structure, and a sense of inevitability, poems that deal with ritual have a ready-made attraction for the formalist poet. Here is a poem by Baron Wormser that says something about the impact of soap opera patterns on the patterns of our lives, and vice versa.

Soap Opera

If each witless age creates an image of itself,
Ours is of a woman crying for help
Amid a crowd of well-groomed friends.
She is hysterical, tormented, saddened, upset.
In a few minutes she will be better
And stay that way until she cries again.
It was nothing that made her cry.
Ralph had told Joan that Bill might die.
She looks at us through harsh light
That jumps off the linoleum and glass.
She is crying again and has locked the door.
She is not ugly or stupid or poor.
That's why she cries like this.
No one has told her what to do,
And she is forced to always look for clues,
To check the way adolescents dress and swear,
To listen to commentators
And remember the news.
She has opened the door.
Tom looks at her and smiles.
They kiss. It might be reconciliation
Or tenderness or thoughtless urge.
Adroit music surges over the throw rugs
And well-waxed tiles. We are convinced.
Happiness is the best of styles.

from *Good Trembling*

Write a ritual poem about a sporting event, a wedding, a holiday meal, a shopping trip. How do you get ready for work, for a test, for a date, for watching the game on television? What were Sunday mornings like when you were a child? Are there rituals at the restaurants or bars you go to? Employ some kind of formal repetition of sound, rhythm, phrase, or line that enhances the feeling of ritual, of routine, that you are describing.

6. List Poems

Inventories and lists are useful ways to brainstorm for a poem and a good journal exercise. Indeed, many successful poems are little more than lists selected, ordered, and phrased for maximum effect. Since lists are forms of analysis and classification, they can help us come to terms with large subjects or issues without resorting to abstract language. The reader receives the impact through the detail. In Shakespeare's *The Tempest*, Prospero threatens to punish Caliban with this list of pains:

For this, be sure, to-night thou shalt have cramps,
Side-stitches that shall pen thy breath up; urchins
Shall, for that vast of night that they may work,

All exercise on thee; thou shalt be pinched
As thick as honeycomb, each pinch more stinging
Than bees that made 'em.

Lists can be narrowly restricted: things in the pantry, in a bureau drawer, on a desk, in a supermarket, in a wallet or pocketbook. Many lists lead to poems that gain their strength not only from the selection but also from careful decisions about which arrangement of items is most telling. Often, successful poems are constructed out of lists that contain items at once literal and figurative, or that mix the two together. Examine William Stafford's "What's in My Journal":

Odd things, like a button drawer. Mean
Things, fishooks, barbs in your hand.
But marbles too. A genius for being agreeable.
Junkyard crucifixes, voluptuous
Discards. Space for knickknacks, and for
Alaska. Evidence to hang me, or to beautify.
Clues that lead nowhere, that never connected
Anyway. Deliberate obfuscation, the kind
That takes genius. Chasms in character
Loud omission. Mornings that yawn above
A new grave. Pages you know exist
But you can't find them. Someone's terrible
Inevitable life story, maybe mine.

Apply some of their techniques to a few list poems of your own. Don't always let logic rule in stringing items together; see where your imagination takes you. Put at least one of your poems in unrhymed, uneven couplets. Consider some of the following ideas: a basket full of gifts (wishes) for someone, an auction catalog for a hypochondriac's estate, a time capsule for yourself to be opened twenty years from now, a vegetable for each month of the year.

Anaphora is a device connected with formulas, rituals, and lists. It is the repetition of a word or words at the beginning of lines. In "Old Lem," Sterling Brown uses the device as a litany to describe the oppression of African Americans in the South by an overpowering white power structure. Here is a section of story that Old Lem tells the narrator:

"They got the judges
They got the lawyers
They got the jury-rolls
They got the law
        They don't come by ones
They got the sheriffs
They got the deputies
        They don't come by twos
They got the shotguns
They got the rope
        We git the justice

> In the end
>   And they come by tens.
>
>   from the *Collected Poems*
>   *of Sterling Brown*

The piling up of "they got" becomes an emblem of the strength of the oppressors who have everything and the oppressed who "got nothing."

Using anaphora, write a poem about some contemporary civic power that appears to be overwhelming.

7. Dramatic Poems/Character Poems

Dramatic poems comes in two major types. One is the **soliloquy**, in which a character speaks (or thinks out loud) to no one in particular. The other type, the **dramatic monologue**, imagines a full dramatic scene in which the occasion for the utterance is clear; we can usually sense that a particular listener is intended, as in a play. Both types are, of course, often imbedded in ficton (as interior monologue) and stage plays.

You are probably already familiar with works like Tennyson's "Ulysses" and Browning's "My Last Duchess." Eliot's "The Love Song of J. Alfred Prufrock" is an interior monologue in which Prufrock's character is revealed while the dramatic situation is subdued. Pretending to be someone else and speaking through that other person requires imaginative leaps and new considerations of language: Just how would that character see the world, meditate, speak? In the following poem, Geoffrey Brock imagines himself into the mind of John Brown, Jr., who is recollecting one of his famous father's punishments:

Flesh of John Brown's Flesh: Dec. 2 1859

We knew the rules and punishments:
Three lashes for lack of diligence,
Eight for disobeying mother

Or telling lies .... *No blood,* he'd say,
and no remission, Came a day
he started keeping my account,

as at a store. And came another
he called me to the tannery:
a Sunday, day of settlement.

I'd paid one-third the owed amount
When he, to my astonishment,
handed the blue-beech switch to me.

Always, the greatest of my fears
were not his whippings, but his tears,
and he was tearful now. I dared

not disobey, not strike him hard.
"I will consider a weak blow
no blow at all, rather a show

of cowardice," he said. *No blood
and no remission.* Thus he paid
himself the balance that I owed,

our mingled blood a token of
a thing that went unnamed: his love.
This nation, too, is his bad child,

fails him utterly, drives him wild
with rage and grief and will be scourged
nearly to death before she, purged,

may rise and stand. *No blood,* I hear
him saying still, *and no remission.*
So hang him today, Virginia: cheer

his body swaying in the air—
tomorrow you will learn what's true:
hanging's a thing he's done for you.

from *Subtropics*

Brock says of the historical account that it "paints a portrait of paternal authority and sacrifice that is both severe and weirdly tender" and allows him a way of getting dramatically at John Brown's madness and terrorism in the service of justice as he saw it. The incident the son relates enables him to accept his father's "martyrdom" as a necessary step to cleansing sin from the body of the nation. John Brown, Jr. also tells us about his own willingness to suffer because of his father's model.

Perhaps it is easiest to begin working into a dramatic poem by transporting yourself into the mind of someone you know or into that of an historical person. Can you imagine Marilyn Monroe's last phone call? Suppose Barack Obama (or another president) had a chance to talk to George Washington; what would they say to one another? Or what about an astronaut's first glimpse of earth from space?

8. Event Poems

Wordsworth tells us that "poetry is the spontaneous overflow of powerful feelings: it takes its origin from emotion recollected in tranquility." In principle that statement is true, depending on one's definition of how long the emotion has to keep before it flows into a poem. Poets do react immediately to immediate events relatively immediately. Wilfred Owens composed "Dulce et Decorum Est"—the most powerful antiwar poem ever written—during World War I. Of course, he did not write it while he was in battle; still, the events were quite fresh in his memory while he was recuperating from war wounds in 1917. (You can find the poem on the Internet or in anthologies of English Literature.)

Writing when close to the events that have created the passion are a way for the poet to deal with those events. Since it is unlikely that between our writing this and your reading it that the world has changed, sometime in your present a significant national or social event has occurred, one that dominates the news (a war, a massive accident, a catastrophe such as a tsunami or earthquake or volcanic explosion that affects thousands). Using such an event as those, one to which you have had a strong reaction, write a poem that reflects your thoughts.

As a sample, read the following poem by a creative writing professor about the massacre in 2007 at Virginia Tech. The poet, Bob Hicok, actually informed the administration of his concerns about the mental health of the murderer who had written worrisome stories for class assignments.

So I know

He put moisturizer on the morning he shot
thirty three people. That stands out. The desire
to be soft. I could tell the guy from NPR
that's what I want, to be soft, or the guy
from the LA Times, or the guy from CNN who says
we should chat. Such a casual word, chat.
I'm chatting to myself now: you did not
do enough about the kid who took your class
a few buildings from where he killed.
With soft hands in Norris Hall killed.
This is my confession. And legs I think
the roommate said, moisturizer in the shower,
I don't know what I could have done
something. Something more than talk to someone
who talked to someone, a food chain of language
leading to this language of "no words" we have now.
Maybe we exist as language and when someone dies
they are unworded. Maybe I should have shot the kid
and then myself given the math. 2 < 33.
I was good at math. Numbers are polite, carefree
if you ask the random number generators.
Mom, I don't mean the killing above.
It's something I write like "I put my arms
around the moon." Maybe sorry's the only sound
to offer pointlessly and at random
to each other forever, not because of what it means
but because it means we're trying to mean,
I am trying to mean more than I did
when I started writing this poem, too soon
people will say, so what. This is what I do.
If I don't do this I have no face and if I do this
I have an apple for a face or something vital

almost going forward is the direction I am headed.
Come with me from being over here to being over there,
from this second to that second. What countries
they are, the seconds, what rooms of people
being alive in them and then dead in them.
The clocks of flowers rise, it's April
and yellow and these seconds are an autopsy
of this word,

                    suddenly.

You will notice that the very ebb and flow of the poem reflects Hicok's attempt to understand the almost unspeakable horror of the event as well as his feeling that he was somehow to blame.

9. Personification Poems

Telling stories through the mouth of animals and inanimate things is an ancient device that enables the narrator to express an idea or emotion from a slant point of view. In "When I was a dinasaur," Joanie Mackowski expresses the short-sightedness of that creature as a way of telling us something of ourselves.

I was stagosaurus, a.k.a. "armed roof lizard" with seventeen
headstones growing from my spine. And not one brain

but two: the first a walnut wedged in my skull:
the other a brick at the root of my sex. I wasn't whole.

And I thought I was a seed pod, that some beak
might crack my husk and make my roots take

root to be a bloom like a sweet pea, purple
and drunk to smell. I didn't foresee the rubble

and the ice, the ages of seep and sludge,
the wonder of photosynthesis and each

new life. I love the orchids best, every bulbous god
They pull from the spines, but I see nothing good

about people. No ceiling arcs
from the bones of their backs,

and each of their brains sprouts a long gray tooth:
to think of the sun, they bite it in half.

                    from *Pool*

Of course, on the literal level, human beings were not coextensive with dinasaurs (from most points of view). Mackowski wasn't concerned, as she says, about logic but about something that "is (1) extinct, (2) still talking, (3) something other than itself." The poem isn't meant as an allegory of Alzheimer's (though her mother suffered from it) but certainly evokes the loss of connectiveness between parts of the mind, memory, and reason.

Try to find speech for a being or thing: an old dog about to be put down, or a rusty car on the way to the junkyard, the last spoonful in a bottle of vanilla extract, a laptop computer built in 1995.

10. Epistolary Poems

Epistolary poems, that is, poems written in the form of letters, can be voiced through invented characters or they can be ways to express deep personal feelings. In the following poem, Krista Benjamin imagines a "Letter from My Ancestors" written in the past and telling her about the American immigrant experience:

> We wouldn't write this,
> wouldn't even think of it. We are working
> People without time on our hands. In the old country,
>
> we milk cows or deliver the mail or leave,
> scattering to South Africa, Connecticut, Missouri,
> and finally, California for the Gold Rush—
>
> Aaron and Lena run the Yosemite campground, general
> store, a section of the stagecoach line. Morris comes
> later, after the earthquake, finds two irons
>
> and a board in the rubble of San Francisco.
> Plenty of prostitutes need their dresses pressed, enough
> to earn him the cash to open a haberdashery and marry
>
> Saide—we all have stories, yes, but we're not thinking
> stories. We have work to do, and a dozen children. They'll
> go on to pound nails and write up deals, not musings.
>
> We document transactions. Our diaries record
> temperatures, landmarks, symptoms. We
> do not write our dreams. We place another order,
>
> Make the next delivery, save the next
> dollar, give another generation—you
> maybe—the luxury of time
>
> to write about us.

> from *Margie*

The idea of a letter not written allows Benjamin to coalesce typical family stories around a familiar experience. The image, as with so many other natural forms, opens a door into the poem. Try an epistolary poem that begins with the word *dear* and

- reviews your qualifications for an imaginary job
- admits that you might have been wrong about something
- is an e-mail that you really do not mean to send

11. Time Warp Poems

Writers in all genres have juxtaposed historical characters to contemporary events, relocating them to our own times. What if Benjamin Franklin found himself in Silicon Valley? What if Ulysses led his mariners to a modern American port, like Baltimore, instead of the land of the lotus eaters? What if the biblical Miriam found herself at a women's rights rally? Such an exercise can be the prelude to humor or to the probing of important, universal issues. Before reading Stephen Bluestone's "Isaac on the Altiplano," consider Bluestone's comments:

> "Isaac on the Altiplano" is but one of countless retellings and elaborations of Genesis 22, the chapter that deals with the sacrifice of Isaac, also known as the "Aqedah" (or binding) in Hebrew. My version is a parallel one that sets father and son in the Andes and makes them Aymara Indians. This Isaac is even more zealous than his father; in this retelling Isaac knows he is to be sacrificed, is impatient for it to happen, and leads the old man to the high place "where air is as thin/as a knife blade and breath is locked in stone."...Obviously this character is wholly invented, but his origin is in Genesis 22, which is a blueprint for one of the most profound explorations in all of religious literature of the relation between God and man and father and son.

Here is the poem:

Isaac on the Altiplano

Say there are high *cordilleras* sharp as glass
against a black sky, a country of lost cities
with the ghosts of children playing on the slopes
of the shining day, places where air is as thin
as a knife blade and breath is locked in stone.

Down below, it is holiday time, with dancers
in flower hats and shawls, women clapping hands,
and men playing flutes; there is *chicha*, too,
the smack of it, along with the graceful prows
of bundle-reed boats on the waters of the Great Lake.

Isaac waits, having come ahead of his father,
impatient to hear the sound of the wind.
Isaac hates the damp cellar of the Andes,
the cobbled keep of the mines; like his father,

he hates the *Aymara* villages, with their bent backs
against the stiff sides of impossible peaks...

And now the sky is near enough to touch;
he turns to watch the old man struggle up behind him
much too slowly, a bird entering darkness
too heavy for wings or the lift of song.

"Here I am," he says to his stiff-legged father,
a pale and brittle figure gasping for breath.

Isaac kneels to be blessed; he laughs
while the gods, like butterflies, converge on the spot,
their yellow wings beating like slow hearts,
their empty veins drinking his love.

from *The Laughing Monkeys of Gravity*

Using historical characters (or literary ones) is not only a common technique in poetry but is frequently the basis for fiction and drama. Try your own biblical story poem.

12. Advice Poems

Poets have found the framework of giving sham council provides an opportunity for irony. We are all familiar with Polonius's cautionary talk with Laertes in *Hamlet*, clichéd advice that says more about the father than it is of use to the son. William Carlos Williams's "Tract" promises to "teach you my townspeople / how to perform a funeral" without any of the folderol usually associated with them. Jessica Goodheart's poem "Advice for a Stegosaurus" is filled with useless counsel considering that it is given so long after the disappearance of dinosaurs.

Never mind the asteroid,
the hot throat of the volcano,
a sun that daily drops into the void.

Comb the drying riverbed for drink
Strut your bird-hipped body.
Practice a lizard grin. Don't think.

Stretch out your tail. Walk, as you must,
in a slow deliberate gait.
Don't look back, Dinosaur. Dust is dust.

You'll leave your bones, your fossil feet
and armored eye-lids
Put your chin to the wind. Eat what you eat.

from *The Antioch Review*

Part of the fun here is that the poem is about another species that may be heading toward extinction because it is shortsighted.

Try your own advice poem. For example: how to write an A essay in fifteen minutes, how to refuse a date without cutting the guy off entirely, how to tell your parents you are quitting school.

13. Picture Poems

Art calls forth art. Composers create compositions based on poems and painters place actual lines from poetry into their paintings. Poets also find in the arts a source for suggestive images. Here is a poem by Billy Collins based on a landscape by a nineteenth-century romantic painter:

The Brooklyn Museum of Art

I will now step over the soft velvet rope
and walk directly into this massive Hudson River
painting and pick my way along the Palisades
with this stick I snapped off a dead tree.

I will skirt the smoky, nestled towns
and seek the path that leads always outward
until I become lost, without a hope
of ever finding the way back to the museum.

I will stand on the bluffs in nineteenth-century clothes,
a dwarf among rock, hills, and flowing water,
and I will fish from the banks in a straw hat
which will feel like a brush stroke on my head.

And I will hide in the green covers of forest
so no appreciator of Frederick Edwin Church,
leaning over the soft velvet rope
will spot my tiny figure moving in the stillness
and cry out, pointing for the others to see,

and be thought mad and led away to a cell
where there is no vaulting landscape to explore,
none of this birdsong that halts me in my tracks,
and no wide curving of this river that draws
my steps toward the misty vanishing point.

Collins does not simply look at the painting and report what he sees in it; he wishes himself into it...a tribute to the power of art, any art. Use a painting, sculpture, or photograph that you admire as the inspiration for a poem. Try to capture in language the energy, technique, and vision of life that the artwork has to offer.

14. Music Poems

A variation of the preceding exercise is to find inspiration for a poem in music, as in Kevin Young's "Black Cat Blues":

> I showed up for jury duty—
> Turns out the one on trial was me.
>
> Paid me for my time & still
> I couldn't make bail.
>
> Judge that showed up
> was my ex-wife.
>
> Now that was some
> hard time.
>
> She sentenced me
> to remarry
>
> I chose firing squad instead.
> Wouldn't you know it—
>
> Plenty of volunteers
> to take the first shot
>
> But no one wanted to spring
> for the bullets
>
> Governor commuted my sentence to life
> in a cell more comfortable
>
> Than this here skin
> I been living in.
>
> from *Virginia Quarterly Review*

Young tells us that the poem "first appeared as part of 'Watching the Good Trains Go By,' a suite of poems written to accompany photomontages by Romare Bearden, the artist." So, the inspiration is from both music and art.

Choose a piece of music that has affected you deeply. Play it over a number of times, paying special attention to its rhythms and emotional colorings. Now try to render those same rhythms and emotions in a poem. Don't write *about* the piece of music; translate it into poetry.

15. Poems on Poems

Poetry itself can evoke poems. We are not referring here only to parodies, though every great poet—particularly those with a distinctive style such as Walt Whitman or T.S. Eliot—has been lampooned. But also poems may evoke answers or sequels, as in Albert Goldbarth's response to Frost's most famous poem:

Stopping by Woods on a Snowy Evening

"...miles to go before I sleep," says Frost,
as if at last, at night,
the eyes shut, and the mind shuts,
and the journey halts. Of course

that's wrong. All day and into dusklight
at this flyway stop, the waterfowl
—as plump as pillows, some of them; and others
small and sleek—have settled, abob

in the wash of the river; and here,
by the hundred, they've tucked their heads
inside a wing: inside that dark
and private sky. The outward flying is done

for now, and the inward flying begins.
All one, to the odometer.

from New Letters

Frost's poem provides a seed for Goldbarth's evocation of a different view of waking and sleeping in the voyage of life.

Take a well-known line of poetry and use it as the organizing image for your own poem.

16. Found Poems

When nothing else works, pushing someone else's language around can start the juices flowing. It can be revealing, too. Here are some things to do:

1. Look for ready-made poetry in your everyday reading. Bulletin boards are good places to look. After you have selected a few of these found poems and copied them into your journal, take some notes on what qualities of expression make them seem poetic. Some possibilities: advertising copy, operating manuals for various products, announcements for auctions, correction notices (apologies) for errors in the daily paper. Pay special attention to material that is highly patterned. The language of food and astrology columns is, in some ways, remarkably poetic.

2. Cut and paste! Take a column from a newspaper or magazine and cut it in half or in thirds lengthwise. Now rearrange the strips of type and look for vivid passages. Slide the strips up and down until effective word combinations appear. Now use them. Line up half-columns from different articles or news stories and see what happens.

3. Sculpt! Download a long article from the Internet. Now, delete the least interesting stretches of language, letting the more evocative words and

phrases reveal themselves. Can you get a poem to emerge by chiseling away the unnecessary words? You could do this on your computer.

4. X-ray! Highlight words in yellow or red to display the words and phrases you find most striking. Now try linking together what you have found into a poem.

We have hardly begun to suggest the various frames for the poems you might want to write as part of your apprenticeship. When you read poetry—and read lots of it—do not concern yourself about the interpretation. Look for the underlying music and the form that attaches the poem to everyday experience: imitation, song, advice, letter, and so on. The types we present here are just a handful of the everyday communications we all make, communications that you intensify in the poem you need to write. On your good days or with luck, the practice may actually turn into something quite good.

> " *The old joke goes: A visitor to New York City*
> *stopped a man carrying a violin case and asked:*
> *'Sir, how do you get to Carnegie Hall?' The man*
> *replied: 'Practice, practice, practice.'*"

Here is "The Poem Queen" by Susan Astor to compare with your attempt at finding the original order:

> The Poem Queen writes a poem a day,
> In her spare time pauses to pray
> It will be read.
>
> She has a soldier and a drone
> To please her when she is alone
> Or in her bed.
>
> Some say hers is a magic throne
> That she eats custard made of bone
> And blossom bread.
>
> She has more power than they know,
> Has found a way to burn the snow;
> Turns gold to lead.
>
> Her pen is her divining rod;
> She uses it to handle God,
> And tame the dead.

> from *Dame*

CHAPTER 7

POETRY PROBLEMS

*"For the student, having a genuine insight into the true
badness of some poems is, I think, a necessary corollary
of having a grasp of what makes good poems good."*

Seamus Cooney

As we have said before and will say again, all good writing is the result of editing and revising. Rarely do we put down in a first draft what will be a finished
work. Even poems that we want to believe are ready to go after we have drafted
them usually benefit from second thoughts and third and.... One poet we
know even continues covertly revising in copies of her published books when
she finds them in a bookstore, taking them from the shelves and surreptitiously
penning in changes. That's a bit of overkill but illustrative of her instinct for
revision and her desire to make her work more perfect.

At the end of the first draft, you will have built only the foundation of the
finished poem. You may not have probed the emotion or thought as fully as
possible. You may have been writing under mistaken impressions of what represents effective poetic practice in these days. Your poem may jingle or drone.

Look at the poem again, honestly, and revise mercilessly. Often, having
solved the technical problems in a poem, we are ready to congratulate ourselves
prematurely. Here are some common problems in the poems of beginning writers (and some experienced ones, too).

 OUT OF TUNE

In all writing the sound and the sense must be inseparable. In poetry, however,
the demand for the bonding is more intense than in the other genres. Flabby,
lifeless diction choices and sounds that clunk will stand as a barrier between the
reader and content. To put it another way, the reader is likely to say what you
have written is not poetry.

Here is an example of clotted writing that undercuts a quite appalling
memory.

The Ancient Dread

Evil, ancient thing,
~~That~~ hid in the dark~~ness~~.
He must have heard me coming,
Searching through the barn for my jump rope
Unknowingly getting closer and closer.
~~He must have~~ coiled tighter and tighter in the dark~~ness~~,
His body becoming a coiled, angry black muscle,
His head erect and ready to strike.

Evil, ancient thing,
That came at me out of the darkness.
I opened the gate of the old stall,
And his black head struck at my bare leg.
My mind took a few minutes to catch up.
My body reacted, I put my hand out to protect myself
And he struck my wrist,
As if to say, "Learn this lesson, girl, and learn it well."

Evil, ancient thing,
That slithered off into the darkness.
His point had been made.
Some primal fear,
Some ancient dread of the legless, stealthy alien
Form overtook me.
I sat down and stared at my puncture wounds.
I knew I would wash them again and again.
As a scream for Mommy rose in my throat,
I realized pee was running down my leg.

This piece, one hesitates to call it a poem yet, appears to be based on a real memory intensified by the mythic enmity between women and snakes. But the execution is wooden and such lines as "My mind took a few minutes to catch up" are flat because they state rather than show. Still, at moments poetry does threaten to break through. We have struck out some lines and words in order to start carving out a sound that fits the sense.

● ● ● ● ●   *EXERCISE*   ● ● ● ● ●

Assume the poem came from a memory you jotted down in your own journal. Remove as much as you can to begin your revision and to capture the snake, the strike, and the horror that will stay with you for the rest of your life. Concentrate on the sound and the division of the lines that help reveal that sound and still keep to the narrative of the piece. Before you start, look again at Chapter 4.

—————————●—————————

We can't leave this section without sharing a bit of Theophilus Marzials's poem, which has been called the worst poem in the English language:

A Tragedy

Death!
Plop.
The barges down in the river flop.

Flop, plop.
Above, beneath.

From the slimy branches the grey drips drop,
As they scraggle black on the thin grey sky,
Where the black cloud rack-hackles drizzle and fly
To the oozy waters, that lounge and flop
On the black scrag piles, where the loose cords plop,
As the raw wind whines in the thin tree-top.

Plop, plop.
And scudding by

The boatmen call out hoy! and hey!
All is running water and sky,

And my head shrieks—"Stop,"
And my heart shrieks—"Die."

At this point, of course, we, too, are ready to cry "stop" and "die." (For those who wish to read the whole poem, google the author.)

 ## Archaic Diction

Some of the more obvious archaic words and phrases in the following poem we have set in italics. Language that is so remote from common usage sounds insincere. Paradoxically, the writer probably chose it because it sounded "poetic," and two hundred years ago may have been considered so. Nonetheless, it is hard to take these formulations seriously now. Though this student's technical skill is apparent, that skill is undermined by flawed diction.

The Thief

The warm, the fevered pillows pushed aside,
I lay amidst the ever-present Night
While his sweet handmaid, his euphoric bride
Beamed through glazed panels with a pallid light.
Mid hoary trees her shadows could be seen
In contrast to that phosphorescent sheen.
I sighed, unshackled from my torpid shrouds,
And sleep's last fetters from the covers fell
Away. As I peered out, a sable cloud
Swirled round the orb—as if its soul to quell.
Who else but Luna would steal o'er my sill
While I, bedazzled, could no more lay still?

Diction like this is often accompanied by the old-fashioned poetic contractions—"o'er," in this case—and by a tendency to disguise experience rather than reveal it. "Glazed panels" are only windows; why not say so? The unidiomatic reversal in the last line halts the reader. Writing like this tends to become formulaic; it expresses abstract actions or emotions rather than particular ones.

Can you find other diction problems in this poem? What revisions (substitutions) do you suggest? Can any of the poem be salvaged, or should the poet begin again? Do you spot any problems in the syntax? Can you solve them?

 ## The Anonymous Voice

Characteristic of much greeting card verse—and of much unsuccessful poetry—is the anonymous voice. The following poem is an example of the kind of writing that sounds as if it could be by almost anyone and is therefore unconvincing. Along with problems in mastering the stanza form, this poem suffers from hackneyed figures of speech, absence of particulars, yearning after vastness, and easy **sentimentality**.

Dreams

In a world of fantasy
dreams, like nets, were thrown
from a vessel hopelessly
adrift and all alone.

To cast a net and catch a dream
is no simple task.
Of any man it might seem
impossible to ask.

My dreams have come up empty,
Worthless, tangled, torn.
—A rend too harsh for charity
—A wound that must be borne.

How long have I been dreaming?
The ship sails out of sight.
Sand's slipped through the opening.
I've dreamed away the night.

A poem like this cannot be improved merely by local substitutions—nor should it be thrown away. The poet needs to begin again with honest materials. What really constitutes the kind of dream vaguely alluded to here? What is a convincing comparison? A fresh, evocative approach is required, one in which the poet leaves behind the world of decoration and soft disguises. In too many poems, the attention to form is not only a superficial attention but also one that limits the novice poet's focus. Overwhelmed by making the rhymed container, the poet has no energy left for the diction and the content.

The following poem is true greeting card verse. It is completely anonymous and offers a generalized sentiment without one concrete image. We, of
course, have sent greeting cards in which the emotion is in the very sending, not
in the words. Unless you are writing for the card market, avoid using language
in this way.

Giving

> I give to you a part of me
>   I give to you my heart
> I'll try to ask for nothing more
>   Than friends that never part
> I'll give to you all my life
>   I give because I care
> I give because a friend like you
>   Is found so very rare.

This verse can be sent by anyone to anyone and is unlikely to be read with
attention.

APPALLING ABSTRACTION

In some ways, appalling abstraction is like greeting card verse, but usually
more urgent. However, the urgency is never convincing because the language
makes no impact, no connection with felt experience. Intellectually clear, the
formulations that follow do not begin to take on the concern for language that
is poetry's province:

> If nurtured,
> The fantasy thrives.
> If neglected,
> The untested dream dies,
> The imagination atrophies,
> The soul perishes.
> It's the same with us.
> Barren years
> Interlaced with frenzied passion,
> Have sterilized our union,
> Distorted our dreams,
> Crushed our raison d'etre . . .

The writer here is working from an inner pain, but none of the specifics
come through to allow the reader to experience the pain. Part of the problem has to do with the lack of music in the lines. Try to scan the fifth and
sixth lines.

Unintentional Humor

Novice poets are sometimes not aware of the ways in which diction can misfire, especially cliché-ridden words and phrases. In an attempt to force on us an emotion, the writer of the following poem uses diction that is found—and belongs— in horror films and comic books:

Inside Out

I feel violence within,
churning.
A knife sits sharp and ready,
burning.
Deep red, warm gushing and
gurgling.
The brook of life silently
running,
Over sharp rocks, soft moss
glowing
To the cold ocean of death,
ending.

Because we associate a phrase like "gushing and gurgling" with literary modes that we don't take seriously, we are kept from taking this poem seriously. We might think of blood "gushing"—but blood "gurgling"? Miscalculations like these come in part from inexperience, in part from laziness—letting ready-made expressions find their way into poems. Ready-made language rarely convinces us that it expresses genuine experience.

A variation of the problem occurs in bathetic writing. Though **bathos** is one of the definitions of excessive sentiment, its first definition refers to the type of work that causes unintended comedy by a mixture of high and low diction.

[from] Beautiful Springs

The north winds are still and the blizzards at rest,
All in the beautiful spring.
The dear little robins are building their nests,
All in the beautiful spring.
The tramp appears and for lodging begs,
The old hen setteth on turkey eggs,
And the horse has scratches in all four legs,
All in the beautiful spring.

J. B. Smiley

The verse starts as a commonplace but serious ode to spring, but the sudden ridiculous picture of the hen and the scratches on the horse's leg are a sudden descent from the high-flown, Wordsworthian images in the first five lines. The bathos is a result of the tyranny of rhyme, which we will illustrate in the section "For the Sake of Rhyme." What effect does the word *dear* have in the third line?

 ## JARRING DICTION

The result of not paying enough attention to connotation and to words in context can be diction that is jarring. The next poem, cast in free verse, mixes diction groups in unattractive ways:

Land Lord Dharma

I kneel
head erect
shoulders straight
hands on thighs
the warrior's posture
he enters
in long white silk robes
he looks so elegant—
from the warrior's shrine
he hands me implements
for my new quarters
first a flashing sword
with a slightly curved tip
to cut neurosis
and allow gentleness
then comes the black pen
with a rolled white scroll
tied with a ribbon . . .

The words "implements" and "neurosis" are in conflict with the poem's general diction. Additionally, "quarters" may be a questionable choice. The gains are obvious when we substitute "blessings" for "implements" and "masks" for "neurosis." Now "cut" seems off, if it wasn't clearly so before. What would be a better verb here? What substitute can you find for "quarters"?

 ## FOR THE SAKE OF RHYME

Solving the puzzle of an intricate rhyme scheme is so exhilarating that you can become lost in a single dimension of a poem. One of the more famous cases occurs in a quatrain by John Close:

Around the gods, each seated on a throne,
The poets, crowned like royal kings they sat.
Around their heads a dazzling halo shone,
No needs of mortal robes, or any hat.

The inappropriateness of the rhyme words "sat / hat" is bathetic and makes us laugh.

The poet who wrote "Departure" conjured up the "braided ballad" form that rhymes *abcb/cede/dfgf* and so forth:

Departure

The smell of guava blossoms
appears to fill the air
and in the wind are waving
the palm leaves . . . and your hair.

I sit on the porch, craving   5
those kisses that you give
and think that these are times
in which it's good to live.

But in the end our crimes
seem to catch up with us,   10
and I must take a trip
with a distant terminus.

I board the hated ship
as you wave from the sand
and dream I cup your bosom   15
and feel it on my hand.

Among the problems lurking in this draft are the following:

1. Line 2 lacks poetic density; that is, the only function of most of the language is to get in enough syllables ahead of the rhyme word.
2. Unnatural (unidiomatic) word order undermines lines 7 and 8. More natural alternatives would be "and think that these are good times to live in" or "and think that it's good to live in these times." The poet has solved the problem of rhyme, but created a new one.
3. Inappropriate diction. The use of "terminus" in line 12 creates a clever rhyme but ruptures the poem's simple diction and earnest tone. It seems far-fetched, and it is.

There are a few other instances of these and related problems in the poem. Can you find them? What kinds of revision would you suggest? Should the poet stay with this demanding form, or should he abandon it?

Rose MacMurray's poem that follows is a more successful handling of the same form. Compare the two efforts (trimeter quatrains) before attempting your own.

Teen Mall-Rats Die in Suicide Pact

After the Mall closed down
they came and built a nest.
Monoxide was a high
and they could charge the rest.

No sweat to say goodbye,
monoxide was a gas.
The mall rats, curled in death,
have solved their maze at last.

We lay a discount wreath.
May their eternity
be one long shopping mall,
one Gold Card spending spree

and may their parents all
sign up for every course
in "Interfacing Grief"
and "Creative Remorse."

When the relentless search for rhyme words drives the poem, the reader (or listener) soon begins to wait for the rhyme rather than follow the sense that the rhyme is meant to fulfil. The tyranny of rhyme in rap or hip hop music appears absurd when read without the intense rhythmic beat.

 THE CLASH OF POETIC ELEMENTS

The clash of poetic elements is a broad category, covering scores of jarring images, moods, senses, rhythms, sounds, and other poetic ingredients. In the following example, the picture being painted and the meter used to reveal it are at odds with one another:

They glide like spirits by the water
Open to the tepid twilight
Bearing alabaster candles:
Rush-like figures clad in white.
Thin and spectral, like the Shee-folk
With their dripping, glowing wands...

This poet, who has control over sound, meter, and language, does not coordinate the elements effectively. Whatever can "glide like spirits" will not move in this insistent, choppy rhythm. The pushy trochaic beat conflicts with anyone's notion of ethereality. A simple lengthening of the lines would help, but getting rid of those initial stressed syllables is the first step in improving the poem. Things can't glide and march at the same time.

 ## WRITING PAST THE POEM

Sometimes poets are unable to throw away what they have put down on paper. They are more willing to revise than to delete. In "Bagged Air," the poet's inventiveness goes beyond the poem's need:

> The signs say no balloons.
>
> You are just another visitor,
> Hunted, fearful of the telltale coughs,
> the dripping of mysterious liquids suspended
> in bags,
> and harried eyes
> of people in white.
> Frailty, mortality, futility,
> the cheap pictures on the wall say it,
> so do the eyes from the beds,
> watching you pass.
> You walk on, holding roses for a shield
> against these exposed truths.
> Brown has begun to claim the healthy pink domain
> of a petal.
>
> Among carefree balloons, even the best
> leak gaseous blood,
> and submit
> to the most basic laws of nature,
> pulling them earthward.
> That admonishing sign is humane—
> stopping those who would give a doomed
> bag of air
> as a gift of cheer
> here.

Most of the poem *shows,* whereas the last stanza mostly *tells.* Can a minor revision of the main part of the poem eliminate the need for the last stanza?

 ## TREASURE BURYING

An otherwise unsuccessful poem often contains buried poetic treasure that might be the basis for a successful poem. In the following piece, the writer employs predictable rhymes and overuses repetition. Moreover, she breaks the logic of her own figurative expressions. Still, one extremely vivid and evocative stanza sings out. We have set it in italics.

Desert Rain Poem

I am the desert
Dry and desolate
Shimmering in the sun
You were rain
And I watched the rain
Coming down
Against my sun-drenched pain

I am the African steppe
Dying into desert
The wind tosses over me
A blanket of sand

Shrouding once verdant trees,
Big dry holes—once lakes
Maybe small seas
Into oblivion

Some fountain of sorrow
Fountain of life
An ancient aching love
Brings on the spring rain
Just to pass my way again

Only searing sun-drenched
Pain, reigns
Raining down on me

I am the desert at night
Cold dark sand
Blows against my stark
Countenance

When I love, I rain
My rains to come
As long as the love
Keeps coming
So will the rains.

Our suggestion to this writer would be to start over again, rebuilding the poem from the third stanza, which could be an effective beginning. Three additional four-line stanzas, if they are equally compact and focused, should do to complete the idea of the earlier draft.

Saying Too Much

Even sophisticated writers can overwrite by saying too much. The following draft is slightly heavy-handed, though it is clearly the work of a careful and skillful writer.

January Thunder

As the heavy presence nears
bare branches falter and twist.
At the first crash of the axe
pines flail and lash,
stoop to the snow.

At the iron boom of the hammer
gusts of summer flare at the window,
ice pellets surge up.
Snow flooded by lightning,
blazes white beyond white.

In a workshop session, the author agreed that eliminating "heavy" and "blazes" would strengthen the poem. Why do you think that the poet agreed? Do you see other possibilities for paring back so that less does more?

 ## The False Start

It should be obvious to a practiced writer that we often find our subject and warm up our language engines only after we have been writing for a while. In composition classes, students are warned about introductions that no longer work when the act of writing has taken the writer in unexpected directions. This type of false start happens in all types of narratives, including poems.

Here is an early draft of a poem by Elizabeth Bennett.

A Small Explosion

Is it a coincidence
This forty years later
soft knock at the door?
the young girl, Makiko
with her father, Yasuo
their car broken down.
I pronounce her name wrong.
Her father explains
it means little jewel.
She looks at me
little jewel, eyes clear

as a freshwater pool
where fish still swim, hair
paint brush straight.
In the kitchen
she takes off her coat
Her T shirt says
Washington A Capitol City.
While her father phones
she plays with my infant son's
Steiff bear, fondles
its stiff fur.
When the baby cries
she makes a face
She pulls her long arms
inside her shirt.
See, I have no arms
she says to make him laugh.

This was not a first draft, nor is it the final one. In the published version, a number of changes have been made. Notice how the poem gets off to a quicker start when the third line becomes the first line. Locate and discuss the other changes.

Small Explosion August 6th, 1985

A knock at the door,
the young girl, Makiko
with her father, Yasuo
their car broken down.
I pronounce her name wrong.
Her father explains
it means little jewel.
She looks at me,
            little jewel,
eyes clear as a freshwater pool
where fish still swim,
hair paint brush straight.
Her T shirt says,
            Washington A Capitol City
While her father phones
she plays with my infant son's Steiff bear,
fondles its stiff fur.
When he cries she makes a face,
pulls her arms inside her shirt,
See I have no arms, she says
to make him laugh.

It is forty years later.

from *Poet Lore*

PUNCH-LINE ENDINGS

Although they can be successful, too often punch-line endings reach for too much or too little. Poets can be tempted to rescue weak or trivial poems by clever resolutions. The next poem leans too heavily on its forced close, a close that isn't strong enough to take the weight.

Lifeguards

Gopher holes blemished our backyard like acne
when the swimming hole
was dry
and it was too hot for kickball
Henry and I
took the hose
and filled them up
to the brim
We waited for gophers
to surface gasping
Patient hours
we sat on our shadows
but never saw
one.

Back then
we didn't know
        of escape tunnels.

The idea of bringing in a new perspective that answers a question is a good one, but the execution falls flat. The shift seems too self-conscious, and, once again, the decision to tell rather than show is part of the problem. What if you retitled the poem with the last line, stopped after "know," and removed the stanza break?

 ## INEFFECTIVE LINE BREAK

It is often hard to detect an unsatisfactory line break without the frequent testing of alternatives. It is easy to cure such diseases as ending on function words (articles, prepositions, conjunctions) for no good reason, calling too much attention to words whose only job is to link more important words together. Most often, line-break problems result in obscuring key images and relationships between images and ideas. Examine the following passage:

I hold a desperate starfish before I toss him back
matched with my hand, our common five-shape
a reminder of where we begin.

Here the writer wants us to observe the relationship between the human hand and the starfish, but both words are lost in the middle of lines. One solution would be to reconstruct these lines:

> Before I toss him back, I hold a desperate starfish,
> our common five-shape, matched with my hand—
> a reminder of where we begin.

There is some strategic improvement in placing the "before" clause in front of the rest. However, "our common five-shape" now has less emphasis, and its proper place in the movement from specific to general has been lost. Stronger yet is this shaping:

> Before I toss him back,
> I hold a desperate starfish,
> matched with my hand—
> this, our common five-shape,
> reminder of where we begin.

The language still needs work, but at least the key words/images—"starfish," "hand," and "five-shape"—are properly emphasized and clearly related to one another. Line break has controlled the emerging picture and idea.

 ## OUT OF ORDER

Lines or sections that are not in a fitting order can cause a poem to lack cohesiveness and focus. Linda Replogle's untitled poem is fairly effective as it stands, but it could be argued that the transposition of stanzas 2 and 3 would make an even stronger poem. Read the poem aloud both ways.

> The old man sits
> at the white kitchen table,
> his eyes big
> behind thick glasses.
>
> Behind him, his wife
> in a large apron
> fries fish
> at the kitchen stove.
>
> He looks out, away,
> into the garden.
> Rain separates him
> from the green hydrangea.
>
> He puts the magnifying glass
> down on the newspaper
> and lifts the cup
> hot from tea
> with his fragile hands.

What are the losses and gains in the suggested rearrangement? What other arrangements are possible?

DERIVATIVE DRIVEL

Many beginning poets get lost in the worst habits of a poet whom they consciously or unconsciously imitate. Usually they capture only the most obvious surface features of a style or technique. The resulting poems are simply clumsy posturings: piles of mannerisms. Of course, the worse the model, the worse the imitation is likely to be. Here is an example of a poet striving for poetic density. The cop-out is at the end.

> Red rock in the brain
> and the proud darkness settles like a sifted house
> deep in the synapse of ultimate mind.
> Do you know what I mean?

And here is ersatz beat generation sprawl:

> I wandered in the big, empty, people-filled city
> an ant in Miami Beach where I saw
> dopers, fat landladies, displaced Californians, cops
> in Porsches right out of tv...and scrawled walls of
> sneering, scarred, fearing, raging...
> pimps and smarmy politicians, supermarket grandmas,
> and I wanted to kick and smash and trash them all!

Most of us will take our "Howl" straight.

These are only a sampling of the many problems that both beginners and experienced poets encounter. We could fill a book with additional instances such as predictable rhyme, lack of unity caused when two poems are pressed into one, and stumbling rhythms. While writing poetry requires more than technical skill, without that skill no amount of vision or largeness of soul will produce a living poem.

We began this unit on poetry by talking about the line—the most obvious signal that we may be in the presence of a poem. It should be clear by now, however, that the mere ragged right-hand margin does not a poem make. To borrow the prestige of poetry by presenting pedantry, political argument, exhortation, or preaching in "poetic" lines—without *attending to craft* in the ways we have explored—is more likely to fool you than your reader. Nor can you just throw words anywhere on a page, break up lines, remove punctuation and capitals letters, and break normal syntax or grammar—and say that you have written a poem, as undoubtedly the writer of the following words thought:

We have to shed ourselves of these

                                            snake

politicians who crawl

                       around

each year

                          and cover up all graft they take...

Impeach those who dip

                                                into

and make

our pockets empty and dishonor

this greatest land of all

where men and women should stand

                                      TALL!!!!!

The less said about this stuff, the better.

"Poetry is ordinary language raised to the Nth power. Poetry is boned with ideas, nerved and blooded with emotions, all held together by the delicate, tough skin of words."

                                              Paul Engle

PART THREE

THE CONCERNS
OF THE STORYTELLER

"It's plotted out. I just have to write it."

◄▬▬▬► MODEL PROSE SUBMISSION

William Sydney Porter
457 McDougal St.
New York, New York 10011
(212)776-3434
ohenry@net.net

Short Story
3,500 Words

The Last Leaf

In a little district west of Washington Square the streets have run crazy and broken themselves into small strips called "places." These "places" make strange angles and curves. One street crosses itself a time or two. An artist once discovered a valuable possibility in this street. Suppose a collector with a bill for paints, paper and canvas should, in traversing this route, suddenly meet himself coming back, without a cent having been paid on account!

So, to quaint old Greenwich Village the art people soon came prowling, hunting for north windows and eighteenth-century gables and Dutch attics and low rents. Then they imported some pewter mugs and a chafing dish or two from Sixth Avenue, and became a "colony."

THE ELEMENTS OF FICTION

"I keep six honest serving men
(They taught me all I knew);
Their names are What and Why and When
and How and Where and Who."

Rudyard Kipling

Although this and the next three chapters are primarily for the writer of prose fiction or nonfiction, many of the principles we present here about structure, narration, character, and other storytelling elements apply equally to poetry and drama. And, as we've indicated previously, all the genres share a foundation in their concern about choices of points of view, effective diction, and appropriate style.

 THE NATURE OF FICTION

Prose fiction contains the hi*story* of one or more characters or something that acts like a character (a talking owl, yellow Rolls-Royce, or computer). The writer shapes that history with the same tools one would use in literal history—except that "people" become *characters,* "talk" becomes *dialogue,* "reporting" becomes *relating* (narrating), and "places" become *settings.* The stories contain descriptions of where and how the characters live, what they do, and what they say, believe, or think:

There was once upon a time a Fisherman who lived with his wife in a miserable hovel close by the sea, and every day he went out fishing. And once as he was sitting with his rod, looking at the clear water, his line suddenly went down, far down below and when he drew it up again, he brought out a large Flounder. Then the Flounder said to him, "Hark, you Fisherman, I pray you, let me live, I am no Flounder really, but an enchanted prince. What good will it do you to kill me? I should not be good to eat, put me in the water again, and let me go."

"Come," said the Fisherman, "there is no need for so many words about it—a fish that can talk I should certainly let go, anyhow." With that he put him back again into the clear water....Then the Fisherman got up and went to his wife in the hovel.

"Husband," said the woman, "have you caught nothing today?"

"No," said the man, "I did catch a Flounder, who said he was an enchanted prince, so I let him go again."

"Did you not wish for anything first?" said the woman.

"No," said the man, "what should I wish for?"

"Ah," said the woman, "it is surely hard to have to live always in this dirty hovel; you might have wished for a small cottage for us. Go back and call him. Tell him we want to have a small cottage, he will certainly give us that."

Jakob and Wilhelm Grimm from "The Fisherman and His Wife"

[You can read the whole story at fairytales4u.com/story/fisherma.htm.]

———————————•———————————

Notice that the Grimms' story has the following elements:

- *time*—a "once upon a time" that is vague but efficient
- *setting*—a hovel by the sea (a place related to the action) in a fairyland with real poverty
- *characters*—the Fisherman, Wife, and Flounder-prince
- *reported actions*—catching Flounder and throwing Prince back
- *dialogue*—revealing the Fisherman's easily satisfied nature and the wife's materialism

In a more complex fashion, Charles Dickens's *Great Expectations,* Virginia Woolf's *To the Light-House,* J. D. Salinger's *Catcher in the Rye,* and J. K. Rowling's Harry Potter series contain these elements. Whether you wish to write realism, magic realism, fantasy, whatever, there is no way around mastering the techniques for presenting the basics.

Of course, the story of your character in fiction will be different from a literal biography. One of the major differences is that in fiction it is legitimate to choose the events and make them come out as you like. The subject of a biography is seldom so lucky. In the story, a fish can be turned into a prince who makes wishes come true. To put the matter another way, in fiction you can travel anywhere you want so long as you can convince your reader to take the trip with you.

Your story may grow from actual or imagined experience(s), character(s), image(s), or concept(s). Whatever generates your story line, you will have to create a **plot** to carry it. As you can guess, we are not using *story* and *plot* interchangeably, as we do in everyday speech. Here *story* is the name we give to imagined lives presented chronologically—an imitation of how we present events in an autobiography, chronicle, or history. Story, in that sense, is A to Z. *Plot*, on the other hand, is the name for the shape we give to the story materials by selection, arrangement, and emphasis. Plot involves (1) *what* parts of the story are told and shown, and (2) *when* each unit of showing and telling is presented to the reader.

In this chapter we present an overview of the elements of fiction, stopping for short examples and a number of exercises along the way. Some of the discussion refers to the stories in Chapter 11. You might want to read them before going on and then again as they are brought into the discussion. Between the overview and the stories are a chapter on problems that can occur in fiction and one on nonfiction.

 ## PLOT AND WHAT IT DOES

> *"The king died and then the queen died is a story.*
> *The king died, and then queen died of grief is a plot."*
>
> E. M. Forster

Though the writing process itself can begin anywhere, we are beginning the discussion of fiction with plot because plot is the vehicle that carries all the other elements. Like a sentence and love, you should know a plot when you see one—though you may be deceived.

Here are several dictionary definitions for *plot*:

1. a secret plan or scheme
2. the plan, scheme, or main story of a play, novel, poem, or short story
3. in artillery, a point or points located on a map or chart
4. in navigation, to mark on a plan, map, or chart, as the course of a ship or aircraft

Beginning writers often take the first definition as the significant one and so think their task as writers is to hide what is going on from the reader until they spring their surprise. The second definition, though accurate, is about as useful as saying that your plot should have a beginning, middle, and end. A rope needs the same thing. The real problem for a writer is *how* to make particular beginnings, middles, and ends.

Strangely enough, the third definition is a bit more to the point; in a way, the plot is the direction in which you have aimed your readers and the distance you want to take them. The fourth definition is the most appropriate of all for writers. Sailors plot a course to get from here to there as safely and efficiently as possible considering their purposes and what difficulties (rocks, narrow passages, land masses) are in the way. What the plot does is to organize the voyage most efficiently.

For your reader, the plot may appear to be the equivalent of the story (the narrative), the sum of all the events that "happen." Even a writer might try to report the chronological story line if asked, "What is it all about?"

"It's the story of this man and woman who are caught in a cave-in. She doesn't like him and, at first, they fight all the time. Then, when they think they are going to die, they fall in love. Then they feel this breeze and then start to—"

The potential reader breaks in:

"Wait a minute. How did they get into the cave in the first place? Why doesn't she like him? How come they didn't feel the breeze right off?"

And when the answers to these questions raise more questions, the writer most likely will say, "Look. You'd better read it." The reason the writer can't satisfactorily tell you the plot by giving the chronological events is the same reason a chocolate chip cookie can't be experienced by having you taste butter, chips, flour, sugar, and vanilla. Because the story is mixed and baked into the plot, it is an error to think that a mere sequence of events is what the work is about.

This common error is understandable, however, because what the characters do is usually the most visible element in the plot. Through these actions the reader sees what the writer has prepared: (1) a conflict or conflicts with complications, (2) a crisis or crises, and (3) a resolution—all contained within a series of actions the characters perform because of their needs and wants. For some readers, the plot is the writer's plan for keeping the characters in danger in order to keep the reader interested. And, for some readers, the only worthwhile plot is the type that keeps them at the edge of their seats or up past midnight waiting for... *what comes next.*

Such plots are not easy to make, and those who, like Stephen King or Sue Grafton, can hold our attention with their plots and satisfy our need to be on tenterhooks deserve our gratitude and praise. They haven't written *Sons and Lovers* or *The Color Purple*, or *Everyman,* but they have entertained us. On the other end of the spectrum, some plots may be made up of subtler actions, not so externally "dramatic." Such plots satisfy us less by presenting a series of slam-bang actions that bring the characters to success or failure and more by expanding our understanding of human circumstances (see Kate Blackwell's "You Won't Remember This" or James Joyce's "The Boarding House").

Both types of plots share with all plots the same purpose: to put the characters in motion so the reader can follow them to a satisfactory—that is, convincing—end. This end must grow from what we have come to understand about the characters' needs, wants, abilities, weaknesses, situation, and so on. Plots provide a line to follow; they explain how and why what is happening is happening; and they involve us with the fate of the characters because the elements that make up the plot connect the character to our world (or wished-for world) in a logical way. By "a logical way" we mean "a *process* to which our minds may give assent without believing." This process need not be revealed to the reader chronologically.

Experienced as well as inexperienced writers may confuse a situation (a premise, image, idea) with a plot, though the experienced writer will soon realize that something is wrong. The following list, for example, contains the root situations for six specific American works. These obviously could be the root situations for a million other works.

1. A young boy runs away from his cruel father.
2. A woman commits adultery.
3. A family is driven from its land.
4. Two best friends grow apart and become enemies.
5. A young woman loses the man she loves.
6. A young black man comes North.

At this point, the preceding situations share one feature—each is a frozen statement of the characters' circumstances. In a plot, however, the situation is in motion.

The situations just listed may be thought of as images or pictures about which the story has yet to be told. Indeed, writers often begin with even less in mind:

1. The seventeen-year locusts come out.
2. A red scarf lying in a bed of white flowers.
3. What if a man always told the truth?
4. An intelligent computer that wants to be fed graphics of food.
5. The last living veteran from World War II.
6. The last living veteran from World War IV.
7. The bag lady who has a Ph.D. in nutrition.
8. Aunt Susan, who disappeared and no one talks about her.

These notebook jottings, the kind of pictures or ideas always popping into our minds, are the stuff from which we might build anything—poems, fiction, essays, or plays.

> "*I think almost always that what gets me going with a story is the atmosphere, the visual imagery, and then I people it with characters, not the other way around.*"
>
> Ann Beattie

Here we should point out that writers work out plots in many ways. Some find out what will happen by writing along until the direction reveals itself, almost magically. Then they go back and make it all connect. Some construct elaborate outlines of each scene and transition and will not begin writing until they know every part of their story. Some start with characters and invent situations and plots for them to act in. Some start with plots and invent characters. Some start with abstract ideas and invent everything else to express those ideas. The starting places, if not infinite, are various, and you will find a way to work that is most congenial and productive for you. It is a sign of inexperience to ask a writer or a workshop leader: What is *the* way to go about developing a plot?

Wherever you start, you have to construct events—opportunities for your characters to be in psychological and physical conflict or motion. Keep in mind, however, that though a plot is made up of events, a mere series of them do not a plot make. Here is an example of a plot that a student outlined:

A. Kane never liked school much and one day had a major fight with Mr. Sonwil, his English teacher.
B. Another time, Kane and Leon, his brother, are wrestling, when Kane kills Leon.
C. Kane moves to NYC where he gets a job washing windows on the Empire State Building.
D. He meets a young woman who is free with her favors.
E. Kane decides to go to night school.
F. The woman goes to Africa with a wealthy man, and there she kills a tiger.
G. Kane goes back to the family farm.
H. One day, while plowing, he unearths a treasure.
I. The next day a bee stings him and he dies.

Each of these is certainly an event. One can even imagine building from this outline a series of scenes in which actions occur (think of the opportunities for action in event C). However, we would be hard put to find any *connections* that make event A flow into event B and B into C, with event C also connecting to event A . . . and so on, until they are so woven together that to pull one strand out would destroy the whole. You might argue, of course, that if one eliminates item F, the events are connected because they happen to one character. Or, they are connected because they happen to the same character in chronological order. Or, that if all the events happen in New York to one character, and one event follows the other, everything will be connected. Such connections in time, place, and character can be virtues, but they do not create a sense that the events have a necessary and logical relationship, a syntax, that allows us to understand the events individually and as a whole. To put it another way, the plot is the clothesline on which you hang the events.

●   ●   ●   ●   ●   *EXERCISES*   ●   ●   ●   ●   ●

1. Take the incidents previously listed and try to find a syntactical relationship between them—some reason that Kane goes to New York and takes such a dangerous job, a reason to go home, a reason to find a treasure, a reason to die. Feel free to drop items out, change them around, and bring items in. Don't expect to end up with anything useful. It is the process of finding the connections and adjusting the events that is important for developing a plot from Kane's biography. Is there anything you can do with the name Kane? Is it necessary to begin telling the story with Kane's school days?

2. Once you have selected the key events and determined their relative importance (show or tell) and their connections, rethink the strategy of your plotline. Will simple chronology suffice? When does the reader need to know that Kane killed his brother? This is a different question from "When did it happen?" Reconstruct your plot as a sequence of revelations to the reader.

3. Create a list of incidents that might surround the following poem:

> Written in Pencil
> in the Sealed
> Railway Car
>
> Here in this carload
> I am eve
> with abel my son
> if you see my other son
> cane son of man
> tell him i

> Dan Pagis from
> *Variable Directions*

In a sense, writers have to construct plots as they might sentences. All the nouns, verbs, adjectives, adverbs, articles, and conjunctions must be in their proper grammatical form and place to produce the effect of a sentence. You don't have a plot until all the parts produce an understanding of what each part is doing in the work. Just as a vase is not the space it contains, so a plot is not the simple addition of events; the plot *contains* and *connects* events.

SETTING

We generally use the word *setting* in two senses. One has to do with the particular "somewhere" in which the characters function for a single scene—the kitchen, the palace, the street. We discuss that kind of "where" later in the chapter. In its second sense, **setting** refers to more than a specific space. It refers to the total environment for your story, with all of its cultural shadings as well as its physical landmarks, contents, and characteristics—medieval Burgundy, turn-of-the-century Sacramento, contemporary cubistic Houston. These settings are not and should not be flat backdrops in front of which the action happens. From the character's point of view, it is not a set but rather their home, a place in which all their senses operate.

An effective setting is intimately related to the plot because what happens to the characters could happen in the way it happens only in that particular setting. James Joyce's "The Boarding House" cannot be divorced from its setting in a Dublin boarding house at the edge of society. The characters know that they are somewhere; therefore, the reader is more inclined to believe in and respond to their lives.

The physical place that the writer invokes in a particular scene is surrounded by a larger environment that the writer may directly or indirectly suggest. In stories such as Edward Jones's "First Day," the particular settings include more than streets and churches. Late twentieth-century Washington, D.C., is a society containing all that "society" means. Such environments are involved in our understanding of what happens to any character.

Chapter 2, "Journal/Research/Invention," provides many suggestions for working toward a control over setting. The following excerpts show how two writers communicate a sense of place:

It was a bad time. Billy Boy Watkins was dead, and so was Frenchie Tucker. Billy Boy had died of fright, scared to death on the field of battle, and Frenchie Tucker had been shot through the nose. Bernie Lynn and Lieutenant Sidney Martin had died in tunnels. Pederson was dead and Rudy Chassler was dead. Buff was dead. Ready Mix was dead. They were all among the dead. The rain fed fungus that grew in the men's boots and socks, and their socks rotted, and their feet turned white and soft so that the skin could be scraped off with a fingernail, and Stink Harris woke up screaming one night with a leech on his tongue. When it was not raining, a low mist moved across the paddies, blending the elements into a single gray element, and the war was cold and pasty and rotten.... The ammunition corroded and the foxholes filled with mud and water during the nights, and in the mornings there was always the next village and the war was always the same.

Tim O'Brien from *Going After Cacciato*

Somewhere in the Bronx, only twenty minutes or so from the cemetery, Maeve found a small bar-and-grill in a wooded alcove set well off the street that was willing to serve the funeral party of forty-seven medium-rare roast beef and boiled potatoes and green bean amadine, with fruit salad to begin and vanilla ice cream to go with the coffee. Pitchers of beer and of iced tea would be placed along the table at intervals and the bar left open—it being a regular business day—for anyone who wanted a drink.

The place was at the end of a sloping driveway that started out as a macadam but quickly diminished to dirt and gravel. There was an apron of dirt and gravel in front of the building, potholed, and on the day of the funeral filled with puddles, and the first ten cars parked there, including the black limousine Maeve had ridden in. The others parked up along the drive, first along one side, then the other, the members of the funeral party walking in their fourth procession of the day (the first had been out of the church, the second and third in and out of the graveyard), down the wet and rutted path to the little restaurant that, lacking only draught Guinness and a peat fire, might have been a pub in rural Ireland. Or, lacking dialogue by John Millington Synge, the set of a rural Irish play.

How in the world she ever found this place was a mystery, despite the question being asked again and again as Billy's friends and family filed in—the women, in high heels, walking on tiptoe down the sloping path, the men holding their wives' arms and umbrellas that had already been well soaked at the side of the grave. All of them, in their church clothes, giving a formal air to the grey day and the ragged border of city trees and wet weeks. All of them speculating: perhaps the undertaker had suggested the place, or someone from the cemetery. Perhaps a friend or relative on her side (few as they were) who knew something about the Bronx, or maybe Mickey Quinn who had his territory up here. But Mickey Quinn denied it, shaking his head, if you can believe there's a bar in any of the five boroughs that he hasn't been to.

The place smelled slightly of mildew, understandable in this weather and with the thick (even in April) bower of trees, but the red-and-green tile floor was immaculate and the wooden bar gleamed under the fluorescent light. One long table draped with white tablecloths and set for forty-nine cut diagonally across the entire length of the room. One large window showed the parking lot full of cars, the other a wood that no doubt ended at a narrow side street or a row of dumpsters behind a row of stores, but seemed from in here to be dark and endlessly deep.

Alice McDermott, *Charming Billy*

We don't mean to suggest, with these examples, that the first thing you do in your story is to lay out the setting in full detail. More often, the impact of setting on the reader is cumulative, as it is in any of Cormac McCarthy's novels set in the West. When the writer has fully imagined the place (even if the place is only imaginary), that necessary sense of "being somewhere" will permeate the writing in hundreds of seemingly incidental details. The two worlds in Ursula K. Le Guin's science fiction novel *The Dispossessed* are her own inventions, but the characters who live there know them with the same sense of their own belonging or alienation as we know the settings of our own lives—or so it seems while we're reading. To put it another way, the reader believes in a setting—natural or imaginary—precisely because the writer has made one in which the characters believe.

If you look back over the examples, you will see that each passage not only conveys a material reality but also projects attitudes and emotion. Places are associated with feelings, often because of the events that happen there. The setting in *Charming Billy*, for example, is not simply a bar. McDermott establishes that it is a dreary place to have a wake, even if it is clean. The isolation in the midst of a giant city begins to suggest the isolation of the characters. The fact that the mourners conjecture about how Maeve found the place tell us of how unpromising the place it is. The menu for the wake suggests that the fare is as limited as the place and it suggests that Maeve lacks imagination or caring about Billy. The narrator's aside about Mickey Quinn suggests an ironic attitude. When handled effectively, then, setting—like everything else—is not only literal, but suggestive. How the characters feel about and relate to the setting is often the "background music" of the work. Setting isn't established and forgotten. (For more about settings, see Chapter 12, "The Elements of Drama," pp. 314–316.)

● ● ● ● ●   *EXERCISES*   ● ● ● ● ●

1. Read the preceding examples again and describe as fully as possible the worlds that the characters live in: material, social, spiritual. For those who want a model of setting up points of view, we suggest you read the entire novel.

2. Draft four descriptions of the same place, such as a shopping mall, a mountain vacation spot, a college or university, or an office. Develop each description through a character's point of view. Let each description register a different emotion or tone: nostalgia, torment, mystery, or humor.

POINT OF ATTACK

Think of your narrative as being composed of two movements. One movement is forward, an unfolding of events in scenes that the characters have yet to experience. From their point of view, the future is unknown, as in *Oedipus* or an episode of *CSI*. In some cases, the audience knows what will happen even when the characters don't. Part of the interest and dramatic tension comes from wondering just when the truth will dawn on the characters. As the characters move forward in time, the writer communicates to the reader (or viewer or listener) past events that are necessary for understanding the characters' present situation. This other movement, sometimes called **exposition** or **backgrounding**, evolves in the process of shaping a plot from a narrative.

The first forward-moving scene that you choose to show the reader is your **point of attack**. You may do a lot of writing during your drafts before you find the moment in the time line of the story at which the plot begins. Where you begin writing anything makes no difference because readers will only know where they began. Ultimately the point of attack is one of your major decisions. Whether you know it before you begin writing or discover it as you write, sooner or later you have to decide where you are going to have your reader begin reading. It's as important an issue as point of view.

Many other decisions follow from this process. Here is a rule of thumb:

> *Have the reader start reading as far along the time line as is consistent with the effects you are trying to achieve.*

The principle of beginning somewhere along the way—**in medias res**—has been distilled from the practice that worked even before Aristotle and still works for us. The *Iliad* begins in the tenth year of the Trojan Wars. Even in fiction writing, where you have a bit more latitude in presenting background than in playwriting, start as late in the chronology of the story as you can.

The following Aesop's fable, "Belling the Cat," gets to its one scene quickly, and that scene is within moments of the story's end.

One day the mice held a general council to consider what they might do to protect themselves against their common enemy, the Cat. Some said one thing and some said another, but at last a Young Mouse stood up and announced that he had a plan which he thought would solve the problem.

"You will all agree," said he, "that our chief danger lies in the unexpected and sly manner in which our enemy comes upon us. Now if we could receive some warning of her approach, we could easily hide from her. I propose, therefore, that a small bell be obtained and attached by a ribbon to the neck of the Cat. In this way we could always know when she was coming and be able to make our escape."

This proposal was met with great applause, until an Old Mouse arose and said, "This is all very fine, but who among us is so brave? Who will bell the Cat?" The mice looked at one another in silence and nobody volunteered.

from Aesop's *Fables*

The story dramatizes the truth that it is easier to suggest a plan than to carry it out. Aesop relies on conventional characters (a foolish young mouse and a wise old one) and a conventional situation—we expect that mice will want protection from cats. The exposition is rapid: time = one day, place = a meeting, situation = an enemy to be frustrated. For the point Aesop wishes to make, we don't have to experience in detail the Cat's deprecations among the legions of mice, the process by which the meeting was called, or even the description of where it is being held (between walls, one is sure). Not only is the point of attack at the first and, one presumes, last meet-ing, but also that meeting is the only scene. Notice where we really enter the action: close to the end of the meeting when the Young Mouse stands to deliver his plan.

This basic principle cannot be repeated too often: *Have your reader enter the story at a point that allows all irrelevant effects to be excluded.* We return to this point shortly.

●　　●　　●　　●　　●　　　　*EXERCISES*　　　　●　　●　　●　　●　　●

List all the information that happened before the point of attack in the following story excerpt.

1. Alice was beginning to get very tired of sitting by her sister on the bank and of having nothing to do: once or twice she had peeped into the book her sister was reading, but it had no pictures or conversations in it, "and what is the use of a book," thought Alice, "without pictures or conversations?"

So she was considering, in her own mind (as well as she could, for the hot day made her feel very sleepy and stupid), whether the pleasure of making a daisy-chain would be worth the trouble of getting up and picking the daisies, when suddenly a White Rabbit with pink eyes ran close by her.

Lewis Carroll from *Alice's Adventures in Wonderland*

2. If you have not read Lewis Carroll, try the same exercise with Edward Jones's "First Day."

————————●————————

For three reasons, it is best to choose as late a point of attack as possible:

1. You have less to account for and avoid many undramatic transitions.
2. You get the reader into the story faster.
3. You increase the tension because the reader waits for the unfolding of both the past and the present.

In Carroll's story, had we met Alice before she got bored and fell asleep, we probably would want to know more about what reading she had just before. And now we'd have a story with different effects. The classic though deliberately amusing case of beginning too early and getting caught in too many explanations is Laurence Sterne's *Tristram Shandy*. Tristram decides to tell his life story from the beginning, his birth. Since he is an inexperienced storyteller, he feels he has to explain how he was conceived, and that decision leads him back and back into the past. As a result, he never gets born in the novel. Remember, the later the entrance, the fewer the explanations.

Getting the reader into the narrative quickly is not simply a matter of exploding into action, as in the following opener:

John grabbed the gun from the wall and shot the two men Swenson had sent to kill him. Then he flung himself out the window, crashing through the convertible top of the Maserati waiting below. Sheila gunned the 460cc engine and squealed away from the curb. The Bolix XG-5 on the other side of the street took off after them.

How did John and Sheila get themselves into this bind? Well, six months before, Karl Ambler had called them and . . . .

Sure, this story begins quickly, but then it comes to a dead halt to orient us. And it starts on such a high pitch that the writer will have a hard time building up the excitement again. In fact, this point of attack feels like the final moment of the final scene. However, in some types of novels and films, such as *The Da Vinci Code*, the slam-bang start does work because the action dominates the narrative (at the cost of a host of other annoying flaws). The point is that a late point of attack need not be a noisy point of attack.

A late point of attack works on your readers' natural curiosity about the purpose of or reason for something they are experiencing. They will trust you to fill in the background if there is something happening in the foreground. Only in rare circumstances will the reader tolerate investing hours of energy in a story before it really gets started. Of course, decisions about point of attack are connected to the nature of the fiction: A novel may begin earlier than a short story. For obvious reasons, in short stories or plays or poems, the point of attack is usually near the concluding event.

Though you never begin at the beginning—can one ever?—you still have to discover the effective point of attack for the work in hand. This technique won't always work, but you will find that the useful initial scenes are those natural to life itself. Start with actual beginnings (weddings, new jobs, births, graduations, vacations); waitings (for friends, dinner, trains, mail, the long-lost cousins, news); movings or relocations (into the forest, into a vehicle, out of town). What better way to begin the story of a wasted life than at a wake, as in McDermott's *Charming Billy*? What happened to bring about Billy's wrecked life? Moments like these involve the kinds of tensions we are all familiar with, allowing readers to enter willingly the truths of fiction.

Also, these are moments connected to change in the lives of our characters. Readers are inclined to suspect that something is up with a character who is starting her first day in school or is developing a crush on someone. Such natural beginnings focus your readers' attention. They raise questions about the future and the past that will pull them into your story.

●   ●   ●   ●   ●   *EXERCISES*   ●   ●   ●   ●   ●

What is the effect of each of the following opening scenes?

1. She was a large woman with a large purse that had everything in it but a hammer and nails. It had a long strap, and she carried it slung across her shoulder. It was about eleven o'clock at night, dark, and she was walking alone, when a boy ran up behind her and tried to snatch her purse. The strap broke with the sudden single tug the boy gave it from behind. But the boy's weight and the weight of the purse combined caused him to lose his balance. Instead of taking off full blast as he had hoped, the boy fell on his back on the sidewalk and his legs flew up. The large woman simply turned around and kicked him right square in his bluejeaned sitter. Then she reached down, picked the boy up by his shirt front and shook him until his teeth rattled.

Langston Hughes from "Thank You, M'am"

2. The king sits in Dumferling town
Drinking the blood-red wine:
"O where will I get a good sailor,
To sail this ship of mine?"

Up and spake an elder knight
Sat on the king's right knee:
"Sir Patrick Spence is the best sailor,
That sails upon the sea."

from the anonymous ballad
"Sir Patrick Spence"

3. It is five o'clock in the morning, Daylight Saving Time. I have been sitting on the balcony of the down-river room on the second floor of the Howard Johnson's motel on Canona Boulevard almost all night. In other cities motels may be escape routes to anonymity, but not for me, not in Canona, and not this morning.

Mary Lee Settle from *The Killing Ground*

"*Anton Chekhov gave some advice about revising a story: first, he said, throw out the first three pages.*"

Ursula K. LeGuin

CHARACTER AND CHARACTERIZATION

We started this chapter with plot and scene because without them your characters drift aimlessly. However, many workshop leaders would argue that we should have begun with character because it is the most important element of the story. We think writers should approach "most important element" with a good deal of skepticism because all the narrative elements are equally important and have to join in a satisfactory manner. Nonetheless, you do well to keep in mind that the story from which your plot grows through exposition (largely *telling*) and scenes *(showing)* is about the life or a portion of the life of characters.

Keep in mind that you are writing fictional autobiography, biography, or history that the reader will take as "real" during the time of reading. For example, *The Great Gatsby* is Nick Carraway's memoir about a fateful summer and *The Grapes of Wrath* is the chronicle of a dispossessed family. Even in pure allegories or the most action-oriented plot, we expect that what happens to the characters and what they do will grow from their natures, or will appear to. The pigs in *Animal Farm* who make up the communist oligarchy do literally wallow in comfort as pigs are wont to. So, whether you create characters to fulfill a situation or a situation to fulfill characters, the reader expects situation and characters to match. By *match* we mean:

1. What the characters do always reflects who they are or what happens to them as the story unfolds.
2. Their natures are understandable both in terms of the conventions of fiction or of what has happened to them. (Remember, the environment or setting is always happening to them.)

They do not think of themselves as characters (usually). From their point of view, they have lived and are living through events, not a plot. In a different sense of the word, of course, they may plan or try to "plot" their lives to reach goals. They may "plot" against some other characters or vice versa. Like people, within the flow of events that you are charting for them, your characters wish to achieve their desires.

There are three possible types of characters in your stories or novels: primary characters, whose story you are telling; secondary characters, who are necessary for understanding the primary characters or carrying out the plot; and "uniformed" characters—doormen, waitresses, crowds—who are in the story to open doors, serve meals, and jostle the other characters—that is, provide a credibly populated fictional world. In a way, this last type of character is a part of the setting. How much time you spend on characterization depends on how much of the story the character carries. (See the section "Functionaries and Stock Characters" on pp. 205–206.)

The word *character* comes from the Greek word meaning "an instrument for marking or engraving." By the fourteenth century the word in English had come to mean "distinctive mark," and by the fifteenth, "graphic symbol." Not until the seventeenth century was it used in anything like our modern sense—the sum of mental and moral qualities—and not until the eighteenth do we find it used in place of *personage* and *personality*. The history of the word suggests that character is something imprinted, impressed upon, or scratched into universal human material to distinguish it from other material. It is the specific in the universal. A character in a literary or dramatic work is a fictional personage whom the reader recognizes by the distinctive traits the author has stamped upon or etched into the raw material. That character is "branded" so as not to be mistaken for anyone else.

A major error of beginning writers is to equate "character" with "actor"—to think that simply because one has given different names to the personages carrying out the plot the task of characterizing has been done. What the writer should strive for is to convince the reader that (1) what happens, (2) where it happens, and (3) to whom it happens are intimately related. In fact, when you inspire in your reader a belief in the character, you usually can get your reader to believe any other aspect of the story. This "belief" we are speaking of refers to recognizing the character's reality in the story rather than its reality as part of the natural world. When we identify and individualize the characters, the reader even can believe in talking flounders.

The writer gives the reader four basic ways of identifying each character. For every Roderick Usher, Ahab, Elizabeth Bennett, Holden Caulfield, Invisible Man, Harry Potter, the writer constructs

- an identifiable way of behaving
- an identifiable way of speaking
- an identifiable appearance
- an identifiable way of thinking

The writer sets up and develops the identification by either (1) telling us information through straight exposition or (2) showing us how the character acts. This showing includes, of course, how the character looks, speaks, and thinks and how other characters respond. All these elements are ultimately connected to the plot because without them what happens would not happen in the way it happens. And so once again, character is plot and plot is character.

In practice, the writer shapes our sense of the character's identity by mixing the basic techniques, as in the following passage:

Much to his surprise, Grant felt relaxed, yet serious.

"We may as well admit it's over, really over this time," he said.

He could see that Alice wasn't convinced that this time was any different from the others. Her hand smoothed her shoulder length hair in a gesture that was part of her little arsenal in such situations. The gesture was always the first step in a delicate series of maneuvers that had kept them together. But Grant had prepared himself. "That's not going to work, you know." He had had enough. He was through.

Even in this brief passage, the writer uses all the tools of characterization. The first sentence presents the narrator's assessment of the situation. He (or she) tells us something about Grant. Then Grant, in his own words, reveals where he stands—and thus something about himself. Alice's actions characterize her or at least Grant's perception of her and, in passing, give us some sense of how she looks while helping us understand the history of their relationship. But it also says something about Grant. We know that up to this point he has been indecisive about ending the relationship and that he had a weakness for Alice's physical charms, which she has exploited in the past. Grant's own words finish the job of establishing a changed situation, and the very way he speaks tells us something about his quiet but firm approach to this difficult moment. The closing sentences appear to be the narrator's report of what Grant is thinking, almost as if Grant had said it aloud. By this point, the reader understands not only that the situation has changed but also a little bit about the nature of both characters. Such moments, repeated dozens of times in any particular narrative, give the reader a sense that a character has a specific psychological and moral organization, an identifiable way of looking at and responding to situations.

One thing to notice about the preceding sample is that it doesn't sit there screaming *characterization*. The ongoing business of characterization gets done while everything else is getting done. Only when a character is first introduced or at special moments in an extended narrative is a long, static section of characterization ever appropriate. Even then, most writers would have the character doing something—going or coming, making coffee, at a meeting...in some way already involved with an event that establishes an element of the plot. Characters are more effectively presented to readers by actions and words than by analytical descriptions.

The problem with long, analytical descriptions is that the audience is given the end product—the summary case history—rather than being allowed to experience the character in action. The writer creates a greater sense of intimacy and engagement when a reader deduces the nature of characters from what they do, think, or say. In life itself, these are the ways we get to know an individual's nature. Indeed, one of the reasons a reader comes to believe in a character is that the writer provides the same kinds of information by which we come to know real people; we don't come to know them through lengthy analyses. Remember, the characters created in a work of fiction are not "real" because they pass the test of measurement against real models. They are fictional personages in whom we agree to believe because of accepted, conventional means the writer employed.

To create these believable characters, you must know more about them than can ever be told or shown to the reader. This in-depth knowledge is particularly true for major characters. The writer sets the game in motion by knowing the fictional personages so well that every move they make, every word they speak, every thought they have grows from a kind of intimate biography that allows the writer to answer the following questions:

1. When and where was the character born? Why does the character have that name? What is the character's background—economically, spiritually, educationally? Does the character have brothers and sisters? What are the family dynamics?
2. What does the character look like? How does the character speak? Move? Relate to others? What are the behavioral tics (like rubbing the side of his nose or hiccuping when nervous)?
3. What does the character do for a living? for fun? for a hobby? to kill time?
4. What is the character's psychological makeup? What are the character's memories—conscious and unconscious (as revealed in dreams and actions)? How self-aware is the character?
5. What significant events shaped the character's views and reactions?
6. *What does the character want and why?*

While all of these questions are important, the last is crucial. (For more on these elements of characterization see Chapter 13, "Dialogue and Its Problems.")

Knowing what your characters want and need can help you find situations that will put them in conflict with other characters or with the environment. It is the question that can connect character and plot, not in the sense that the pursuit of a goal is all that makes for a story line, but in the sense that knowing what the character wants and needs (even if the character doesn't) is the key to knowing how that figure will react to various circumstances. In Bel Kaufman's "Sunday in the Park" (pp. 269–272), what the woman, "she," really wants is paradoxical—a sensitive man who can beat the daylights out of the bully. As in life, the clash between the wants and needs of a character and the blocking forces of nature, social conditions, or the wishes of other characters is what creates tension. Without tension, stories and life are ho-hum—which is acceptable in life but not in stories.

Once you know your character, you will be able to present that character as a unique being rather than just as a type (see "Functionaries and Stock

Characters"). And once you know your character that well, you cannot avoid keeping to what may be the only unbreakable rule in fiction: *The character must always behave according to his or her nature as the writer has established that nature.* Tom Sawyer may leave off being a romantic and become a cynic, but we'll have to see how that happened. Indeed, how that happened may be the story or part of it. Merely for the convenience of the writer in a single scene, a character who studied atomic physics cannot ask another physicist: "By the way, who was Einstein?"

Writers, particularly novelists, often develop elaborate journal sketches of their characters' lives so that they can give those characters the degree of complexity, the multiple edges required for the type of fiction they are writing. Often they discover potential scenes or plot directions. In sum: individuality, consistency, and complexity result in successful characterization. They give the reader the opportunity to believe in the character.

You should, however, avoid the temptation to push everything you used in a character sketch into your story. The sketch is there only as a reference, a resource. The materials in the sketch must be used selectively and suggestively. You will need to choose or invent representative items that economically stand for many omitted possibilities. Essentially, doing the sketch will give you the knowledge and the insight necessary to set the character in motion. You can draw on that insight as you follow the character through a series of actions and reactions.

●   ●   ●   ●   ●   *EXERCISES*   ●   ●   ●   ●   ●

1. Write three elaborate character sketches in your journal. Make one of the characters approximately your own age, one five years younger, and one five years older. Two of them should be the same sex as yourself, the other of the opposite sex. Answer all of the questions listed on p. 193 as well as others that you think of.

2. Test out your character sketches with someone else. Find out what the sketch has not covered or made clear about your characters.

3. Make a list of situations in which each character might find him- or herself. In making the list, consider the kind of problem or set of circumstances that will best reveal what the character is made of.

4. Have one of your characters look in the mirror and record what he or she sees (some first-person introspection). *Note:* This device has become a cliché— useful in practice sessions, dangerous in serious work.

"I plot the first 5 or 6 chapters quite minutely, and also the end. So I know where I am going but not how I'm going to get there, which gives characters the chance to develop organically, as happens in real life as you get to know a person."

Joanna Trollope

Action

The characters' actions are part of the materials that constitute plot. In a narrative, every action must be convincing in this double way: (1) It must be consistent with what we know or will come to know about the character's inner state; and (2) it must be necessary to the development of the plot and the revelation of meaning.

Actions are related to motivations and reveal character. In James Joyce's "The Boarding House," (pp. 264–269) when Mr. Doran passes Jack Mooney, the brother of the girl he has compromised, he notes Jack's powerful arms and remembers how violent he could be. We realize that Mr. Doran is a physical coward as well as a moral one and that he will marry Polly. In Tony Earley's "Just Married" (pp. 275–277), the serenity of the old couple in their wrecked car reveals their acceptance of life's assorted accidents. Their story of love and faithfulness over fifty years of being married to others evokes the doubt and foreboding in the husband and wife who have helped the old couple. Will they be so faithful? Do they hold in their hearts a deep love for someone else? In this story, the action of the old couple affects the thoughts of the younger couple.

Actions are directly related to motivations. In Edward Jones's "The First Day" (pp. 272–275), the mother takes the child to kindergarten at the wrong school not only because she does not understand the concept of school zones but also because she wants her daughter to go to the school close to her church. We learn about her desire to provide a better life for her daughter by the care she takes in dressing her and in buying the school supplies. Certainly love motivates her, but just as telling is the fact that she can neither read nor write. She does not want her daughter to be a victim of ignorance as she is. We understand the pain the lack of these skills brings her because of her embarrassment when she asks for help in filling out the school forms. Overcoming the embarrassment becomes a sign of her pride and strong character.

● ● ● ● ●   *EXERCISE*   ● ● ● ● ●

From one of the character sketches you have drawn up, develop a scene in which a character trait—impatience, for example—is revealed in action or actions. See if, at the same time, you can show how that trait developed.

The Outer View: Appearance

In life, appearances are important, even if they are deceiving. When we meet people, they strike us first as images, and it is this first impression that we usually remember. In fiction, even a single detail (Huck Finn's ragged pants) gives the reader some tangible image to hang on to. Such details usually hint at other aspects of the character or situation. In the collection of physical features that meets the eye is something of the essential individual.

The amount and kind of detail about your character that you present to the reader needs to be carefully measured and selected. Beginning writers tend to go to extremes, either (1) giving their characters too much of a physical embodiment or (2) neglecting to visualize their characters altogether, often insisting that the reader's imagination will fill in the detail. The writers who go overboard elaborate the appearance of the character far beyond what the reader needs. In fact, just as with scene setting, when a writer lays out pages of excruciating detail about the character's appearance, the reader is likely to lose the essential picture. When there is simply too much for the reader to remember, the story slows to a crawl. On the other hand, a character who is totally faceless (except for age and sex) has so many possibilities that the reader is left without anything to hold on to. Readers are also confused when too many different characters are described one right after another. Think of what happens when you are introduced at a party to an entirely new group of people. In a first-person narration, the reaction of the observer can tell us both about her and the other characters.

The following physical description suggests the nature of a character:

Zadok Hoyle presented a fine figure on the box of carriage or hearse, for he was a large, muscular man of upright bearing, black-haired and dark-skinned, possessed of a moustache that swept from under his nose in two fine ebony curls. On closer inspection it could be seen that he was cock-eyed, that his nose was of a rich red, and that his snowy collar and stock were washed less often than they were touched up with chalk. The seams of the frock coat he wore when driving the hearse would have been white if he had not painted them with ink. His top hat was glossy, but its nap was kept smooth with vaseline. His voice was deep and caressing. The story was that he was an old soldier, a veteran of the Boer War, and that he had learned about horses in the army.

from Robertson Davies, *What's Bred in the Bone*

Nothing is directly said about Hoyle's personality here, though the narrator has begun to show the character in a way that allows us to draw inferences we will test later in the novel. What Hoyle does to maintain his clothes suggests his pride in his appearance, as does his posture. The "fine figure" is an image that he has worked hard to create. Nonetheless, we receive the impression of a man who is competent within a limited sphere and who can be endearing (note the qualities of his voice).

Make a list of expectations about Zadok Hoyle from the materials presented in the paragraph. After each, answer the question, "What makes you think so?" Notice that Davies comes right out and *tells* us what Hoyle's appearance is rather than trying to find more "subtle" ways (i.e., having Hoyle look in a mirror or seeing Hoyle's appearance through another character's eyes).

● ● ● ● ●   *EXERCISES*   ● ● ● ● ●

Ask the same questions about the following passages. For each, note how much is told, how much shown. What role does appearance play in each passage?

1. She smelled his shaving cream and felt his dry mouth on her cheek and turned to smile up at him. He was dressed in his gray gabardine suit. She noticed that he'd missed a spot on his chin, a little gray tuft that would grow ragged by mid-afternoon, causing him to shave again. His white shirt was dazzling in the early morning light. He stood, his left hand resting lighly on her shoulder, reading Page One of the Washington newspaper. The headlines parsed, he turned to the editorial page; fifteen seconds there, nothing of consequence. He glanced at the Op Ed, his eyebrows rising once. Then he returned to Page One, something there had caught his eye. All of this with one hand on her shoulder, the newspaper open on the kitchen table, and the radio describing the President's preparations for a visit that day to a labor union convention in Puerto Rico.

Ward Just, *In the City of Fear*

2. When Mary Graving was sober, her face was too decided and twitchy to look good with the large plain earrings she always wore. She thought she was generally too grim-looking, and her earrings looked too cheerful at

the edges of her face. Now that she was drunk, though, and wearing a red dress, her face felt hot and rosy. Her smile stayed stuck on, and she knew that the earrings—a new pair, especially cheap, not from Bagley's in Duluth but a product of the Ben Franklin Store in Rachel River—looked fine. She was not beautiful but she was all right.

Carol Bly from "The Last of the Gold Star Mothers"

The Inner View: Thought

A reader knows the action of a character's mind in two basic ways: (1) The narrator *reports* what a character thought, dreamed, or felt; and (2) the narrator directly *presents* the flow of the character's thoughts as a playwright might present a soliloquy. Sometimes the narrator may present the flow as an **interior monologue**—an apparently realistic narration of the complex flow of diverse thoughts, feelings, and images welling up within the character. **Stream of consciousness** is the extended form of interior monologue often going on for whole chapters, as in the works of James Joyce, Virginia Woolf, and William Faulkner. (This technique has fallen out of fashion.) Both give the reader insight into the character's reponse to their situation or the action, information that the other characters do not have. Because the technique reflects how our own minds might leap from thought to thought, the flow of the interior monologue need not be logical.

An omniscient narrator can enter the mind of any character, but in most fiction the narrator chooses one character as a point of psychological reference, limiting our access to the thoughts (feelings, dreams) of that individual, as in Kate Blackwell's "You Won't Remember This." Jumping back and forth among the minds of many characters is undesirable because it puts extra demands on the reader's attention. On the other hand, shifting from the mind of one character to another often occurs when the juxtaposed points of view are important to the plot. In "The Boarding House," Joyce's decision to take us into the minds of three characters because his story is largely about their different perspectives and their understandings of one another. Notice that in recording his characters' thoughts, Joyce rarely tags the passages with phrases like "he thought" or "she pondered." The narrator slips into the character's mind and, with a minimum of fuss, tells us what's going on. Here are Mrs. Mooney's thoughts as she prepares to maneuver Mr. Doran into a proposal to Polly Mooney:

There must be reparation made in such a case. It is all very well for the man: he can go his ways as if nothing happened, having had his moment of pleasure, but the girl has to bear the brunt. Some mothers would be content to patch up such an affair for a sum of money; she had known cases of it. But she would not do so. For her only one reparation could make up for the loss of her daughter's honour: marriage.

Joyce's report of her thought comes very close to authorial comment, another means of characterization that we will discuss later in this chapter. His intention, however, is to bring us close to Mrs. Mooney's thoughts, not to access them directly. The pronoun "she" signals that these are her thoughts. Of course, in first-person narration, the narrators have no difficulty expressing what is in their own brains.

A more typical handling of a character's thoughts is this passage from "You Won't Remember This":

> They took her back to her room, a small soft-beige room with gentle lighting. She got into bed and yawned luxuriously. Her body felt light and free. She happened to notice her foot and saw how thin it was again, how white and delicate with its tracing of blue veins. For a moment, she felt full of impatience, ready to leap up and run out to do all the things she used to take pleasure in doing. But in reality, she was so tired she could not even lift her hand. Now she would sleep and when she woke, her child would be there and she would nurse it and do everything for it.

In this story we know what Angelina is thinking because the narrator reports her feelings and thoughts. We are a slightly more distant from the character's mind than in "The Boarding House" because we are aware that the narrator is reporting the thoughts rather than presenting them as a form of **indirect discourse**, reported dialogue. (see "Indirect Discourse," pp. 202–204.) We know of the character's inner life but at arm's length. The emotional cost of this technique is the distancing; the virtue is that it can move the narration along faster and fits Angelina's own sense of distance from her body.

●　●　●　●　●　　　*EXERCISES*　　　●　●　●　●　●

1. Report the thoughts of two characters you have sketched. Work the thoughts into the flow of a scene with dialogue.

2. Write interior monologues for two of the characters you have sketched, one of each sex.

Dialogue

What characters say to one another is a key way of dramatizing them, putting their needs and wants into action. Whereas action, appearance, and thought reveal the character in ways that heighten his or her individuality, dialogue insists that we see the character in immediate relationship to others. We might say that speech is the way in which thought becomes action. Dialogue used merely as a way of presenting **exposition** (facts necessary for the reader to understand the plot) will be stilted and boring.

The writer who uses dialogue well understands that it performs multiple tasks. Let us say two characters are talking about whether or not to go to Boston. Ideally, the way they talk about going to Boston should carry the plot forward, reveal character, focus relationships, carry thematic implications, and—if convenient—provide some exposition. However, dialogue that only serves the purpose of exposition and to break up solid lines of narration tends to be clunky. (See Chapter 13, "Dialogue and Its Problems," for a discussion of exposition in playwriting.) If a stretch of dialogue isn't working on many levels, then dialogue is not likely to be the best tool to use at that point.

Here's a passage from the short story "Corn" developed through conversation between Toby, his wife René, and an old farmer. Notice how René's doubtfulness and Toby's attempt to appear down to earth and the farmer's desire to make money fit together without spelling these desires out. The situation is that Toby and René have been arguing about the best way to cook corn.

"We'd like to set up our stove, go pick some corn, and cook it right here. We'll pay you, of course. It's kind of a scientific experiment." The Lab let Toby scratch its ears.

The old man considered the proposition. René just shook her head back and forth. The dog left Toby and sniffed at her legs.

"Could be danger of fire," the farmer said.

"He's perfectly right, Toby. You're perfectly right, sir," René said. "We're sorry to have bothered you."

"But if'n I brought over the hose, we can set your getup right next 't the field and I could dowse any fire quicker 'in you can say . . . corn."

"How much?" Toby said.

"Ten be too much?"

"Throw in a dozen ears of corn?"

"You pick 'em."

"Done."

Toby backed the station wagon next to the field, set up the Coleman stove, attached the propane canister, filled their largest camping pot with water from the farmer's hose, and set it to boil.

Though it is clear from the context that Toby is some distance from being a farmer, the quick fencing about price and amount shows him trying to act as he imagines a farmer would act. René's desire to flee the scene is signaled by her rapid acceptance of the farmer's apparent rejection. The farmer's willingness to accommodate them, despite the danger of fire, is a signal that either he wants the money or has another motive that will reveal itself later in the story. As well as information, the dialogue reveals undercurrents—**subtext**—that the reader grasps without the narrator slowing the action to analyze the desires or goals of the characters' statements.

The passage also illustrates some conventions of dialogue. Notice how a paragraph indentation signals a shift in speaker. Though in some cases writers will run the speeches of different characters in the same paragraph or bury a character's speech in a narrative passage (see Coover's "Grandmother's Nose," pp. 284–289), normally each speech has its own paragraph. This convention is a way of helping the reader keep the characters straight. We are so used to it that it has become an unconscious expectation when we read. As writers, we need to be helpful in these most ordinary ways.

Notice also how the **designators** or **dialogue tags**—the words that tell us who is speaking—are simple and sparse. A single instance of "said" is all that the exchange between Toby and farmer needs, in part because there are only two speakers and in part because the dialogue is quick and sharp, like a duel. Beginning writers tend to become heavy-handed with these tags, no doubt out of a false worry about repetition. They try to juice up their prose by being inventive when they should be almost silent. "He snarled" and "she groused" and the like should be used sparingly, if ever.

Not only are elaborate designators more comic than helpful, but they also signal the writer's insecurity about whether the reader will respond properly to what the characters have said. The writer is shouting, "Get it?" When the writer has shown the state of mind or the tone of voice in the dialogue, it is not necessary to do so in the designator. If the writer hasn't shown them in the dialogue, then the dialogue needs revision. (Older fiction did tend to use designators with adverbs, but contemporary authors are much more sparing of them.)

The designator in the following speech is both redundant and silly:

"For God's sake, please don't go, Lettie," he implored in a piteous voice.

"He said" is sufficient. When the designator remains almost invisible, the reader is in closer contact with the dialogue and therefore with the characters. In fact, the writer can increase direct contact by judiciously dropping the designator altogether, as we have seen in the passage about cooking corn.

You will want to read the extended discussion of how to create expressive dialogue in Chapter 13, "Dialogue and Its Problems." Keep in mind that the dialogue is what characters *do* to one another; it is part of the action.

● ● ● ● ●   *QUESTIONS*   ● ● ● ● ●

1. Look at the designators in "Sex Education," pp. 50–59. How many only need "she said"?

2. What are the surface and subsurface meanings (text and subtext) in the dialogue from Earley's "Just Married" when we first meet the old couple (pp. 275–277)?

● ● ● ● ●   *EXERCISE*   ● ● ● ● ●

Write two pages of dialogue for any two characters. Create a simple conflict (should they go someplace or not; should they buy something or not). Do not use designators for any of the characters' speeches.

Remember: The characters know what they are doing and what their situation is, so they are not likely to talk about it directly. Show your dialogue to someone else to see if they can understand the situation and keep track of each character. Better yet, read the dialogue aloud with someone else as you might a play.

———————●———————

Keep in mind that the dialogue in your work occurs in the scenes, and the scenes are fundamentally play-like moments. As in a play, give your characters something to do as well as something to say.

Indirect Discourse

The technique a writer can use to avoid unnecessary dialogue is to report or have a character report (as in a play) what characters said to one another. The technique is called **indirect discourse**. Let us suppose that you have developed a scene in which one character (A) has to tell another character (B) about what a third (C) said from an earlier scene. Since the readers already have heard the information, they need not hear it elaborated again so that your story drags. Here is the flat beginning of the scene presented in dialogue:

Addie entered the room where Franklyn was setting the table.
"Hi, Frank."
"Hi, Addie."
"How you feeling?"
"O.K., I guess. And you?"
"O.K."
"How did it go with Scotty?"
"I went over there and we started to talk."
"What did she tell you?"
"It's not what she told me. It's what happened."
"What happened?"
[Now Addie launches into a long retelling of a squabble that turned into a shoving match while Frank either fiddles his thumbs, the reader forgets he is there, or Frank interrupts with "and then what happened."]

With indirect discourse you can quickly get over such repetitious or dramatically weak material:

Addie entered the room where Franklyn was setting the table. And after they exchanged greetings she told him what had happened with Scotty—including the business about the fight.

Indirect discourse is also a technique for avoiding the presentation of any dialogue that would be downright tedious or purely informational (not characterizing). In some instances, this technique serves when characterization is called for but the use of dialogue would force you to invent speeches for other characters. Notice in the following example how dialogue and indirect discourse are combined for maximum flavor and efficiency. A son has come home late:

> "I'm only an hour after I promised, Ma. What do you want from—"
> "It wasn't you who was doing the waiting."
> "But, Ma, I'm eighteen."
> He might be eighteen, she told him, but he wasn't a very grown-up eighteen. Because if he was he would understand exactly how she felt. What with no husband and Marcy and Joe gone heaven knows where, he should plan his time a little better. In any case, he was home now and she wanted him to get down to his homework right away. At least one of them would amount to something....

The narrator can go on for quite a while like this, presenting information as well as a communicating a sense of the character without having to worry about the mother's exact words or the son's responses.

In the following example, Flannery O'Connor captures Mrs. May's attitude toward her tenants the Greenleafs as she expresses herself to someone who, we assume, is an acquaintance in town:

> Mr. Greenleaf's pride in them [his boys O.T. and E.T.] began with the fact they were twins. He acted, Mrs. May said, as if this were something smart they had thought of themselves. They were energetic and hard-working and she would admit to anyone that they had come a long way—and that the Second World War was responsible for it. They had both joined the service and disguised in their uniforms, they could not be told from other people's children. You could tell, of course, when they opened their mouths but they did that seldom. The smartest thing they had done was to get sent overseas and there to marry French wives. They hadn't married French trash either. They had married nice girls who naturally couldn't tell that they murdered the king's English or that the Greenleafs were who they were.
>
> "Greenleaf"

Not only does O'Connor give us information about the Greenleaf boys, but also exposes the grudging respect and disdain Mrs. May has for them when she talks about them. Though her talk is reported, we can hear the language with which she speaks of them.

As a general rule, save dialogue for what only dialogue can accomplish—the direct confrontation of the characters. Indirect discourse is often the more effective choice for advancing the narrative.

● ● ● ● ●   *EXERCISE*   ● ● ● ● ●

Finish what the mother who is criticizing her son tells him. Then break into a brief dialogue in which she demands an explanation as to why he was late. Then use indirect discourse to report his story.

Other Means for Characterization

So far we have reviewed the direct means of characterization: what a character looks like and what that character does, thinks, and says. Often the delineation of a character is aided by what other characters say and think about him or her. In "The Boarding House," Joyce presents Mr. Doran's character, in part, by providing Mrs. Mooney's estimate of it. In "Sex Education," we observe Aunt Minnie through the eyes and evaluations of her niece.

Another technique requires a delicate hand: *authorial comment*. It has the advantage of great economy, but the disadvantage of seeming coercive—as if the author doesn't trust our understanding. James Joyce allows himself this method in a well-known line from "The Boarding House": "She [Mrs. Mooney] dealt with moral problems as a cleaver deals with meat." Of course, Joyce's simile comparing her character to a cleaver has its own dramatic brilliance since her husband had been a butcher.

> " *To write cracking dialogue you have to have a good ear. Listen to the way people speak, how they go off on tangents, how they pause, how they coin sayings or aphorisms, even how they interrupt each other. Written well, dialogue explains a character.*"
>
> Alan Gibbons

Functionaries and Stock Characters

In selecting characters and building them, you can exploit what the reader is likely to know already. Indeed, to have your narrator demonstrate, for instance, that an aging mercenary soldier is cynical about the glory of war is to ignore that we know this characteristic by convention, just as we know that dissolute younger brothers of murdered noblemen might be the logical suspect in a mystery. Because your work is not the first your readers have read, you can rely on such types for less important characters, giving the readers' imagination and experience some room for filling in the gaps. Foxes are clever and hungry—*always*.

Most of the figures who populate your work are merely functionaries: the drunk showgirls at Gatsby's parties, for example, or Mrs. Mooney's other boarders. At one level, functionaries may be part of the scenery; on another level, they may have a line or two. The writer is best off relying on the reader's knowledge of the function or the type so that the figure can be sketched in quickly:

> The waitress brought our drinks and we got down to business. It was difficult to talk in whispers because a well-dressed and well-lubricated stockbroker was telling all the world why the market had crashed. Leroy wanted to go to another bar but I thought it would be a waste of time. He was annoyed and at every other word he'd ask me to repeat what I just said. He didn't touch his martini so I took it.

Had the writer said anything more than this about the waitress and stockbroker, we would feel our attention diverted from the central issue of the scene. Usually, unless the functionaries have a significant role in the plot, the most effective technique is to pass over them quickly.

Using **stock characters**, on the other hand, requires more complex decisions. Stock characters are derived either from commonly held generalizations about racial or social types or from conventions of literature. Sometimes it is difficult to separate the generalization from the convention, as in the following list: the disrespectful servant, the braggart, the tough prostitute with a heart of gold, the silent cowboy, the snobby Harvard grad, the randy farmer's daughter, the incorruptible but sarcastic private eye, the Step 'n Fetch it; the effeminate cross dresser, the geek, and so on. On the one hand, stock characters can easily become mere reflections of popular prejudices. On the other hand, stock figures can behave so according to type that they never become characters with their own wants. Plots driven by stock characters tend to be allegorical or popular but such stories often become predictable, boring, or like comic books and games with avatars. Novels like those of Tom Clancy in which the plots are driven by single-dimensional characters usually don't stay in the mind for long. (On the other hand, they do sell in the millions.)

A social type (the dull professor or the airhead yuppie), of course, will not offend the reader as may the racial, religious, or sexual stock character. Offensive or not, such stock figures can play major roles in satire or comedy. The dirty old man lusting after a young bride has supplied the central focus for many plots. When you want only a stock response, use a stock character, but weigh the risks involved.

The stock character can also provide the seed from which the writer builds a more complex character. Just as our understanding of real people may begin with placing them in general categories by which we first know them (gender, age, occupation, class), so may we begin developing our fictional people by first seeing them as types and then learning about them as individuals. For an extended discussion of this process, see the section on stock characters in Chapter 12, "The Elements of Drama."

●   ●   ●   ●   ●   *EXERCISES*   ●   ●   ●   ●   ●

1. What characterizing techniques does Earley use in "Just Married" to turn the stock elderly couple into more complex characters?

2. There is a fine line distinguishing stock characters, an artistic convenience, and stereotypes, a potentially hazardous playing on prejudices. How would you categorize each of the following? How might you turn them into more complex characters?

- a. a redheaded, gum-chewing waitress
- b. a dumb jock
- c. a computer geek
- d. a male nurse
- e. a television evangelist
- f. an aging spinster
- g. a punk rocker
- h. a Puerto Rican thief

Naming Characters

Finding appropriate names is not a trivial task, since your reader is often attracted or distracted by the name itself and by its seeming "rightness" for that particular character. A name must have credibility without being a cliché, and sometimes the name may have significance or suggestiveness. In choosing names, the writer must consider:

1. cultural stereotypes (if only to avoid them)
2. historical authenticity (Is the name right for the times?)

3. regional probability (Is a small-town Texan named "Melvin"?)
4. socioeconomic signals (Is "Poindexter" the trucker?)
5. symbolic overtones (Is "Joshua" leader or wimp?)
6. auditory features (What's an "Ebenezer Scrooge"?)

The following list includes names of characters from drama, fiction, and poetry. For the characters you know, check the "ring" of each name against the traits of the character. For the others, make a list of traits you would expect and then find out how close your portrait comes to the original.

1. George F. Babbitt
2. J. Alfred Prufrock
3. Becky Thatcher
4. Willy Loman
5. Harry Potter
6. Quentin Compson
7. Stephen Dedalus
8. Luke Skywalker
9. Nick Adams
10. Joseph Andrews
11. Lemuel Gulliver
12. Moll Flanders
13. Isabel Archer
14. Oliver Twist
15. Holden Caulfield
16. Daisy Buchanan

Beware of names that are overly allegorical—Lancelot Hero—as well as names that do nothing to distinguish your character—Bill Smith, Sam Smyth, Joan Jones, Joy Jakes. In the latter case, the reader may become lost in the forest of one syllable names.

A useful technique to find names for your characters is by "researching" in telephone directories, local newspapers, and blogs. Mix first names and last names. Try out your characters' names on your friends or an instructor.

The Relationship of Character, Plot, and Setting

Since fictional characters are "represented" persons, their lives are limited to the fictional work or works that shape them. A character is "real" in terms of the imagined environment, not necessarily in terms of the world we know intimately or the larger world that we know something about. The reality of Angelina's pregnancy is bound up with the environment in which Blackwell places her: the impact she has on *that* world and that it has on her. It is easy to grasp this point when we consider fairly exotic settings (like the grandmother's house in Coover's "Grandmother's Nose") and nonnaturalistic characters. However, the same truth holds in the more familiar world created by Bel Kaufman. The reality of the character is *inside* the story, not *outside* it. This means, in part, that the things the reader needs to know about a character are limited to the larger unity of the story. Not every character, as we've already pointed out, is given the same attention, the same degree of rounding.

The situation (or conflict) that shapes the plot also limits or controls what readers need to know about the character; that is, those matters that bear on the circumstances at hand. As writers, we will know much more about these characters than the plot allows us to share with the reader. Our concern for overall unity and focus will help us select just what must be known about each character. When the first word the old woman in "Just Married" speaks is "well" and the old man answers "well," Tony Earley gives us all we need to know about their imperturbability.

●   ●   ●   ●   ●   *EXERCISE*   ●   ●   ●   ●   ●

Reread "Sex Education" (pp. 50–59) and develop a scene between Aunt Minnie and her wayward son Jake when she finds him after he runs away. Be sure you describe him and develop how her attitudes about sex may have affected him. What does she do to convince him to come home?

> *"Each of my characters comes from somewhere, and where they come from, good or bad, has a large part in forming who they are, and who they can become."*
>
> Nora Roberts

 A NOTE ON THE NOVEL

Writing a novel involves all the techniques of writing shorter fiction—character and scene development, narration, dialogue—plus the demands brought on by the sheer magnitude of your promise to tell a long story. From a purely commercial point of view, when you undertake a novel, you commit yourself to writing a minimum of 40,000–60,000 words, or 150–200 double-spaced pages. And for some of the subgenres of the novel, like the historical romance, you may need to write 100,000 or more words because the reader expects a substantial beach book. Even with word processing, the task is daunting when you think of the time involved in writing the original draft and then revising it, probably more than once.

However, the more serious challenges are not those of filling up pages. While a short story generally focuses on a single event involving only one or two major characters, a novel enters far more fully into the imitation of an unfolding life (or series of lives) while it places that unfolding in an elaborated setting that traditionally includes social background. The novelist must exercise intense concentration over a long period of time to manage the intricacies of characters' lives in an expanded plot. Authors of long fictions, even more than writers of short stories, must truly live with their characters.

Generally speaking, you will need to do much more prewriting than might be necessary for a short story. Since novels tend to imitate either biographies, autobiographies, or histories, you have to determine how your imagination will substitute for the nonfiction writer's research. Of course, you will need to do much of the same kind of research (see Chapter 2) to create a sense of authenticity. And you will have to be flexible: Because you will be working on the manuscript for months, even years, your reading will expand your writing tools, and your experience of the natural world and the world of your novel will deepen. While you are drafting, you will make discoveries about your characters and the moral, physical, and intellectual world(s) they inhabit. Rigid adherence to a plan over the months and years of the writing process that novels require is likely to be a foolish faithfulness.

Though you want to jot down notes as ideas come to you for all writing projects, writing a novel calls for even more note taking. Much more is happening, more characters are moving across your stage, more time has passed since you set up the action. Think of yourself as the person who takes care of the props in a play or the continuity in a film. Like such managers, you need to know what your character was wearing and had in her purse in the last scene. Or, since four years have gone by since Jay Gatsby left for the war, how does he find out where Daisy is living? The sheer volume of events, props, and characters, and the time that elapses between writing Chapter 1 and Chapter 10, qualitatively change the task before you. Some authors dedicate a journal to keeping track of their ideas and plans for a novel, and then for keeping track of their progress (see Steinbeck excerpt, pp. 19–20).

If you have read this far, you already know that you have to study the genre and subgenre in which you plan to write. Particular subgenres—mystery, adventure, science fiction, romance, historical—are subdivided into even more types, and you should master the conventions and expectations of the audience (even if you intend to upset those expectations). You should have read in the genre for a long time before you try, let us say, an adventure story. If you try to write in a subgenre just because it is popular, let's say something like the Harry Potter series, you will probably create a manuscript that will gather dust in your computer files.

A good part of your preplanning should involve especially careful thinking about who is going to tell the story (see Chapter 3). For example, if you are going to have to do a great deal of exposition (as in an historical novel), a first-person point of view may cause difficulties. How are you going to get a piece of information to your narrator? On the other hand, a story about growing up or a hard-boiled detective story may flow easily in the first person. If your point of view in a short story is not working, you have relatively little revising to do. But going back after writing a hundred pages of a novel can be a burden so daunting that you might give up.

Normally, but not always, you will tell your novel in the past tense. Though you might have a prologue in the present tense to set the atmosphere, telling a whole novel in the present tense usually puts off a reader and poses exposition problems for the writer. It's been done, of course, but seldom successfully. Page after page of "she meets John and they go to the zoo where they look at the monkeys" creates unnecessary demands on the reader's attention. The novel has no emotional resting place. Everything appears to be so important and significant. Everything is happening now. The present tense may work in some short stories but, ultimately, it tends to create an evenness in the prose, an immediacy that allows for no hills and valleys.

All the decisions regarding plot, point of attack, character and characterization, and setting that we have already discussed become increasingly complicated when you tackle a novel. Perhaps the most important decision is to determine what to show and what to tell—and to be sure you know why. Because the novelist has to create a more sustained illusion of time passing, decisions about scene and summary are far more complex than they are for short stories. And, of course, such decisions must be made over and over again.

As a practical matter, what you show will be in scenes that combine description, narration, and dialogue (or interior monologue). Each scene will exist to reveal character and present action. If information is conveyed, it will be conveyed as a side effect of the scene. The scene must never appear to exist for the purpose of giving the information. When Hawthorne, in *The Scarlet Letter*, creates the scene in which Chillingworth doctors Hester and attempts to pull from her the identity of Pearl's father, we also learn about Chillingworth and Hester's marriage.

Most novels have twenty to forty major scenes of two to ten or more pages. Often one scene, with attendant description and exposition, makes up a chapter. If you find your scenes are a page or less and/or you have dozens in a chapter, you probably are writing scenes that exist only to give information (either to the reader or the other characters) or to provide a transition to another scene. In either case, the brief scenes are probably only for exposition and should be eliminated in favor of having your narrator simply tell the reader the key information at the start of the next scene: "After he bedded down the elephant, he went to the local pub" is probably sufficient for a transition. It's unlikely that we will need to see a scene in which your character decides to go to the pub and then dresses and then walks to it.

Some novelists develop a complete life for each character: birthdate, parents, schooling, allergies, and so on. Many of your characters will exist only to help your major characters in their conflicts or to serve the plot. Ask yourself if it is really necessary to give a complete physical description of the doorman who appears only in a single scene. If you do need supporting characters, try to make those characters serve several functions. For example, Jordan Baker in *The Great Gatsby* not only serves as a foil to Daisy Buchanan, not only delivers necessary expository material, and not only becomes Nick Carraway's date for the summer (a parallel "love" story), she is also one of the characters who illustrates the decadence of contemporary society (she cheats at golf). A less sophisticated novelist might have employed several characters to fulfill these various roles.

Warnings: Do not revise while the novel is developing. When you discover in Chapter 4 that you need to revise one or more earlier chapters—anything from the name of a character to adding a scene—just put down a note to yourself to make the revision. Continue writing as if you had already made the change. Why? Because when you get to Chapter 5 and 6 and so on, you will find other revisions necessary for the earlier chapters. If you keep revising you will never finish the novel. (Word processing has the advantage of letting you return to the earlier chapters and drop in notes to yourself about the changes that will be needed and then jumping back to where you were.)

The challenge of the novel, then, brings a mixture of pleasure and pain. Most fiction writers (but certainly not all) learn to control the essential elements of their craft by working first in the short story, then going on to the longer form. The rewards of building a peopled edifice in words are enormous, but the writer who accepts the challenge must camp out for a long season in those construction sites of the imagination, through bad weather and occasional strikes, while the structure takes shape.

●　●　●　●　●　*EXERCISES*　●　●　●　●　●

1. Prepare a chapter outline for a novel based on Hemingway's "A Very Short Story." Include comments on new characters, new scenes, and point of view.

2. Prepare dust jacket copy for your novel. This task should force you to focus on the essentials. (Read a dozen or so book jackets before you do yours.)

3. Develop a plot of four to five pages using the news article on pp. 33–34 as the foundation. Or, reread Krista Benjamin's "Letter from My Ancestors" (p. 148) about the American immigrant experience and develop a chapter outline for a *bildungsroman* (a novel tracing the entire life of a character.)

> "*Fiction, like sculpture or painting, begins with a rough sketch. One gets down the characters and their behavior any way one can, knowing the sentences will have to be revised, knowing the characters' actions may change.*"
> John Gardner

CHAPTER **9**

NARRATION AND ITS TECHNIQUES

> "*At one time I thought the most important thing was talent. I think now that the young man or the young woman must possess or teach himself, training himself, in infinite patience, which is to try and to try until it comes right.*"
>
> William Faulkner

This chapter extends the discussion of techniques for writing your narrative—the interaction of a situation (focused at the point of attack), setting, and characters, as plotted through alternating units of telling and showing: exposition, flashback, scene, and summary. In this process, almost anything can go wrong.

 EXPOSITION

Writers need ways to communicate information that will round out their readers' understanding of the unfolding story, which is told primarily through scenes and linking summaries. Most often this information has to do with events that precede the point of attack. The writing that supplies this information is called exposition ("the back story" in drama); we have touched on this already. In Joyce's "The Boarding House," five introductory paragraphs supply family background necessary to our full comprehension of the dramatized events. We are told about

212

Mrs. Mooney's unfortunate marriage, the reputation of the boarding house, and Polly's character and situation. The events that follow make sense—a particular kind of sense—because of what has been revealed. Of course, exposition will continue throughout a piece, either as transitions between scenes or within them. The task is to find strategies for making the exposition interesting in itself…or as brief as possible.

Exposition is almost always handled by *telling,* whereas scenes are conveyed by *showing.* Some of your most difficult decisions will involve discovering (1) how much of what happened before the point of attack is necessary to tell, (2) when to tell it, and (3) how to tell it most effectively and least obtrusively.

There are two kinds of information that the reader needs. First is the information about the world we all live in that bears upon the characters. If you are writing a story that involves, let's say, mountain climbing, how much does the reader need to know about Nepal, crampons, rappelling, hypothermia, atmospheric conditions? How much can you expect the reader to know already? How much can be gleaned from context? You need to gauge the reader's knowledge about the most relevant information, avoiding dull explanatory passages that stop the action. When in doubt, expect the best of the reader. If you assume that you have to explain where New York City is, you will never make your way through the writing of a story.

Some fiction depends on introducing the reader to relatively unknown settings, the unfamiliar details engaging the reader's imagination. For example, novelist Dick Francis has made a career of letting his readers experience the world of horse racing. In works like these, the absorbing of new information is a central pleasure. A valuable technique is to develop a character or characters who are engaged in learning information so that we are seing it through their eyes or their struggles to learn the information. A classic case is Daniel Defoe's *Robinson Crusoe,* which gains much of its power from having us learn the same things that Crusoe must learn to survive.

Most short fiction, however, needs to tell us only that, for example, the main characters are a couple with one child who live across from Central Park and read *The New York Times* every Sunday ("Sunday in the Park"). Your reader can intuit a lot from this little bit. In longer stories with more complex plots (as in a novel), the writer might spend time on even more exposition. In a subtle and amusing way, Hemingway's "A Very Short Story" is almost all exposition because it is a condensed novel and he has to tell us a good deal for us to understand the situation. (Man and woman fall in love, man goes off to war, woman doesn't wait, each suffers the consequences.) "Sex Education" is mostly exposition, which the narrator learns in the process of growing up. On the other hand, does Kate Blackwell in "You Won't Remember This" have to tell us how Angelina got pregnant?

The second type of information the reader needs is information about the lives and circumstances of the characters *in the story:*

> Once upon a time, in a distant kingdom, there lived a princess who was an only child. Her name was Esmeralda and in every way save one she was the most fortunate of young persons.
>
> Phyllis McGinley from *The Plain Princess*

Who, where, and *when* need to be established in almost every piece of fiction (including narrative poetry and drama), and little is ever gained by hiding this material from the reader. Making puzzles out of basic information, a novice's idea of creating mystery, more often loses the reader altogether. Look at the first paragraph of Bel Kaufman's "Sunday in the Park" (pp. 269–272) to see how sure-handedly the basic expository work can be done and smoothed into the point of attack. In fact, effective exposition in itself can please readers and appear to be dramatic.

However much you tell the reader about the background, you will know ten times more than you can tell. Your job is to anticipate the reader's needs as the story unfolds and to offer the right information—and no more—in the right place.

Again, most expository information is revealed by summary overviews of conditions, backgrounds, and settings. Directness is a virtue; don't waste time inventing cute ways to make a simple point:

No: He walked up to the door. When the tall woman answered it, he handed her his card. She read on it: "Will E. Seridy, 7803 Wilson Lane, Exterminator."

No: Will looked into the handsome reflection that showed him a six-foot man of thirty-two with an intriguing cowlick of reddish hair.

These passages call more attention to the means of communicating the facts than to the facts themselves. The reader can see the writer is struggling with the exposition. The following attempt is simpler, yet far more effective:

Will Seridy walked up to the front door. A handsome man of thirty-two, the lanky exterminator had reddish hair that fell in a cowlick. He handed the tall woman who answered the door his card.

Save your creative effort for more important struggles than finding cute ways to give the reader information necessary so that the story may move forward.

Providing exposition is like giving your readers a map orientation before you show them where they are going: "You are right here. Now from this point...." Notice how quickly Nathaniel Hawthorne's famous short story "Young Goodman Brown" sets the action in motion:

> Young Goodman Brown came forth at sunset, into the street of Salem village, but put his head back, after crossing the threshold, to exchange a parting kiss with his young wife.

We learn the central character's name, where we are, that he is going on a trip just before dark—an unusual time for beginning a journey—and that he is newly married. Since it is an unusual time to set forth, we are already aware that something is up. (In fact, he is going to a black mass and will meet with the devil.) In many works, like folk ballads (see p. 189), thrusting us into the action is conventional.

Frequently, exposition is not placed at the beginning of a work, as our examples so far might indicate. Though chronologically it can convey information that precedes the point of attack, structurally exposition comes at the point the author feels is strategically effective. Blackwell in "You Won't Remember This" starts us in the last days of Angelina's pregnancy and then returns to fill us in on the information about her gradual descent into passivity. In fact, the sections of the story leading up to the day she gives birth are a type of flashback.

FLASHBACKS

Usually, a **flashback** dramatizes events that happened before the point of attack in a work or a scene. While exposition may or may not be presumed to occur in the mind of the character, a flashback is always presumed to be about an event a character or characters remember. A memory like "as she reached for the peanut butter, Josie saw again the knife-scarred kitchen counter on which rested the fixings of all those homemade snacks her mother used to give her" is not yet a flashback but rather a piece of generalized exposition. It contains no events. Flashbacks are remembered **scenes** that interrupt the ongoing action. They serve expository purposes, certainly, but they dramatize rather than just report about something in the past.

> As she reached for the peanut butter to make Henry his snack, she remembered when—was she just thirteen?—her mother handed over the tools of the trade and the responsibility.
>
> "No more waiting on you hand and foot," she said.
>
> Josie was stunned. The words and the kindly, loving look in her mother's eyes seemed in conflict. She walked over to the counter and picked up an apron. "Which do you put on first, the peanut butter or the jelly?"
>
> Today, she still imitated her mother's kitchen habits, though in everything else she had gone her own way.

Because flashbacks occur in the character's mind under the pressure of present circumstances, the reader assumes that whatever is revealed in the interrupting scene has some importance to the emotional development of the character as well as the developing action. That is, a flashback should contain emotional facts, not simply material information. Where you place the flashback—or other exposition of past events—will be a step in the experience you are creating for the reader.

The techniques for moving in and out of flashback scenes deserve special attention. You should get in and out of a flashback as quickly and directly as possible. Many times you can simply cut to the flashback, particularly if you use a typographical means (such as italics) to hold the flashback material. Here is an example of this technique. Miriam, at Phyllis's wedding, remembers a past event. Note the decision to put this flashback in the present tense for additional emphasis.

Miriam heard the minister say, "Do you, Phyllis"—She is standing at the punch bowl wondering why she came. She wants to be at the lab or back in her room listening to Bach. She sees the frenetic dancing and Robin talking animatedly at the other end of the room. Someone touches her on the shoulder and she turns to see Frank and he is saying, "Do you want to . . ."

And then she heard Phyllis saying "yes" and wondered how things would be now if she had said "yes" to Frank.

Normally you will cast flashbacks (and everything else) in the past tense. This is what readers are used to and what is easiest for them to follow. However, as in the previous illustration, we note a growing tendency in contemporary fiction to use the present tense in narration and flashbacks.

Readers are also used to the simple conventions that introduce interrupting scenes: "He remembered the time when . . . ," "She wished she could get back to when she was everybody's favorite, like on the day that . . . ," "The smell reminded her of . . . ," and so forth. Here is a movement backward from Joyce's "The Boarding House":

It was not altogether his fault that it had happened. He remembered well, with the curious patient memory of the celibate, the first casual caresses her dress, her breath, her fingers had given him. Then late one night as he was undressing for bed she had tapped at his door, timidly. She wanted to relight her candle at his for hers had been blown out by a gust. It was her bath night. She wore a loose open combing-jacket of printed flannel. Her white instep shone in the opening of her furry slippers and the blood glowed warmly behind her perfumed skin. From her hands and wrists too as he lit and steadied the candle a faint perfume arose.

●   ●   ●   ●   ●   ●   *EXERCISES*   ●   ●   ●   ●   ●   ●

1. Invent one or two flashback scenes for Bel Kaufman's "Sunday in the Park."

2. Imagine a character you have developed in a character sketch getting ready to meet his new girlfriend's, or her boyfriend's, parents for the first time (or some similarly critical situation, such as getting ready for a college interview, a promotion review, or a trip to the doctor). Move your character through a believable landscape (or cityscape) and into the building and room where he or she will wait to meet the others. The character is apprehensive. Since this episode is your reader's introduction to the character (and the whole story), your writing must serve many functions at once without being too obvious. The character might be reminded of something in the past (which you could develop in a flashback), might notice certain details in the office building or home, might wish to escape the situation or else be eagerly looking forward to it. Keep the action moving. All aspects of fiction writing except dialogue can play a part here. If you use dialogue, keep it to a minimum. See Exercise 3 for some planning ideas.

3. Inspector A arrives at the home of Mr. and Mrs. X. He has come to interview them about their reported theft of a painting. Describe Inspector A's arrival at the X estate, his impressions of the owners from what his trained eye notices as he approaches the front of the house, enters, walks through the entrance hall or lobby, and is shown into the sitting room, where he waits for Mr. and Mrs. X to join him. Through physical details, the inspector is building an understanding of the people he is about to meet. You might as well have a butler answer the door. Prepare a sketch, such as the one on p. 218, to help you visualize the situation.

▶ SCENE AND SUMMARY

In *Writing Fiction*, R. V. Cassill tells us that scenes "bring the action and sometimes the dialogue of the characters before the reader with a fullness comparable to what a witness might observe or overhear" [as at a play]. Summary passages, on the other hand, "condense action into its largest movements." They tend to telescope events rather then present them in dramatic detail as scenes do. Janet Burroway, in her book *Writing Fiction*, considers "scene" and "summary" as ways of treating time: "A summary covers a relatively long period of time in relatively short compass; a scene deals with a relatively short period of time at length." Burroway believes that, though a summary is a useful device, scenes are absolutely necessary. As a practical matter, however, it is difficult to narrate without mastering both.

Scenes create the illusion of an unbroken stretch of time and action, usually in a single place. Summary passages stitch scenes together while performing expository work. In your scenes you make your work come alive. A crucial task for the writer is to determine which material demands development in a scene

SKETCH OF GROUND FLOOR LAYOUT; SITTING ROOM SCENE OF THEFT

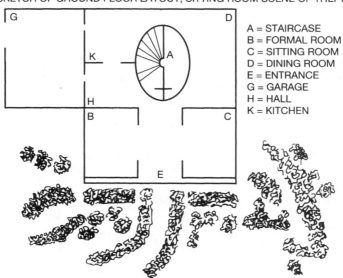

A = STAIRCASE
B = FORMAL ROOM
C = SITTING ROOM
D = DINING ROOM
E = ENTRANCE
G = GARAGE
H = HALL
K = KITCHEN

and which requires only summary handling. The principle of economy operates here: Scenes should be chosen to perform multiple tasks, and no plot should have more scenes than it needs. Of course, deciding how much is needed is about as easy as picking exactly the chocolates you want to eat from a five-pound box of candy. You may have to take a bite of all of them first.

On the pages that follow, we discuss the development of plot through scenes in three short stories: Joyce's "The Boarding House," Jones's "First Day," and Hemingway's "A Very Short Story." Though we mainly concentrate on the selection and juxtapositioning of scenes, we will pay attention as well to point of attack, exposition, flashback, summary, and characterization. Scenes, of course, assume "scenery," the physical places and its contents. Our discussion here is intended to help you look at these issues as a writer. You might want to reread each story before reading our discussion.

————————●————————

"The Boarding House" is a clear example of economy in scene selection. It is built out of four scenes in the ongoing present into which are embedded past scenes and some observations about past events. The story begins slowly, as Joyce takes a leisurely five paragraphs to give us the background of the situation in which Mrs. Mooney and her daughter Polly find themselves. However, if we study these expository paragraphs carefully, we see that Joyce has established a vivid personal situation inside a larger cultural one. Mrs. Mooney's aim is to get Polly married to the "right" man rather than sexually involved with many men, at the same time running Polly past a number of potential husbands until the right one gets trapped. The moral environment of the story is one of Joyce's main concerns.

Only after presenting the background and the initial portraits of Polly and her mother does Joyce focus the story through dramatized scenes as the marriage trap is finally sprung. The first scene establishes the time—Sunday morning—in which all of the unfolding action occurs. We see the respectable-looking churchgoers out on the street, while the fallen establishment that Mrs. Mooney runs is being aired out. We receive a detailed description of the breakfast remains, and we hear about the frugal measures Mary takes under Mrs. Mooney's instruction. The images of propriety ("gloved hands") clash with the images of egg streaks and bacon fat, intensifying thematic concern with the distance between outward appearances and inner truths. So, too, the expansive gesture of the open windows and ballooning lace curtains conflict with the pettiness of putting "the sugar and butter safe under lock and key." Joyce's scene contains precise images that not only render the place concretely—materially—but also suggest the moral issues of his story.

Embedded in this scene is Mrs. Mooney's reconstruction of the previous night's conversation with Polly. Joyce does not dramatize that scene; we get none of the conversation and only the barest summary of what happened. Nonetheless, we know exactly what happened.

Scene 1 continues with Mrs. Mooney planning her attack on Mr. Doran. She knows that she holds all the cards of moral pressure. She and Polly have been silent accomplices in the pursuit of a proper marriage for Polly. Their plan is based on a reading of Mr. Doran's character and an intimate knowledge of how important reputation is in Dublin. The morally repugnant scheme depends on the concern for appearances, and it reinforces the superficiality of those appearances. Ironically, Joyce has Mrs. Mooney consider that she has just enough time to blackmail Mr. Doran and still make it to church by noon. She sees no inconsistency between the two acts.

We get to know Mr. Doran a bit through Mrs. Mooney's ruminations. The second scene presents Mr. Doran in his room puzzling over his fate. We learn that Polly had come to see him after discussing their sexual relationship with her mother the night before, and that she had told him about the mother and daughter conversation. He is remembering his confession to a priest, examining the overall situation, and retracing the steps of his involvement with Polly. Within this second scene is a flashback—Doran's vivid recollection of the night he succumbed to Polly's seductive behavior. The second scene concludes with Mary's arriving to summon him to see Mrs. Mooney.

The third scene, Mr. Doran's journey down the stairs, intensifies his anxiety, especially as he passes Polly's brother Jack, a man capable of violence who has threatened anyone who would jeopardize his sister's reputation. Jack, we gather, is the strong-arm version of his mother.

Between the third scene and the concluding scene, we know that Mrs. Mooney and Mr. Doran have had their little chat. However, Joyce chose not to present it, trusting the reader to feel the full weight of the inevitable through silence.

Instead of following Doran into the parlor for his confrontation with Mrs. Mooney, we visit Polly's room and enter Polly's thoughts. We see her preparing for the news that is bound to come. It is an emotional moment for her, but her complex imaginings of the future are left unspecified. Joyce leaves us to ponder the kind of relationship these two can have, given the questionable foundation on which it is built. Mrs. Mooney's voice breaks through Polly's reverie, announcing that Mr. Doran has something to speak to her about.

In shaping this story, Joyce has made a series of decisions about plot. Mrs. Mooney, of course, has a plot, but Joyce's plot focuses the ongoing action as close to the climax as possible. The beginning of the story lies in the long distant past (Mrs. Mooney's own disappointing marriage and her society's attitudes toward sex and marriage); the plot focuses that story in the time between breakfast and morning mass. The concentration increases the intensity, a useful principle of plotting to keep in mind.

●   ●   ●   ●   ●   *QUESTIONS*   ●   ●   ●   ●   ●

1. Joyce uses dialogue sparingly in this story. What does he save it for?

2. Joyce allows access to the thoughts of each of his three main characters. How is this omniscient technique handled? Why is it necessary? (Note: The selected scenes do not show the characters interacting.)

3. If Joyce began the story with Mrs. Mooney's marriage, how long would it have to be?

●   ●   ●   ●   ●   *EXERCISES*   ●   ●   ●   ●   ●

1. Invent the two "missing" scenes: the conversation between Mrs. Mooney and Polly and the one between Mrs. Mooney and Mr. Doran.

2. Imagine Jack Mooney's perspective on what has been going on. Develop one or two scenes from his point of view.

———————————●———————————

Ed Jones chooses scenes in his story even more thriftily than Joyce did. "The First Day" is built around six scenes, one of which is extremely brief:

1. Preparing for the first day of school
2. Going to school
3. Arriving at school and being told that it is the wrong one
4. Going to the designated school
5. Registering the child
6. Leaving the child

Preparing for the first day at school is really a flashback scene because at the point of attack, the opening sentence, they are already on their way. The effect is to put the characters in motion before slowing down to set the background, another useful technique. The narrator is the grown-up child who is looking back and trying to recapture the feel of that day as her younger and more naïve self might experience it. The narrator tells us that she "learned to be ashamed of her mother" as a young child. However, we come to understand that now she is proud of her mother's fierceness and courage. In fact, the central paradox of the story is pride coexisting with the shame. The detail in the preparation scene is rendered with loving detail (colors, food, school box) which suggests that Jones thought carefully about what a little girl might remember and what would excite her. We learn also that the child is fatherless and that fact, as we read on, accounts for the mother's combination of sternness and indulgence. She has to be both parents. The narrator mentions in passing the fact that she has sisters, which tells us something of the difficulty this single-parent family faces. Though Jones doesn't tell us at this point that this is an African-American family, the detail tells us it is (Dixie Peach hair grease and the plaits). When the mother slaps the child for using a street label (dykes) for Miss Mary and Miss Blondelle, the speaker reveals that her mother wanted her to be proper and respectful.

The brief second scene, in which the child sees none of the children she knows on the way to school, suggests that something is amiss, a kind of foreshadowing. We also get a hint that the mother chose Seaton Elementary because it was across from her church. In a later scene we will learn the reason for the assumption.

The scene at Seaton school opens with a sentence that is meant to establish another point about how the child looks at the world. She is keenly aware of and impressed by what she takes to be the fancy dress, "out of . . . *Ebony*," worn by the school administrators and teachers. At the same time, if we haven't figured it out previously, the writer lets us know again that this is an African-American mother and child in an African-American community. The later revelation about the mother being illiterate is foreshadowed in her tiff with the school administrator. We will realize that the mother tries to cover up her failure to understand the concept of school districts (and, perhaps, inability to read notices sent to homes about where a child is to go) when she says: "If I'da wanted her someplace else, I'da took her there." She is a proud woman and that makes her later admission at the other school more powerful. We learn one other aspect of the mother's character: She may respect authority but she doesn't bend to it.

The next scene is so short one might think Jones could skip it. Why not jump to the new school and save the transition? Partly the scene shows the mother's decisiveness when she knows she is licked on what ultimately is a minor point. She hurries the child off to the correct school. The speech "One monkey don't stop no show" we take as a way of saying the bureacracy will not defeat her and that there is more than one way to skin a cat. She is a woman who keeps the primary goal in mind and will not be distracted by trifling road blocks.

To this point the scenes serve the following dramatic purposes: (1) They show us the situation and key facts while revealing aspects of the mother's character; (2) they foreshadow complications, the details of which we will not understand until the fourth scene; and (3) they set up the block to the characters fulfilling their wants and needs. In the fourth scene we see the mother overcome the obstacles, at a price. She has to admit that she can't read or write. She has to reveal her shame to her daughter. She has to beg someone for help. We notice that the narrator also reveals another quality of her mother. She is prepared with all the documents she might need and some that she doesn't need, like the public assistance payments—documents that, ironically, she cannot read. Also, instead of telling us that the family is on public assistance, Jones has us learn the information through the action of presenting the papers. Having overcome the blocks to achieving the goal caused by her illiteracy, the mother and child reach their goal.

The final scene, though apparently anticlimatic, actually adds to the immense ache one feels at the end. In the first place, when we hear that the mother will pick up the child at noon, it is borne out to us that this is only kindergarten and we understand the struggles the mother will have to go through for her children in the future. We also learn why and how the child learns to be ashamed of her mother and when the shame began. The women out of *Ebony* and her mother's darned socks and loud shoes, her mother's illiteracy, and everything she will learn directly and indirectly at school combine to "learn" the daughter to be ashamed. This bitter irony, however, is softened by the story itself which tells us that the narrator adult has finally transcended her younger self and is intensely proud of her courageous mother. Otherwise, why tell the story as lovingly as she does?

●   ●   ●   ●   ●   *EXERCISES*   ●   ●   ●   ●   ●

1. Why does the woman who fills out the form for the mother seem "so much happier" and why does she take the money? In the same scene, in what way does the other child's staring fit the narrator's understanding of how the first day experience affected her? What would happen to the story if the first sentence were left out?

2. Try to write a synopsis of this story in one paragraph. What elements would the reader who only looks at your summary miss?

3. Expand the scene on the way to the second school. Keep in touch with Jones' characters and maintain the same narrative style.

Ernest Hemingway's "A Very Short Story" appears to violate some earlier practices we have suggested: The scenes are many and brief, and the key characters are stock characters. However, we take the story to be a summary that relies on us knowing something about the events that render them typical. In parody, satire, and allegory, the characters exist to drive home a message, and so we do not expect the writer to develop them in the same way as we might in another type of story. The story and the plot are simple: Boy meets girl; boy loses girl. The wartime setting provides the set, so to speak. The characters—a young, wounded solder who falls in love with the young nurse—have been used in a thousand stories and movies. The events are quite what we might expect, and the scenes are almost like a movie scenario (an art film, no doubt, because the heroes are not reunited), mostly narrated rather than shown. Here are a few of the scenes or presumed scenes:

1. An opening on the hospital roof with a wounded soldier and a young girl who have fallen in love (or, at least, fallen in sex) and who have sex
2. The operation scene
3. Settling into a type of hospital domesticity
4. A scene in the church (the Duomo)
5. The letters arriving
6. A scene in which they talk about their wedding plans and decide to hold the marriage after he has a job in the States
7. A quarrel scene on the train
8. A trip home
9. Luz returns to hospital
10. Luz is seduced by an Italian major (of course)
11. Luz writes a dear John letter
12. The major dumps Luz
13. Luz writes to America to tell the young soldier (now former) about the end of the affair
14. The boy takes a ride through Lincoln Park and makes love to a salesgirl who gives him gonorrhea

In fact, Hemingway touches upon so many expandable scenes one could almost write a novel from "A Very Short Story." In a way, he demonstrates how the shortest plot contains a long story.

Hemingway condenses a typical story (it probably reflects his own experience of being jilted) into a small area to show us that it was a typical pattern during and after the First World War. He expects us to understand that war brings on feelings of impermanence, isolation, and separation that put people under intense pressure to seize the moment and rush into romantic relationships. The scenes that rush along, tumbling over one another, capture the intensity of a wartime romance. The plot is driven by the sequence of scenes, but readers have to supply the elaboration and connections from their experience with literature and life.

But, once the war is over, the romance is likely to cool. It's an old story. The assumed scene in which we are told that Luz and he agree to wait, linked to the scene when they have the fight, suggests that it is Luz who convinces him to go back to America without her. Because Hemingway reveals none of their back story, we don't know either character's motives based on an elaborately presented background. What the characters did before the war, what they will do in the future (except have some unfortunate sexual encounters) we know nothing of, nor need we. The characters don't need to be three-dimensional because in this story what counts is what they do, not why they do it. It's wartime is a sufficient reason. The beginning scene is a lesson in how a few, well-selected details can suggest all we need to know for the occasion, as in a political caricature. Hemingway shows what he needed to show to engage the reader.

Despite the brevity of the scenes, Hemingway does dramatize those that are a bit longer. In the opening scene we learn that the affair has already begun, that the war is on (the search lights), and that they have been having some kind of party on the roof (the bottles which we assume are wine bottles). In a later scene, we see them in church where, we assume, they are praying for his safe return. Hemingway sketches the moment by letting us know that there are other people and that it was "dim and quiet." After the armistice, when he gets the letters, sorts them, and reads them, Hemingway neatly sums up their content in a sentence that, considering later events, becomes ironic: "They were all about the hospital, and how much she loved him, and how it was impossible to get along without him, and how terrible is was missing him at night." An experienced reader will intuit that a reversal has been foreshadowed. In a later moment, after the major ditches her, Luz's unanswered letter to Chicago suggests that she is both regretful and hopes to reopen communications and, perhaps, revivify their relationship.

The plot begins on the roof with a love affair and comes to an end in lust and venereal disease. The brief and suggested scenes allow us to see the curve of events over a longer period of time than one might expect in "A Very Short Story."

●　●　●　●　●　　　*EXERCISES*　　　●　●　●　●　●

1. How is "A Very Short Story" not short? Why might Hemingway have decided to move the story along so rapidly? How does he indicate that the others have empathy for the couple? Why is the narrator omniscient? Are there any indications that Hemingway might have had his tongue in his cheek when he wrote this story?

2. Describe the transitions from event to event. What does Hemingway assume you know? Put in one or two such suggested but not stated transitions.

3. Every paragraph, in fact almost every sentence and sometimes part of a sentence, contains a scene. Choose one and expand it with detail. As much as you can, keep to the Hemingway voice.

● ● ● ● *ADDITIONAL EXERCISES* ● ● ● ●

1. Examine the structure of scenes in Blackwell's "You Won't Remember This." How many scenes are there? What does each accomplish? What kind of material is summarized? How are events handled that occur before the ongoing present time of the story?

2. Earley's "Just Married" is really one large scene surrounded by an opening and a short final scene. Why might Earley have structured his story that way?

VERISIMILITUDE

We could have dealt with this topic in any of the previous sections because the writer's successful handling of characterization, plot, setting, and scene creates **verisimilitude,** the feeling that both individual elements and the whole fiction is *like the truth*. Of course, in creative nonfiction your story elements and overall story *are* the truth.

A historian or biographer has to report literal reality, something that anyone else who has found the same evidence would report. (Differing interpretations, of course, are another matter.) Fiction writers have only to give the impression that their fictive history or biography follows the rules of evidence. Therefore, while writers cannot be arbitrary, they need not prove that the facts can be tested in the chemistry lab or FBI files. Verisimilitude is like NutraSweet: It needs to taste like sugar but not *be* sugar.

Inexperienced writers often waste energy trying to re-create literal reality rather than an impression of it. Experienced writers understand that, for the sake of a good story, readers are willing to suspend their disbelief in the "facts" of the fictive world. Thus readers already do half the job of producing a feeling of reality. For example, because we tell stories about our parents to others, we accept easily the appearance of storytelling that we find in Jones' "The First Day."

Readers don't task writers with explaining which chemical laws allow a prince to be turned into a flounder, or how a spaceship can go faster than light, or what motivates a white whale to go around eating legs. Readers never ask how first-person narrators can remember verbatim conversations that happened two or ten or thirty years ago. We could not read Coover's "Grandmother's Nose" if we stop to ask how all the non-naturalistic and naturalistic events can coexist. The little girl believes that the wolf can talk and so do we.

In fact, when the writer goes about nervously matching the fictive world to the phenomenal world, the reader begins to question the fiction. It is best not to explain how it happens that your character can fly. Just let your hero fly early and late, have Lois Lane believe it, and we'll believe it so long as we are convinced that the unbelievable fact works in the story.

Interestingly enough, a story will lack verisimilitude only if our flying character doesn't fly when, for example, abandoned on a lonely desert island (unless, of course, the writer has created a reason the character cannot fly in that particular circumstance).

Verisimilitude is maintained as long as the writer is careful about the following matters:

1. *The characters should behave consistently from scene to scene* (not just in one scene), or the reader must be prepared for a deviation from an expected behavior or trait. A character who has been a coward throughout cannot suddenly save a child from a runaway horse just because the writer has discovered that the situation requires the child to be saved and grow up to invent the electric lightbulb. Nor can the writer finesse the point by saying "something just came over him." If you haven't done it in the first place, you need to **foreshadow**—to find some way to suggest the possibility that the coward can be brave. In brief, a story begins to lack verisimilitude when the special identity of the character is ignored merely to satisfy the plot.

2. *Surprising plot elements shouldn't pop up merely to get out of a dead end.* The long-lost, rich uncle can't be made to appear just when the newlyweds are about to go down for the third time. (See **deus ex machina** in the Glossary.)

3. *All the props are planted before they are needed.* The gun doesn't just happen to be in the purse. Either we see it put into the purse, or we are convinced by other means that it is likely to be there. (Incidentally, if we are shown a loaded gun in a purse, it had better go off sometime in the story.) This principle is a variation of number 2.

4. *The outside reality that the story calls on the reader to know is rendered accurately.* When a writer depends on the reader's knowledge of outside facts for some of the internal effects of the story, then the facts must (a) have verisimilitude in the story and (b) accurately reflect outside reality. A chase scene in New York City that has the pursuer's car traveling due east on Broadway (mostly a north-south street) is likely to offend the experienced reader's sense of reality with no gain for the fiction. Readers will more easily accept Superwoman deflecting bullets with her bracelets than they will accept that she did it on the border between Alabama and Arizona. Unless your first person narrator is a mind reader, he or she can't know what someone else is thinking unless told. The need for accuracy cannot be overstressed. If your readers catch you in a factual mistake, you may lose them.

5. *Your characters must interact with the environment or "set" you have created for them in credible ways.* If a scene occurs in a howling gale on the deck of a schooner, don't have them whisper to one another. If your

characters are two recluses in a house full of cats, the cats will be rubbing up against the characters' legs, scratching at the Victorian sofa, and sniffing around the hamburger. One of your recluses will be forever shooing the cats away. For more on how characters interact with their world, see Chapter 12, "The Elements of Drama." The essential point is that we believe in characters who see, hear, taste, touch, and smell the world in which the writer has placed them.

Creating verisimilitude requires that you plot (or replot) so the "equipment" necessary to move the story—straw, cellphones, attributes, experience, ray guns—does not magically or awkwardly appear in the scene just at the moment needed. If you don't plan (or go back and fix up), the sudden appearance of the new element will unpleasantly surprise the reader: "How did that knife get there? Did I miss something? Why would George kill Andrea? I think the writer got stuck." When you have destroyed verisimilitude in this way, readers begin to ask the kinds of questions that destroy belief in your story.

As you can see, foreshadowing in both a limited sense (getting the gun into the purse) and a more profound sense (suggesting changes in relationships) is at the heart of creating an impression that the story is like reality.

Unsophisticated writers often try to justify an event—a coincidence, for example—that is not convincing in the story by saying, "But that's the way it happened." Strange though it seems, some things, like coincidence, happen more in "real" life than they can in fiction or, to put the issue another way, coincidence happens differently in life than it can in fiction.

For example, in real life you might be broke and alone in a big city, let's say Chicago. Night is coming on. Your family can't be reached because they've gone to Nepal on vacation. Besides, you don't even have enough money to make a call. You are getting frightened as you walk the Loop in the crowd of homeward-bound people. Suddenly a hundred-dollar bill swirls down in the stiff breeze off Lake Michigan and lands right at your feet. Saved! Once in a billion times you have won the lottery of life. In real life, the chance may be a billion to one, but there is room in reality for that statistical *one*.

In plotting, there are no statistics. Everything that happens, even a coincidence, is part of the writer's plan. The writer deals out the hundred-dollar bills for the character. The reader of a story would feel that the happy coincidence just described occurs only because the writer could not think of another, more logical solution to the character's dilemma. The wind-blown inheritance, no matter how well disguised, is a cop-out, a way of rescuing the character that does not grow from the situation (except that Chicago is windy) or from the character's identity. Because the writer has not plotted well, the surprise that has been sprung on us is not satisfying: No amount of foresight could have predicted it in this story.

In contrast, the surprise that grows from an inevitable but unanticipated event at the climax of the story is one of the pleasures you provide your reader, who says, "I should have realized that." Some stories are aimed directly at this pleasure—for example, O. Henry–type short stories or James Bond novels. But the surprise that is not inevitable, the surprise that readers cannot kick themselves for having missed because it was foreshadowed, the surprise that seems to exist only to keep the action going or to get the characters offstage—that kind of surprise destroys verisimilitude. In a way, what the reader says to the writer is "I'll suspend my disbelief, but only if you help me."

● ● ● ● ●   *EXERCISES*   ● ● ● ● ●

1. Can you think of ways to use such an unexpected event as the windblown money without injuring the reader's sense of verisimilitude? For example, what if you did not use the event at the end of a story but at the beginning? Work out the first paragraph of a story that has the event as its central incident. Can you think of any other ways to give the event verisimilitude?

2. List the ways in which the authors convince (or fail to convince) the reader that the following potentially unlikely circumstances are in fact likely:

    a. Mr. Doran's accepting the trap set for him rather than just moving out of the boarding house to avoid marrying Polly

    b. Little Red Riding Hood feeling she is in a real world talking to a wolf

    c. The mother becoming the bully at the end of "Sunday in the Park"

3. What techniques does Hemingway use in "A Very Short Story" so that we accept his story's reversals? Can you find elements of foreshadowing?

*"I guarantee you that no modern story scheme,
even plotlessness, will give a reader genuine
satisfaction, unless one of those old-fashioned plots
is smuggled in somewhere. I don't praise plots as
accurate representations of life, but as ways of
keeping readers reading. One of my students wrote
a story about a nun who got a piece of dental
floss stuck between her lower left molars, and who
couldn't get it out all day long. I thought that
was wonderful. The story dealt with issues a lot
more important than dental floss, but what kept*

*readers going was anxiety about when the dental
floss would finally be removed. Nobody could read
that story without fishing around in his mouth
with a finger."*

Kurt Vonnegut, Jr.

 ## PROBLEMS

In this section we discuss some typical problems of beginning writers. Some of these are illustrated here. Some would take an entire story to illustrate, so we have merely described the problem. In a sense, we are protecting the guilty and saving you from reading too much ineffective prose.

Needless Complication

A misguided sense of what makes for verisimilitude, or a desire to surprise the reader, can lead a writer to give a character an unconvincing action. In the following opening passage, the student writer is so intent on piling up details and creating a suspenseful mood that he fails to build the character and situation in a truly plausible way:

> Brian brushed his long blond hair out of his eyes, then quietly opened the door to his bedroom. He was tall and rather thin. As he gently closed the door, he thought himself lucky that his parents hadn't heard him come in two hours late from his date. The room was consumed by darkness except for the narrow streak of light along the bottom of the door. He turned and tip-toed over to his desk.
>
> He opened the drawer slowly and began to carefully sort through the disarray. It was hopeless, groping about in the darkness, so he reached over and drew the curtains open slightly. Moonlight shown in illuminating the scene. Bending over to look into the drawer, he spied them—a small bottle of pills in the back right hand corner. He pulled the pills out of the drawer and set them on his nightstand.

You undoubtedly spotted any number of problems in style, diction, and even grammar and spelling. But the conceptual failure would remain even after you smoothed out the rough spots. Here it is: Brian is searching for drugs in *his* desk. When the reader learns this, the elaborate description of the search becomes unconvincing. Brian should know just how to get his hands on the bottle. After all, he hid it. All the business about a hopeless disarray and letting in the moonlight rings false once we discover what he is actually doing.

No matter what genre you are working in, you have ultimately to decide what and how much telling detail you need. A useful technique is to fill your scene and then, in later drafts, whittle out the inessentials. What the reader does not see won't hurt you.

Misuse of Dialogue

Too often in premise or adventure fiction, the characters are just pieces on the writer's checkerboard. As a result, dialogue serves only obvious expository purposes. Because the writer of the following material is so concerned that the reader understand the situation, the dialogue seems to exist only for that purpose:

> "Colonel Yeshnick, I refuse to sign this visa for Donnis to defect to the United States," responded General Alexeev in a rejecting manner.
>
> Colonel Yeshnick replied placatingly, "Sir, he will be immigrating, not defecting to the United States, and you are the only one left from the Premier on down who has to approve it. Sir, with all due respect, you promised him that he would be allowed to leave if he would not retire from athletics until after the Olympic Games. Not only did he compete, but he won the silver medal, and also set a new...."

The dialogue seems forced and artificial because it is. It is in the service of exposition that could be handled more smoothly in another way. In fact, the entire story is told primarily through conversations between these two officers, while Donnis, the character whose fate is at stake, hardly gets any attention. Even though we are always hearing voices, we are never getting in touch with characters. They are doing the narrator's work. Note also the awkward, heavy-handed use of designators.

Here is a shorter example of dialogue being used, obviously and clumsily, to do the work of exposition.

> "You must be that Penny fellow from Bangor. I'm Mrs. Johnson. We're the caretakers. Wipe your feet. Give me your coat. The Cables are expecting you. Come with me."

This passage can also serve to illustrate another ineffective use of dialogue: the attempt at verisimilitude that comes from trying to detail the most trivial kinds of "actual" speech. In this category we include those interchanges of "hello" and "goodbye" that have no emotion or characterizing energy. Just because it is easy to make these exchanges sound authentic is no reason to use them in a piece of fiction. Better a few instances of indirect discourse—the narrator's "after saying hello" or "after stating his business" or "the introductions having been made"—than a tedious reproduction of speech. Rarely would we need to belabor this part of a scene or transition, and even more rarely would we need to have it dramatized. (See Chapter 13, "Dialogue and Its Problems.") We can't say too often that dialogue is part of the action; it is what characters do to each other.

Sudden Comfort

Beginning writers often call too much attention to the contrivances that their stories depend upon. We have read too many stories in which, within the course of seven or eight pages, morose lovers or spouses become suicidal, and when they need a weapon to blast themselves out of their misery, the author conveniently provides one—all this just as the story is about to end.

Case in point: Bill's wife has left him. He regrets that he has been a drunk and a bully, often forcing himself on her in brutal ways. But now, seeing that she has moved out, he convinces himself that all is lost. His tortured mind leads him to set up a romantic dinner for himself and an imaginary version of his wife. Just before he brings that special bottle of wine to the table, something draws him to a nightstand: "Bill reached under the drawer and pulled off an object that had been obviously concealed." Well, of course, this mysterious object is identified a few sentences later as the "32 caliber pistol" that he fires into his temple. End of the story. How convenient for Bill and for the author. (If Bill is the first-person narrator, the reader faces an additional shock.)

The sudden appearance of a gun or any other fortuitous plot saver happens, in part, because the story is weak and skeletal to begin with. However, only in first drafts, when the flow of events is taking on a shape, are such conveniences forgivable. Then it's time to recognize the problem and do something about it, such as the following:

1. To revamp the whole story because it is hackneyed
2. To create a plausible reason, long before it is needed, for a gun to be available, and to build that reason into the story with some subtlety
3. To avoid depending on the gun gimmick altogether

Sudden Omniscience

Once you have established a perspective from which events and information are revealed, you must stick to it. One student writer made his main character, Connor, the central intelligence. We go where he goes, see what he sees, and have access to his thoughts and feelings. Connor, who runs a bar, has decided to walk Katherine, one of his waitresses, to her car. It's late at night:

> As he walked her to where she had parked her rental car, he could see from her face that she was still upset over the night's events.

But wait! Nothing that comes earlier in the story allows Connor to know that she is driving a rented car. The narrator has moved too far outside of the limited perspective chosen for this story. We wonder whether this information has special importance (it doesn't) or is simply an attempt at verisimilitude or narrative density. Keep in mind that while detail creates the reader's sense of verisimilitude, too much or irrelevant detail only confuses him.

Ping-Pong

Shifting the point of view too rapidly, especially without any clear reason for breaking the convention of maintaining a single point of view throughout a scene (if not an entire work), disorients the reader and strains credibility.

In one student work, we are asked to follow the path of a mysterious killer, taking things in through his perspective: "The night sounds were a calming friend to him" and "he noticed a car light stop on the bridge above him" and "his adrenaline began to flow freely" establish the reader's focus. When the author writes "After the killer had ascended the sloping hill up to the bridge, his form became visible to the stranger waiting for him...," we are momentarily jolted by the shift in perspective, and to no good end.

The same type of mistake occurs in the following scene, in which a policeman, Bob Bryant, is questioning Miss Lee about the death of her boyfriend. Bryant is the story's central intelligence whose perspective the reader shares.

> Boy, you're losing your touch and your sensitivity, Bob told himself. "I'm sorry to bother you, but we need to ask you some more questions. Can you think of any reason why someone would have wanted Wayne dead?"
>
> Miss Lee seemed calmer now, but she never got over her agitation during the half hour she spent with Bryant.

Unless Miss Lee's agitation is shown outwardly (and it isn't) or somehow Bryant perceives it, we shouldn't be told about it.

Pogo Stick

Beginning writers often feel the need to sketch in many short scenes, presenting some bit of information in each but not developing any of them fully enough to further the plot or deepen the character. This quick jumping around from scene to scene without a clear direction only confuses the reader.

In the Bob Bryant story discussed earlier, an early scene in the station house contains a celebration of Bob's successful "sting" operation in which a major narcotics organization was busted and the leader shot. The only purpose of the scene is to establish that Bryant is a policeman, a fact that is easy to communicate when his present case is first mentioned. None of the other details in the scene have any relevance later on. In "A Very Short Story," Hemingway does present many brief stories, but they are connected by time and the overall action of the love story.

Wrong Technique

In the same story treated in the "Sudden Omniscience" section, the author has attempted to reproduce Connor's thoughts rather than simply characterize them:

"God it's hot," thought Connor, "maybe I should think about investing in an air conditioner for the joint. Yeah, and I oughtta set the temperature way low. The girls wouldn't be wild about it, but I bet business would triple. Hah—I'm a damn funny guy."

These thoughts read too much like self-conscious speech; even Connor's habits of pronunciation are reproduced. Better to simplify:

Connor wondered if he should buy an air conditioner. If he had one, he would set it way low. The girls wouldn't be wild about it, but business would probably triple. Connor was pleased with his own cleverness.

Notice how the revised second and third sentences come across clearly as Connor's thoughts even though they aren't given designators, quotation marks, or verbal quirks. The narrator has slid quietly in and out of Connor's mind.

Descriptive Clutter

Like needless complication, sometimes the search for verisimilitude ends in massed details that only slow the story down while the reader is forced to pay attention to "realistic" trivia. Here is an example:

> He went back to the van. The door on the driver's side was slightly rusting near the bottom front corner. He opened the door, climbed in, and closed the door. The sound of vibrating steel resounded throughout the car.

For this story, we don't need to know the degree or exact placement of the rust, nor the three steps the character takes to get behind the wheel. Essentially, the writer's job is to get him moving again. So, "He got back in the van and winced as the rusty door slammed shut" would do it.

Another kind of clutter comes from trying to introduce too many characters at once. Here is the opening of a novel that causes more confusion than clarification, especially since some of the characters mentioned here are never heard of again.

> Dolly McKee's timing was less than perfect. Sam Parker was just getting to the part of his meeting with the president that Ken Meyers had been patiently waiting to hear about.
>
> "I'm sorry to break in," Dolly said, her hand on the doorknob, little more than her birdlike face visible as she leaned into the room. "Levi says he's got to talk to Ken. He's upset about something. It sounds important. Can you handle it, or should I call Simpson?"
>
> Sonofabitch, Meyers thought. What a time for a housekeeping problem. Just when Parker might say something about whether Babcock was planning to reappoint him. He told Dolly to show the black man into his office.

Even though one might argue that these characters are real to one another, such a barrage of names, labels, and pronouns will raise any reader's anxiety level—and for no good reason.

Other Problems

We have no space to illustrate the story in which one action follows another and yet nothing happens. That is, the events don't reveal character or shape an understanding of some issue. Nor will we ask you to consider the other extreme: the story that constantly screams out its meaning by glossing every action and every physical detail as if the writer felt obliged to present both the story and its interpretation. Nor the kind in which the author has gone back and disguised all the evidence we need to make any sense out of what's going on, as if bewildering the reader is a worthy goal if one can later show how cleverly the writer has obscured the information. These and other problems take whole stories to illustrate. In any case, a reader, classmate, teacher, or editor will be quick to point out the myriad of difficulties in your work that interfere with effective story telling.

It is easy to go wrong in telling stories because so many demands come to bear at the same moment—character development, plot, exposition, description, narration. You can't let down your guard and cruise for a while, because what is said on page 20 has to connect with page 6 and both with page 23. You need constantly to anticipate, recognize, and then solve the problem during your revision. Of course, recognizing a problem you created in drafting is not always easy. Be tough on yourself.

"Books aren't written, they're rewritten. Including your own. It is one of the hardest things to accept, especially after the seventh rewrite hasn't quite done it..."

Michael Crichton

10

CREATIVE NONFICTION

> "*The word 'creative' refers simply to the use of literary craft in presenting nonfiction—that is, factually accurate prose about real people and events—in a compelling, vivid manner. To put it another way, creative nonfiction writers do not make things up; they make ideas and information that already exist more interesting and, often, more accessible.*"
>
> Lee Gutkind

 THE NATURE OF CREATIVE NONFICTION

"Creative nonfiction" describes a host of familiar subgenres including essay, personal essay, memoir, anecdote, and journal entry. In one sense, the term identifies an old bias that writing nonfiction is somehow a lesser creative activity than writing poetry, fiction, or drama. However, if we go back less than three centuries, we discover that writers like Daniel Defoe and Henry Fielding were borrowing the prestige of nonfiction for the new form, the novel, that they were developing. *Tom Jones* purports to be biography, and *Moll Flanders* comes to us in the guise of a slightly edited memoir by an untutored woman. The form in which the fiction is cast immediately confers reality—verisimilitude—on the narrative. After all, people do keep diaries, write history, and exchange emails. Put it another way: All your fictions come from real places, you and the universe. So, fiction and creative nonfiction are two sides of the same coin.

The term "creative nonfiction" reminds us once more that all writing can be creative and that the barriers between one genre and another are porous, as Tony Earley suggests in his postscript to the short story "Just Married" (p. 277). The foundations—precise word choice, style, structure—that we have discussed in all the previous chapters link nonfiction to the other genres and entail just as much problem solving, selection, and invention. From this point of view, a more useful term would be "literary nonfiction," suggesting that the distinction is not between creativity and noncreativity but between nonfiction written primarily to pass on information and nonfiction in which information serves other purposes. Look, for example, at the following two paragraphs, both describing the same event:

In April 18, 1906, a big earthquake struck San Francisco. Buildings collapsed and residents evacuated the city. However, Alice Eastwood stayed behind. She was botany curator for the California Academy of Sciences which had this major national collection of botanical specimens. Heroically, she gathered 1000 before the building collapsed. These botanical specimens can be viewed by the public to this day. This is an illustration of the commitment of collectors who shaped the American museum.

On April 18, 1906, at precisely 5:12 a.m., a massive earthquake tore through the San Francisco Bay area. Within minutes, downtown San Francisco was in flames. One after another, buildings collapsed. Terrified residents by the thousands fled their burning city. But one woman, a 47-year-old botany curator named Alice Eastwood, was seized by a different impulse. She left the safety of her Berkeley home and, dressed in the long skirt befitting a proper woman of the time, rushed across the bay toward the raging fires. Her destination was the museum where she worked, the California Academy of Sciences, repository of one of the country's most extensive collections of botanical specimens.

By 7 a.m. Eastwood had reached the smoke-filled academy building. Unable to use the crumbling marble stairs, she painstakingly inched her way along the iron railings until she reached the sixth floor. There she feverishly gathered more than 1,000 records and specimens. For hours, via a makeshift pulley, she lowered items to the street below. "The earthquake didn't frighten me" Eastwood later recounted. "What scared me more was losing my life's work." At last conditions forced her out of the building and she made a mad dash to join her rescued treasures. By 2 p.m. the Academy of Sciences was completely destroyed. But today those same botanical specimens, saved from a burning museum, can still be viewed. They survive thanks to the heroic efforts of an otherwise anonymous, but most assuredly dedicated museum curator.

Marjorie Schwarzer, *Riches, Rivals, and Radicals*

The first example is a report on a heroic event. The second example is meant to allow us to share the excitement of the event and to be involved in the heroic act. Such historical writing goes beyond the simple facts and allows us to share an experience, the dedication of a museum curator.

We don't mean to erect a brick wall between writing to report information and creative nonfiction. "How-to" subgenres can have a literary dimension even while their thrust is to provide the facts of the case. Many restaurant reviews, medical or exercise columns, and sports columns transcend—as reading experiences—the information and advice they contain. The additional dimension can come from the entertainment the essay gives us, from the aesthetic satisfaction we receive because the piece is so well written, or from our sense that the facts may add up to more than appears on the surface.

Creative nonfiction is likely to be the natural outgrowth of research, diaries, and journal work. In fact, your journal writing, if it is more than a flat record of events, is one kind of creative nonfiction. The very journal that Anaïs Nin kept (see pp. 28–29) partly to be a seedbed for stories and novels, with selection, revision and polishing surpassed her fiction. Though creative nonfiction comes in many packages, today it is most fequently thought of as short, sometimes fragmentary writing offered up with some kind of insight or emotional charge. That is, it has much the flavor of a journal entry.

A nonfiction counterpart to the novel is a work like Norman Mailer's *The Executioner's Song,* in which history is reimagined with a novelist's tools and techniques. Michael Herr's *Dispatches* (a series of highly stylized personal essays about the journalist's experiences in Vietnam), Ernest Hemingway's *Death in the Afternoon* (a mixture of narration and meditation on bullfighting), and Annie Dillard's *Pilgrim at Tinker Creek* (a meditative journal with fine observations of nature)—all represent different types of book-length creative nonfiction.

Contemporary creative nonfiction is most often—though, as we have seen, not always—told in the first person or with the strong sense of an "I" present. The unreality, if you will, of such nonfiction is that it purports to be literal, a "real" picture of what people did, felt, and thought. The very neatness of a piece like Rita Dove's "Loose Ends," however, should expose how she selected and shaped to reveal the events.

For years the following scene would play daily at our house: Home from school, my daughter would heave her backpack off her shoulder and let it thud to the hall floor, then dump her jacket on top of the pile. My husband would tell her to pick it up—as he did every day—and hang it in the closet. Begrudgingly with a snort and a hrrumph, she would comply. The ritual interrogation began:

"Hi, Aviva. How was school?"

"Fine."

"What did you do today?"

"Nothing."

And so it went, every day. We cajoled, we pleaded, we threatened with rationed ice cream sandwiches and new healthy vegetable casseroles, we attempted subterfuges such as: "What was Ms. Boyers wearing today?" or: "Any new pets in science class?" but her answer remained the same: I dunno.

Asked, however, about the week's episodes of "MathNet," her favorite series on Public Television's "Square One," or asked for a quick gloss of a segment of "Lois and Clark" that we happened to miss, and she'd spew out the details of a complicated story, complete with character development, gestures, every twist and back-flip of the plot.

Is TV greater than reality? Are we to take as damning evidence the soap opera stars attacked in public by viewers who obstinately believe in the on-screen villainy of Erica or Jeannie's evil twin? Is an estrangement from real life the catalyst behind the escalating violence in our schools, where children imitate the gun-'em-down pyrotechnics of cop-and-robber shows?

Such a conclusion is too easy. Yes, the influence of public media on our perceptions is enormous, but the relationship of projected reality—i.e., TV—to imagined reality—i.e., an existential moment—is much more complex. It is not that we confuse TV with reality, but that we prefer it to reality—the manageable struggle resolved in twenty-six minutes, the witty repartee within the family circle instead of the grunts and silence common to most real families; the sharpened conflict and defined despair instead of vague anxiety and invisible enemies. "Life, my friends, is boring. We must not say so," wrote John Berryman, and many years and "Dream Songs" later he leapt from a bridge in Minneapolis. But there is a devastating corollary to that statement: Life, friends, is ragged. Loose ends are the rule.

What happens when my daughter tells the television's story better than her own is simply this: the TV offers an easier tale to tell. The salient points are there for the plucking—indeed, they're the only points presented—and all she has to do is to recall them. Instant Nostalgia! Life, on the other hand, slithers about and runs down blind alleys and sometimes just fizzles at the climax. "The world is ugly,/ And the people are sad," sings the country bumpkin in Wallace Stevens's "Gubinnal." Who isn't tempted to ignore the inexorable fact of our insignificance on a dying planet? We all yearn for our private patch of blue.

Rita Dove from "A Handful of Inwardness" in *The Poet's World*

The opening anecdote about her daughter is the dramatic lever for Rita Dove's observation that television is attractive because it is so condensed and simple. Although everything in the piece is drawn from life, the elements are carefully selected to achieve the same effects of scene, tension, and character that a fiction writer wishes to create. As writers we are aware that the details, including the dialogue, are carefully distilled from dozens of such homecomings to make us experience the parent's sense of frustration.

Before reading on, take another look at "Loose Ends" and list all the elements that suggest we are dealing with an event transformed by memory, selection, imagination, and purpose.

Here is our list:

1. "For years" is obviously hyperbole, created for dramatic effect. Children don't behave the exact same way for years or watch the same programs for years.
2. Dove actually calls her anecdote a "scene" to signal us that she is creating a typical event, not an actual one.
3. "Thumped" and other words are chosen for dramatic effect.
4. The dialogue is offered as typical rather than as the perfectly remembered language of a specific conversation. This technique allows Dove to avoid the issue of whether an actual dialogue can be accurately remembered. Unlike a reported conversation in which the exact words have legal, political, or social import, in creative nonfiction readers suspend their incredulity for the sake of the truths in the narrative.
5. *Lois and Clark* is probably one of many television shows that Aviva enjoyed with members of her family. Dove chooses this one not only for the appeal of the specific but also to suggest something precise about her daughter's interests—beyond mathematics.
6. Dove makes the anecdote convincing through such selection and specificity. The diction and images ("life, on the other hand, slithers about...") appear chosen for effect as they are in a poem. (It's no accident that Rita Dove is, as a matter of fact, a poet of national stature.)

Though creative nonfiction uses many of the techniques we have come to associate with fiction—scene setting, character development, narration, and dialogue—these elements in nonfiction are more often (and more obviously) shaped in the service of the writer's message, as in Rita Dove's piece. Nonetheless, the reader must agree to believe that the events rendered happened as the writer reports. We are not suggesting that the writer violates the truth—which is the essential promise or contract of nonfiction—but rather that no writing that we would wish to read sitting before a fire on a chilly evening ever fully represents a slice of life. Selection and compression distort the reality of the minute-by-minute passage of time, the flow of sensation, and thought. Indeed, the conceptual level of a memoir is most likely a present-day overlay on a distant experience. The truth is the truth of memory and the truth of the revealed self. (See Philip Gerard's piece "The Fact Behind the Facts" on pp. 252–255 for an extended examination of "truth" and "the revealed self.")

In the following memory piece, a selection from *Fathering Words: The Making of an African American Writer* (St. Martins Press, 2000), the poet E. Ethelbert Miller does not attempt to render a sharply etched picture but rather a record of memory itself and how it skips about as each memory evokes another:

The day after my brother died, Carmen, one of his neighbors, said she saw him walking his dog. My brother Richard, who had changed his name to Francis, loved animals and so he took the name of the saint he loved.

Growing up in the South Bronx it was important to believe in something, and so my brother decided to believe in God. I met God one afternoon on Longwood Avenue in the Bronx. It must have been around 1958 and I was attending P.S.39, which was near streets like Beck, Kelly, and Fox. Longwood Avenue was the "big street" and I was not permitted to cross it alone. I was in one of those grades in school where you took naps and the teachers gave you cookies when you were good. On the day I met God I had been standing on the corner for almost an hour afraid to cross Longwood Avenue. All my school friends were gone and I was alone with cars passing by and the dark evening creeping in like one of my sister's boyhood lovers. I was afraid to cross the street without holding someone's hand, and so I did something my brother was good at doing. I started praying to God. I asked God to come for me to help me cross the big street. If he did, I promised I would be good for the rest of my life. I would never steal or lie. I closed my eyes and only opened them when I heard my father running across the street, cursing and trying to fix his clothes at the same time. When I was little I thought my father was God.

Sitting in the back of a black limousine, parked on a hill in a cemetery near Yonkers, on a cold day in December 1985, I saw my father cry for the first time in my life. It was one of those moments when the world slows down and you notice the color of air. You stare at your hands and wonder how long you will live or which member of the family you will bury next. My father, Egbert Miller, dressed in black, his shoes polished in a way he could never teach my brother or me, sat in the limousine waiting to return home after Richard's funeral. I watched him raise his hands and heard him mumble one word, "gone." Maybe this is how God will end the world. He will say one word and end everything. No fire or rain. I listened to my father, repeating one word and knew he would never be comforted again. Little did I know that another black limousine would come for me in two years. It would take me to my father's funeral. On that day I would begin to search for my own words in order to make sense of my loss. All the men in my family were suddenly—gone.

In the past whenever I was troubled I could sit down and write a few poems. But what I am recovering from now is a different type of heart surgery. Sorrow and grief can be found in the place within the blues where words end and moans begin. The singer is speechless because the hurt is so bad. The only thing one can do is ride the song.

The stream of Miller's recollections assume a meditative tone, as if told to us at a quiet moment in the day when the speaker is relaxed and among family or friends, almost as if at a wake. Notice how he moves from picture to picture without logical connectives, as in a poem. In a way, the "creative" part is how Miller chips out all but the essentials.

At the other end of the spectrum, James Jones' essay, which appears on the surface to be a news report from Vietnam, reveals his helplessness and despair.

The Beggar Woman

I had seen her on the Sunday, when I was walking back to the hotel for lunch. It being Sunday, there was almost nobody on the street. That made her more noticeable. I was as inured to beggars as the next man. In fact, I had just turned down two ladies with credentials, begging for some Catholic orphanage. If you did not get hardened to the beggars, you would have no money left at all—and you still would not have made a dent in them. But this one was not begging. She was standing, leaning against a shuttered Sunday storefront. I was across the street from her.

Something about her posture caught me. I thought I had never seen anyone look so beat. She stood with her head against the grillwork of the closed store, her face in the corner angle the grill made with the masonry. And she didn't move.

She seemed vaguely familiar, as if I might have seen her up the street near the hotel or the Times office, where the beggars congregated. She was dressed like any Viet woman, a conical straw hat, black trousers, a ragged *ao-dai*. There was no way of telling how old she was. An old US Army musette bag stuffed with something hung from her left shoulder, and she had a bundle of what looked like rags in her other arm.

I watched her a full four minutes, I timed it, and she did not move. Then her shoulders heaved themselves up slowly and fell, as if she were drawing a breath, and she became motionless again.

I wondered if she could be dying, standing there. Instinctively, like some animal reacting, I took a thousand-piastre note out of my wallet and crossed the street and touched her on the shoulder.

Her hand came up. I put the bill in it and patted her on the shoulder. Only then did her head come up, and she looked at me with such a dumb, wordless despair that it was as if someone had thrown acid in my face. I have never seen such a destroyed heart, such ravagement of spirit on a person's face. I turned and walked away, realizing belatedly that there had been a scrawny baby in the bundle.

I got as far as the corner before I could get myself stopped, or put my head in order. The baby didn't bother me. The baby didn't matter. It was the woman. I could not even put into thoughts what I was feeling. Most of us have defenses in our personalities. Usually, we have layer after layer of them. Even when we are dying, we can still put some last personality defense on our faces. This was a face from which the last, bottom layer of defense had been peeled away like an onion.

I took the rest of the money I had with me, four thousand piastres, and walked back to her and put that in her hand with the other note. She did not even look at it, and raised her face again, and her face did not change. However much money it was, it would not be enough. She knew it, and I knew it. It might keep her going for a week, maybe even longer, that was all. Somewhere under her defenselessness some part of her seemed to be trying to tell me she appreciated my concern.

I walked away, wondering what kind of hope I'd hoped to give. There wasn't enough money to help her. Not now. The United States had not helped her. Neither had the French. The South Viets hadn't helped her, the North Viets hadn't helped her, the VC had not helped her. And what any of them or all of them might do for future generations would not do her any good at all.

She was all of Vietnam to me.

The piece is more than a report that there are beggars in Vietnam. Jones transforms it to an indictment of the war.

● ● ● ● ●   *EXERCISES*   ● ● ● ● ●

1. Use Dove's essay as a model for your own consideration of the significance of MySpace or computer avatars.

2. Use Miller's piece as a model for juxtaposing your own memories.

3. Write a factually based essay on a contemporary political event in the mode of Jones with suggestions of your reactions to the event.

> "*The compression of the brief form, completely familiar to poets and to those who read poetry, gains a fine elasticity in nonfiction. Tone can range from somber to whimsical, lament to praise. Anything writers can do with long forms has parallels in brief forms.*"
>
> Peggy Shumaker

HOW THE WRITER CONVINCES THE READER

Exposure of Self

The "I" in a personal essay promises to be really you, not a character created to tell the story. You cannot say, "Hey, mom, it's a story I made up." She knows better. The "fictions" in creative nonfiction provide little distance between the actual you and the reader. To create a sense of authenticity, you have to look for the real feelings and beliefs and be willing to risk appearing foolish, ignorant, weak, mean-spirited, or any other of the hundreds of human frailties to which we are all prone. You, not your character, will show the warts to the reader even if, as we know, the self in the piece is hardly the whole truth. For example, in "The Fact Behind the Facts" (pp. 252–255) Philip Gerard is exposing his youthful naïveté as a reporter who thought he had all the facts but did not know the most important fact.

Or even more disturbing to some people might be the following passage.

I was twenty-five years old. He [Al] was thirty-eight. He was a black man, the son of a coal miner from Dolomite, Alabama.... I was a young white woman from Long Island working at Boston's anti-poverty agency. We had met ten months earlier, in June, and moved in together in October to an old Victorian house just past Brighton Square. I had a two-year-old daughter who couldn't say "Al." She transposed the consonant and vowel and called him "La." He got home from work first and would greet her upon her return from nursery school every day with a snack of Hawaiian punch and animal crackers. They cooked soul food, hooked rugs, and watched football together. He taught her to ride a bike and change the oil in the car.

Cecilia Cassidy from "Dialysis and the Art of Life Maintenance"

Though certainly not as unusual as it once was, some blacks and whites will react negatively to this piece because it describes a mixed-race sexual relationship (among other things). But even if the writer could write the piece without the facts of race, she must take the risk of exposing herself to rejection, or even danger, in order to render the emotions truly.

If the personal essay is not honest, the reader will spy out inauthentic emotions and react negatively to easy truths, such as "this teaches us to respect good writing and remember to call our mothers."

Testable Elements Hold Up to the Test

In presenting nonfiction to the public, you must make sure that your handling of events, dates, locations, and other people's attitudes stand up to scrutiny. In a work of fiction, readers may excuse a writer for creating a nonexistent intersection in a well-known urban neighborhood, but they will be far less tolerant in a work that purports to be rooted in fact. Similarly, unless you are from an alternate universe, you can't say you remember your father buying a new Studebaker in 1990 when the company had ceased operation in 1966. Or, "it was October 2002 when two hijacked jets slammed into the Twin Towers and ended my childhood innocence." And for the writer to claim "well—I always remembered it as being 2002" or "whatever" does nothing to mend the broken contract between writer and reader. If a person you are writing about was born in Hoboken, don't relocate to Newark for effect. In science fiction, investigators may find weapons of mass destruction in Iraq, but in a personal narrative, you can't have discovered them. (For additional examples, review "Verisimilitude" in Chapter 9.)

Anecdotes Must Feel Universal

Though readers can be engaged in and entertained by the colors and textures of the unfamiliar, the writer must make a connection between the freshness of the material and the familiarity of the felt experience—the shareable human element. In Naomi Nye's "Mint Snowball," we see the world of the old drugstore ice cream counter as filtered through two memories, her mother's recollections of her grandfather and Nye's recollection of her mother's stories. The familiar element here is the longing for a world lost.

Mint Snowball

My great-grandfather on my mother's side ran a drugstore in a small town in central Illinois. He sold pills and rubbing alcohol from behind the big cash register and creamy ice cream from the soda fountain. My mother remembers the counter's long polished sweep, its shining face. She twirled on the stools. Dreamy fans. Wide summer afternoons. Clink of nickels in anybody's hand. He sold milkshakes, cherry cokes, old fashioned sandwiches. What did an old fashioned sandwich look like? Dark wood shelves. Silver spigots on chocolate dispensers.

My great-grandfather had one specialty: A Mint Snowball which he invented. Some people drove all the way in from Decatur just to taste it. First he stirred fresh mint leaves with sugar and secret ingredients in a small pot on the stove for a very long time. He concocted a flamboyant elixir of mint. Its scent clung to his fingers even after he washed his hands. Then he shaved ice into tiny particles and served it mounded in a glass dish. Permeated with mint syrup. Scoops of rich vanilla ice cream to each side. My mother took a bite of minty ice and ice cream mixed together. The Mint Snowball tasted like winter. She closed her eyes to see the Swiss village my great-grandfather's parents came from. Snow frosting the roofs. Glistening, dangling spokes of ice.

Before my great-grandfather died, he sold the recipe for the mint syrup to someone in town for one hundred dollars. This hurt my grandfather's feelings. My grandfather thought he should have inherited it to carry on the tradition. As far as the family knew, the person who bought the recipe never used it. At least not in public. My mother had watched my grandfather make the syrup so often she thought she could replicate it. But what did he have in those little unmarked bottles? She experimented. Once she came close. She wrote down what she did. Now she has lost the paper.

Perhaps the clue to my entire personality connects to the lost Mint Snowball. I have always felt out-of-step with my environment, disjointed in the modern world. The crisp flush of cities makes me weep. Strip centers. Poodle grooming and Take-out Thai. I am angry over lost department stores, wistful for something I have never tasted or seen.

Although I know how to do everything one needs to know—change airplanes, find my exit off the interstate, charge gas, send a fax—there is something missing. Perhaps the stoop of my great-grandfather over the pan, the slow patient swish of his spoon. The spin of my mother on the high stool with her whole life in front of her, something fine and fragrant still to happen. When I breathe a handful of mint, even pathetic sprigs from my sun baked Texas earth, I close my eyes. Little chips of ice on the tongue, their cool slide down. Can we follow the long river of the word "refreshment" back to its spring? Is there another land for me? Can I find any lasting solace in the color green?

Naomi Shihab Nye, *Mint*

All of us have experienced moments that stick in the memory (a first smell or taste, a great catch, a family story of a better time) that is forever evoked by later experiences. It is this evocative power of memory we recognize and share with Nye. The mint snowball becomes her emblem that something is lost in contemporary life, or at least in her life.

When readers feel that they are sharing an experience not as voyeurs but because something like it has happened or could happen to them, they feel enriched. Of course, tell-it-all stories of the famous—frequently more fictional than nonfictional and popularly held to lower truth standards—often describe lives that could hardly be our own. For most of us, however, the interest and pleasure come from less pyrotechnic experiences. We are more likely to succeed because of honesty, close attention to the virtues of accuracy, and careful thought and selection of detail.

VIRTUES IN NONFICTION

If the entries in the following list sound like virtues of fiction as well as of nonfiction, of course that is because the distinction is fuzzy around the edges. In fact, contemporary philosophers and critics would say that there is no pure fiction or nonfiction. That may be true on the cosmic level, but for writers, practical differences exist at the working level.

Here is our list:

1. Creative nonfiction often tends to sound like conversation or musing, as in a journal entry or a letter. The style is closer to the colloquial or the familiar than in academic or business writing. However, we do accept the intrusion of more latinate diction and phrasing as well as a greater mix of diction levels than we are likely to be comfortable with in fiction. Rita Dove's "devastating corollary" is more formal than conversational, while the following sentence mixes levels effectively: "The salient points are there for the plucking." In "Chinese Medicine" (Chapter 11, pp. 278–284), Hilary Tham translates Chinese phrases into English, a convention that would be intrusive in a story but is perfectly acceptable in nonfiction of all types.

2. While fiction should "show not tell," creative nonfiction writers may specifically, though not always, state a thesis, a point they are trying to prove. Sometimes they will tell you exactly what it all means, as in the Dove, Nye, or Gerard pieces. Still, the most effective creative nonfiction does a good deal of showing, re-creating the event(s).

3. As we have discussed in more detail earlier, despite a carefully limited use of fictional elements, the writer promises to be as honest as possible about the events, emotions, and beliefs that the piece reports. It takes courage to tell an audience of strangers that your father kept a mistress, as Hilary Tham does in her memoir

4. The writer is almost always talking in the first person and, except for comic writers, tends not to wear a mask. In fact, of course, even the nonfiction writer creates a mask (persona), but the reader is not intended to feel that a mask exists. At the end of the piece, we think we can say: Dove or Tham *believes* so and so. As an illustration of different effects of mask, look at Tham's prose portrait of her father in "Chinese Medicine" and then at her poem about him (pp. 139–140). Notice how the personal anger is more diffused by the cooler tone Tham employs to tell about her father's desertion. This difference resides partly in the effect of the memoir's first person singular, which becomes the plural "our" and "us" late in the poem. In some ways, of course, the bitter final two lines of the poem and the understatement and control of that bitterness have more impact and tell a much different story to the reader than does the prose.

5. In most creative nonfiction, the writer often uses the story to explore an idea, to meander through a great number of considerations and reconsiderations, and to digress. In effective fiction, we feel that everything must fit the plot. In nonfiction, the writer might start in one place and end up in a completely different place with a new cast of characters. Often we are in the presence of a mind in the process of thinking, and a piece may feel unshaped (though the lack of shape should be a fiction

and a disguise). The structure of much creative nonfiction, when it is not strictly narrative/chronological, is the structure of discovery. Notice how Tham's "Chinese Medicine" starts off as if it is to be about growing up in a Chinese household but changes into a piece about discovery, disappointment, and anger. A variation is in Gerard's "The Fact Behind the Facts" where he uses his own foolishness as the springboard to describe issues in reporting and memoir.

PROBLEMS IN CREATIVE NONFICTION

Among the many problems that can sink a piece of creative nonfiction, the following are most weighty (and often just like the problems one finds in fiction):

1. *Poor storytelling that grows from lack of detail, ineffective selection of events or detail, clunky dialogue, and too much explaining:* We have discussed these elements in Chapter 9 and in this chapter.

2. *Factual elements that fail the truth or reality test as in the following sentence:* "While I drank my tea, I pressed the seashell to my ear as I anxiously opened one of mother's bibles to the first page." Try opening a book with one hand while drinking tea and pressing something to your ear. Pure invention is usually thought of as cheating. In 2005, Oprah Winfrey interviewed James Frey, the author of *A Million Little Pieces,* a memoir of his substance abuse, and endorsed his book as a reflection of social reality. It turned out that the book was loaded with events that had not happened to him. Frey was roundly criticized and Oprah felt that she had been conned. The principle is that readers feel swindled when what is alleged to reflect real events turns out to be fiction. (Of course, we are not concerned when fiction turns out to reflect real events.)

3. *Off-putting tone, especially mawkishness:* "I closed my eyes and urged my mind to wander back to those glorious summer days when I and the world were younger." "Urging" one's mind like one urges a horse appears rather a rough way to treat one's mind. Also avoid obvious attempts to impress the reader as in the following: "The strong scent of roses hindered my walking any farther in this old, well-trodden road in an ancient country. The teasing and the beckoning of this wild robust aroma captured my imagination." Not among the least of the problems in this prose is its failure to capture our imagination. (See also Chapter 4, "Language Is Your Medium.")

4. *The other side of that coin is flat writing, as in the following:* "The main mystery of my friend's life centered around his daily routine and one could tell the time by his odyssey from the Red Line Metro to his domicile in the apartment complex on East West Highway which sat at the

complex juncture defined by Wisconsin Avenue and Chevy Chase Section Four." Beyond the fact that "odyssey" does not exactly conjure up the image of a "daily routine" (unless meant ironically), the language and sentence structure are more suitable to case histories or legal reports (and not very precise ones, at that).

5. *When trying to create intensity or excitement, the writer may actually create a sense that the emotions are inauthentic—that is, false.* Consider the following:

> The dirty wooden box I carried into my house yesterday might have stayed at the estate auction if I'd known what it contained. I bid on it only because I had this weird sense of knowing its contents. Curiosity nearly got the best of me before I got it inside. I hurriedly opened the heavy domed lid.

Apart from any other difficulties in the passage, the author pretends to feelings that she could not have had, since the box turns out to contain memorabilia from her grandmother proving the truth of a pleasant childhood memory. So, surely she would have bid on it. About her mystical sense of knowing its contents—another reason to bid on it—we also have some doubt. The sum is that the reader comes to sense in the prose an attempt to create excitement in us with unreal report of the narrator's feelings at the time. Later on the same writer reports that following the experience, "I heard the blood running through my head...." How often has that experience happened to any of us?

6. *The piece fails as a whole to connect to universals and so has a true aimlessness, like a friend walking in and telling us, "Yesterday I got a dent in my fender."* We have neither the space nor the unkindness to print a long example, but the piece of nonfiction about the box cited in number 5 goes on to reveal that her grandmother's stories were based on fact. Gosh! That's the type of "true" anecdote that reports the facts but leaves us saying "So?" A variation of this problem is a story so private that though it may be gripping for you, your family, and friends, it lacks a context that will grip a larger audience. Look at the following series:

   a. My uncle Fred ran off to Arizona and married another woman without divorcing his first wife.

   b. My mother never talked in front of us kids about Uncle Fred, who ran off to Arizona and married another woman without divorcing his first wife.

   c. My mother never talked in front of us kids about Uncle Fred, her brother, who ran off to Arizona and married another woman without divorcing Aunt Sally, my father's sister. I knew it was wrong of me, but I kept in contact with him. However, I never told my parents.

The last in the series starts to have possibilities because it evokes the truths of family secrets and betrayals. For another example, look at Hilary Tham's anecdote about her threat to charge her husband for housework. Without the context of the other memories, it lacks power and becomes more of a cocktail party anecdote. Or, consider what would happen if you removed the last paragraph from Nye's piece (pp. 245–246). It would then be just a report her mother's memories of a lost recipe.

In a way, of course, what we are telling you here is a truth of all writing: You have to have something interesting to say, and you have to say it well. The prior condition for doing both is to do some serious observing and thinking about both the exterior and the interior worlds.

● ● ● ● ●   *EXERCISES*   ● ● ● ● ●

1. Starting with a family story of a lost opportunity or skill, write a memoir of how that story affects your vision of your life now.

2. Using Gerard's piece "The Fact Behind the Facts" at the end of this chapter, write a personal experience that leads you to consider best practices in some profession or activity.

    FINDING MATERIALS

Reading

It goes without saying but we'll say it anyway: Read widely in historical and contemporary literary nonfiction. Examine the classic models of Seneca, Plutarch, Montaigne, Addison and Steele, Lamb, Emerson, Thoreau, Orwell, and E. B. White. Attend to such contemporaries as Truman Capote, Annie Dillard, Peter Matthiessen, Barbara Ehrenreich, and Frank McCourt. You read not only to develop a wider sense of the possibilities in creative nonfiction (subject matter, form, and technique), but also to develop your knowledge of the areas that you mean to pursue in your own writing.

Exploring Yourself

In creative nonfiction, you can make an essential connection between your responses to experience and your reader's curiosity. If you handle the writing task well, this curiosity will lead to the reader's imaginative engagement with your responses. What do you have to share? Who are you? Think of all of the ways in which you interact with other people, the various roles you play as family member, friend, lover, student, political partisan, employee, leader, patient, shopper, borrower or lender, athlete, hobbyist, worshipper, and writer. In each of these roles, and in so many others, you have particular stories to tell that can connect you with readers who have found themselves in similar roles.

What irks, pleases, or perplexes you? How do you celebrate holidays? Birthdays? What are your feelings and thoughts at weddings, anniversaries, or funerals? In what areas do your most passionate feelings lie? What pictures in the family album get you most upset or bring you the most joy? Why? This is the kind of work you can begin working on in your journal and later develop with greater attention to form and audience.

Interviewing, observing, and researching other people will provide ample material for third-person nonfiction narratives. You should learn some of the basic techniques of the interview. With carefully recorded quotations, you can provide real voices that make the character portrait and the whole essay convincing.

● ● ● ● ●   *EXERCISES*   ● ● ● ● ●

1. Use Hilary Tham's "Chinese Medicine" as a springboard for your own tale of conflict between cultures or generations.

2. Reread Hilary Tham's piece and her poem "Father" (pp. 139–140). Take an experience that you have had when you were disappointed in someone you love. Write about the experience first as nonfiction, then as either fiction or poetry.

———————————●———————————

On the surface, creative nonfiction seems as open-ended as "free" verse. It appears that anything goes; all a writer has to do is put down a personal experience in any form whatsoever. However, to move an audience, a personal essay or journal piece requires the same old precisions of observation, language, and shaping that any other successful writing demands.

> *"Writing creative nonfiction is all about carpentry, about nailing the pieces of narrative together with transitions, about spiking the past to the present to clarify both, about gluing surface events together to add strength and depth and meaning."*
>
> Shane Borrowman

We end with Phillip Gerard's piece. Pay particular attention to how the narrative backstops the general principles of nonfiction writing. In a way, his creative nonfiction is also a lesson in writing nonfiction and serves as a review of the chapter.

The Fact Behind the Facts
or
How You Can Get It All Right and Still Get It All Wrong

PHILIP GERARD

I was a cub reporter for a small weekly newspaper, fresh out of college, where I had studied anthropology and English literature and taken not a single course in journalism. My editor was an old-fashioned newspaper man, the kind you might find in one of those old black-and-white films with fast snappy patter in which everyone is constantly saying things like, "Sweetheart—get me rewrite!" One day he hung up his phone and said across the newsroom, "Go over to the high school—some kid just saved his girlfriend from a burning car. Get me a hero story." I'm quoting him to recreate the sense of urgency that came across, but of course that's a trick, a convention of the genre. It's been years and I'm trusting my memory to give me the gist of what he said, the way a writer usually must in any memoir—and "hero story" were key words.

So I chugged over to the high school in my washed-out yellow1962 Ford Falcon and there, indeed, in the parking lot sat the scorched hulk of a car, still smoking. Fire engines were pulled up nearby and a crowd of students and teachers had gathered. I got to work.

I interviewed the fire fighters, the boy who had saved his girlfriend, the girlfriend herself, the guidance counselor, and other witnesses. I got the license number of the car, wrote down its make and model and described the damage. I noted the shadow of the gym slanting across the tarmac, the temperature and clouds and the size of the crowd. My notes were copious and thorough, much longer than the story I would write.

Back at the office, I typed up an account of the incident and it ran on the front page with a photo and a headline about boy-hero saving girl—my first front-page byline. My career was launched. Puffed up with professional pride, I celebrated. I don't remember where, but very likely I hoisted a few beers at the Deer Park Tavern, a local watering hole where we used to hold our weekly staff meetings over lunch.

In any case, some years later I was sitting at that same bar enjoying a beer and a sandwich when a stranger took the stool beside me. He said, "I know you," and I was pleased to be recognized. "You wrote that story about the burning car," he went on, and I admitted that yes, I had. "Well," he said, "it was a great story. You got everything right except one thing."

What was that, I wanted to know?

"The guy set the car on fire himself."

According to him, the boy-hero and his girlfriend were having a spat. In a fit of anger, he locked her in the car and then set it ablaze. Almost immediately he had second thoughts, and so he smashed the passenger side window and hauled her out. And that was what everybody else saw: the rescue and the two of them making up.

I asked around and got confirmation from various other people around town who remembered the incident. Mostly they laughed about it, figuring the girl wasn't ever in any real danger. It was just one of those stupid things that guys do when they're tumbling in and out of love.

But I was mortified. That stranger's words felt like a spanking. I had reported every detail exact and true. I had verified every fact in the piece. I had described the scene as I had witnessed it with my own eyes. All these years later, I don't remember many of the details, but I do remember how hard I worked at the time to get them right.

Every fact was true, and yet the story was utterly false.

I had forgotten a fundamental truth about stories—or maybe I hadn't yet learned it: *Backstory drives present action.* I had assumed I was coming in at the beginning of story, that the sequence of events began with the car catching fire. In fact, I was entering a story already in progress for hours, days, maybe weeks before I stepped onto that parking lot and smelled the reek of charred automobile. That was already the first act curtain.

I think of that experience whenever I am tempted to draw too neat a conclusion, whenever I see a story whose arc is just too perfect, whenever I find myself working too fast, or proving out my own preconceptions. There is a kind of gravity that pulls us toward a well-shaped narrative, a pleasing closure. We encounter a set of facts and almost immediately are tempted to overlay a pattern on them, one of several stock patterns we have come to recognize, as if we already see the headline in our mind's eye: *Boy-Hero Saves Girl From Burning Car.*

Sometimes the facts do indeed point to an obvious story. But more often there is a larger true thing, a Big Fact, behind the Facts of the Case. It is this fact behind the facts that determines the meaning of all the other facts, creates a context for interpreting what our eyes are seeing and what our informants are telling us, and dictates the true syntax of a story.

For every story, like every sentence, has a syntax: a dynamic architectural cohesion that determines meaning, based on three qualities that every word in a sentence has—as does every element of a story:

1. Sequence: in what order the elements are arranged, and where in that sequence any particular element fits.
2. Priority: the importance of any element relative to other elements.
3. Relationship: a special connection to each other element and to the story as a whole.

You can see at once that *priority* involves a sequence of subordination—this thing is *more* or *less important than* that other thing. And of course to say that implies a relationship or lack of one between any two elements—and assumes you have discovered all the elements, including that first big fact that colors all the others individually and collectively.

Finding the fact behind the facts is crucial in both public and private stories.

Our culture has become so infatuated with memory that we writers too often begin and end our research there. I realize that caveat even now, recounting my little story about the burning car and wondering just how much of my memory to trust—did he really break the window glass to get her out? Since I tell the story only to illustrate how I got something very wrong, and I am not claiming any consequence for the incident itself, I will leave it drawn anecdotally, rather than commit to the research I would feel obliged to do if I were naming names and writing about it as an *event* rather than as a cautionary tale, for then it would affect others' lives and you, the reader, would have the right to a full and accurate accounting. I would check out other newspapers of the time (the one I worked for went out of business and its archives were destroyed), track down people who might have attended that high school in those days, consulted the alarm logs of the local fire department.

Memory can be warped, it lies, it tells us what we want to hear. So part of this essay is a call to work beyond personal knowledge and thus beyond memory, to test that memory against other evidence in the world. Memory will rarely match that evidence very neatly, but this is a good thing. Discrepancy between memory and other evidence is not a problem—it's the point. The reckoning, the true story, lives in the space of the contradictions.

Bloggers now report their opinions as facts and don't really see the difference. The media reports the trivial facts of celebrities' lives and so many more important facts simply go unreported in our world. Our government is obsessed with secrecy, with hiding facts, often facts that are or should be quite public—like the heartbreaking fact of military coffins being unloaded from transport planes at Dover Air Force Base, week after week.

There are layers of factualness: the box of parts from which we construct a story, and the intelligence behind the facts that determines how we shape those parts into a meaningful whole.

Even if you strive honestly and diligently to get your facts straight, to write from good research and personally persuasive knowledge of backstory, you'll still get something wrong. But that's the only chance you have to get it right.

If you begin by fudging facts, you've already drifted one degree off true. Like a ship with a minor compass error, the farther you travel, the farther out of true your story becomes, and after you've traveled far enough you are miles away from the true course. Worry the little facts, get them right, fret over being exact.

Had I been a better reporter that long-ago day, I might have asked some simple questions: How did the fire start? Do cars usually just burst into flame? How was it that she was in the car and he was outside it? How was she locked in?

I might even have thought to ask him, "Did you set the fire?"

And perhaps the most important question I failed to ask them both was this one: "What were you doing just *before* all this happened?"

"*But aside from the fun that comes from committing shameless acts of libel against your family and acquaintances, creative nonfiction is great because it lets you tell your own stories. I think it's just about the best way of letting others know who you are, and one of the most lasting.*"

Dustin Michael

CHAPTER 11

STORIES AND NONFICTION

You Won't Remember This

KATE BLACKWELL

Angelina lay in a green canvas chair in her garden and watched a white butterfly play among her flowers. She had never in her life sat still long enough to watch a butterfly; even as a child, she was always busy. "High strung," her mother used to tell her, "you were a high-strung child." "It's so good to see you sit," her mother said now, as though her sitting meant Angelina was content. In fact, she felt like a creature that had been washed up on a strange and beautiful shore. Her body was swollen from all the liquid it retained in the summer heat. She had no energy even to think. The baby seemed torpid as well; it no longer struggled inside her, but occasionally gave a languid kick as though to remind her it was still there, in no hurry to come out.

At first, when she found out she was pregnant, she had reacted in the same brisk, efficient manner she was known for in her professional life. She chose an obstetrician, a well-known, respected doctor, and assembled a wardrobe of maternity clothes, many of them borrowed from friends since she did not expect to wear them again. She read books on the first nine months of life, studying pictures of the fetus at each stage in its growth, trying to relate them to the changes in her own slim body, to the thickening and swelling and soreness, to the ugly spots that appeared on her face, to the shift in her sense of balance that caused her to be always conscious of the way she walked and stood and sat.

At night, before she and her husband went to bed, they practiced the exercises for childbirth they learned in a special class. They were both determined to do everything right, her husband especially. "No, you're not relaxed enough," he would say, holding up her leg under the knee and letting it drop. "You need to relax more. Take a deep breath." Then, while she practiced the little panting breaths she had been taught, he would hold his face close over hers, panting, too, his eyes fixed, his mouth opening and closing like a fish's.

She went to work every morning as usual, coming home a little more tired each day. "Why don't you take off these last few weeks?" her husband suggested. "You don't want to be too tired when the baby comes." But she kept going to the office until the doctor told her the swelling was too great; she would have to stay at home where she could keep her legs up. "It won't be long now," he said.

By then, her mother had come to help her finish getting ready. "You just sit. I will do everything," her mother said, making Angelina remember how it had been when she was a child and her mother did everything. She did not argue, but sat while her mother cooked their meals and prepared the room where the baby would sleep. "I feel guilty letting you do all this work," she said, watching her mother weed the garden in the heat of the day. "Don't be silly," her mother replied. "That's what I'm here for." And Angelina did not protest anymore, but lay quietly inside her great body, watching the white butterfly flit around her garden, never stopping anywhere very long, only an instant, before flitting on again.

Her mother went out and bought everything the baby would need and came back and showed Angelina the little white T-shirts and flowered kimonos with strings that tied at the bottom and a few exquisite tiny gowns with tucks and embroidered rosebuds. "They'll be used only once, you know," she told her mother, and then regretted saying this because it seemed she was ungrateful.

"Oh, and look at this," her mother said, holding up a length of yellow satin ribbon. "It's for the bassinet." The white wicker bassinet that had been Angelina's when she was a baby. Her mother had given it away but found it again, in someone's attic, and brought it to her. "I thought you might like to have this," her mother had said. "I remember so well when you were a baby in this bassinet."

While her mother was out shopping, she rested in the white bedroom she shared with her husband. Everything in this room was white; the walls and ceiling were painted white, the shutters that enclosed the windows were white, even the bedspread was white. One afternoon, while she was resting, a fly got trapped in the room. It hurled itself frenziedly against the window panes, trying to get out; then careened around the room, ricocheting off walls and ceiling. The black fly seemed particularly horrible in all the white. But she did not have the energy to get up and let it out, or kill it. When her mother returned, Angelina in was in tears, lying on the white bed. "Why, what's wrong? Is it the baby?" her mother asked. Angelina did not answer, only lay there, tears streaming down her face.

Her mother stroked her forehead. "Can I get you anything?" She did not seem to notice the fly. "I'll bring you a glass of iced tea." On her way out of the room, her mother picked up a magazine and killed the fly, neatly, with one stroke, on the window sill. Angelina fell asleep in the silence that followed the death of the fly.

When she could not stand sitting anymore, she took her heavy body out for a walk, moving slowly in the wet heat, her mind unusually alert. She noticed everything, all the elaborate details of the downtown neighborhood where she and her husband lived—the window boxes planted with fern and geranium, the filigreed porch lamps, the iron fences, the carved stone lions on either side of a door, the subtle colors of the houses, mauve, salmon, fawn, honey.

During these walks, she felt curiously at a distance from everything, the way a traveler might feel traveling alone in a strange country. The feeling was not unpleasant. Inside her swollen body, she knew she was free to go anywhere, to look at anything, without fear or self-consciousness, the way she imagined a man must always feel. She no longer avoided the glances of strangers on the street or closed her ears to their remarks. When men with dancing eyes grinned at her as they passed, she smiled radiantly back at them. She knew they were not looking at her.

One day, passing a restaurant a few blocks from her house, she glanced in the window and saw a man she knew sitting at the bar. He was a heavy, dark, sensual man, older than she was; she had had a short affair with him before she married her husband. She stood at the window watching the man, thinking maliciously that if he looked up and saw her now, he would be ashamed and embarrassed. While she watched, standing close to the glass, the man stood up and she saw that he was with a woman, a thin, pretty, red-haired woman, who was laughing at something the man had said. They laughed together so heartily that Angelina began to laugh, too. She was still laughing when they passed her, on their way out of the restaurant, almost touching her. The man did not even glance at her, and she knew that she was right: she had become invisible. She walked slowly home, dragging her body through the oppressive heat, stopping often to rest because the baby's weight now pressed like boulders on her legs.

At home, her mother had changed into a pearl-gray dress and darkened her lashes. She thought how young and attractive her mother looked. In the middle of the table, her mother had placed a cut-glass bowl filled with deep pink roses from the garden and beside the bowl, a pair of heavy silver candelabra. "How beautiful everything is," Angelina said.

Her mother looked at her anxiously. "You've been gone a long time. Shouldn't you rest? Can I get you anything?"

"I'm going to sit outside," she said and went out into the garden and sank her enormous body into the green canvas chair, the only chair in which she could now be comfortable. Even here, she felt restless, as though all of her nerves were on edge, and she wanted to scream. Nevertheless, by the time her mother came out with a glass of cold tea for her, she lay still, her eyes closed.

When she woke, she heard her mother and her husband talking in the kitchen. Their voices were low and intense. "Maybe she'll decide not to go back to work at all," her mother was saying. Her husband said, "Oh, she's too good at what she does. She'd be bored at home. We'll get a nanny for the baby." "Yes, but she ought to take some time off," her mother insisted. "She's always tried to do too much. I worry about her." "Don't worry," her husband said. "She'll be fine. I promise you."

She listened in a detached way. It was as though they were discussing someone she did not know. Then she became irritated listening to the argument. She struggled to get out of her chair, but fell back heavily each time she tried. She began to laugh at her clumsiness; her laughter grew loud and shrill, until it was almost hysterical. Her husband and her mother came running out into the garden. "Are you all right?" her mother asked. Her husband bent over her, his eyes large and anxious, his face close to hers. "I'm fine," she sobbed, trying to control herself because of the pain that had started in her side. "When are we going to eat? I'm starving," though she had not thought of food until that moment. Her mother said, "I'll put it on right away," and hurried back into the house. Her husband begged, "Tell me how you feel." He put his hand on her stomach where the baby was moving continuously, causing tiny ripples like waves just under the skin. Immediately, he took his hand away, and she thought, *It won't be long now.*

At dinner she ate ravenously, tearing off chunks of bread and putting them into her mouth with pieces of tender veal. Her husband and her mother looked at her thoughtfully. "She certainly seems to be eating for two tonight," her mother said. "Yes," her husband agreed, "everything she does affects the baby." He paused and her mother said, "You've prepared yourselves so carefully. You've thought of everything, including the birth itself. You even know how to breathe!" Her mother laughed. "These things used to be handed down from mother to daughter. But I was knocked out the whole time. I wouldn't know what to say."

Angelina was so full that her stomach pressed painfully against her ribs, pushing up under her lungs so she could hardly breathe. She sat very still thinking if she did not move, she could not suffocate, but the pressure increased until she felt her stomach might rise into her throat. She tried to breathe using the little panting breaths she had been taught in the class, but they did not help. She felt dizzy and gripped the arm rests of her chair to keep from falling over. "Here's to a wonderful dinner," she heard her husband say. He looked flushed and handsome in the candlelight, and she could tell from his voice that he was a little drunk. "And here's to many more good dinners," her mother responded gaily. She held up her glass. Angelina's husband held up his, too, and after a moment, Angelina picked up her glass of tea. She had a brilliant smile on her face, despite the fact that she was suffocating. They reached toward each other, but the table was too large for the glasses to touch.

"Don't you want some coffee?" her mother asked. "No, thank you," Angelina said, getting up from her place. "Please excuse me." She went into the garden, carrying her enormous body slowly and carefully, breathing in small shallow breaths through her mouth. Outside it was dark; all around her were the bright unwinking lights of houses and apartment buildings and above, the glow of the city had turned the sky a vivid pink, as though there were a fire somewhere. A siren wailed, making her think of the way a wolf's howl must sound in the wilderness. I am not used to this, she thought. I have never known any of this before.

She paced slowly over the swept brick, panting as the pain rose, breathing deeply when it receded. You will not feel pain, they had told her in the class, only pressure, as the baby tries to get out, and you will handle it by breathing and by concentrating on something. Now she realized they had deceived her, the way people sometimes deceive children by telling them it won't hurt or it will only hurt for a minute.

When her husband and her mother came out onto the porch, she was walking slowly around the small garden, staring fixedly at the ground. Her husband came out to her and said, "It's the baby, isn't it?" When she did not reply, he said, "Don't you want to come inside and lie down?" He reached out to touch her but she drew back with such a fierce mute stare that he went quickly back up on the porch.

"Why does she have that look on her face?" asked her mother in bewilderment. "She's concentrating, that's all," said her husband. "There's nothing to worry about. After all, women used to drop their babies in the middle of a field and go right on working." Her mother turned to him with a shocked look and he said quickly, "I'm sorry. I don't know why I said that."

After a few minutes, her husband went out to her again. "We ought to call the doctor now, darling." Angelina gave him another terrible look and went on with her pacing and he went inside and called. "I'm afraid she's beginning to panic," he told the doctor. "She won't speak to me." But the doctor reassured him. "That's natural. She's concentrating. Just find out how far apart the contractions are and call me back."

Her husband made himself a large drink and took it into the living room, where her mother sat holding a magazine. "I can't watch her anymore," her mother said. "There's nothing I can do to help her." She began to weep soundlessly. "Please don't cry," her husband said. "Everything is fine. Maybe you could go and see whether her bag is ready." Yes, I'll do that," her mother said, wiping her eyes. She glanced at the stopwatch he was holding. "What on earth is that for?" "It's to time the contractions," her husband explained. Her mother shook her head sorrowfully. "I'm sorry I can't help you," she said as she started upstairs. "I was knocked out the whole time. I really don't know anything about it."

Angelina continued walking, taking deep sighing breaths and holding her belly until another pain came and then she breathed in quick gasps and let her arms fall to her sides because she could not stand to touch herself. Her husband walked beside her with his stop watch, trying to guess when the contractions came from the changes in her breathing. After a while, he said, "Eleven minutes. They're eleven minutes apart," and went back inside to call the doctor. When he left, she looked up quickly at the glowing red sky that seemed to have grown brighter, more livid, since she began to pace. Then her womb contracted and she lowered her head and clenched her fists. It took all her determination to keep moving. Her husband stood on the porch and watched her plodding around the garden holding her enormous stomach, her legs like an elephant's, her head bent onto her breast. Just like an animal, he thought, and quickly stopped himself and thought instead about the baby, his child, that was about to be born.

Though she did not want to leave the garden, she was finally too tired to walk and she let her husband help her into the car. She lay on her side in the back seat, no longer trying to keep track of the pains as she had been taught, of the way each one approached, swept over her, and receded. She heard her husband talking to himself. "We're into the second stage now. Contractions five minutes apart. Doing fine." She kept her eyes open and stared at the fantastic designs of light that played on the car seat when they passed a neon sign or street lamp. "How's it going back there?" her husband asked. But she said nothing. She remained mute even after they reached the hospital, never speaking when they strapped her onto the table under the brash lights, or when the nurses touched her with their cool needlelike hands, or when the doctor gave instructions in his calm objective voice. At last, when volcanic eruptions seized her just before the baby was born, she broke her silence and uttered terrific neighing grunts of pleasure.

After that, she lay quietly, her eyes shut. When she opened them, her husband was bending over her, his face close to hers, his large dark eyes glowing with tears. She looked at him, wondering what she wanted to say to him.

"Hello," she said finally.

"We have a baby," he replied, as though in answer to a question.

"Yes," she said.

"You were wonderful," he said.

"No," she objected. "I wasn't."

"It's over now. Everything's fine."

Angelina felt terribly angry about something. She looked around the room for the first time; everything was white: white walls and ceilings, white lights, doctor and nurses in white, her husband white except for his dark eyes above the white mask. She too was covered with white as she lay on the table.

"Don't you want to see her?" her husband asked. "She's beautiful. She looks just like you."

Angelina lifted her head and stared at the baby, wrapped in white, lying on her stomach which was now flat and lifeless. All she could see was the baby's head, shiny and pointed, covered with long black hair.

"Like me? Don't be silly," she said and lay back again.

A nurse picked up the baby and put it in the bend of Angelina's arm. Angelina studied its angry red face and swollen slits of eyes through which the baby seemed to regard her hostilely. Suddenly, like a small furious animal, it burrowed its face into her side. She pushed it away, horrified.

"You plan to nurse your baby, don't you?" the nurse said.

"Of course she does," her husband replied. "We've read all about it. We know it's the best way."

She lay completely passive while they pulled the sheet down from her breast and turned her so the baby could reach the nipple. At first, the baby could not find what it wanted; it gnawed at the side of her breast and the skin under her arm, until the nurse took the nipple in her fingers and shoved it into the baby's mouth. Angelina cried out at the sharp pain when the baby clamped onto her tender flesh. Then she sobbed in great noisy gasps while the baby pulled and sucked, stabbing her repeatedly with pain.

Her husband tried to wipe away her tears with his sleeve. "Darling, sweetheart, don't." He looked distraught. He rushed off and came back with tissues with which he dabbed at her face. After a while, the baby fell asleep, exhausted, and the nurse picked it up. "We'll bring her to you in your room in about an hour," the nurse told her. "Please don't," Angelina said. "I want to sleep."

The nurse glanced at her and went out carrying the baby. "You'll feel better after you rest," her husband said. "I'm going to call your mother now." He kissed her and hurried away.

They took her back to her room, a small soft-beige room with gentle lighting. She got into bed and yawned luxuriously. Her body felt light and free. She happened to notice her foot and saw how thin it was again, how white and delicate with its tracing of blue veins. For a moment, she felt full of impatience, ready to leap up and run out to do all the things she used to take pleasure in doing. But in reality, she was so tired she could not even lift her hand. Now she would sleep and when she woke, her child would be there and she would nurse it and do everything for it. Angelina made a little mewing sound in her throat. It was all so irresistible, yet it had nothing to do with her. She lay listening to the rushing traffic on the street below her window, which sounded like waves beating on a shore, and thought of a white beach, an inlet curled like a woman's fingernail, and a jutting of bleached rock on which a still dark figure lay.

Then the nurse came in with the baby. Angelina felt a stirring in her breasts. Gingerly, she put her lips to the baby's forehead. The baby's warmth shocked her and she drew back, but she couldn't resist and kissed the baby again. What was it she had been thinking about? She couldn't remember. How strange. Someone had warned her: You won't remember, afterward. She had thought they were talking about the pain.

A Very Short Story

ERNEST HEMINGWAY

One hot evening in Padua they carried him up onto the roof and he could look out over the top of the town. There were chimney swifts in the sky. After a while it got dark and the searchlights came out. The others went down and took the bottles with them. He and Luz could hear them below on the balcony. Luz sat on the bed. She was cool and fresh in the hot night.

Luz stayed on night duty for three months. They were glad to let her. When they operated on him she prepared him for the operating table; and they had a joke about friend or enema. He went under the anesthetic holding tight on to himself so he would not blab about anything during the silly, talky time. After he got on crutches he used to take the temperatures so Luz would not have to get up from the bed. There were only a few patients, and they all knew about it. They all liked Luz. As he walked back along the halls he thought of Luz in his bed.

Before he went back to the front they went into the Duomo and prayed. It was dim and quiet, and there were other people praying. They wanted to get married, but there was not enough time for the banns, and neither of them had birth certificates. They felt as though they were married, but they wanted everyone to know about it, and to make it so they could not lose it.

Luz wrote him many letters that he never got until after the armistice. Fifteen came in a bunch to the front and he sorted them by the dates and read them all straight through. They were all about the hospital, and how much she loved him, and how it was impossible to get along without him, and how terrible it was missing him at night.

After the armistice they agreed he should go home to get a job so they might be married. Luz would not come home until he had a good job and could come to New York to meet her. It was understood he would not drink, and he did not want to see his friends or anyone in the States. Only to get a job and be married. On the train from Padua to Milan they quarreled about her not being willing to come home at once. When they had to say goodbye, in the station at Milan, they kissed goodbye, but were not finished with the quarrel. He felt sick about saying goodbye like that.

He went to America on a boat from Genoa. Luz went back to Pordenone to open a hospital. It was lonely and rainy there, and there was a battalion of arditi quartered in the town. Living in the muddy, rainy town in the winter, the major of the battalion made love to Luz, and she had never known Italians before, and finally wrote to the States that theirs had been only a boy and girl affair. She was sorry, and she knew he would probably not be able to understand, but might someday forgive her, and be grateful to her, and she expected, absolutely unexpectedly, to be married in the spring. She loved him as always, but she realized now it was only a boy and girl love. She hoped he would have a great career and believed in him absolutely. She knew it was for the best.

The major did not marry her in the spring, or any other time. Luz never got an answer to the letter to Chicago about it. A short time after he contracted gonorrhea from a salesgirl in a loop department store while riding in a taxicab through Lincoln Park.

The Boarding House

JAMES JOYCE

Mrs. Mooney was a butcher's daughter. She was a woman who was quite able to keep things to herself: a determined woman. She had married her father's foreman and opened a butcher's shop near Spring Gardens. But as soon as his father-in-law was dead Mr. Mooney began to go to the devil. He drank, plundered the till, ran headlong into debt. It was no use making him take the pledge: he was sure to break out again a few days after. By fighting his wife in the presence of customers and by buying bad meat he ruined his business. One night he went for his wife with the cleaver and she had to sleep in a neighbour's house.

After that they lived apart. She went to the priest and got a separation from him with care of the children. She would give him neither money nor food nor house-room; and so he was obliged to enlist himself as a sheriff's man. He was a shabby stooped little drunkard with a white face and a white moustache and white eyebrows, pencilled above his little eyes, which were pink-veined and raw; and all day long he sat in the bailiff's room, waiting to be put on a job. Mrs. Mooney, who had taken what remained of her money out of the butcher business and set up a boarding house in Hardwicke Street, was a big imposing woman. Her house had a floating population made up of tourists from Liverpool and the Isle of Man and, occasionally, *artistes* from the music halls. Its resident population was made up of clerks from the city. She governed the house cunningly and firmly, knew when to give credit, when to be stern and when to let things pass. All the resident young men spoke of her as *The Madam*.

Mrs. Mooney's young men paid fifteen shillings a week for board and lodgings (beer or stout at dinner excluded). They shared in common tastes and occupations and for this reason they were very chummy with one another. They discussed with one another the chances of favourites and outsiders. Jack Mooney, the Madam's son, who was clerk to a commission agent in Fleet Street, had the reputation of being a hard case. He was fond of using soldiers' obscenities: usually he came home in the small hours. When he met his friends he had always a good one to tell them and he was always sure to be on to a good thing—that is to say, a likely horse or a likely *artiste*. He was also handy with the mits and sang comic songs. On Sunday nights there would often be a reunion in Mrs. Mooney's front drawing-room. The music-hall *artistes* would oblige; and Sheridan played waltzes and polkas and vamped accompaniments. Polly Mooney, the Madam's daughter, would also sing. She sang:

> *I'm a ... naughty girl.*
> *You needn't sham:*
> *You know I am.*

Polly was a slim girl of nineteen; she had light soft hair and a small full mouth. Her eyes, which were grey with a shade of green through them, had a habit of glancing upwards when she spoke with anyone, which made her look like a little perverse madonna. Mrs. Mooney had first sent her daughter to be a typist in a corn-factor's office but, as a disreputable sheriff's man used to come every other day to the office, asking to be allowed to say a word to his daughter, she had taken her daughter home again and set her to do housework. As Polly was very lively the intention was to give her the run of the young men. Besides, young men like to feel that there is a young woman not very far away. Polly, of course, flirted with the young men but Mrs. Mooney, who was a shrewd judge, knew that the young men were only passing the time away: none of them meant business. Things went on so for a long time and Mrs. Mooney began to think of sending Polly back to typewriting when she noticed that something was going on between Polly and one of the young men. She watched the pair and kept her own counsel.

Polly knew that she was being watched, but still her mother's persistent silence could not be misunderstood. There had been no open complicity between mother and daughter, no open understanding but, though people in the house began to talk of the affair, still Mrs. Mooney did not intervene. Polly began to grow a little strange in her manner and the young man was evidently perturbed. At last, when she judged it to be the right moment, Mrs. Mooney intervened. She dealt with moral problems as a cleaver deals with meat: and in this case she had made up her mind.

It was a bright Sunday morning of early summer, promising heat, but with a fresh breeze blowing. All the windows of the boarding house were open and the lace curtains ballooned gently towards the street beneath the raised sashes. The belfry of George's Church sent out constant peals and worshippers, singly or in groups, traversed the little circus before the church, revealing their purpose by their self-contained demeanour no less than by the little volumes in their gloved hands. Breakfast was over in the boarding house and the table of the breakfast room was covered with plates on which lay yellow streaks of eggs with morsels of bacon-fat and bacon-rind. Mrs. Mooney sat in the straw armchair and watched the servant Mary remove the breakfast things. She made Mary collect the crusts and pieces of broken bread to help to make Tuesday's bread-pudding. When the table was cleared, the broken bread collected, the sugar and butter safe under lock and key, she began to reconstruct the interview which she had had the night before with Polly. Things were as she had suspected: she had been frank in her questions and Polly had been frank in her answers. Both had been somewhat awkward, of course. She had been made awkward by her not wishing to receive the news in too cavalier a fashion or to seem to have connived and Polly had been made awkward not merely because allusions of that kind always made her awkward but also because she did not wish it to be thought that in her wise innocence she had divined the intention behind her mother's tolerance.

Mrs. Mooney glanced instinctively at the little gilt clock on the mantel-piece as soon as she had become aware through her revery that the bells of George's Church had stopped ringing. It was seventeen minutes past eleven: she would have lots of time to have the matter out with Mr. Doran and then catch short twelve at Marlborough Street. She was sure she would win. To begin with she had all the weight of social opinion on her side: she was an outraged mother. She had allowed him to live beneath her roof, assuming that he was a man of honour, and he had simply abused her hospitality. He was thirty-four or thirty-five years of age, so that youth could not be pleaded as his excuse; nor could ignorance be his excuse since he was a man who had seen something of the world. He had simply taken advantage of Polly's youth and inexperience: that was evident. The question was: What reparation would he make?

There must be reparation made in such case. It is all very well for the man: he can go his ways as if nothing had happened, having had his moment of pleasure, but the girl has to bear the brunt. Some mothers would be content to patch up such an affair for a sum of money; she had known cases of it. But she would not do so. For her only one reparation could make up for the loss of her daughter's honour: marriage.

She counted all her cards again before sending Mary up to Mr. Doran's room to say that she wished to speak with him. She felt sure she would win. He was a serious young man, not rakish or loud-voiced like the others. If it had been Mr. Sheridan or Mr. Meade or Bantam Lyons her task would have been much harder. She did not think he would face publicity. All the lodgers in the house knew something of the affair; details had been invented by some. Besides, he had been employed for thirteen years in a great Catholic winemerchant's office and publicity would mean for him, perhaps, the loss of his job. Whereas if he agreed all might be well. She knew he had a good screw for one thing and she suspected he had a bit of stuff put by.

Nearly the half-hour! She stood up and surveyed herself in the pierglass. The decisive expression of her great florid face satisfied her and she thought of some mothers she knew who could not get their daughters off their hands.

Mr. Doran was very anxious indeed this Sunday morning. He had made two attempts to shave but his hand had been so unsteady that he had been obliged to desist. Three days' reddish beard fringed his jaws and every two or three minutes a mist gathered on his glasses so that he had to take them off and polish them with his pocket-handkerchief. The recollection of his confession of the night before was a cause of acute pain to him; the priest had drawn out every ridiculous detail of the affair and in the end had so magnified his sin that he was almost thankful at being afforded a loophole of reparation. The harm was done. What could he do now but marry her or run away? He could not brazen it out. The affair would be sure to be talked of and his employer would be certain to hear of it. Dublin is such a small city: everyone knows everyone else's business. He felt his heart leap warmly in his throat as he heard in his excited imagination old Mr. Leonard calling out in his rasping voice: "Send Mr. Doran here, please."

All his long years of service gone for nothing! All his industry and diligence thrown away! As a young man he had sown his wild oats, of course; he had boasted of his free-thinking and denied the existence of God to his companions in public-houses. But that was all passed and done with...nearly. He still bought a copy of *Reynolds's Newspaper* every week but he attended to his religious duties and for nine-tenths of the year lived a regular life. He had money enough to settle down on; it was not that. But the family would look down on her. First of all there was her disreputable father and then her mother's boarding house was beginning to get a certain fame. He had a notion that he was being had. He could imagine his friends talking of the affair and laughing. She *was* a little vulgar; some times she said "I seen" and "If I had've known." But what would grammar matter if he really loved her? He could not make up his mind whether to like her or despise her for what she had done. Of course he had done it too. His instinct urged him to remain free, not to marry. Once you are married you are done for, it said.

While he was sitting helplessly on the side of the bed in shirt and trousers she tapped lightly at his door and entered. She told him all, that she had made a clean breast of it to her mother and that her mother would speak with him that morning. She cried and threw her arms round his neck, saying:

"Oh Bob! Bob! What am I to do? What am I to do at all?"

She would put an end to herself, she said.

He comforted her feebly, telling her not to cry, that it would be all right, never fear. He felt against his shirt the agitation of her bosom.

It was not altogether his fault that it had happened. He remembered well, with the curious patient memory of the celibate, the first casual caresses her dress, her breath, her fingers had given him. Then late one night as he was undressing for bed she had tapped at his door, timidly. She wanted to relight her candle at his for hers had been blown out by a gust. It was her bath night. She wore a loose open combing-jacket of printed flannel. Her white instep shone in the opening of her furry slippers and the blood glowed warmly behind her perfumed skin. From her hands and wrists too as she lit and steadied her candle a faint perfume arose.

On nights when he came in very late it was she who warmed up his dinner. He scarcely knew what he was eating feeling her beside him alone, at night, in the sleeping house. And her thoughtfulness! If the night was anyway cold or wet or windy there was sure to be a little tumbler of punch ready for him. Perhaps they could be happy together....

They used to go upstairs together on tiptoe, each with a candle, and on the third landing exchange reluctant good-nights. They used to kiss. He remembered well her eyes, the touch of her hand and his delirium...

But delirium passes. He echoed her phrase, applying it to himself: "*What am I to do?*" The instinct of the celibate warned him to hold back. But the sin was there; even his sense of honour told him that reparation must be made for such a sin.

While he was sitting with her on the side of the bed Mary came to the door and said that the missus wanted to see him in the parlour. He stood up to put on his coat and waistcoat, more helpless than ever. When he was dressed he went over to her to comfort her. It would be all right, never fear. He left her crying on the bed and moaning softly: "*O my God!*"

Going down the stairs his glasses became so dimmed with moisture that he had to take them off and polish them. He longed to ascend through the roof and fly away to another country where he would never hear again of his trouble, and yet a force pushed him downstairs step by step. The implacable faces of his employer and of the Madam stared upon his discomfiture. On the last flight of stairs he passed Jack Mooney who was coming up from the pantry nursing two bottles of *Bass*. They saluted coldly; and the lover's eyes rested for a second or two on a thick bulldog face and a pair of thick short arms. When he reached the foot of the staircase he glanced up and saw Jack regarding him from the door of the return-room.

Suddenly he remembered the night when one of the music-hall *artistes*, a little blond Londoner, had made a rather free allusion to Polly. The reunion had been almost broken up on account of Jack's violence. Everyone tried to quiet him. The music-hall *artiste*, a little paler than usual, kept smiling and saying that there was no harm meant: but Jack kept shouting at him that if any fellow tried that sort of a game on with his sister he'd bloody well put his teeth down his throat, so he would.

Polly sat for a little time on the side of the bed, crying. Then she dried her eyes and went over to the looking-glass. She dipped the end of the towel in the water-jug and refreshed her eyes with the cool water. She looked at herself in profile and readjusted a hairpin above her ear. Then she went back to the bed again and sat at the foot. She regarded the pillows for a long time and the sight of them awakened in her mind secret, amiable memories. She rested the nape of her neck against the cool iron bed-rail and fell into a reverie. There was no longer any perturbation visible on her face.

She waited on patiently, almost cheerfully, without alarm, her memories gradually giving place to hopes and visions of the future. Her hopes and visions were so intricate that she no longer saw the white pillows on which her gaze was fixed or remembered that she was waiting for anything.

At last she heard her mother calling. She started to her feet and ran to the banisters.

"Polly! Polly!"

"Yes, mamma?"

"Come down, dear. Mr. Doran wants to speak to you." Then she remembered what she had been waiting for.

Sunday in the Park

BEL KAUFMAN

It was still warm in the late-afternoon sun, and the city noises came muffled through the trees in the park. She put her book down on the bench, removed her sunglasses, and sighed contentedly. Morton was reading the *Times Magazine* section, one arm flung around her shoulder; their three-year-old son, Larry, was playing in the sandbox: a faint breeze fanned her hair softly against her cheek. It was five-thirty of a Sunday afternoon, and the small playground, tucked away in a corner of the park, was all but deserted. The swings and see-saws stood motionless and abandoned, the slides were empty, and only in the sandbox two little boys squatted diligently side by side. *How good this is,* she thought, and almost smiled at her sense of well-being. They must go out in the sun more often; Morton was so city-pale, cooped up all week inside the gray factorylike university. She squeezed his arm affectionately and glanced at Larry, delighting in the pointed little face frowning in concentration over the tunnel he was digging. The other boy suddenly stood up and with a quick, deliberate swing of his chubby arm threw a spadeful of sand at Larry. It just missed his head. Larry continued digging; the boy remained standing, shovel raised, stolid and impassive.

"No, no, little boy." She shook her finger at him, her eyes searching for the child's mother or nurse. "We mustn't throw sand. It may get in someone's eyes and hurt. We must play nicely in the nice sandbox." The boy looked at her in unblinking expectancy. He was about Larry's age but perhaps ten pounds heavier, a husky little boy with none of Larry's quickness and sensitivity in his face. Where was his mother? The only other people left in the playground were two women and a little girl on roller skates leaving now through the gate, and a man on a bench a few feet away. He was a big man, and he seemed to be taking up the whole bench as he held the Sunday comics close to his face. She supposed he was the child's father. He did not look up from his comics, but spat once deftly out of the corner of his mouth. She turned her eyes away.

At that moment, as swiftly as before, the fat little boy threw another spadeful of sand at Larry. This time some of it landed on his hair and forehead. Larry looked up at his mother, his mouth tentative; her expression would tell him whether to cry or not.

Her first instinct was to rush to her son, brush the sand out of his hair, and punish the other child, but she controlled it. She always said that she wanted Larry to learn to fight his own battles.

"Don't *do* that, little boy," she said sharply, leaning forward on the bench. "You mustn't throw sand!"

The man on the bench moved his mouth as if to spit again, but instead he spoke. He did not look at her, but at the boy only.

"You go right ahead, Joe," he said loudly. "Throw all you want. This here is a *public* sandbox."

She felt a sudden weakness in her knees as she glanced at Morton. He had become aware of what was happening. He put his *Times* down carefully on his lap and turned his fine, lean face toward the man, smiling the shy, apologetic smile he might have offered a student in pointing out an error in his thinking. When he spoke to the man, it was with his usual reasonableness.

"You're quite right," he said pleasantly, "but just because this is a public place..."

The man lowered his funnies and looked at Morton. He looked at him from nead to foot, slowly and deliberately. "Yeah?" His insolent voice was edged with menace. "My kid's got just as good right here as yours, and if he feels like throwing sand, he'll throw it, and if you don't like it, you can take your kid the hell out of here."

The children were listening, their eyes and mouths wide open, their spades forgotten in small fists. She noticed the muscle in Morton's jaw tighten. He was rarely angry; he seldom lost his temper. She was suffused with a tenderness for her husband and an impotent rage against the man for involving him in a situation so alien and so distasteful to him.

"Now, just a minute," Morton said courteously, "you must realize...."

"Aw, shut up," said the man.

Her heart began to pound. Morton half rose; the *Times* slid to the ground. Slowly the other man stood up. He took a couple of steps toward Morton, then stopped. He flexed his great arms, waiting. She pressed her trembling knees together. Would there be violence, fighting? How dreadful, how incredible.... She must do something, stop them, call for help. She wanted to put her hand on her husband's sleeve, to pull him down, but for some reason she didn't.

Morton adjusted his glasses. He was very pale. "This is ridiculous," he said unevenly. "I must ask you..."

"Oh, yeah?" said the man. He stood with his legs spread apart, rocking a little, looking at Morton with utter scorn. "You and who else?"

For a moment the two men looked at each other nakedly. Then Morton turned his back on the man and said quietly, "Come on, let's get out of here." He walked awkwardly, almost limping with self-consciousness, to the sandbox. He stooped and lifted Larry and his shovel out.

At once Larry came to life; his face lost its rapt expression and he began to kick and cry. "I don't *want* to go home, I want to play better, I don't *want* any supper, I don't *like* supper..." It became a chant as they walked, pulling their child between them, his feet dragging on the ground. In order to get to the exit gate they had to pass the bench where the man sat sprawling again. She was careful not to look at him. With all the dignity she could summon, she pulled Larry's sandy, perspiring little hand, while Morton pulled the other. Slowly and with head high she walked with her husband and child out of the playground.

Her first feeling was one of relief that a fight had been avoided, that no one was hurt. Yet beneath it there was a layer of something else, something heavy and inescapable. She sensed that it was more than just an unpleasant incident, more than defeat of reason by force. She felt dimly it had something to do with her and Morton, something acutely personal, familiar, and important.

Suddenly Morton spoke. "It wouldn't have proved anything."

"What?" she asked.

"A fight. It wouldn't have proved anything beyond the fact that he's bigger than I am."

"Of course," she said.

"The only possible outcome," he continued reasonably, "would have been—what? My glasses broken, perhaps a tooth or two replaced, a couple of days' work missed—and for what? For justice? For truth?"

"Of course," she repeated. She quickened her step. She wanted only to get home and to busy herself with her familiar tasks; perhaps then the feeling, glued like heavy plaster on her heart, would be gone. *Of all the stupid, despicable bullies,* she thought, pulling harder on Larry's hand. The child was still crying. Always before she had felt a tender pity for his defenseless little body, the frail arms, the narrow shoulders with sharp, winglike shoulder blades, the thin and unsure legs, but now her mouth tightened in resentment.

"Stop crying," she said sharply. "I'm ashamed of you!" She felt as if all three of them were tracking mud along the street. The child cried louder.

If there had been an issue involved, she thought, *if there had been something to fight for.... But what else could he possibly have done? Allow himself to be beaten? Attempt to educate the man? Call a policeman? "Officer, there's a man in the park who won't stop his child from throwing sand on mine...."* The whole thing was as silly as that, and not worth thinking about.

"Can't you keep him quiet, for Pete's sake?" Morton asked irritably.

"What do you suppose I've been trying to do?" she said.

Larry pulled back, dragging his feet.

"If you can't discipline this child, I will," Morton snapped, making a move toward the boy.

But her voice stopped him. She was shocked to hear it, thin and cold and penetrating with contempt. "Indeed?" she heard herself say. "You and who else?"

The First Day

EDWARD JONES

In an otherwise unremarkable September morning, long before I learned to be ashamed of my mother, she takes my hand and we set off down New Jersey Avenue to begin my very first day of school. I am wearing a checkeredlike blue-and-green cotton dress, and scattered about these colors are bits of yellow and white and brown. My mother has uncharacteristically spent nearly an hour on my hair that morning, plaiting and replaiting so that now my scalp tingles. Whenever I turn my head quickly, my nose fills with the faint smell of Dixie Peach hair grease. The smell is somehow a soothing one now and I will reach for it time and time again before the morning ends. All the plaits, each with a blue barrette near the tip and each twisted into an uncommon sturdiness, will last until I go to bed that night, something that has never happened before. My stomach is full of milk and oatmeal sweetened with brown sugar. Like everything else I have on, my pale green slip and underwear are new, the underwear having come three to a plastic package with a little girl on the front who appears to be dancing. Behind my ears, my mother, to stop my whining, has dabbed the stingiest bit of her gardenia perfume, the last present my father gave her before he disappeared into memory. Because I cannot smell it, I have only her word that the perfume is there. I am also wearing yellow socks trimmed with thin lines of black and white around the tops. My shoes are my greatest joy, black patent-leather miracles, and when one is nicked at the toe later that morning in class, my heart will break.

I am carrying a pencil, a pencil sharpener, and a small ten-cent tablet with a black-and-white speckled cover. My mother does not believe that a girl in kindergarten needs such things, so I am taking them only because of my insistent whining and because they are presents from our neighbors, Mary Keith and Blondelle Harris. Miss Mary and Miss Blondelle are watching my two younger sisters until my mother returns. The women are as precious to me as my mother and sisters. Out playing one day. I have overheard an older child, speaking to another child, call Miss Mary and Miss Blondelle a word that is brand new to me. This is my mother: When I say the word in fun to one of my sisters, my mother slaps me across the mouth and the word is lost for years and years.

All the way down New Jersey Avenue, the sidewalks are teeming with children. In my neighborhood, I have many friends, but I see none of them as my mother and I walk. We cross New York Avenue, we cross Pierce Street, and we cross L and K, and still I see no one who knows my name. At I Street, between New Jersey Avenue and Third Street, we enter Seaton Elementary School, a timeworn, sad-faced building across the street from my mother's church, Mt. Carmel Baptist.

Just inside the front door, women out of the advertisements in *Ebony* are greeting other parents and children. The woman who greets us has pearls thick as jumbo marbles that come down almost to her navel, and she acts as if she had known me all my life, touching my shoulder, cupping her hand under my chin. She is enveloped in a perfume that I only know is not gardenia. When, in answer to her question, my mother tells her that we live at 1227 New Jersey Avenue, the woman first seems to be picturing in her head where we live. Then she shakes her head and says that we are at the wrong school, that we should be at Walker-Jones.

My mother shakes her head vigorously. "I want her to go here," my mother says. "If I'da wanted her someplace else, I'da took her there." The woman continues to act as if she has known me all my life, but she tells my mother that we live beyond the area that Seaton serves. My mother is not convinced and for several more minutes she questions the woman about why I cannot attend Seaton. For as many Sundays as I can remember, perhaps even Sundays when I was in her womb, my mother has pointed across I Street to Seaton as we come and go to Mt. Carmel. "You gonna go there and learn about the whole world." But one of the guardians of that place is saying no, and no again. I am learning this about my mother: The higher up on the scale of respectability a person is—and teachers are rather high up in her eyes—the less she is liable to let them push her around. But finally, I see in her eyes the closing gate, and she takes my hand and we leave the building. On the steps, she stops as people move past us on either side.

"Mama, I can't go to school?"

She says nothing at first, then takes my hand again and we are down the steps quickly and nearing New Jersey Avenue before I can blink. This is my mother: She says, "One monkey don't stop no show."

Walker-Jones is a larger, newer school and I immediately like it because of that. But it is not across the street from my mother's church, her rock, one of her connections to God, and I sense her doubts as she absently rubs her thumb over the back of her hand. We find our way to the crowded auditorium where gray metal chairs are set up in the middle of the room. Along the wall to the left are tables and other chairs. Every chair seems occupied by a child or adult. Somewhere in the room a child is crying, a cry that rises above the buzz-talk of so many people. Strewn about the floor are dozens and dozens of pieces of white paper, and people are walking over them without any thought of picking them up. And seeing this lack of concern, I am all of a sudden afraid.

"Is this where they register for school?" my mother asks a woman at one of the tables.

The woman looks up slowly as if she has heard this question once too often. She nods. She is tiny, almost as small as the girl standing beside her. The woman's hair is set in a mass of curlers and all of those curlers are made of paper money, here a dollar bill, there a five-dollar bill. The girl's hair is arrayed in curls, but some of them are beginning to droop and this makes me happy. On the table beside the woman's pocketbook is a large notebook, worthy of someone in high school, and looking at me looking at the notebook, the girl places her hand possessively on it. In her other hand she holds several pencils with thick crowns of additional erasers.

"These the forms you gotta use?" my mother asks the woman, picking up a few pieces of the paper from the table. "Is this what you have to fill out?"

The woman tells her yes, but that she need fill out only one.

"I see," my mother says, looking about the room. Then: "Would you help me with this form? That is, if you don't mind."

The woman asks my mother what she means.

"This form. Would you mind helpin me fill it out?"

The woman still seems not to understand.

"I can't read it. I don't know how to read or write, and I'm askin you to help me." My mother looks at me, then looks away. I know almost all of her looks, but this one is brand new to me. "Would you help me, then?"

The woman says Why sure, and suddenly she appears happier, so much more satisfied with everything. She finishes the form for her daughter and my mother and I step aside to wait for her. We find two chairs nearby and sit. My mother is now diseased, according to the girl's eyes, and until the moment her mother takes her and the form to the front of the auditorium, the girl never stops looking at my mother. I stare back at her. "Don't stare," my mother says to me. "You know better than that."

Another woman out of the *Ebony* ads takes the woman's child away. Now, the woman says upon returning, let's see what we can do for you two.

My mother answers the questions the woman reads off the form. They start with my last name, and then on to the first and middle names. This is school, I think. This is going to school. My mother slowly enunciates each word of my name. This is my mother: As the questions go on, she takes from her pocketbook document after document, as if they will support my right to attend school, as if she has been saving them up for just this moment. Indeed, she takes out more papers than I have ever seen her do in other places: my birth certificate, my baptismal record, a doctor's letter concerning my bout with chicken pox, rent receipts, records of immunization, a letter about our public assistance payments, even her marriage license—every single paper that has anything even remotely to do with my five-year-old life. Few of the papers are needed here, but it does not matter and my mother continues to pull out the documents with the purposefulness of a magician pulling out a long string of scarves. She has learned that money is the beginning and end of everything in this world, and when the woman finishes, my mother offers her fifty cents, and the woman accepts it without hesitation. My mother and I are just about the last parent and child in the room.

My mother presents the form to a woman sitting in front of the stage, and the woman looks at it and writes something on a white card, which she gives to my mother. Before long, the woman who has taken the girl with the drooping curls appears from behind us, speaks to the sitting woman, and introduces herself to my mother and me. She's to be my teacher, she tells my mother. My mother stares.

We go into the hall, where my mother kneels down to me. Her lips are quivering. "I'll be back to pick you up at twelve o'clock. I don't want you to go nowhere. You just wait right here. And listen to every word she say." I touch her lips and press them together. It is an old, old game between us. She puts my hand down at my side, which is not part of the game. She stands and looks a second at the teacher, then she turns and walks away. I see where she has darned one of her socks the night before. Her shoes make loud sounds in the hall. She passes through the doors and I can still hear the loud sounds of her shoes. And even when the teacher turns me toward the classrooms and I hear what must be the singing and talking of all the children in the world I can still hear my mother's footsteps above it all.

Just Married

TONY EARLEY

Late one night, the summer my wife and I lived on the mountain, we saw a deer standing on the traffic island at the end of our street. We saw the headlights of a car coming up the highway. We saw the deer fidget and leap into the light.

By the time we made it to the wreck, the old woman had called 911 on the car phone. The old man held on to the wheel with both hands and stared straight ahead through the webbed glass of the windshield. On the old woman's knee was a large drop of blood shaped like an apostrophe.

"Well," said the old man.

"Well," said the old woman.

"I guess I wrecked your car."

"But it was just a car," she said. She patted his hand.

"We just got married," he said.

"Tonight," she said. "Six hours ago. In Huntsville. We stayed too long at the reception."

"Everybody was there."

"All the grandkids. His and mine. We didn't want to leave."

The old man almost smiled. "Well," he said. "We did and we didn't."

"That's true enough," she said. "But we had a grand time."

"We've been married for a hundred years," he said.

"Just not to each other."

"I was married forty-nine years. She was married fifty-one."

"That makes a hundred. Isn't that something?"

"We were high school sweethearts."

"We just didn't get married."

"Not until tonight, anyway."

"Because of the war."

"I was on a destroyer in the Pacific."

"That's why we didn't get married."

"I had to leave before we figured things out."

"We didn't get anything decided."

"And when I came back, she was married."

"Oh, you make me sound so bad. It wasn't like that. We just never decided anything."

"I didn't mean it like that. I knew Frank. We played ball together. Frank was a good man."

"And Nell was a good woman. I always liked Nell."

"I was always faithful to Nell."

"Of course you were. Of course you were faithful to Nell."

"We were married forty-nine years and I was always faithful."

"Nell and Frank died last year," she said.

"Within a week of each other."

"Isn't that odd?"

"Then one day I just up and wrote to her. And she wrote me back and said she had been thinking about writing to me."

"And I was. Isn't it funny the way things work out? Sometimes you can almost see the plan."

"I still have her letter. It's in my suitcase. In the trunk."

"I put his letter in my safety-deposit box."

"Oh, it's just a letter."

"Not to me."

The old man tapped the steering wheel once with his forefingers. "Let me tell you something," he said. "I always knew she was the one. I was married forty-nine years, and I loved my wife, but I always knew she was the one."

"And I felt the same way about him. I always knew that he was the man for me."

I saw my wife glance up at me. I could tell she was wondering if I was the right man, or if there was a better man, a different life, waiting out there somewhere. And I could tell she knew I was thinking the same thing.

"You just can't say those things," the old woman said.

When the ambulance came, we walked up the highway and looked at the deer. It had slid on its side maybe fifty yards up on the road. A sharp piece of bone stuck out of one of its legs. The eye staring up at us seemed made of dark stone. We stared at the deer, and we sneaked looks at each other. We didn't talk. In the woods beside the highway, we could hear small living things moving beneath the leaves. We could hear the cicadas and the crickets and the tree frogs and the night birds calling out, all the breathing creatures looking for something in the dark.

———————————●———————————

The following commentary by Tony Earley appears at the end of the story in the anthology *New Stories from the South*. It tells us a good deal about the relationship between fiction and nonfiction, about how easily they flow from one to the other. What do you make of his casting the "true" event as if it might not be genuine? See the exercise on p. 225.

Okay, suppose there was this writer, who, while living one summer on top of a mountain in Tennessee, was stricken in the middle of the night by a craving for a frozen burrito and a Diet Coke. And suppose this writer, as he approached the highway near his home, happened to see a car traveling at a high rate of speed strike a deer. What if inside the wrecked car the writer found a man and a woman, both in their seventies, who had been married earlier that evening and were on their way to their honeymoon? And what if these hypothetical newly-weds told this hypothetical writer a story much like the one in this anthology? If you found out that the writer appropriated the story of these strangers, added a fourth character to provide symmetry and dramatic tension, and sold it to a magazine as fiction, would you think less of him than if he had told you that the whole thing was a product of his imagination? What if the writer told you that he drove to the motel where the couple had reservations and made arrangements to pay for their breakfast? If such a writer existed—and I'm not saying he does—your opinion might determine whether or not he told you the truth.

Chinese Medicine

HILARY THAM

I learned about love from my parents. I learned that love was unstable as water, that fathers were heroes one day, taking you out to feast at restaurants or to the beach on an unexpected Sunday; that the next day, they will disown you and call you an unbearable burden. I accepted that fathers were to be waited upon, hand and foot, at the brief twilight hour when they were home for their bath and dinner, before they left again "for business." It was an unquestioned rite in our house that we boiled hot water for our father's bath, placed his towel and fresh boxer shorts ready to his hand. It was our way of life that fathers had to be catered to and pampered, for they were the earners of wages. I learned early that fathers had temper tantrums, that they smashed and broke things if they did not get their way, that they threatened to leave the family, something that mothers never do.

Mothers were the opposite of fathers: they were dull as walls and furniture. They nagged, they disciplined, they had a moral or proverb for every occasion. If I complained as a child about something being "not fair," she'd say, "*Hak gau dau sek, baak gau dong joi.* The black dog steals the food, the white dog gets punished." (The world is not always fair or just.)

"*Choi kar m'chip hak, chut lo mo kwai yan.* Refusing to receive guests at home, on the road, no hosts or patrons." (Do unto others as you would have them do unto you.)

On prudence and saving for a rainy day, she gave us this proverb: "*Sek gai daan, m'sek gai na.* Eat the eggs but not the mother hen."

She had worldly wisdom: "*San don yau chek shi, sai kai mo chek yan.* In the forest, there are straight trees; in the world, there are no straight persons." Do not be too trusting—*tai ngan sik yan.* Wear eyes when meeting people. On the other hand, we were to be sensitive to others' needs, and not to be *dhin dhang dham,* an electric lightbulb staying brightly lit when lovers wanted to be alone in the dark.

My mother had proverbs for love, too. Often, on seeing lovers hand in hand in the public gardens, she would shake her head and say with a tolerant smile, "*Yau ching yam seui baau.* With love, drinking water fills the belly." I think she envied the euphoric time when lovers think they can be happy with love alone, though she'd warn us it was most unrealistic. One cannot live on love alone, echoing the English proverb "When poverty knocks at the door, love flies out the window."

My mother believed that one must make allowances, especially in a marriage. Since one was not perfect, one could not expect perfection or perfect happiness. She used to say, "*Daan ngan lou tai louh poh, yat ngan hoi, yat ngan mai.* The one-eyed man viewing his wife." (He keeps one eye blind to her faults.) She urged her children to study hard, for that was our only road out of poverty, a landscape she had grown too familiar with since her marriage. She stressed the need for a career, our own earning power, especially for us girls; she wanted us to avoid her fate, being chained to a loveless marriage, having to suffer a feckless husband. "Never stay with a man who hits you. The moment he lays a hand on you, you walk out the door. Or you are not my daughter."

My father never hit my mother, not because he did not want to. In some of their altercations, I have seen him poised with raised hand and voice to strike her. But he was prevented by her courage and reactions. She never flinched or cowered from him. She always grabbed a weapon, once a ceramic vase, once a large pair of scissors, and promised him she would harm him, she would spill his blood and his life, if he touched her. He believed her and shunted his violence aside, smashing many radios, gramophone records, once his brand-new TV set.

Until my early teen years, I believed they fought about money. I was not aware there were other conflicts underlying the fight over housekeeping money. When I was thirteen, my mother made me her confidante and shared with me her hopes and her betrayals. It was my stumbling accidentally onto one of the betrayals that thrust me into the role of secret sharer, and later, fierce champion that has been mine ever since.

I was thirteen the year I discovered there were dark secrets underlying the calm and easy rhythms of our very ordinary lives. I think this eventually led to my need to become a writer, to fill out the shapes and shadows beneath the surfaces people present to the world.

At thirteen, I wanted things and people to be what they seemed. Change bothered me. My body bothered me. It was changing, filling out. I was suddenly growing hair in strange places. My secret fear then was that I was changing into a beast, like Kafka's cockroach man. I asked my brother and he told me, from his vast experience of having lived two years more, that it was a natural thing; that even our parents had armpit and pubic hair.

Wanting confirmation, I asked Mother and she explained that I was not turning into an animal, just into a woman. She showed me how to crumple and pulverize cheap rice-chaff paper into coarse feminine napkins to catch the blood my body would begin to expel every month. She said rich women used soft, absorbent cotton napkins, Modess, instead of hard rice-chaff. I had naïvely assumed from the "Because…" ads that the elegant ladies were modeling dresses for that brand name.

I hated the physical process of becoming a woman. Month after month, I had "accidents" that mortified me, embarrassed me. It was made worse by the fact there would be no end to this process for the next forty years, an eternity to a teenager. At that time, a newspaper article brought me comfort. In Sweden, the first sex-change operations had been performed successfully. Though they were to change men into women, I felt cheered and confident that Western medicine would have achieved the ability to do the opposite operation by the time I grew up and saved enough money. I resolved to have my sex changed. This decision must have become embedded in my subconscious. Years later, when I was picking my baptismal name, I chose the uni-sexual name of Hilary.

Mother offered to let me have my hair permed. I think she sensed my difficult adjustment to puberty. Most of my friends had curly hair: the Malay girls came by theirs naturally, the Chinese girls artificially. Mongolian straight black hair is a dominant genetic trait and I had hair that stubbornly refused to curl, however much I braided it. We all wanted curly hair and despised what we had. Only when I came to America did I realize that our long, straight black hair was a thing of beauty to Western eyes. I had begged Mother for a permanent. She refused because we couldn't spare the money. I knew her offer was her "handful of raisins," the sop she used for getting us children to swallow bitter medicine.

In my experience, Chinese medicine always came in the form of a huge bowl of bitter black broth with stomach-turning ingredients like earthworms, cockroaches, scorpions, creepy-crawly things, fungi, and roots, simmered in a clay pot for hours to condense the bitterness. One almost had to get well fast to avoid another dose of the evil-smelling, evil-tasting liquid. Mother would give us a packet of sweet golden raisins as a treat after, but the raisins never quite erased the bitter aftertaste of the medicine.

My friend Swee Hoe recommended the Mei Wah Beauty Salon on Kapar Road. It was located above the Bata Shoe Store in a row of three-story shophouses by the market. I climbed the stairs and turned off the first landing. The stairs continued up to private apartments above; I could tell by the shoes parked by the stairwell. In Malaysia, you take off your shoes before entering a private home.

It was my first visit to a beauty salon and I was overwhelmed by the smell. It was as if someone had washed the floor with *eau de cologne* after a herd of cows had used the place as a bathroom. The salon assaulted the eyes as well: bright pink walls, bright pink linoleum floor, bright pink plastic seats, sinks, hair-dryers, rollers, brushes. Contrast was provided by snippets of black hair on the pink floor around each seat. The horror was amplified by mirror-covered walls.

There were two customers, both their heads and faces hidden by pink beehive hair-dryers and women's magazines. There were two girls in pink smocks, both Chinese. One had dyed her hair red and it looked most incongruous with her sallow complexion. The other girl smiled and asked me in Cantonese how I wanted my hair done. I showed her my pin-up of a magazine model, an English girl whose beauty I yearned for, the high nose, the deep large green eyes, the light brown hair; I hoped to achieve the look of her lustrous curls. The salon girl shook her head, not unkind. She must have been used to customers coming in with unrealistic dreams. She said my hair was not long enough for that style. I picked one she suggested from her folder. She told me her name was Su-lin and started to pin and clip my hair. Then she shampooed it, rolled it in tight curlers, and drenched the curlers with pink perm solution (the source of the cow urine smell). She seated me under a steel contraption with a mass of dangling black wires, clamped a wire to each roller, handed me a bundle of magazines, and told me it would take thirty minutes for my hair to be "electrified." The Chinese word for perming is to "electrify the hair." I looked at my reflection in the mirror and decided I looked like Medusa in an extreme state of shock.

A long time later, or so it seemed to me as I sat in an odor of burning hair and ammonia, Su-lin released me, rinsed my hair (still in rollers), and stuck my head inside a pink beehive blow-dryer. I watched the other women taken out of their beehive captivity and their transformation as their rollers were removed and their hair fluffed out and styled. I began to read my magazines.

Looking up from an irritatingly arch article on "What Men Like in Women," I saw Father in the doorway. Actually, I saw his reflection in the mirror as I was sitting with my back to the door. I returned to my magazine and decided to let him surprise me when I had achieved my transformation.

I was happy he had come to take me home. At the time, my father outshone all the storybook heroes in my eyes. He played the saxophone (self-taught) in the local band; he was a lead actor in the Amateur Chinese Opera Association. He told magnificent stories and took me on outings with his large group of friends in their beautiful cars. He was a leader in the group even though his only means of transportation was a bicycle. He spent money freely and bought presents for me on those outings. His friends were as lighthearted and always game for adventure as he was.

I was disappointed when Su-lin finished my hair. Reality did not match my hopes. I was doubly disappointed when I looked for Father and he was not there. Su-lin said no one had come in after me.

I told Mother about the curious appearance and disappearance of Father at the Mei Wah Beauty Salon. She became very still for a moment, then she continued to spoon rice into my bowl. When I pressed her for an explanation, she admitted that she had known for five years that he kept a mistress above the Mei Wah.

I was not ready for such adult knowledge, though I must have subconsciously picked up earlier hints so that her statement had the force of truth, the click of the final piece in the jigsaw puzzle fitting into place. I protested the impossibility of it, the unreason of it. I tried to make my adults fit the rules of my then simpler universe.

"Is she more beautiful? What's she got that you haven't got?" I couldn't understand my father's betrayal. Mother was beautiful by Chinese standards: she still had a lovely figure. (Later she became heavy after six pregnancies, too little exercise—housework drudgery is not exercise; it does not burn calories—and too much starch in the diet.) She waited on Father, trained us to wait on Father hand and foot, and treated him as the most important person in the household (except when they had their fights). She kept the house neat and clean; she did not waste his money. What more, I argued, childish in my fear of change and loss, could a man want?

Mother showed me a photograph of Father's Badminton Club. Badminton is a serious sport in Malaysia. For us, the International Thomas Cup is as big a deal as the World Cup in England or the Superbowl in America. I'm still rather proud that I played for the varsity team in my first year in college. Whether we won or lost the season is a total fog to me. Strange, thinking back on it now. But I've realized and grown to accept this fact about myself: I am not a fiercely competitive person. I want to excel, to do well, to make the grade. But I am content at that level; it does not bother me that I am not the best; it does not bother me that there are others above me (as long as the number is not too many). I think this habit of being content was drilled into me by Mother's favorite proverb, "*San ko wan yow yat san ko.* Tall mountain, there's another mountain taller." (Do not be arrogant: you may be the best here, but somewhere, there is someone better than you.)

When Mother pointed out a woman in the Badminton Club photograph as my father's mistress living above the Mei Wah Beauty Salon, I stared. The woman was plain. She had a square face and a square body. Her eyebrows were bushy, her eyes too small, and her mouth too large.

"She's ugly. How can he prefer her to you?"

My mother must have asked herself this question many times. And worked her way to a painful, partially correct answer. "Men like change. Men like admiration. They need admiration and will choose it over devotion and a good housekeeper every time."

"You admire Father," I said. It seemed as obvious as mentioning that the sky was blue.

Her answer shocked me.

"I stopped admiring your father years ago. When Second Daughter died. When she was sick and he did not care enough to come home to take her to the doctor. It's hard to admire a selfish man who takes food from his children's mouths to take other women out for dinner. All these years, week in and week out, I am begging him for housekeeping money. Each time I beg, another piece of my heart turns to stone."

Years later, I would realize how this constant feeling of powerlessness in her life had embittered her. She was a woman whose intelligence, passion, and perceptions knew little outlet except secondhand, through her children. Surrounded by children and neighbors and relatives, my mother was essentially alone. She had to maintain the façade of a happy household to save the "face" of my father, of our family. My mother had a strong sense of integrity, of dignity. Until she turned to me as a receptive listener, there had been no one with whom she could share her hurt and shame at having an unsatisfactory husband; no one with whom she could speak the truth and not "lose face."

I sat while my rice grew cold and hard. I felt betrayed by both parents. My father in betraying my mother had betrayed me. I felt honored by my mother's telling me adult secrets. Yet the feeling was tinged with resentment. I felt burdened, weighed down, legs trembling like a colt carrying an overfed man. Looking back, I can name the thing I subconsciously grasped at the time. She made me grow up before I was ready.

"I would not stay after such betrayal," I said, quick to judge her. Thirteen is not an ideal confidante. At thirteen, there is only black and white, no varying shades of gray and compromise. Mother showed me a little of women's realities in 1959. Divorce was a social disgrace and rare. It was available for men whose wives cuckolded them, but few men wanted to "lose face" in such a drastic way. It was the social norm for men to have more than one woman. My father's lack of money was the only bar to his having concubines. A woman with little education and no children could become a house servant at subsistence pay. A woman who left her husband and children for such a position would be vulnerable to unwanted male attentions; she would have a full belly but she would have "no face" to meet the eyes of the world. My mother explained that she could not abandon us children to the hardships a second wife would inflict on us; she could not earn enough to take us with her. Women who were dependant on their husbands had to shut their eyes (and mouths) to things like mistresses. My mother was progressive in her outlook. She believed fervently that times were changing. She was determined on equality for her daughters—we were to have as much education as we could attain. She knew daughters needed it more. She had sworn her daughters would not suffer as she had to.

I had never thought much about Mother—she was just there, like the roof over our heads. She sheltered, she scolded when we were out of line, she controlled our lives. It jarred me to learn she was powerless in a man's world. Compared to Father, who could come and go as he pleased, love whom and where and when he pleased, she was like a household pet constricted by invisible fences, her power real only to her children and her pots and pans.

In my own marriage, I have had a tiny taste of her lifelong powerlessness and the rage that seeps up with being caged. After the birth of our daughters, I stopped working to stay home full-time. It was my choice to be with my babies, yet I had an underlying uneasiness at having no income, no career of my own. One day, I purchased a trash compactor to reduce the bags of trash I had to haul to the curb each Tuesday night. My husband was shocked at the price: three hundred dollars for an unnecessary luxury. He felt I should have asked his permission (which he would have refused) before buying the contraption. He said that in future, I was not to buy anything over two hundred dollars without his okay. My mother had sensitized me. I recognized the male power play: first, to demean what I did in our household as of little worth, not meriting a labor-saving device. My husband did not subscribe to the macho myth that the "Man of the House" takes out the trash. In this and many practical aspects, ours is a very Asian household. The second part of the power play demoted me from equal to subordinate, from spouse to child, someone who needed to ask permission before action. My reaction was to demand that he pay me a salary (retroactive, please) at the going rate for full-time housekeepers. "Fair's fair," I said, "if you are going to treat me like an underling, then I want my underling's pay to call my own; money I can use to buy trash, much less trash compactors, if I so desire." In fairness to my husband, he was not consciously seeking to belittle me or reduce my self-worth. He was thinking of being prudent with money, saving for the children's college educations. But if I had acceded to his restrictive proposition, my sense of self-worth would have been eroded and we would have stepped onto the slippery slope of resentment, of feeling betrayed and unloved, that is the beginning of the breakdown of many marriages. I have to thank my mother for the lessons she taught me, consciously and unconsciously.

That was the only time I had my hair permed. I decided I preferred having straight hair. I also gave up the idea of changing myself into a man. I stopped liking raisins; I was a grown woman, and could take my Chinese medicine in all its bitterness.

See also Tham's poem, "Father" on pp. 139–140.

Grandmother's Nose

ROBERT COOVER

She had only just begun to think about the world around her. Until this summer, she and the world had been much the same thing, a sweet seamless blur of life in life. But now it had broken away from her and become, not herself, but the place herself resided in, a sometimes strange and ominous other that must for one's own sake be studied, be read like a book, like the books she'd begun to read at the same time the world receded. Or maybe it was her reading that had made the world step back. Things that had once been alive and talked to her because part of her—doll, house, cloud, well—were silent now, and apart, and things that lived still on their own—flower, butterfly, mother, grandmother— she now knew also died, another kind of distance.

This dying saddened her, though she understood it but dimly (it had little to do with her, only with the inconstant world she lived in), and it caused her to feel sorry for these ill-fated things. She used to think it was funny when her mother chopped the head off a chicken and it ran crazily around the garden; now she didn't. She no longer squashed ants and beetles underfoot or pulled the wings off flies and butterflies, and she watched old things precious to her, like her mother, with some anxiety, frightened by the possibility of their sudden absence. Since dying was a bad thing, she associated it with being bad, and so was good, at least as good as she could be: she wanted to keep her mother with her. If her mother asked her to do something, she did it. Which was why she was here.

She also associated dying with silence, for that was what it seemed to come to. So she chattered and sang the day through to chase the silence away. A futile endeavor, she knew (she somehow had this knowledge, perhaps it was something her grandmother taught her or showed her in a book), but she kept it up, doing her small part to hold back the end of things, cheerfully conversing with any creature who would stop to talk with her. This brought smiles to most faces (she was their little heroine), though her mother sometimes scolded her: Don't speak with strangers, she would say. Well, the whole world was somewhat strange to her, even her mother sometimes; it was talk to it or let the fearful stillness reign.

Though the world was less easy to live in than before, it was more intriguing. She looked at things more closely than she had when looking at the world was like looking in at herself, her eyes, then liquid mirrors in a liquid world, now more like windows, she poised behind them, staring out, big with purpose. To be at one with things was once enough, sameness then a comfort like a fragrant kitchen or a warm bath. Now it was difference that gave her pleasure: feathers (she had no feathers), petals, wrinkles, shells, brook water's murmuring trickle over stones, not one alike, her mother's teeth (she hadn't even seen them there in her mouth before), the way a door is made, and steps, and shoes. She thought about words like *dog, log,* and *fog,* and how unalike these things were that sounded so like cousins, and she peered intensely at everything, seeking out the mystery in the busyness of ants, the odd veiny shape of leaves, the way fire burned, the skins of things.

And now it was her grandmother's nose. It was a hideous thing to see, but for that reason alone aroused her curiosity. It was much longer and darker than she remembered, creased and hairy and swollen with her illness. She knew she ought not stare at it—poor Grandma!—but fascination gripped her. Such a nose! It was as if some creature had got inside her grandmother's face and was trying to get out. She wished to touch the nose to see if it were hot or cold (Grandma lay so still! it was frightening); she touched her own instead. Yes, dying, she thought (though her own nose reassured her), must be a horrid thing.

The rest of Grandma had been affected, too. Though she was mostly covered up under nightcap, gown, and heaped-up bed-clothes as though perhaps to hide the shame of her disease, it was clear from what could be glimpsed that the dark hairy swelling had spread to other parts, and she longed—not without a little shudder of dread—to see them, to know better what dying was like. But what could not be hidden was the nose: a dark bristly outcropping poking out of the downy bedding like the toe of a dirty black boot from a cloud bank, or from snow. Plain, as her grandmother liked to say, as the nose on your face. Only a soft snort betrayed the life still in it. Grandma also liked to say that the nose was invented for old people to hang their spectacles on (Grandma's spectacles were on the table beside her bed, perched on a closed book), but the truth was, eyes were probably invented to show the nose where to go. The nose sat in the very middle of one's face for all to see, no matter how old one was, and it led the way, first to go wherever the rest went, pointing the direction. When she'd complained that she'd forgotten the way to Grandma's house, her mother had said: Oh, just follow your nose. And she had done that, and here she was. Nose to nose with Grandma.

Her grandmother opened one rheumy eye under the frill of her nightcap and stared gloomily at her as though not quite recognizing her. She backed away. She really didn't know what to do. It was very quiet. Perhaps she should sing a song. I've brought you some biscuits and butter, Grandma, she said at last, her voice a timid whisper. Her grandmother closed her eye again and from under her nose let loose a deep growly burp. A nose was also for smelling things. And Grandma did not smell very nice. On the way I also picked some herbs for tea. Shall I put some on? Tea might do you good.

No, just set those things on the table, little girl, her grandmother said without opening her lidded eye, and come get into bed with me. Her voice was hoarse and raw. Maybe it was a bad cold she was dying of.

I'd rather not, Grandma. She didn't want to hurt her grandmother's feelings, but she did not want to get close to her either, not the way she looked and smelled. She seemed to be scratching herself under the bedding. It's…not time for bed.

Her grandmother opened her near eye again and studied her a moment before emitting a mournful grunt and closing it again. All right then, she mumbled. Forget it. Do as you damn well please. Oh dear, she'd hurt her feelings anyway. Her grandmother burped sourly again and a big red tongue flopped out below her swollen nose and dangled like a dry rag on a line, or her own cap hanging there.

I'm sorry, Grandma. It's just that it scares me the way you look now.

However I look, she groaned, it can't be half so bad as how I feel. Her grandmother gaped her mouth hugely and ran her long dry tongue around the edges. It must have been—*fooshh!*—something I ate.

She felt an urge to remark on her grandmother's big toothy mouth, which was quite shocking to see when it opened all the way (so unlike her mother's mouth), but thought better of it. It would just make her grandmother even sadder. She'd said too much already, and once she started to ask questions, the list could get pretty long, not even counting the parts she couldn't see. Her big ears, for example, not quite hidden by the nightcap. She remembered a story her grandmother told her about a little boy who was born with donkey ears. And all the rest was donkey, too. It was a sad story that ended happily when the donkey boy got into bed with a princess. She began to regret not having crawled into bed with her poor grandmother when she begged it of her. If she asked again, she would do it. Hold her breath and do it. Isn't there some way I can help, Grandma?

The only thing you're good for, child, would just make things worse. Her grandmother lapped at her nose with her long tongue, making an ominous scratchy sound. Woof. I'm really not feeling well.

I'm sorry...

And so you should be. It's your fault, you know.

Oh! Was it something I brought you that made you sick?

No, she snapped crossly, but you led me to it.

Did I? I didn't mean to.

Bah. Innocence. I eat up innocence. Grandma gnashed her teeth and another rumble rolled up from deep inside and escaped her. When I'm able to eat anything at all...foo...She opened her eye and squinted it at her. What big eyes you have, young lady. What are you staring at?

Your...your nose, Grandma.

What's the matter with it? Her grandmother reached one hand out from under the bedding to touch it. Her hand was black and hairy like her nose and her fingernails had curled to ugly claws.

Oh, it's a very *nice* nose, but...it's so...Are you dying, Grandma? she blurted out at last.

There was a grumpy pause, filled only with a snort or two. Then her grandmother signed morosely and grunted. Looks like it. Worse luck. Not what I had in mind at all. She turned her head to scowl at her with both dark eyes, the frill of the nightcap down over her thick brows giving her a clownish cross-eyed look. She had to smile, she couldn't stop herself. Hey, smarty-pants, what's funny? You're going to die, too, you know, you're not getting out of this.

I suppose so. But not now.

Her grandmother glared at her for a moment, quite ferociously, then turned her head away and closed her eyes once more. No, she said. Not now. And she lapped scratchily at her nose again. In a story she'd read in a book, there was a woman whose nose got turned into a long blood sausage because of a bad wish, and the way her grandmother tongued her black nose made her think of it. Did her grandmother wish for something she shouldn't have?

I sort of know what dying is, Grandma. I had a bird with a broken wing and it died and turned cold and didn't do anything after that. And living, well, that's like every day. Mostly I like it. But what's the point if you just have to die and not be and forget everything?

How should I know what the damn point is? her grandmother growled. She lay there in the heaped bedding, nose high, her red tongue dangling once more below it. She didn't move. It was very quiet. Was she already dead? Or just thinking? Appetite, her grandmother said finally, breaking the silence. And the end of appetite. That's it.

That was more like the Grandma she knew. She had lots of stories about being hungry or about eating too much or the wrong things. Like the one about the little girl whose father ate her brother. He liked the dish so much he sucked every bone (now every time she ate a chicken wing, she thought of that father). The little girl gathered all the bones he threw under the table and put them together and her brother became a boy again. Grandma often told stories about naughty boys and cruel fathers, but the little boy in this story was nice and the father was quite nice, too, even if he did sometimes eat children.

Her grandmother popped her eye open suddenly and barked in her deep raspy voice: Don't look too closely! It scared her and made her jump back. She'd been leaning in, trying to see the color of the skin under the black hairs. It was a color something like that of old driftwood. Look too closely at anything, her grandmother said, letting the dark lid fall over her eye once more and tilting her nose toward the ceiling, and what you'll see is nothing. And then you'll see it everywhere, you won't be able to see anything else. She gaped her jaws and burped grandly. Big mistake, she growled.

The thing about her grandmother's nose, so different from her own, or from anyone's she knew, she thought as she put the kettle on for tea, was that it seemed to say so much more to her than her grandmother did. Her nose was big and rough, but at the same time it looked so naked and sad and kind of embarrassing. She couldn't figure out exactly *what* she thought about it. Grandma's talk was blunt and plain and meant just what it said, no more. The nose was more mysterious and seemed to be saying several things to her at once. It was like reading a story about putting a brother back together with his licked bones and discovering later it was really about squashing bad ladies, one meaning hidden under another one, like bugs under a stone.

With a pestle she ground some of the herbs she'd brought in a mortar, then climbed up on a chair to get a cup down from the cupboard. Her grandmother's nose was both funny and frightening at the same time, and hinted at worlds beyond her imagination. Worlds, maybe, she didn't really want to live in. If you die, Grandma, she said, crawling down from the chair, I'll save all your bones.

To chew on, I hope, her grandmother snapped, sinking deeper into the bedding. Which reminds me, she added, somewhat more lugubriously. One thing your grandmother said, as I now recall, was: Don't bite off more than you can chew.

Yes. But *you're* my grandmother.

That's right. Well—*wuurpp!*—don't forget it. Now go away.

Leave me alone. Before I bite your head off just to shut you up.

This dying was surely a hard thing that her grandmother was going through, one had to expect a little bad temper. Even her grandmother's nose seemed grayer than it had been before, her tongue more raglike in its lifeless dangle, her stomach rumblings more dangerously eruptive. It was as though she had some wild angry beast inside her. It made her shudder. Dying was definitely not something to look forward to. The kettle was boiling so she scraped the mortar grindings into the cup and filled it full of hot water, set the cup on the table beside the bed. Here, Grandma. This will make you feel better. Her grandmother only snarled peevishly.

Later, when she got home, her mother asked her how Grandma was feeling. Not very well, she said. A wolf had eaten her and got into bed in Grandma's nightclothes and he asked me to get in bed with him. Did you do that? No, I sort of wanted to. But then some men came in and chopped the wolf's head off and cut his tummy open to get Grandma out again. I didn't stay, but I think Grandma was pretty upset. Her mother smiled, showing her teeth, and told her it was time for bed.

Was that what really happened? Maybe, maybe not, she wasn't sure. But it was a way of remembering it, even if it was perhaps not the best way to remember poor Grandma (that nose!), though Grandma was dying or was already dead, so it didn't really matter.

She crawled into her bed, a place not so friendly as once it was, but first she touched her bedstead, the book beside it (Grandma had given it to her), her pillow, doll, felt the floorboards under her feet, convincing herself of the reality of all that, because some things today had caused her doubt. No sooner had her feet left the floor, however, than there was nothing left of that sensation except her memory of it, and that, she knew, would soon be gone, and the memory of her grandmother, too, and some day the memory of her, and she knew then that her grandmother's warning about the way she looked at things had come too late.

PART FOUR

THE CONCERNS OF THE PLAYWRIGHT

 NO EXIT HEARING

> Hearing room. On a table a pile of thick
> "Interim Reports." On a blackboard is
> printed: "Hearing for the Interim
> Report." Chairs and a folding table. A
> podium with a mike. The sound of a dev-
> ilish chuckle. It fades as EDWARD en-
> ters. He is middle-aged. Looks around
> and sighs wearily.

EDWARD

It's always the same.

> HE sits. Thrums his fingers. Sees the
> Reports, retrieves one, tests its weight,
> and returns to his seat. Turns pages rap-
> idly. MARIE-JANE enters. She looks
> around. Purses her lips, nods her head
> and sits. Says to the world:

MARIE-JANE

Can you tell me what's wrong with people? Don't they care?

EDWARD

In my opinion, the question is—

MARIE-JANE

Don't they care?

EDWARD
(reading)
They've lost hope of--

MARIE-JANE

Hope be damned. I wouldn't miss a chance to have my say. I
insist on it. Even if I didn't have to. Civic duty and all
that. Bring me one of those, young man.

EDWARD

What?

MARIE-JANE
(shouts)
I said! Bring one of those to me, young man! My George was
completely deaf too until he went up . . . I believe, though I
don't care. If he went up or down. Probably down. Serves him
right. May still be deaf.

CHAPTER **12**

THE ELEMENTS OF DRAMA

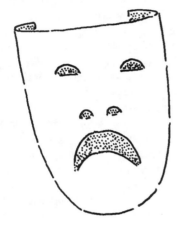

"*I don't get it.*"

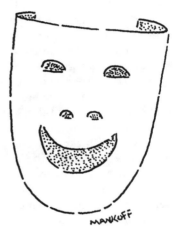

"*You never get it.*"

"*The art of the dramatist is very much like the art of the architect. A plot has to be built up just as house is built— story after story; and no edifice has any chance of standing unless it has a broad foundation and a solid frame.*"

Brandar Matthews

THE NATURE OF DRAMA

Drama has the same rudiments as poetry or prose; all three are rooted in the techniques that writers use to engage audiences. Playwrights (who may become poets or prose writers on other days) also keep journals, read, and research. From the writer's point of view, the boundaries between genres have no border guards. A story can appear to be a memoir and a poem may sound and look like prose; when a novelist shows instead of tells in a scene, he is writing a play; poets write dramatic monologues. *The Glass Menagerie*, for example, is a poetic memoir in the shape of a play. For the writer, the critical categories are not especially helpful because at bottom all are related to performance and story telling.

What is most useful for the beginning writer in any genre is a grasp of how the technical mastery needed for each is different. Poets need to listen to sounds with extra attention and learn to manage line breaks dramatically. Prose writers have to learn to vary the mass of the words on the page and the techniques that will speed the readers on their way. For most playwrights the only way to master the technical advantages and limits of the stage (or camera) is to involve themselves on a working level in the theater (or film, or television, or radio).

In some capacity—acting or moving sets, directing or running a camera—you should become engaged in the production of dramatic work so as to experience its freedoms, conventions, energies, and limits. Working in the media, even as a gopher (go-for coffee, go-for a script, go-for a chair) or as a spear carrier, will make you more sensitive to the problems that your collaborators face. These collaborators are the artists who will design your living room, light it, and dress and direct the actors who, in turn, must kiss with convincing passion as if an audience were not watching. Once you have spoken lines that make no sense, or stood about in a scene with nothing to do, or changed a set for the third time in fifteen minutes—once you have been exposed to the *physical reality* of the media—you are more likely to be sensitive to such difficulties and to construct your plays to avoid them. You will begin to think performance.

Of course, you can argue that the reader of a poem or story performs your work mentally; however, the reader's performance does not have to be limited by talent, space, or material. This state of affairs is far different from having a director, sound technician, lighting technician, costumer, set designer, and actors among your host of ultimate collaborators. These other contributors literally and figuratively put on (embody) your words.

Consider the following action: "They walked into the living room and kissed passionately. Then they began to remove their clothes." Think of the difference between your response to this action (1) brought to your mind's eye through print and (2) brought to your senses as it *happens* before you on stage or screen.

As a reader, you can allow your imagination to build on the writer's material, you can decide to read more quickly to see if the couple will be interrupted or more slowly to savor the experience, and you can interrupt the experience by putting down the book and then picking it up again. Or you can skip it. Of course, you could close your eyes at the nudity in a play if you know it is coming (though, we suppose, you could close your eyes immediately and reduce your time exposure). In any case, our reaction to actual nudity is bound to be different than to imagined nudity. In reading you have some degree of safety and control because you can easily put a distance between yourself and the potential impact of the writer's words. At some level, you are always conscious of holding a book or magazine and looking at the printed page.

In plays and films, the illusion of life-going-on is the result of other people doing something with the writer's words. As a member of an audience, you are confronted by something *happening*. You are a *witness* to real people as well as characters stripping before you. The pressure and the pace of the production absorb your attention. Images and voices from outside of you run at someone else's pace and create the particular illusions of life-going-on that are different from the illusions of fiction.

As we have pointed out, one way to master the particular illusions of drama so as to exploit them is to have hands-on experience in theater and film. Another step is to read books intended for professionals—actors, directors, designers—to know their language and concerns. The more familiar you are with their world, the more you can do to ensure that your narrative will be produced and performed as you have conceived it.

In the sections that follow, we touch only lightly on matters discussed in the poetry and prose chapters. If you have turned to this chapter first, you may want to refer back to those discussions of plot, sound, point of view, character, point of attack, scene, and setting. Here we stress how these same elements need to be reconsidered for dramatic presentation. Among other plays, our discussions will refer to Joyce Carol Oates' *Procedure* and Michel Wallerstein's *Off Hand* in Chapter 14, as well as to some of the short stories and poems appearing earlier in the book.

> *"Writing a play, you start with less, so more is demanded of you. It's as if you have to not only write a symphony, but invent the instruments as well."*
>
> David Ives

STORYTELLING WITH PEOPLE AND THINGS

The word *drama* retains the force of its original meaning in Greek—"to do." You write out your script to communicate with those who will *do* the play for the audience. If you happen to publish the play to be read, it is a by-product of your collaboration. And if you write, direct, and act in a one-person play or monologue. your writer-self, director-self, and actor-self are different people when each is doing his or her job. It is best, then, to think of your play as being similar to a musical score: signs placed on paper that show others how to perform your work. You can't ask the musician to play notes or make sounds that the instrument can't produce.

Don't fall into the trap of thinking that playwriting is simply telling stories on a different instrument and without having to cover a page from margin to margin. It is certainly true that the narrative you want your collaborators to present for you contains many of the same elements discussed in the other chapters. Like fiction, a play has the following elements:

1. A *story* out of which you carve a *plot*
2. in which *characters*
3. are in *conflict*
4. because they want to achieve their individual *desires*
5. about some object and/or idea and/or emotion.

The wants and needs of the characters are based on beliefs that the author and the audience may or may not share. Willy Loman in *Death of a Salesman* believes that personality—being well liked—can bring success and excuses lying and stealing, and that what people think of you is more important than what you know or what you can do. Arthur Miller's point of view appears to be that this kind of search for outward success—measured by money—prevents Willy from recognizing his real talents and needs. The struggle to achieve at any cost a materialistic version of the American Dream results in a tragically empty life. Ironically, Willy's wants and needs actually block him from achieving happiness. We come to know Miller's point of view because of what happens to Willy Loman.

Such a combination of (1) controlling ideas in the characters plus (2) a set of circumstances (obstacles) and conflicts is called the **premise**. The dramatic premise triggers the actions the audience sees on the stage or in the film. Because Willy has followed his beliefs, he has—by his lights—failed. At the point of attack, he no longer can go on as a salesman either emotionally, mentally, or physically. He is thinking of suicide. At that very moment his son Biff returns. In *Death of a Salesman* the combination of Willy's beliefs, his traits, and the circumstances are the seeds from which grow the conflicts, the flashbacks, and all the other actions we observe that lead to Willy's suicide. The elements of the premise, then, can be seen as an opportunity, a potential, for something to happen.

Though we might find the basic concept of premise to be useful for any type of storytelling, the *dramatic* premise requires an especially intense combination of triggering forces at the point of attack. For example, it is much more critical in a dramatic presentation for the point of attack to be as close to the climax as possible. At most the playwright usually has only a few hours of audience attention for showing the story. In effect, the majority of the events and the development of essential character traits will have happened before the curtain rises. A late point of attack creates great pressures. In an actual ten minutes or two hours, the playwright must have the characters reveal all the information necessary for us to understand who they are and what they are doing (the exposition) and do and say the things that will bring on the dramatic conclusion. The pressure of compressing so much into a limited time has, as we shall see, both advantages and drawbacks.

Playwriting is so linked to the material presence of actual time, spaces, sounds, and people (actors)—life-going-on—that it has unique energies and limits. Many a writer successful in another genre (Henry James, for example) failed in playwriting by not mastering the particular life, effects, and affects of drama. What might be dismissed as merely mechanical differences are quite complex and can cause important changes in the writer's decisions about developing and presenting character and plot.

The following discussions about how one might adapt stories from fiction to drama will begin to illustrate this point. (We suggest you read each piece of fiction before you read the discussion.)

1. "Belling the Cat" (p. 186)

The fable is based on the following ideas: (1) If a solution to a problem cannot be put into effect, it is a foolish suggestion, and (2) an inexperienced person (in this case, a young mouse) is more likely to propose a foolish solution than is an experienced one. These ideas are dramatized through the plot that they shape. The setting is minimal, as is the characterization. You can read the fable in a minute, absorb the truth of the premise (which is stated directly), and move on. It is the idea in the premise that dominates the characters and circumstances.

If you wanted to turn the fable into a dramatic work, keeping the same characters (mice and cat) and circumstances, what problems would you have? (Jot down a few ideas before going on.)

Though not the most important, the most obvious problem is that you would have to teach mice to talk. *Solution:* Make a cartoon using human voices. *Or:* Dress human beings in mouse costumes. *Or:* Let the human beings simply think of themselves as mice. Such problems can be solved by dozens of conventional techniques (as in *Peter Pan, Equus, Cats,* or *The Lion King*). A good principle to follow when trying to solve such mechanical problems is simply to borrow a convention the audience is used to.

The more difficult "dramatic" problem is how to activate the premise so that it can occupy the stage or screen for more than a minute or two. The typical solution would be to expand the number of scenes and develop the characters. For example, to show us the precise nature of the dilemma, the playwright might add a scene in which the Cat decimates a group of the mice as they are raiding the kitchen. Or, perhaps the dramatization will begin with Young Mouse and Old Mouse as father and son. Old Mouse tells Young Mouse not to make a fool of himself at the meeting. What has motivated Old Mouse to do that? Young Mouse is fresh out of Rodent College, where he majored in conflict resolution and felines. He has returned, full of piss and vinegar, to put his academic training to practical and immediate use. Perhaps the first scene will begin just slightly before the meeting. The last scene will show the mice actually trying to bell the cat (as we see in one of the cartoon versions). The visible block is that Cat is bigger. Somehow, though, in the process of developing the material, we have changed a part of the premise. It's not just about wisdom; it has come to involve a conflict between education and experience, new ways and old ways, sons and fathers, the natural world and extravagant hopes.

Inexorably, the move from a fictional premise to a dramatic premise will bring changes—additional actions, a reshaping of emphasis, and different ways of developing character. We are by no means suggesting that dramatizing a piece of fiction always requires expansion. It almost always requires contraction of some events and expansion of others. For example, the film *Moby Dick* eliminates vast sections of Melville's novel and changes the impact.

In the end, the experience we will receive from *Belling the Cat*/Movie will be different from the experience we get from *Belling the Cat*/ Fable because the audience's expectation of the media has been met. We will see and hear the movement rather than imagining it. Also, because the Old Mouse and the Young Mouse will be present to us, we do not expect to be told one is older and one is younger. The director will make sure we can see that. In fact, the characters won't be telling us anything we can see for ourselves. We might, however, expect to see Young Mouse actually try to *do* the belling. The block to his achieving his goal will be visual: The cat is big and he is small.

Ironically, then, it is no praise to say of the dramatic version that it is exactly like the original.

●　●　●　●　●　　　*EXERCISE*　　　●　●　●　●　●

Choose a different fable—for example, "The Tortoise and the Hare" or "The Traveler and the Bear"—and develop a dramatic premise for it.

2. "Sunday in the Park" (pp. 269–272)

The thematic element of Kaufman's premise is this: At bottom, no matter how much they may praise and encourage the civilized virtues of intellect and gentleness, some women really want a man to protect them (another way of saying to be manly or macho). Because Bel Kaufman has chosen to tell the story from the wife's point of view, we are as surprised as the wife is to find her more "primitive" nature surfacing after the bully faces down her husband, Morton. The insight—the epiphany—works in the short story because the woman's sudden *conscious* awareness *is* the point. In a way, the premise is not the revelation of her desire for a manly man, but the fact that she wasn't aware of the depths of her dissatisfaction.

Taking the same premise for a play, however, would require major changes and expansion. For example, the antagonist (the bully) in the story has a simple function: He forces Morton's choice of whether to fight for his family's right to share the sandbox in peace or to walk away. Once you put the bully into the flesh of an actor and the actor starts walking on stage or through the film, you need something more for him to do than this single action. You might, of course, shape the action so that the bully comes on only toward the end of the scene but, for the purpose of this discussion, let's assume that the bully must be present for a longer period so that his action does not appear gratuitous—mere bullying for the sake of showing power.

In order for the character to be present to the audience for a longer period of time, the dramatist will have to increase the bully's active role. What would happen, for example, if instead of separate benches, as in the story, there was only one bench to share and the bully had entered and joined the couple? What kind of byplay would occur among them as they jostled for room? What are the emotions evoked when people have to share territory? Would the bully sit on Morton's *Times*? Might Morton and his wife try to placate the man? Might Morton offer him a section from his *Times*? Would the bully resent this offer because he senses both Morton's and Morton's wife's condescension? Is the bully (a construction worker) sick and tired of the "college boys" telling him that the concrete isn't mixed properly? Perhaps, after all, he isn't merely a bully; he has a grievance. Are Morton and his wife regentrifying the construction worker's neighborhood and slowly driving out the working class? Notice how the very fact that the bully will be physically present generates questions that begin to affect the premise.

In a ten-minute skit or a comedy show, such elaboration probably would not be needed, but the presence of a character who is more than a functionary increases the playwright's obligation to account for that character.

More important, if the premise has to do with the woman's sudden recognition of her more "primitive" desires, a way has to be found to let the reader directly experience what the narrator only reports: "It was more than just an unpleasant incident, more than defeat of reason by force...it had something to do with her and Morton, something acutely personal, familiar, and important." At the very same time the playwright must (1) find ways to reveal how the woman is hiding her true desires beneath what she believes she ought to desire, and (2) convince the spectators to accept that, with the same evidence they have, she can fail to draw the same conclusion until the very end. (For the audience, seeing what she doesn't see increases the dramatic tension. When is she going to find out what is so clear to us?)

It might appear, then, that the playwright needs only to organize and expand the events in preparation for the wife's moment of realization, ignoring (as the narrator of the story can) the husband's wants and presence. Because Bel Kaufman focuses the events through the woman's point of view, the reader is not concerned about the husband. Since a play normally has no narrator to focus the point of view, the husband will be *present to the audience,* and his presence must be fulfilled. The playwright should not suddenly throw a spotlight on the wife and filter out his presence. The audience won't forget the husband's reality as quickly as a reader would because he is physically present and his point of view must be acknowledged through his action or words.

Since the bully creates an occasion for the wife to realize her true feelings but is not directly involved in the important developments in the marriage, the playwright may feel there is no problem getting him off stage. But surely the husband cannot be treated like a functionary. He is directly involved in the conditions that lead to the wife's recognition. To dramatize the wife's dissatisfaction, to put it into action, the playwright is going to have to show us the relationship. The husband's wants will become important, if only to make us interested in the conflict. Perhaps he and the wife will need a scene before the bully enters to give the audience a sense of the prior relationship. And once the husband's prior set of circumstances are revealed, he acquires importance in the dramatic presentation. Inevitably, his importance will lead to adjustments in the premise and in the resolution, because he shares the audience's attention with the wife. How is he going to react to her self-realization? Would he say: "I'm signing up for refresher karate lessons. I would have done it long ago if you'd have let me. I should never have let myself get out of shape." In that case, to the premise must be added new ideas and circumstances: Sometimes a man's civilized behavior merely reflects a woman's overt desires. Given a chance he'll revert to manliness.

Here is the principle: The playwright must account for *all the characters who have been involved in the conflict that springs from the premise.* Servants, spear carriers, and other beings who function in the plot only as mechanisms do not, of course, need to be accounted for, because they don't have a unique identity in relationship to the premise. In the process of accounting for the major characters, however, other aspects of the premise will begin to change.

● ● ● ● ●   *EXERCISES*   ● ● ● ● ●

1. Since the wife's recognition alone is not likely to suffice for the ending, we will have to create something that gives the husband an ending in relationship to her new premise: I want a man. He might have a recognition: "You got what you created and I'm comfortable being a wimp." Or, he might throw her over his shoulder and take her off the stage. Plan an ending for a dramatic version of "Sunday in the Park." Be sure to work up what the husband wants. Try to keep the play to one set.

2. Write an analysis of "The Boarding House" (pp. 264–269) based on the premise that men must be trapped into marriage, which is a type of "reparation" for the satisfaction of the male's sexual desire. Given that the story is extremely subtle, list the scenes that might have to be developed to present the characters' emotions to the audience's senses. Write one of the scenes (e.g., Doran's confession to the priest).

3. Create a treatment (a scene-by-scene outline) for a movie version of "The Boarding House." As you select your scenes, keep in mind that you are trying to suggest in another medium the effects of Joyce's short story. For a model, read Joyce's "The Dead" and see John Huston's film rendition of the story.

4. Assume that "The Boarding House" characters live today—let us say at an exclusive but small and seedy college dedicated to the arts and overrun with mice, not donors. What kind of premise might you come up with that captures the spirit of the original if Mrs. Mooney runs some kind of off-campus establishment (small apartment house in a former mansion) and Mr. Doran is an assistant professor who is coming up for tenure? Outline your version of the play.

———————●———————

Whether you adapt or create your own premise, situation, and characters, the principles will be the same: You will need to develop a premise suitable for the demands of a presentation. Though the fundamental elements of narrative construction will remain the same as in fiction (see Chapter 9, "Narration and Its Techniques"), the pressures of dramatic presentation will determine how you go about developing the plot.

By this point it should be clear that when you intend to tell stories with real people and things, you must constantly be alert to the impact of the visual. The illumination of characters and plot in dramatic media is more than a matter of transferring your narrative into dialogue and stage directions.

A Final Note

As it is in fiction, the point of attack in drama is generally as close to the climax of the story as the playwright can make it. Try to structure the events so that as much of the story as possible has happened before the curtain rises or credits end. The less that needs to be shown, the less time the production will take and the fewer the actors and sets required. The drawback is that you have to find dramatic ways to provide the back story (the exposition) to the audience.

> *"Society is inside of man and man is inside society, and*
> *you cannot even create a truthfully drawn psychological*
> *entity on the stage until you understand his social*
> *relations and their power to make him what he is and to*
> *prevent him from being what he is not. The fish in the*
> *water and the water is in the fish."*
>
> Arthur Miller

 ## CHARACTERS

As we have already discussed, a character is the sum of "characteristics" that create for an audience some sense that the personages in stories, narrative or dramatic, are present and distinct. (See Chapter 9, "Narration and Its Techniques," for more about this aspect of character.) Just as in other narratives, the playwright builds a sense of the characters' reality by having them behave in a manner consistent with their development in the plot. In Ibsen's *Hedda Gabler*, Hedda behaves in a self-centered, independent way, reflecting characteristics attributable to her upbringing as a general's only child. In part, her suicide is understandable as an outcome of (1) that independence and her refusal to allow another man to dominate her and (2) her fear of public exposure. These characteristics are seen in actions before her suicide.

A flesh-and-blood person will play Hedda. This special condition—actor plus the role the actor plays—creates for the playwright special opportunities and problems. Unless something about a character's physical appearance is extremely important, the playwright need only sketch it in. The director will choose the actors for gross distinctiveness (sex, age, looks) in accordance with the plot. Obviously, except in a radio presentation, the audience will not have to visualize these elements. The actor will provide the accent and the details (makeup, costume, sex, stature, and mannerisms) that a narrator constantly has to supply in fiction. Nor does the dramatist have to provide details to help the spectators visualize actions. The actor (and the other collaborators) present them directly to the senses. On the surface, then, it might appear that since half the job is done by others, all sensible writers would become playwrights.

The freedoms from some writing tasks actually create terrible responsibilities because, for most dramatic presentations, in what they say and do the characters have to carry forward almost all the elements of both the premise and the plot. Everything is compressed into the showing—characteristics, relationships, and conflicts. In some ways, condensation for effective dramatic presentation is closer emotionally and artistically to the demands of poetry than to fiction.

In small compass, the following radio advertisement shows how much can be compressed into the characters and the situation that unfolds through them, all in a continuous time. We have decided to call the playlet "The Teeth of the Problem."

> TIME: *The present*
> SCENE: A restaurant. Sounds of dishes clattering and other restaurant noises in the background.)
>> MAN: Hi. Sorry I'm late.
>> WOMAN: Oh, that's O.K. This is a nice place.
>> MAN: Speaking of nice places—
>> WOMAN: Uh-huh?
>> MAN: I got the brochures. Here's Jamaica, the Virgin Islands, Martinique.
>> WOMAN: I have a [pause] "brochure" for you, too.
>> MAN: (*reading*) "When Your Child Needs Braces"? What is this?
>> WOMAN: Your child needs braces.
>> MAN: Eric?

WOMAN: That's what Dr. Marshall says.
MAN: Darn. What's that going to cost?
WOMAN: Oh, the price of a nice cruise.
MAN: Which means—
WOMAN: Right.
MAN: Diane, we need this trip.
WOMAN: Uh-huh.
MAN: We've waited five years for it.
WOMAN: Eric isn't too happy about this either.
MAN: I know. Is there any way we could swing both?
WOMAN: I don't see how, honey.
VOICEOVER: *For anyone who has ever said there isn't enough money, now there is. Sovran has half a billion dollars to lend.*

Notice how much narrative is compressed in the playlet:

Situation: A couple have been planning for a Caribbean cruise for some time and have saved money for it. They have sacrificed to raise Eric, and they may need this trip for the health of their marriage and their own mental health. The husband has gone to the travel bureau and picked up information; the wife has taken their son to the dentist. Previously they had planned to meet for lunch and discuss the trip.

Complication: Their son needs braces.

Crisis: They don't have enough money to meet their responsibility and also to take the trip they have worked for.

Conflict: Do they give up their trip or have their son grow up with crooked teeth?

Climax   (and resolution): A **deus ex machina**—the bank—arrives to say there is enough money because the bank is willing to make loans.

Premises: (1) You can fulfill your responsibilities to others and yourself if you have enough money. (2) Some pleasures, such as a vacation, may actually be responsibilities. (3) If you are responsible, you are rewarded with pleasures and the apparent conflict really isn't one.

It is not fanciful to say that the plot of the playlet we experience here grows from the attributes of the characters. Both are responsible people (they have saved for their trip and take good care of Eric). The husband appears to be a bit less responsible than the wife. He is the one who picks up the brochure, and he also seems, at least for a moment, to be the one less willing to give up the trip. So we have a potential dramatic conflict. The wife is the one who takes Eric to the dentist, she arrives on time, and she has apparently already determined that the money is to be spent on Eric. Their need for a vacation comes from the very fact that they are married (rather a stock situation, which may reflect the audience's understanding of reality). Their dilemma, paying for the braces, comes from the fact that they have had Eric and are responsible enough to take him to a dentist. Plot and character are related.

The message from the bank (a conventional *deus ex machina*) fulfills their needs in terms of their character traits. Anybody as responsible as they have already shown themselves to be can have a slice of the half billion. Such people pay their debts. The principles on which the bank operates—the subtext of the message announced to the audience—is obvious and neatly self-fulfilling.

Note how much of the couple's past, present, and future is condensed into a single minute of presentation, some twenty lines of dialogue. For the playwright to pack all this into such short compass requires a sense of how to create for the audience the images that it can instantly understand. As we will see, the dramatic presentation does not (usually) contain a narrative point of view to provide additional comments, to filter out accidental impressions, or to focus the audience's attention. Essentially, the whole task of storytelling has to be done with what the characters say and how they act. Notice how much faster the advertisement plays than it took you to read the analysis. Speed intensifies dramatic tension.

●   ●   ●   ●   ●   *EXERCISE*   ●   ●   ●   ●   ●

Continue the scene after the bank's message, showing what would happen if the wife decided it would be irresponsible to take out a loan and the husband protested. (Consider what situations and premises would make her decide this, and be sure to keep to the characteristics already established for both of them.)

 PRESENTING CHARACTER

Beginning playwrights often forget how much the revelation of character traits can be condensed through exploiting the opportunities that the actor's physical presence affords. The actor interrelates with the environment and other characters while speaking dialogue. Indeed, the playwright is responsible for preparing conditions that will give the actors opportunities for **stage business**—something to *do*. The stage business need not be spelled out in detail for the actor or director but should be inherent in one or more of the following:

1. The dress, physical habits, and condition of the characters. (Has one of them a cold and is the other a hypochondriac? Is one dressed elegantly?)
2. The physical action called for at a particular point. (Might one play the guitar or a video game?)
3. The place in which the characters find themselves. (Is it a hospital waiting room?)
4. The relationships among the characters. (Are they married or just living together?)

The more physical the action, the less "business" the actors will have to think up for themselves (and the less they have to say because we see what they are doing). In a screenplay set in Montana, the actors hunting on horseback for wild buffalo will have little difficulty finding things to do when the cameras are rolling.

If your play occurs in a palace, however, and the issue is whether the king will abdicate or not, the actors might find the stage business less obvious. Granted that what the characters say to one another will be a kind of doing, their talking for two hours about the problem is likely to put a strain on the director's and actors' ingenuity for creating visual effects to keep the audience awake. Now give the king a cold (almost too obviously symbolic) and a large briefcase into which he is placing papers from his desk. A servant (let's make him a wise fool) comes and goes, bringing handkerchiefs (a king does not use Kleenex), drinks, and news.

> SERVANT: These are the last clean ones, your highness.
> KING: I suppose I should get used to using Kleenex. Bring me that wastebasket.
> SERVANT: You should get used to fetching your own.

The king's habit of command is revealed, as is the changing situation to which he must soon become accustomed. The servant's "forgetting" to say "your highness" in the second speech indicates his realization that the situation is changing. Might not the king's posture stiffen also? Does he touch the crown he is wearing? Suddenly, there are things for the actors to do whether or not they are speaking—objective realities for their inward attitudes and emotions. Remember, though, that these outward manifestations of the plot and character ought not be mechanical. Don't say that the queen pulls at her nose unless you know why she does it and how the other characters might react to so unqueenly a gesture.

Obviously, stage business is most effective when it is the result of clearly thinking through the character's inner cast of mind. In *The Caine Mutiny Court Martial,* Captain Queeg's disturbance is expressed by the business of rolling the two ball bearings in his hand; the same action suggests psychosexual disturbance. His uncontrolled manipulation of the bearings triggers the past for him. Both what he says and what he does reveal to the military jury that Queeg is mentally ill, leading to the acquittal of the mutineers. In this case, stage business that grows from character leads to revelation and resolution.

● ● ● ● ●   *EXERCISES*   ● ● ● ● ●

1. Create a scene in which a student is trying to get a better grade from a teacher. Let us see within the first five lines of dialogue the student's need (or needs) but not the reasons for it. The teacher does not want to give the student a passing grade but does not wish to say so. You may reveal this fact at any point.

Now create things for the characters to handle and do that will indicate their inner natures. Bring us to a point at which the teacher can convincingly tell the student about the "F" because now he or she wishes to.

2. Imagine that you are directing a television version of the radio ad on pp. 302–303. Write out directions for how you want the actors to appear and what you want them to do. Include directions for a scene to be shot in a restaurant, their kitchen, or their bedroom. Change the dialogue as necessary (remember we can see what's happening). Try to keep to the same performance time.

 ## STOCK CHARACTERS AND CHARACTER DEVELOPMENT

Stage business can create the audience's sense of distinctive traits in what is really a stock character, a stereotype from life or literature. (For more on stock characters, see pp. 205–206.) The shy, awkward maid whose role is to serve tea becomes a presence when she invariably spills it. If she is not fired, the audience makes judgments about the people who pay her salary. One bit of business starts to create a potential for more stage business revealing even more characteristics. The playwright is continually shuttling between the character's business, the internal state that the business indicates, how the other characters react, their internal state, and on and on. In the course of a play's development, a character like Shakespeare's Falstaff (the stock bragging soldier), may acquire a sharper identity because while inventing things for the actors to do the playwright delves further into the source of the traits behind the visible effects.

In fact, even those characters you originally conceive of as having complex attributes need to be revealed first through their stock attributes, moving from the type to the individual. The actors will be dressed as kings, servants, slatterns, hippies, policemen—something that categorizes them. They will be washing dishes, driving a BMW to work, jogging, sleeping, carrying a load of books, preparing a corpse for burial, looking at paintings. In the first few moments the audience will judge the characters by their dress, their looks, what they are doing, what is around them. In the same few moments the audience will be trying to absorb the environment (set) and to figure out what the issues are. Anything easily and quickly recognizable—the stock characteristics—orient the audience, just as they would in daily life. The beginning of the play is no time to present the "To be or not to be" soliloquy. The revelations about Hamlet's interior landscape are so complex that they would be lost until we are comfortable with his exterior.

In Michael Wallerstein's ten-minute play *Off Hand* (pp. 346–352), for another example, the two characters are seen in their expected roles—older woman and young man. They behave as if they are looking at the pictures in a knowledgable way. The Woman is brusque to a stranger. The Man is forward in his questioning as a younger person might be, and he doesn't have the deference the Woman expects. Their differing view of the two paintings suggests she likes more naturalistic art. Even in a short play like *Off Hand*, the dramatist starts us in familiar territory and moves us into unfamiliar territory.

Since the audience usually has no narrator to explain characteristics, nor can it flip back the pages and control the display of information, the playwright has to reveal the characteristics in stages. You might want to think of this gradual revelation as similar to how an image slowly emerges on Polaroid film. The image is already there; it must be developed. Of course, sometimes the revelation we have is a horrifying ratification of our first perception as the characters do more. Nurse A, the experienced nurse in *Procedure* appears to be totally cool and and almost inhumanly mechanical. Her chilly personality, almost unbelievably chilly, is revealed when we learn that the dead man is her father. The dramatic process is fairly typical; the unfolding of the events creates an opportunity to see aspects of a character that can attract or repel us. Putting it another way, we can say that the playwright's plot creates opportunities for the audience's understanding to develop and change.

Of course, the characters may "change" in the sense that events they have experienced will or will not modify their perceptions of past events, the other characters, their own condition, or the decisions they should make. We learn why Nurse A can be so "professional." Her father is not beloved. Nurse A will always be an iceberg. The one who might change is Nurse B who, having gone through the experience once, may herself become more professional. This will be a change of behavior, not of fundamental characteristics since we are likely to feel that she'll always be more sympathetic and emotional than Nurse A. Shakespeare's King Lear, on the other hand, does appear to undergo a basic change. He appears to soften and become more capable of love and pity. But does he change, or do we see hidden traits revealed? The role that Lear has had to play as a king has disguised his loving nature (a softness that his two wicked daughters understand). When the "king" is beaten out of him, Lear's loving side stands revealed.

● ● ● ● ●   *EXERCISES*   ● ● ● ● ●

Take two of the stock characters in the list on p. 206. Put them in a laundromat, waiting to use the only working dryer. Both their wash loads are finished at the same time. Problem: Who is going to use the dryer first?

1. Create dialogue based on what the audience might expect such characters to do and say.

2. Now assume that after a while, one of the characters realizes that he or she is behaving like a stock character. Give that character something to say or do that indicates this realization.

3. Go back to the dialogue you wrote for number 1 and revise it to indicate the character's potential for having such a realization.

Some Final Points

One of the reasons a play appears so raw when you read it, perhaps even emotionally crude, is that the attributes of the characters, like musical notes in a score, can gain timbre—that is, subtlety—only from the player and the context of the presentation. In Ibsen's *A Doll's House*, Nora's slamming the door after she leaves her husband appears **melodramatic**, overdone, when we read it. When we experience the actual sound, it appears almost understated. This strange alchemy is in part the result of the fact that we can see her husband react to the sound. The playwright who attempts to show a character with the same narrative subtlety as one would in fiction is attempting to provide what the medium is not intended or able to carry. In a play, the writer needs to paint with a much broader brush.

The playwright should not expect that an important element of character slipped in subtly at the beginning of a play and never reinforced is going to enable the audience to understand another element of character or plot at the end of the play. Remember, the audience does not have the luxury of stopping the film or play to say, "Let's see that again because my attention slipped and I missed what happened." Or, "I see what happened, but what does it mean?" Or, "Now that we've gotten to this point of the play, I appear to have missed something. Let me flip back to see what it was." Of course, you could see the play or film on a DVD, which will afford you an opportunity to move back and forth to shed light on an action or character. However, it is highly unlikely that you would because you would then destroy your pleasure in the on-going action.

Finally, characters on a page ultimately will have to be turned into actors on a stage or in film. As a practical matter, you cannot multiply characters in a play with the same degree of freedom as you can in fiction. The cast of thousands is not possible on the stage and seldom is in film. For one thing, budgets are not likely to be big enough. More important, unless the "characters" are merely part of the scenery, the audience cannot meet too many in such a short period of time and keep them all in mind. (Think of what happens when you meet ten new people at a party.) Certainly it is easier to keep track of four characters than of forty. Many theaters with an interest in new plays suggest that the play require no more than five to six actors. While this fact has little to do with the artistic considerations that ideally should concern the writer, in the less than ideal world another character means another actor to pay, costume, and find a place on stage for.

> *Remember: A late point of attack is one technique for avoiding the necessity of multiplying characters.*

CHARACTERS IN PLACE AND TIME

For condensation and characterization, a playwright exploits the fact that an actor "puts on" the character and moves in real space and real time.

> SHEILA: There are a lot of memories in this room.
> BEN: There certainly are. Remember when we bought that piece?
> SHEILA: Oh, Ben, we need to talk now.

Sheila has come home determined to tell her husband that she is leaving him. She enters the living room that contains all the objects they have collected during six years of marriage. The actor *sees* those objects that the designer has placed on the set. (Remember that to the actor in the role of a character, it is a living room, not a set.) If the playwright remembers the small statue the couple bought on their last trip to Stockholm, the actor playing Sheila may have something to pick up and handle lovingly to indicate her state of mind. Her remembrance may well be revealed not in precise terms but as a *reaction* that suggests her emotion—and then her immediately conflicting emotions as she replaces the statue on the mantle, turning off Ben's efforts to re-create the past.

The awareness of physical place and objects has to be matched by the playwright's awareness of time. At the simplest level, if an actor goes off to change a costume (to the character it is a change of *clothes*), the other actors must have something to do that advances the plot or the audience will grow restive in the real time that it takes to make the costume change. A planned silence that the playwright uses to reveal character, advance plot, or create tension is different from silences imposed by the fact that the characters have nothing to do or must cross space without something to say. A real minute can appear to be hours to an audience (or actor) unless the dramatic minute has something in it that advances the plot.

Sometimes the very fact of "real" versus "stage" time can be used to create exciting effects. In the following scene, the climax of Christopher Marlowe's *The Tragicall History of Dr. Faustus,* Faustus is about to pay with his soul for the bargain with the Devil, a bargain that has given Faustus wealth, power, sex, and knowledge. As we pick up the action, his friends are leaving: They say "farewell" and exit.

The clock strikes eleven.

> FAUST: Ah, Faustus,
> Now has thou but one bare hour to live,
> And then thou must be damn'd perpetually!
> Stand still, you ever-moving spheres of Heaven,
> That time may cease, and midnight never come;
> Fair Nature's eye, rise, rise again and make

Perpetual day; or let this hour be but
A year, a month, a week, a natural day,
That Faustus may repent and save his soul!
O lente, lente, currite noctis equi
(Run slowly, slowly steeds of the night.)
The stars move still, time runs, the clock will strike,
The Devil will come, and Faustus must be damn'd.

After twenty-one more lines, at most another two to five minutes, we (and Faustus) hear the clock strike again:

FAUST: Ah, half the hour is past! 'T will all be past anon!

And, then after another eighteen lines—perhaps one minute of acting—we hear the clock strike midnight. We are told that an hour has gone by, but only ten minutes or so have gone by in real time. The difference creates a sense of speed that fits the situation.

The next part of the action manipulates the opposite effect of time. Keep in mind during the following scene that the clock's bell will be tolling steadily but with greater intervals between each of the twelve strokes than in real time.

                    The Clock striketh twelve.
O, it strikes, it strikes! Now, body, turn to air,
Or Lucifer will bear thee quick to hell!
                Thunder and lightning
O soul, be chang'd into little water-drops,
And fall into the ocean—ne're be found!—
My God, my God, look not so fierce on me!
                    Enter DEVILS
Adders and serpents, let me breathe awhile!—
Ugly hell, gape not!—Come not, Lucifer!—
I'll burn my books!—Ah, Mephistophilis!
                Exit DEVILS with him.

The director will ask the actor to stretch out this speech so it will take as long as possible, dragging out Faustus's final moments agonizingly. (If you want to explore the dramatic moment further, you can find the play at http://www.gutenberg.org/dirs/etext97/drfst10a.txt.)

In a production, the manipulation of the difference between stage time and real time creates tension in the audience that is equivalent to the tension in Faustus. The speeding up of time acts out his desire to hold time back. Dragging out the time that it would actually take to strike twelve from thirty seconds into two or three minutes increases the tension unbearably. Just as Faustus fearfully waits for Mephistopheles, the great forecloser on souls, so do we. The device that Marlowe uses so effectively is a rather standard technique in many films, particularly the ones in which a bomb is about to go off. We have learned to accept the convention that time in a narrative does not equal literal time.

● ● ● ● ●   *EXERCISE*   ● ● ● ● ●

Plan a five-minute scene in which the devil is waiting for Faustus. Faustus will come in at the end. The devil's concern is that Faustus will beg God to forgive him and so be saved. Aside from his desire to have Faustus's soul, try to give the devil a personal reason for concern. We will hear the clock that Faustus hears, but we will hear it at a tempo you decide on. Invent other characters if you need to.

 BEATS

On stage and in film you can signal the passage of time through a variety of conventional devices. On the stage, the lights or the curtain can be lowered and raised; in film, fades or cuts serve the same purpose. Five or five hundred years can pass in an instant. The breaks in the flow of the action work much as a chapter break might, allowing us to focus on key elements in the plot rather than the transitions. The fact that the audience accepts such devices is useful in two ways: (1) The few minutes of a curtain's dropping and raising is accepted as the hours it would take for a character to go from New York to Chicago or the years it takes for a character's hair to grow white; and (2) it allows the writer to account for the time it might take a character's traits to modify. In effect, the audience accepts that, during the break in the time flow signaled by the convention, people have gotten from one place to another and hours, days, or years have gone by. Such devices allow you to compress twenty years of story events into a few hours of performance.

Such conventional devices work as a kind of gravitational force holding scenes and acts, the large conventional units, firmly to the needs of the plot.

Directors often speak of a play as if it were a piece of music made up of **beats**, smaller units of dramatic time. From the playwright's point of view, beats are the essential working unit of the play. It is like the line in poetry and the sentence in fiction. The sum of the beats is the play. Each beat contains a revelation of a mood, relationship, or an action that advances our understanding of the plot. Each beat resolves some tension and leads to another beat until the end. Let us say, for example, that you are writing a car chase scene for a film. The villains are after the heroes, who are trying to rendezvous with a helicopter that will fly them to safety.

1. Beat 1. The Blues (the villains) are chasing the Greens (our heroes). The Greens approach a railroad crossing. A train is coming. The Blues are catching up and one of the villains is just raising his Glock. The Greens cross the tracks and The Blues screech to a halt.
2. Beat 2. The Greens' car develops a flat. The heroes frantically work to change the tire. The Blues are under way again and rapidly closing. Just as they round the curve, the tire is fixed and the heroes are back on the road.
3. Beat 3. The chase continues and the villains are catching up. In the distance we see the helicopter. One of the heroes carefully aims and shoots out the front tires of the villains' car, which overturns. Just ahead now is safety.
4. Beat 4. The heroes' car squeals to a halt next to the helicopter. With happy smiles on their faces they start to run to the cabin. In the helicopter we see the head villain raise a submachine gun.
   And so on.

Constructing by beats is equally necessary in less action-filled playscripts, as in the following scene from Harold Pinter's *The Collection*. Note how rapidly the beats follow on one another. The beats are punctuated with a pause.

> SITUATION: Harry enters his apartment and goes to a phone, which we have heard ringing. It is late at night.
> HARRY: Hello.
> VOICE: Is that you, Bill?
> HARRY: No, he's in bed. Who's this?
> VOICE: In bed?
> HARRY: Who is this?
> VOICE: What's he doing in bed?
> (*Pause*)
> HARRY: Do you know it's four o'clock in the morning?
> VOICE: Well, give him a nudge. Tell him I want a word with him.
> (*Pause*)
> HARRY: Who is this?
> VOICE: Go and wake him up, there's a good boy.
> (*Pause*)
> HARRY: Are you a friend of his?
> VOICE: He'll know me when he sees me.

HARRY: Oh yes?
(*Pause*)
VOICE: Aren't you going to wake him?
HARRY: No, I'm not.
(*Pause*)
VOICE: Tell him I'll be in touch.
(*The telephone cuts off.*)

In the first beat, the Voice fails to give Harry what he wants—an answer to his question. In the second beat, Harry is forced into the unreasonable position of having to respond to the Voice's questions without having received an answer to his. In a sense, he is defeated. The beat ends when the Voice treats Harry as a servant by asking Harry to wake Bill. Harry, quite understandably, tries to establish equality but is again defeated when the Voice does not answer the question; instead, the Voice reasserts his position of authority. Harry is not a "boy." In the next beat Harry again tries to establish his equality, but his question receives an unexpectedly indirect answer—an answer that is almost threatening. Harry's last speech in this beat is a question because he has not really been given an answer. But "Oh yes?" also has in it an assertion of its own—that is, you had better tell me more. In the next to last beat, the Voice refuses to give that information and Harry reestablishes his equality by refusing the Voice's request. In the final beat the Voice wins by cutting Harry off after making a demand that Harry cannot fulfill. Since the Voice has never given his name, who can Harry say called? We end with a feeling that something bad is going to happen.

As the Pinter excerpt demonstrates, a beat is like the clenching and unclenching of a hand. Sometimes the struggle between the characters is obvious, ending in violent words or actions; sometimes the struggle is simply for a mastery of the situation. Each time the beat unclenches we see a momentary restoration of some type of balance, a relaxation of tension. This relaxation is a small instance of the large resolution we expect at the end of the play. In the Pinter play, the hanging up of the phone literally disconnects the characters and releases the immediate tension. The playwright will, of course, vary the degree of tension in each beat, trying to reach the most intense beat (the climax) as close as possible to the resolution, the final unclenching.

● ● ● ● ●   *EXERCISES*   ● ● ● ● ●

1. If you haven't done so already, read Joyce Carol Oates's *Procedure* in Chapter 14 (pp. 339–345). Analyze the beats.

2. Think of a board game whose rules you know well (Trivial Pursuit, Monopoly, Scrabble, chess). Now take two or three characters who are in conflict about something (for example, whether or not to divorce, whether or not to rob a bank, whether or not to sell their business, whether or not to kill their hostage). Write a scene in which your characters are playing the game or kibitzing. You might also have your characters waiting for someone to arrive or waiting for a phone call with important information (waiting creates tension in the actual and dramatic worlds). What would happen in your scene if one of the characters did not know the game or did not play it well? If you haven't done so already, add a third character who is making something (a cake, a house of cards, a bookshelf, a bomb). *Note*: You should know how to make or do whatever you have your character making or doing (research the process).

 SETTING

> *"I think that as a playwright, if I detail that environment, then I'm taking away some from them [designers]. I'm taking away their creativity and their ability to have input themselves, not just to follow what the playwright has written. So I do a minimum set description and let the designers create within that."*
>
> August Wilson

We already discussed in Chapter 8 ("The Elements of Fiction," pp. 182–185) the idea of a setting or place for your scenes as an active element in your narrative. You may wish to review that section before continuing here. From your characters' point of view, the setting is not a series of words, it is a real place with real temperatures, furniture or grass, sirens or crickets. The setting in the fiction becomes a set in the play, a workplace prepared for the actors who will assume the fictive roles. (Film allows for actual places to become sets.)

In printed versions of plays, you might see the following description of a set:

SCENE: A court apartment in Los Angeles in the West Adams district. The room is done in white—white ceiling, white walls, white overly elaborate furniture—but a red wall-to-wall carpet covers the floor. A wall bed is raised. Upstairs, two doorless entrances stand on each side of the head of the bed. The right entrance is to the kitchen; the backstage area that represents the kitchen is shielded by a filmy curtain and the actors' dim silhouettes are seen when the area is lighted. The left entrance will be raised and offstage right at the head

of a short flight of stairs and a platform which leads into the combination bedroom–dressingroom–closet.

Ed Bullins from Goin'a Buffalo

You may even have seen more elaborate descriptions using words such as *stage
left*, *curtain*, and *scrim*. Most of what you are reading in such cases is probably
the playwright's description of the set from the first production of the play. It is
unlikely that Ed Bullins had that specific a set in mind when he was first writing
the play. Most likely, he thought of his play as happening in a "court apartment." Perhaps he also had in mind that the rooms would be painted white,
have a red carpet, and contain ornate furniture.

In many cases, the playwright has a much sketchier notion, a notion
more related to a sense of the place in which the action occurs rather than a
theatrical set:

> Galileo's scantily furnished study. Morning. GALILEO is washing
> himself. A barefooted boy, ANDREA, son of his housekeeper, MRS. SARTI,
> enters with a big astronomical model.

Bertolt Brecht from Galileo

From this description, a set designer may well build a set just as detailed
as the one we see described in Bullins's play.

When you are drafting, you probably are wasting energy if you spend
large amounts of time working up a set, though you need to be highly conscious of the place your characters are in because they will be conscious of
that place whether it be a mountaintop or their living room. Some playwrights, like some novelists, actually draw out rough designs of the place
where the action occurs, but they do so to give themselves a sense of what the
character is seeing, not in order to become set designers. Though the matter
is not the playwright's primary concern, producers do worry about a play's
meeting the needs of the available space and money.

Beth Henley's *Crimes of the Heart* might well have first caught someone's
eye because the entire play takes place in an old-fashioned kitchen:

> MEG: What's the cot doing in the kitchen?
> LENNY [MEG's sister]: Well, I rolled it out when Old Granddaddy got
> sick. So I could be close and hear him at night if he needed something.
> MEG (*glancing toward the door leading to the downstairs bedroom*): Is
> Old Granddaddy here?
> LENNY: Why, no. Old Granddaddy's at the hospital.

The door, of course, actually leads offstage. And, if we are experienced
with theatrical reality, we also assume that the cot is in the kitchen to provide a
place on which several people can sit at once, perhaps saving a set change to a

living room when the characters may need to lie down. By the end of the beat, however, from the audience's point of view the door leads to a bedroom and the cot is there for the reason stated. (In fact, Grandfather never actually appears in the play.) From a producer's point of view, *Crimes of the Heart* focuses the whole world of the characters in a relatively simple, inexpensive set.

Many theaters specifically request that the plays submitted to them be doable in simple sets with a bare stage or a few pieces of furniture or unit sets in which various places or times can be suggested or acted on different parts of the stage. Playwrights who make sets too specific ignore the reality that stages will vary enormously both in shape and size. All these variables suggest that you can waste a good deal of energy being too specific about details of setting that are not absolutely relevant to the particular actions of the characters.

Imagine yourself, for example, as a producer for a local small theater faced with the following description of a set:

> SCENE: William Hurt's study. At stage left is a small Queen Anne writing table, two by three feet, and next to it is a Chippendale chair with petti-point seat done in subtle shades of blue and rose. The pattern is a fleur-de-lis in the manner of Rogette. The carpet is a Bengali with dominant mauve colors. Stage right is a large bookcase containing the complete works of Dickens with Dore woodcuts. Upstage is a padded door, the type that one sees in libraries and music halls, the only exit from the room. Stage front are two matching leather chairs with an end table between them. On the table is an ivory chess set with the pieces spread on the inlaid board. The game in progress is a repeat of the famous Spassky/Fisher "Indian Defense" played during the Tunisian challenge....

While one might argue that the playwright needs to think of the setting in such detail, almost as a novelist might, writing it out is largely a waste of time. In any case, the director and set designer will probably ignore the elaborate detail.

The following notation will be sufficient for your purposes:

> SCENE: William Hurt's study. A small antique desk and chair, a bookcase filled with a matched set of books, other bookcases and two chairs separated by a low table on which a chess game is in progress.

Finally, keep in mind that the setting for the play is more than a visual environment. It influences how the characters are feeling, what they say and do. Possibilities for characterizing grow from the fact that the environment may contain smells; it may be hot or cold, light or dark. The playwright can exploit the fact that the characters can react to all the physical elements even when they are not talking about them. (In fiction, the narrator has to remind the reader continually that such physical elements are operating.)

● ● ● ● ●   *EXERCISE*   ● ● ● ● ●

Return to one of the scenes you wrote for the television version of the radio advertisement. Write dialogue for the husband and wife that will be a response to the following facts: It is twelve degrees out and the wife is wearing a new perfume. Remember, these facts are known to them before the scene opens.

"The greatest rules of dramatic writing are conflict, conflict, conflict."

James Frey

13

DIALOGUE AND ITS PROBLEMS

"I've never written anything, but I think I have a good ear for dialogue."

"Suit the action to the word, the word to the action..."
Shakespeare, *Hamlet*, III, ii, 17–18

DIALOGUE: THE ESSENCE OF DRAMA

When you write a stage play, most of what you are going to write is dialogue. Here is what your dialogue must do:

1. Contain all the necessary exposition, including what happened before the point of attack, between scenes and acts, and offstage (though the audience can be told some things through sounds, such as a gunshot offstage).
2. Reveal almost everything about the characters' feelings, beliefs, needs and wants.

In other words, the dialogue contains both exposition and action.

From the playwright's point of view, dialogue is not "talk," although the actor is, of course, "talking" the character's words. In fact, transcriptions of how people actually talk are difficult to follow because most of our talk lacks shape, that is, purpose in relationship to a plot. We may indulge ourselves with idle talk, but *dialogue* must be idle only for a purpose. Every line of dialogue serves (or appear to serve) one or more of the following dramatic purposes:

- To reveal the character's nature
- To reveal the character's needs and intentions
- To have an impact on another character or characters

Much of the playwright's work goes into shaping the plot so that the dialogue is what the characters will *do* to each other. If the dialogue contains information (exposition) that the audience needs for understanding the state of affairs, that information usually will be a by-product of the interaction among the characters. Even in a screenplay, in which the characters' action can be more physical, the dialogue must be treated as a type of action.

Ideally, each speech a character makes will contain both a **text**—an intended message directed at the other character(s)—and a **subtext**—which conveys the characters' real feelings, needs, and attitudes.

SON: Can I do the dishes after I talk with Joanne about the test tomorrow?
MOTHER: Do you want to borrow my car on Saturday?

The visible messages—the text—are requests for information. Clearly, however, the son is also trying to put off a task by suggesting that doing the dishes is not as important as doing homework. His real intention (talking with Joanne) is the subtext. The mother's subtext is so clear that it needs no analysis. The questions, as it turns out, are not questions at all.

Even if the other characters do not grasp the subtext, the audience will, consciously or unconsciously. As we saw earlier, each character has an agenda, and this agenda will be reflected in both text and subtext. Just as the surface of what we say to others is only the window into what we really mean, so too for what characters say to other characters.

The opening scene from Noel Coward's *Blithe Spirit* illustrates the technique. In the play, Charles Condomine, a writer, is talking to his second wife, Ruth, while they have cocktails before guests arrive. Their previous dialogue has been about how Charles got the idea for an interesting character in his last novel. Elvira, Charles's first wife, is dead.

1. RUTH: Used Elvira to help you—when you were thinking something out, I mean?
2. CHARLES: Every now and then—when she concentrated—but she didn't concentrate very often.
3. RUTH: I do wish I'd known her.
4. CHARLES: I wonder if you'd have liked her.
5. RUTH: I'm sure I should—as you talk of her she sounds enchanting—yes, I'm sure I should have liked her because you know I have never for an instant felt in the least jealous of her—that's a good sign.
6. CHARLES: Poor Elvira.
7. RUTH: Does it still hurt—when you think of her?

(*Numbering added.*)

Before you go on, think about what this beat establishes. Of course, the overt purpose (text) is simply that Ruth is asking for information about her predecessor, information that the audience learns also. But we sense other, complex messages. A director and an actor preparing the beat for a rehearsal might analyze the subtext as follows:

1. Ruth is really asking if Elvira had the same importance as she does as Charles's creative helper. In a way, Ruth is indicating her concern about something in their relationship. Perhaps she wants to or needs to be told that she is not simply a "second" wife but someone unique.
2. Charles does not catch the subtext at first, and so answers unthinkingly. If he does not modify or correct what he has begun to say, he will have answered "yes" to Ruth's question. That answer would indicate there is nothing unique in their relationship. He realizes immediately that he has been insensitive (does he see a *look* in Ruth's face or a sudden

stiffening of her posture?) and in midsentence modifies his statement. The problem is that he can't really correct what he has already said. In any case, he either has to be unfaithful to the memory of his first wife or lie to his second wife.

3. Ruth tries to appear merely inquisitive, as if she is not jealous. Obviously, however, she is thinking about her dead "competition."

4. Charles's question responds to Ruth, but the word *wonder* tells us that something has flashed across his mind about the differences between his wives.

5. Ruth indicates her jealousy precisely because she raises an issue that no one has raised, and the audience will tend to doubt people who deny an emotion no one has accused them of feeling. In short, we don't believe the text of someone who "protesteth too much."

6. Charles appears not to respond to what Ruth has said but to the train of thought set off by his previous statement. In fact, we might feel that Ruth has started a chain reaction different from the one she expected. (*Note:* Charles responds to what he is thinking, not to the other character's dialogue. He is starting to say what he *has* to say, not what the logic of the dialogue appears to call for.)

7. Ruth has recognized that she has set off a chain of associations in Charles. The text tells us that she is thinking of his well-being. The subtext tells us that she wants some kind of assurance for herself.

Without anyone telling us what they are like, the text and subtext in the dialogue allow the audience to see that the characters are debonair, intelligent, and witty. The subtext also creates a sense of mystery revealed rather than stated. Something is going on that has caused Ruth to push the conversation in this direction. The information also creates tension because (1) we wonder what the characters really mean, what they may be hiding in the way of feelings or facts; (2) or we wonder when another character will catch on to what we know is really being said; (3) or we wonder when characters will realize something about themselves that we have already figured out.

The most effective dialogue does all the above. In sum, creating the subtext—suggesting without telling—is a large part of the playwright's work. Effective dialogue will show not tell.

●　●　●　●　●　　*EXERCISES*　　●　●　●　●　●

1. Before reading the following passage from *Blithe Spirit*, review the preceding passage and ask yourself: What is the first word that Charles should say in his answer to Ruth? Now read on:

CHARLES: No, not really—sometimes I almost wish it did—I feel rather guilty—

RUTH: I wonder if I died before you'd grown tired of me if you'd forget me so soon?

CHARLES: What a horrible thing to say . . .

RUTH: No—I think it's interesting.

CHARLES: Well, to begin with I *haven't* forgotten Elvira—I *remember* her very distinctly indeed—I remember how fascinating she was, and how maddening—I remember how badly she played all games and how cross she got when she didn't win—I remember her gay charm when she had achieved her own way over something and her extreme acidity when she didn't—I remember her physical attractiveness, which was tremendous—and her spiritual integrity which was nil . . .

RUTH: You can't remember something that was nil.

CHARLES: I remember how morally untidy she was . . .

RUTH: Was she more physically attractive than I am?

CHARLES: That was a very tiresome question, dear, and fully deserves the wrong answer.

RUTH: You really are very sweet.

CHARLES: Thank you.

RUTH: And a little naive, too.

2. Analyze this dialogue as we have done for the previous passage. Note that Ruth's question ("I wonder . . . ?") really contains two questions. Is Charles's answer a dramatically effective one? Has anything about their emotional relationship been established? Who, if anyone, has "won" points during the beat? How do you know?

3. Assume that Charles says, "Yes, Elvira was more physically attractive." Write a beat for that answer.

4. Take the following situation and write dialogue for the characters. The scene is a dorm room or shared apartment. The situation is that roommate A is trying to get roommate B to leave the room for the evening but does not want to say why. Remember that the audience at some point has to be let into the reasons for A's action and B's response.

> "*The speech we hear is an indication of that which we don't hear. It is a necessary avoidance, a violent, sly, anguished or mocking smoke screen which keeps the other in its place.*"
>
> Harold Pinter

PRINCIPLES AND COMMON ERRORS

Your Exposition Is Showing

The characters should not tell each other expository information *simply* to transfer that information to the audience. Unless you have a character who has just come into the story and therefore is ignorant of the facts and needs to know them, you must remember that the characters are usually aware of what has happened to them and to each other. Nothing is so absurd as one character telling another:

> "John, do you remember when we had our children—Annabelle, Hermes, and Philo?"

No dialogue destroys an audience's sense of verisimilitude more than characters telling each other about what they obviously must know. The audience suddenly becomes aware of itself: "Oh, I'm watching a play, and the characters are telling me stuff I have to know." Instead of following the characters, the audience becomes conscious of the exposition because the playwright has failed to find a reason in plot and character for slipping in this necessary information. The audience begins to think *about* the play instead of emotionally participating *in* it.

Look at the following scene, for example, in which a couple are having an argument about moving to the town where the wife's parents live.

> JOAN: You are not being fair, Mike.
>
> MIKE: Joan, the issue of fair has nothing to do with it. Your parents do not have a single socially redeeming quality between the two of them.
>
> JOAN: What do you mean my parents do not have any redeeming qualities? Why do you try to hurt my self-esteem like that?
>
> MIKE: That is easy, Joan, your father is loud and obnoxious. Your mother, on the other hand, cannot stick to a subject. She comes totally out of the blue with ideas.
>
> JOAN: Mike, you are being totally unreasonable. The last time my parents were over you had a great time.
>
> MIKE: Joan, do you remember the last time we were with your parents? It was at our wedding reception and that was almost six months ago.
>
> JOAN: Is that so?
>
> MIKE: Do you remember how your dad's Polish jokes almost caused my Uncle Joe to throw him through a window? And Uncle Joe had come all the way from New Zealand to be with us. Aunt Sylvia was not any happier and she came all the way from Buffalo, Joan.

Aside from any other problems you may have noticed with the dialogue, Mike's speeches are clearly addressed to the audience, since Joan would surely remember the last time they saw her parents as well as other facts, such as her own name. And if she does not, we have to know why.

One way of communicating such expository information naturally is to imbed the information in the dialogue as part of the tension between the characters. Assume Mike and Joan have often talked about the wedding and that it always comes up in their spats.

> MIKE: I still feel like hiding when I think about it.
> JOAN: It was six months ago, Mike. I am tired of hearing about it.
> MIKE: Your dad had to know my mother was Polish.
> JOAN: He was just trying to be friendly.
> MIKE: If it was not our wedding, I think my Uncle Joe would have thrown him out the window.
> JOAN: It was only a Polish joke, Mike.
> MIKE: Poles are not dumb. Chopin. Milosc.
> JOAN: You tell them yourself.
> MIKE: It's different, Joan.
> JOAN: You just do not like my dad.
> MIKE: My uncle did *not* come all the way from New Zealand to be insulted.
> JOAN: Do not change the topic.
> MIKE: We are not moving to Urbana. I do not like your mother either.

Though the dialogue still needs work, such as contractions, in the rewritten version the audience is beginning to overhear characters who know what their situation is. The information is now within a dramatic beat within which the actors can appear to speak spontaneously; it feels like an outgrowth of Joan and Mike's argument. Notice the technique of each character only mentioning the name of the other once or twice.

In short, dialogue must appear to be talk for the characters' purposes, not for the benefit of the audience. When they create dialogue, most playwrights adhere to a primary dramatic convention: Between the characters and the audience is a wall. The space inside that wall is the real, the only world. Each time the dialogue lapses into obvious exposition, a crack appears in it. Too many cracks and the audience will begin to wonder why the playwright didn't try to write a novel instead of promising a play.

Note: The limits of dialogue as a tool for revealing the exposition has led modern dramatists to bring back the chorus as a device for revealing opinions and information. But the chorus in a modern play is usually one person, a kind of "stage manager." If your plot involves long stretches of time (as in a history play) or a great deal of exposition (as in a thriller), you may wish to construct the plot so as to use a narrator. For examples see *A View from a Bridge, Equus, Amadeus,* or *Frost/Nixon.* Such a technique appears less clumsy than long stretches in which the characters simply tell the plot to each other. Remember, though, that stage narrators should not provide simply the narrative bridges for the plot's sake; they should be characters who belong to the play's structure. This convenient device can be a burden since the playwright will also have to account for the narrator. In drama, as in the other genres, there are no free rides.

Contractions and Formality

You do not want your characters to speak as if they are delivering dedications or eulogies. Unless you deliberately intend that your characters demonstrate formal traits, they will elide their speech. In any case, if the playwright doesn't do it for them, the actors will change "it is" to "it's" and "cannot" to "can't," especially if the formality appears merely to be the playwright's adhering slavishly to the absurd rule that one should "never use a contraction in writing." In Mike and Joan's dialogue, not using contractions causes their speech to sound formal, more like a debate than an argument between lovers. Note how stiff even the revised dialogue is if you read it aloud.

Even with the contractions, their lines of dialogue still often sound as if they are reading from a prepared script. Mike's use of the phrase "single socially redeeming quality" (in the first version) is stiff and intellectual, to say nothing of how difficult it is to speak. Though your characters may talk formally because of their natures or because the plot has reached a point that requires a formal address (see "Long Speeches," p. 329), the playwright must prepare the dialogue so it appears to have come from that character at the moment. In other words, the playwright has to plan the dialogue so that it seems unplanned, spontaneous.

●   ●   ●   ●   ●   *EXERCISE*   ●   ●   ●   ●   ●

Assuming that Joan is not stuffy, rewrite the first version of her dialogue. Now assume that Mike tends to be stuffy and rigid because he thinks that formal speech is a sign of education and class. Rewrite Mike's dialogue to let the audience know that his formality is a bone of contention between them. (You may want to assume that Mike is self-educated.)

> *"I write plays because dialogue is the most respectable way of contradicting myself."*
>
> Tom Stoppard

Interruptions and Other Ways of Creating Verisimilitude

Dialogue is usually most effective when it follows the *patterns* rather than the content of conversation. Your dialogue is felt as "real" not because it reports what people actually say but because it follows the *way* people talk, the structures of conversation. Just as in actual conversation, your characters' dialogue may be interrupted, may fail to follow from what others have just said, or may appear to be illogical and unreasonable. One reason Mike and Joan sound so stilted is that they skip no steps in what they say to each other. Notice how one word is echoed in each speech as if they had to prove they were listening. (Go back and circle the repeated words in the first version.)

The devices for achieving an appearance of spontaneity are taken from the conversational patterns of people in real life. They

- interrupt each other and finish the sentences of others.
- trail off and repeat themselves.
- do not directly respond to the question asked.
- say things that are the result of a line of thinking not directly related to the conversation.
- use contractions.
- use pronouns; that is, they are aware of what is present to them.
- respond to a look on another's face or to something the other does.
- blurt out.
- use double entendre.
- obviously lie.

There are a host of other verbal habits we have and a useful way to acquire them for your dialogue is to listen carefully for the patterns.

Let's apply some of these patterns to part of Mike and Joan's dialogue:

> JOAN: It was six months ago, Mike. I'm tired of hearing—
> MIKE: He had to know my mother was Polish.
> JOAN: Dad was just trying to be friendly. He doesn't mean—
> MIKE: If it weren't...wasn't our wedding, I think my Uncle Joe
> would have thrown him out the window.
> JOAN: It was only a Polish joke.
> MIKE: Right out the window.
> JOAN: You know my father doesn't—
> MIKE: Yah, I know your father. Well, Poles are not dumb. Chopin.
> Milosc. And...and...hundreds of other people.
> JOAN: You tell them yourself. And stop interrupting me!
> MIKE: Copernicus!

Because interruptions, repetition, and self-correction are so typical of our actual conversational habits, they are the most obvious way of creating verisimilitude and of making your dialogue less formal. However, beware of overusing these techniques. And be sure that *what* the character was about to say is clear before the next character interrupts.

> ROBIN: What if we get caught?
> THADEUS: That's—
> ROBIN: If the police take me home my father is going—
> THADEUS: Police? What are—
> ROBIN: Are you sure it will be O.K.?

Though it is clear that Robin is frightened, it is never clear to the audience what Thadeus was about to say. In fact, the actor who plays Thadeus will look like a fool if Robin's timing is a bit off; he'll have to drag out the word being interrupted. Notice, however, that when Thadeus interrupts Robin, we understand that he was about the say "to give me hell" or some such thing. Be sure to give the character enough words before being interrupted so that the actors playing both the interrupter and interruptee can establish a natural timing.

Beginning playwrights, particularly those who have worked in fiction, often give their characters dialogue that would be used only if the characters were blind. Not only do the characters continually use one another's names, but they mention objects that the audience can see, and name actions as well as respond to them.

> JACK: Here's your martini, Barbara.
> BARBARA: I wanted an onion in the martini, Jack.
> JACK: Try the martini first, Barbara.
> BARBARA (*sips*): Now that I've tried it, Jack, what?
> JACK: What do you think, Barbara?
> BARBARA: I still want an onion in my martini, Jack.
> JACK (*knocks the martini from her hand*): You ungrateful bitch.
> BARBARA: Why did you knock the martini from my hand?

This dialogue sounds as if it were written for a novel without a narrator (not a particularly good idea) rather than a play with an audience who would see the events. (Even in a novel, the description of actions would be in the narration not the dialogue.) Notice, also, the unnecessary repetition of the person's name each addresses. Once should do the job. Such dialogue is a sure sign of inexperience with stage or film.

Fake Dialogue or the Dialogue Dummy

Everything that characters say must serve their needs. When a character says a line of dialogue only to break up a long speech or when a character simply sets up another character's speeches, the playwright is committing two fatal errors in one: The actor who serves up the gopher ball feels like a fool ("Why am I saying this?"), and the audience begins to wonder whether they are observing a ventriloquist's dummy or a character with needs and wants of his or her own.

Ask yourself why Beth is saying the italicized speeches in the following dialogue:

> BETH: The pitcher has my goldfish in it right now. You'll have to use a mixing bowl.
> KEVIN: Looks like one of them has gone to paradise.
> BETH: *Paradise?*
> KEVIN: He is a floater.
> BETH: *Floater?*
> KEVIN: Dead.

Not only has the writer taken too long to establish a small point, but Beth appears simply to be feeding Kevin lines. Now add the following to Kevin's last bit of dialogue before the word *dead*: "Are you listening to me?" At this point Beth's denseness begins to make sense.

● ● ● ● ●　　*EXERCISE*　　● ● ● ● ●

Return to Beth's second speech. It also appears to be merely a placeholder. Write something for her to say that will give us a sense of her needs and advance the scene. If necessary, rewrite Kevin's speeches.

Designators, or Stealing the Actors' and Directors' Jobs

The words the characters say should indicate their emotional state. Being overly elaborate in designating how the speech should be said is usually a blunder. The director or actor will ignore the designator unless the playwright's command to use a special tone of voice is absolutely necessary. Observe the following:

> BARBARA (*concerned*): What do you want to do tonight?
> SAM (*only half listening*): How about us going to Seaside tonight, Diane?
> BARBARA (*shocked by what she hears*): Diane?
> SAM (*embarrassed and placatingly*): I can't believe I said that.
> BARBARA (*angry and puzzled*): What can't you believe you said?
> SAM (*in a squirming voice*): What I just said.
> BARBARA (*questioning*): Who's Diane?

SAM (*whining because he knows he's trapped*): Diane is a friend.
BARBARA (*incredulous*): A friend?

Many of the designators merely sound ridiculous; how does someone say something in an "angry but puzzled" voice?

The rule of thumb is never to use a designator unless the dialogue you write for a character normally would be said in a different tone of voice:

SAM (*softly*): Help.

In fact, a good discipline is to avoid designators altogether, especially when you are creating the playscript. Often writers use elaborate designators to avoid the work needed to ensure that what the characters *say* indicates their emotion. This principle also should be observed in writing dialogue for narrative fiction.

Long Speeches

Usually you will avoid long speeches. However, beats do occur during which characters may talk on for some time because:

1. A character has asked another character a question calling for a long answer.
2. They are making a formal speech as part of the plot (as in a play that contains a trial).
3. Part of their nature is to be long-winded.
4. The playwright has decided to use the device of the soliloquy (a technique not often employed in contemporary playwriting).

Most of the time, however, your characters will be interrupted, challenged, or simply waiting for responses. As a result, most of the individual speeches will be relatively brief alternating lines, what the Greeks called *stichomythia*. For a classical example look at Creon's and his son Heman's argument in *Antigone*. If you find your characters simply giving large blocks of information, it is likely that the dialogue is dialogue only in form.

Grunting and Pausing

Since the actors will create any extra sounds they need for (1) pacing, (2) transitions, (3) laughing or crying, or (4) responding to the action and dialogue, you should avoid indicating grunts and wheezes, conversational placeholders. *Uhh, ohhh, ehh, ahh, er, ahhhh,* and other self-interrupters are not needed and look absurd on the page. If you wish an actor to pause, write "(*Pause*)" at the proper point or ellipses (...).

In the following dialogue, the writer appears amateurish, forcing effects on the actor or reader typographically. In this scene, Barbara and Sam are at the beach. Obviously, Sam is horsing around.

> BARBARA: So where, *uhhhhh*, did we, *ha-ha*, decide to go tonight, Mike?
> SAM: *YUK! YUK!* very funny.
> BARBARA: I'm *soooooo* sorry, *ha! ha!*.........hey cut that out you, don't you dare throw me in the water. I've got my contacts in! Ok, ok, I love you too, I said I love *yogglogglober glub glub gurgle gurgle!*

It would have been sufficient for the writer simply to let the actors know what is happening and allow them to supply the sounds to fit the action. Of course, if the play is meant as a parody, the excesses may be justified. *(Note:* Also avoid representing non-word sounds in fiction.)

Accents, Dialect, and Verbal Tics

The one area in which dialogue should be like conversation is in its imitation of social, regional, or national speech habits. It hardly needs saying that characters should have intonations, accents, grammar, diction, and syntax appropriate to their general background, the circumstances in which they find themselves, and their intentions. Without good reason, a waiter with a seventh-grade education is not likely to speak like a Harvard graduate.

When you give a character an accent that is merely a matter of pronunciation, you need only indicate in the description of the character what accent is necessary:

> FORSYTH P. WILLOWBY, a cadaverous-looking man of about forty who speaks with a Boston accent.
>
> PRISCILLA HESTER GARARD, a thirtyish blond who affects a southern accent. Nonetheless, one can detect her Brooklyn accent.

Presumably, you have given this information to the director because the characters' particular accents are important in the play. The information will be sufficient and the playwright does not need to indicate the pronunciation through phonetic spelling. In fact, the playwright should not do so. The actor will work out the proper accent according to the playwright's directions about where the character is from (Boston, Alabama, or Russia). It is the director's job to cast an actor who can produce the desired accent.

The writer's task becomes more difficult if the character's origins require a dialect. Unlike an accent (how the words are pronounced), a dialect involves different vocabulary, grammar, syntax, and elisions, which will have to be provided for the actor. Obviously, the writer either has to be intimately familiar with the dialect or do research on it.

Swearing and Vulgarity

One way contemporary playwrights create verisimilitude is by writing dialogue that contains the words people use in real life but not in "polite" society or before their grandmothers. Words that once were forbidden are now staples for naturalistic plays; in fact, they are almost conventions for creating a feeling of reality. As with all other diction decisions, the type of swearing or vulgarity, if any, your characters will do depends on what they are like and how they would respond verbally to the situations in which they find themselves. You have to take your chances on your audience's reaction. The producer will not choose to do your play if strong sexual language is inappropriate for the audience (e.g., an audience composed of the school board in a small Missouri town). However, if the audience feels your characters should react to misfortune with contemporary swearing and you have them saying "gee whizzes" when a hammer strikes a finger, then you may unintentionally cause laughter. The audience expects something stronger.

Never have your characters swear just because *you* wish to shock or to create the impression that your play is realistic. The audience will hear the author swearing, not the character. Of course, your character may be the type who unconsciously or unknowingly uses non–drawing-room diction or uses it deliberately for effect. That's part of his character. A good rule of tongue is to ask yourself why this particular character is swearing at this time. As with accents and dialects, don't use swear words unless you have an ear for their natural, idiomatic use—a wag might say "their proper use."

Locker Room Raillery

Though in real life we often chatter at one another in a mocking but friendly way, on paper—and on the stage—this type of wisecracking appears forced, though an individual character may deliver wisecracks as an aspect of his or her personality (as Hawkeye does in *M*A*S*H*). Effective humor occurs when (1) the characters seriously say something that the audience finds absurd or (2) the character is truly witty, as Algernon is in Oscar Wilde's *The Importance of Being Earnest:*

> JACK: I am in love with Gwendolen. I have come up to town expressly to propose to her.
> ALGERNON: I thought you had come up for pleasure? . . . I call that business.
> JACK: How utterly unromantic you are!
> ALGERNON: I really don't see anything romantic in proposing. It is very romantic to be in love. But there is nothing romantic about a definite proposal. Why, one may be accepted. One usually is, I believe. Then the excitement is all over. The very essence of romance is uncertainty. If ever I get married, I'll certainly try to forget the fact.

Algernon intends the humor of his absurd statement as a comment on attitudes toward love. He means to be witty, and his wit is rewarded with our laughter. At the same time, of course, his triviality is revealed.

That wit is a far cry from the following rather crude and forced locker room raillery:

> KEVIN: Hey, asshole. Have you seen my Kleenex?
> SPARKY: Up yours, Kev. You wanna go to Eben's for a couple of brews? The broads are easy.
> KEVIN: You're so dumb you can't even get easy.
> SPARKY: Who struck out with Lena the Hyena? A nerd can make it with her. Face it, you got the sex appeal of a dustball . . . .

The author of this dialogue might want to argue that the characters are meant to sound embarrassingly crude. As walk-on, walk-off characters, Kevin and Sparky could produce a mild discomfort, the embarrassed laughter that characters who are making fools of themselves produce. However, if the audience had to spend much time in their company, they would soon be more irritated than interested or concerned, just as if they met such people in real life.

In any case, the appeal to reality is not convincing. The mere fact that people really speak exactly as you report does not make the fictional or dramatic dialogue effective. A character who is meant to be boring must still be interesting in a way that does not bore the audience.

"Moving around is good for creativity: the next line of dialogue that you desperately need may well be waiting in the back of the refrigerator or half a mile along your favorite walk."

Will Shetterly

● ● ● ● ●   *EXERCISES*   ● ● ● ● ●

1. Read the following scene from *The Day They Shot John Lennon*.

Scene from
The Day They Shot John Lennon

JAMES MCLURE

The date is December 9, 1980, the day John Lennon was shot. Shortly after the shooting was announced people began to gather across the street from his apartment house on Seventy-second Street in New York City. Some were fans; some were merely curious. They stood around for hours; they talked to strangers who stood near them; some cried.

One of those gathered that fateful day was Fran Lowenstein, whom the author describes as thirty-five years old, "a native New Yorker and all that implies. Tough, sensitive, a feminist and a member of the Woodstock generation who is also looking for a meaningful relationship." She works as a secretary.

Fran strikes up a conversation with Brian Murphy, who is "in advertising." The author tells us he is "given to quick opinions and stances of self-confidence though he is basically a confused individual looking for love." He is thirty-three.

By the time the scene below begins, among the topics Fran and Brian have talked about are Lennon's music, their jobs, the bars they frequent, politics, and modern painting. Their interaction continues:

> FRAN: It's like spirals within spirals y'know. I mean I see images tumbling by. I see myself as a little girl on a visit to my grandmother's in Queens and we go to the park. And it's green and beautiful and my father's with me. Big, and young and strong. And whenever I think of that I think of "Penny Lane," it's like, that's the way it felt. (*Pause.*)
>
> BRIAN: I know. It's like background music for our lives. I remember at my first high school dance and I was all sweaty and scared and I was gonna walk across the room to ask Richie Woodall to dance with me. And they started playing "Hey Jude" over the P.A. system. It was a Catholic dance. I think the nuns thought it was about St. Jude. The saint of lost causes.
>
> FRAN: (*Passionately.*) Maybe that's what all this is. A lost cause. The sixties. The peace movement. Look what's happenin' now in the Middle East. El Salvador. Are we any closer? Are we getting there? Take a look at the E.R.A.? Are we getting there? Three-Mile Island. Are we getting there? How can we say we're civilized when we continue to hold people back. Because of sex, because of race. Is that getting us anywhere? Increased military spending, weapons for defense. (*Laughing.*) And the joke is we're all afraid of the bomb! We blame everything on "They." The Pentagon—"They"! The CIA—"They." But we all have to take responsibility for the society in which we live. All America wants to do is go to the movies! Is that getting us there? Where's the leadership? Where's the dialogue? We're not talking. We're not listening. We're missing the whole point. It's not the sixties. People are just burying their heads in the sand. People will do *anything* rather than be here now. (*Pause.*) Are we getting there? No. People are just going to the office and making money...People suck.
>
> BRIAN: (*impressed*) Wow. You know, you're a very passionate woman.
>
> FRAN: Well, what did you expect? Someone dumb?
>
> BRIAN: No, it's just that women—

FRAN: Oh brother, here we go. It's just that women what?

BRIAN: Just that women that you meet in bars—

FRAN: Hey! You didn't meet *me* in a bar! Right? Get it?

BRIAN: But you said you *go* to bars.

FRAN: I go to bars. I wasn't born in a bar. Right?

BRIAN: It's just that I think you're very smart and very passionate and very attractive. And I don't meet women like that.

FRAN: Where do you meet your "women," Brian?

BRIAN: Bars. I meet my women in bars.

FRAN: Well, then maybe that's *your* problem, Brian. Maybe you're meeting those kind of women—the passionate, attractive, intelligent kind of women but since you're just living for the night, maybe you don't see them for what they are.

BRIAN: Hey. Who're you kidding? You go to bars. You have drinks. You meet guys.

FRAN: That's right, Brian. And I'm the passionate, attractive, intelligent kind. (*He touches her arm.*)

BRIAN: Look babe, I didn't mean to—

FRAN: Don't touch me.

BRIAN: O.K. I won't touch you.

FRAN: Boy I hate your kind.

BRIAN: My *kind*? My *kind*? Boy if that isn't sexual stereotyping I don't know what is.

FRAN: Granted. Sexual stereotyping. But in your case, it works.

BRIAN: Oh yeah? And what is my type?

FRAN: You're—the button-down-collar-junior-executive-climbing-the-ladder-of-success-but-I'm-really-the-sensitive-young-man type. That's your type. I'll bet you haven't been to a museum in a million years.

BRIAN: For your information just last week I went to the Museum of Modern Art.

FRAN: Oh yeah. What did you see?

BRIAN: Paintings.

FRAN: What kind of paintings?

BRIAN: Modern paintings.

FRAN: Oh Jesus. What a fake. What a liar. I bet you weren't even at Woodstock.

BRIAN: I was too!

FRAN: Everybody has their little scheme don't they? Tell me, does this line work a lot? This I-like-art line? Does that work on everybody?

BRIAN: No. Just you.

FRAN: Well, it wasn't working on me. I can assure you of that.

BRIAN: Yeah, come to think of it, now, I've seen you before. Sure yeah. I see you all the time in the bars.

FRAN: You don't see me at bars.

BRIAN: Sure I do.

FRAN: You do not.

BRIAN: The Adams Apple, Michaels, Maxwells, The Meat Place, Martys, The Satyre, Pegasus, sure you're there all the time. You're not special. I thought you were but you're not. You're like all the rest.

FRAN: Fuck you.

BRIAN: My pleasure.

FRAN: One thing though.

BRIAN: Huh.

FRAN: If I'm like all the rest...so are you. (*Pause.*)

BRIAN: Look, I'm sorry...I don't know what we got so excited about...I mean...You're a nice girl.

FRAN: Woman.

BRIAN: Woman! Woman! Woman! (*Pause.*) Look...wanna smoke...I've got some gum...spearmint...Look I'm not like this...maybe I am. I didn't used to be. I don't meet women like you. I felt alive in the sixties. That's why I came here. I wanted...I wanted...then I met you. I mean. Something. In common. I don't know. Maybe not. I don't want to go to work. I wanted to talk. (*She accepts cigarette. He lights it.*) I mean. Life goes on.

a. Assume you are the director and that you are discussing the intention behind each speech with the actors who play Fran and Brian because they want to know how to play the tone and gestures best suited to their parts. They have asked the following questions that you have to answer.

BRIAN: In the speech beginning "I know" why do I tell Fran who St. Jude is? Since I know who St. Jude is, am I only setting up her speech? Or is something happening that makes me say that? Or should the writer redo the dialogue?

FRAN: In my long speech, do I really know what I'm talking about or am I simply spewing out words that I've heard?

BRIAN: What was Brian going to say when he starts talking about women? When Fran breaks me off and I start again, have I changed what I was going to say the first time?

FRAN: Why is Fran so uptight after her long speech? Up to that time she seems to have been getting along all right with Brian. In fact, Brian appears to be trying hard to please.

BRIAN: Starting with "My *kind*," when Brian gets angry back, is he serious or is that part of his come-on? And when Fran asks him about the museum, is he putting her on or has she caught him in a lie?

FRAN: Is this attacking and putting down of men one of the reasons that she doesn't get her man? Are her politics always so much up front—perhaps as a defense—that they cut off innocent conversation? Or is there *no* relaxing with her?

BRIAN: When he says he saw her in bars, it's clear that he's striking back because he feels put down. But why does he mention all the bars? And what does he mean when he says "You're like all the rest"?

FRAN: Is she the kind of person who says "fuck you"?

BRIAN: Sure she is, but something more important. His answer just feels like a placeholder, a setup. I don't know why he says it from his point of view.

b. In this scene, Fran and Brian have been struggling over something. What is it? How is it resolved?
c. Why is Brian's last speech so chopped up and so illogical?
d. Picking up on Brian's last speech above, write a beat for the time it will take them to smoke the cigarette. Don't forget that they are holding a vigil outside John Lennon's apartment house.

2. We have a new way of conversing, the Internet. Chat goes back and forth, perhaps hovering between real speech and dialogue (shaped speech). Create an Internet dialogue of two pages or so between two characters. One of their frustrations might be trying to talk and yet feeling limited by the time it takes to keyboard and send a message and then receive a reply. Think of a situation in which at least one of the parties wants something and the other does not want to give it.

3. Your character is in a restaurant with a significant other. They have not been getting along well before dinner. In fact, they have gone out to neutral ground to hash out the situation. They are receiving exceptionally slow service. The waiter has finally given them a basket of rolls. Five in fact. They each have eaten two and then one says to the other: "Do you want the last one?" Write the dialogue that ensues.

———————•———————

A CHECKLIST FOR CREATING NATURAL OR FLOWING DIALOGUE
1. Allow characters to interrupt or finish each other's speeches.
2. Stop a thought in mid-sentence or have a character repeat a word or sentence.
3. Have a character not respond to the other character.
4. Search for better word.
5. Respond to the look on the other's face or something the other does.
6. Give the speaker some stage business while they are speaking.
7. Use indirect discourse to avoid dialogue dummy or create a character

who needs the information (e.g., a detective, someone who has been away, just moved into the neighborhood.)

8. Keep designators simple.

9. Avoid step dialogue in which characters constantly pick up a word from the previous speech or repeat part of the previous speech before going on.

10. Beware of long passages in which characters recite to other characters information—including information about feelings or social attitudes.

11. Remember that each character comes from a position so that his or her response should be in character.

12. Avoid writing something for the actor to say that may be funny but is not in character.

> "*Words of the whole play are like a piece of music—they create sounds, rhythms, tones that are heard and physically felt. They also create images. In this way, dialogue is also poetry, whether or not it rhymes or has a definite meter.*"
>
> Carol Korty

14

PLAYS AND SCREENPLAYS

"Why? You cross the road because it's in the script—that's why!"

Joyce Carol Oates's *Procedure* and Michel Wallerstein's *Off Hand* are typical of the short plays now popular in noncommercial theater, particularly the types of theaters that are most likely to put on dramas by beginners. Such plays are the equivalent of the short-short story you find represented by "Sunday in the Park" (pp. 269–272) or "Just Married" (pp. 275–277), and the technical demands are the same as those for their longer relatives. Both short plays in this section present (1) the pressure of an intense dramatic moment (2) containing the exposition of a past. Before each play we discuss aspects of playwriting that the play itself illustrates. We follow each play with an expanded discussion of techniques and with several exercises, and we introduce each play with some brief comments to heighten your awareness of its key features.

 ## PROCEDURE

In *Procedure* the immediate need to prepare the deceased for the morgue is also the occasion for revealing the special past relationship between the deceased and one of the nurses. The exposition is simple. We find out the following:

1. The place is a hospital.
2. The characters are nurses preparing a body prior to the "family" coming to see it.
3. An experienced nurse is training an inexperienced nurse.
4. The experienced nurse is apparently cold and indifferent; the inexperienced nurse is emotional.
5. The procedures are not simple and must be done in a certain order.

However, the stage business that goes on in the play is not like dusting a room or pouring drinks. The preparation of the corpse is appalling work but does keep the dialogue from being mere talk. Oates's careful exposition is the occasion for an even more appalling denouement. (Don't worry, the corpse is really dead.) *Note:* How the director would represent a corpse and some of the procedures on stage is of no more concern to the playwright than how a sword fight should be choreographed. The body may be an actual nude person or a dummy or a nude person partly hidden behind a screen. Or the body may be imaginary and the actions mimed.

Procedure

JOYCE CAROL OATES

CHARACTERS

A.—late twenties or early thirties
B.—younger and less assured

TIME & PLACE

The present.
A hospital room, and a nurses' lounge.

LIGHTS up. In a hospital bed, motionless, lies the BODY of a man. He is not elderly; perhaps in his sixties. An IV tube is attached to one of his nostrils:

another tube snakes beneath the bedclothes, in the region of his groin. There may be a white screen partly enclosing the bed. A bedside table, with a minimum of items on it. From stage right enter two nurses' aides—A. and B. A. is in her late twenties or early thirties; brisk, self-assured, practiced in her movements. B. is not only younger but less assured; her movements are occasionally faltering and timid, but not excessively. B. is in every sense the apprentice, determined to learn PROCE-DURE, and eager to acquit herself well. Both A. and B. are healthy, even husky young women, and both exhibit near-faultless posture. Between them THEY are carrying the "Death Pack" equipment—a kit out of which items (see below) will be taken, plus a small laundry hamper, a large paper bag, two white sheets, a stretcher and litter straps.

The predominating color of the set is white: stark, dazzling white. The nurses' uniforms, stockings, shoes; the dead patient's gown; the bedclothes. A penumbra of darkness surrounds.

A. and B. approach the bed, B. just perceptibly hesitant.

A.: (*Sharp, clear, mechanical voice.*) PROCEDURE. Open the Death Pack. (*B. opens the Death Pack.*) Take out the DO NOT ENTER sign. (*B. does so.*) Affix to outside of patient's door.

(*B. takes out the sign, which measures about 12"by 8", "DO NOT ENTER" in bold black letters; hangs from the outside doorknob of a door at the rear.*)

B.: (*Nervous smile, breathless laugh.*) I guess—anybody out in the hall, they'd sure know what we were doing.

A.: (*Freezing B. out by continuing, in the same voice.*) PROCEDURE. Remove the contents of the Death Pack and set on available surface in patient unit.

(*B. follows A's instructions, fumbling now and then; conspicuously not looking at the dead man.*)

A.: One wrapping sheet. Absorbent cotton. Padding. Bandage rolls. Safety pins. Death tags.

B.: (*Softly, as if dead man might overhear.*) This is—my first time. My first—(*Gestures awkwardly, abashedly.*)

(*A. gives B. a look of reproof. A beat.*)

A.: PROCEDURE. Remove treatment equipment, if any, from patient unit.

(*B. detaches IV tube, etc., with A.'s assistance; pushes equipment to the side.*)

A.: Lower the head rest, leaving a single pillow.

(*B. lowers head rest, fumbling a bit. Forgets to remove a pillow.*)

    A.: LEAVING A SINGLE PILLOW.

    B.: (*Quickly.*) Oh yes—sorry!

(B. places one pillow on the floor; the dead man's head lolls, which alarms her. As A. gestures impatiently, B. adjusts the head. Her facial expression is taut, but does not betray distaste.)

    B.: Poor guy—wonder who he was!

    A.: (*Continuing, perhaps more forcibly; in an incantatory, ritual-like manner.*) PROCEDURE. Place the body of the deceased in as natural a position as possible—arms at sides (*A. and B. do this. B. A bit timidly.*); palms turned toward thighs. (*B. does this.*)

    B.: (*Breathlessly.*) Wonder *why*—"palms toward thighs."

    A.: (*Coolly.*) PROCEDURE. (*A beat.*) Close eyelids gently.

    B.: (*Nervous laugh.*) Gee—whyn't they have us do this *first?*—so, y'know, the—, the—, *he* isn't looking at us, like! (*Tries to close eyelids, without success.*) Oh my God—they won't *close.*

    A.: (*As before.*) Close eyelids gently.

    B.: (*Tries again.*) Oh mister, I wish you'd c-cooperate, I'm just kind of, kind of—NERVOUS. (*SHE succeeds in shutting both eyelids.*) Hey—O.K.! Thank God.

(*B. holds out her hands, for A. to see how they are shaking. But A. is indifferent.*)

    A.: PROCEDURE. If the deceased has dentures—

    B.: (*Pointing, frightened; as one eyelid opens slowly.*) Oh—he's waking up!

(*A., though exasperated with B., says nothing. In a quick, fluid, decisive manner SHE draws her fingertips down over both the dead man's eyelids; this time both eyelids remain shut.*)

    B.: Oh!—how'd you do that? (*Pause; abashed.*) Well—I guess I'll learn.

    A.: If the deceased has dentures, these should be cleaned and—

    B.: (*Nervous attempt at humor.*) They *all* have dentures, seems like!

    A.: (*Continuing, without inflection.*)—cleaned and replaced in mouth.

    B.: (*Misunderstanding, leans over to peer at dead man's mouth preparatory to timidly poking her fingers into it.*) Oh—mister! You're gonna have to ex-cuse me—

    A.: (*Irritated, but maintaining decorum.*) Dentures should be cleaned and REPLACED. (*As if in an aside, now that she is not repeating instructions from the handbook.*) You must know—dentures are not *in* the patient's mouth. (*Points to bedside table.*)

    B.: Oh! Sorry! (*B. locates dentures in a glass on the table. Picks them up hesitantly. Holds to light.*) They look O.K. to me. I mean—clean.

(*Peering; with a shivery laugh.*) Must be weird, wearing 'em. False teeth!

A.: (*Coolly, as if making a pronouncement.*) Nothing is "weird" in this place.

B.: (*Approaching patient.*) Well, excuse me, mister, gotta put these back *in*. So that your folks, coming to see you in the—the—downstairs—

A.: In the morgue.

B.: —so they'll see you at your best.

(*B. mimes replacing dentures in mouth. [Specific action may be hidden, or disguised, by portable bed screen.] Has difficulties, murmuring to herself.*)

B.: Oh—damn—I just don't know *how*. Like, in real life, this guy'd do it *himself.* (*To A., pleading.*) Y'know—he's still warm. His mouth, I mean. Inside. Wet too—saliva. (*A pause. B. backs away, suddenly frightened.*) Oh God—that's a dead man!

A.: (*In official voice.*) Sometimes, with the dead, dentures cannot be replaced. (*Looking on as B. tries gamely again.*) DO NOT FORCE.

(*B. fumbles dentures, drops to floor.*)

B.: (*Aghast.*) Oh God! I'm sorry!

A.: (*Picking up dentures, setting on table, continuing as before.*) PROCEDURE. Replace top bedding with draping sheet.

(*B. covers body awkwardly with large sheet, removes other sheet. The next several steps are done under the sheet, with some difficulty, and distaste, by B.*)

A.: Remove patient's pajamas. (*B. does so, folding and thrusting them into a laundry hamper as quickly as possible.*) Press bladder gently to expel accumulated urine. (*B. does so.*) Remove catheter. (*B. does so.*) Place cotton pads over rectum and genitalia to absorb feces and urine which will be expelled as sphincters relax.

B.: (*As she is doing this.*) Oh!—oh dear. I guess we had a little accident.

(*A. tosses B. a towel or more absorbent cotton. B. wipes, under the sheet.*)

B.: (*Trying not to appear repelled.*) It's just so—oh geez what can you *say*. You start out life soiling your diapers and you end—

A.: Clean old adhesive markings from skin, if any.

B.: (*Peering under sheet.*) Poor guy—he's got 'em. (*B. busies herself with this task.*)

A.: Prop sagging jaw with folded pads.

B.: That's how *my* mouth comes open, if I sleep on my back! I hear this wet-sort-of noise, y'know, in my sleep, it wakes me up sometimes, or, a minute later, I'm *snoring*—(*As SHE props up dead man's jaw, with some initial difficulty.*) I'm gonna be so worried someday, when—if—

A.: Pad ankles with cotton and tie together with bandage.

B.: (*As SHE does this.*)—I'm married, or something. (*Pause.*) My father, he snores so you can hear it through the whole—

A.: (*Making out tags, deftly.*) PROCEDURE. Tie one signed tag to right great toe (*Gives B. the tag.*)—tie one signed tag to left wrist.

B.: Why *two*? The toe and the wrist aren't gonna get separated, are they?

A.: Roll body gently to side of bed. (*A. helps B. do this.*) Place one clean sheet diagonally under body. (*Pause.*) DIAGONALLY under body. (*Pause.*) Roll body back to center of sheet.

B.: (*Shivering.*) He's still warm—some places. Just his fingers and toes, and his face, are *real* cold. (*Pause.*) Looks like kind of a nice guy, don't he?—'course any man, no matter how cruel, he's gonna look nice, peaceful, sort of, in a weird way, like a *woman*, at a time like this. Y'know what I mean—?

A.: (*Freezing B. out.*) Fold upper corner of sheet loosely over the head and face—(*As THEY do so.*)—the lower corner over the feet (*Etc.*)

B.: (*Almost giddy with strain, waving to patient.*) Bye-bye!

A.: Secure the arms at the sides by bringing the right and left corners of the sheet over to complete the wrapping.

B.: (*Performs this action swiftly, keeping pace with A.'s words.*) Yeah! Right!

A.: Fasten sheet with safety pins. (*Tosses pins to B.*) Fasten additional signed tag to outside of sheet. (*Etc.*) If dentures could not be replaced, wrap in gauze, identify, pin dentures next to tag. (*Etc.*)

B.: He could be anybody now . . . .

A.: Lift wrapped body to stretcher.

B.: Here's the hard part, huh? (*A. and B. lift body, lay on stretcher, which is on the floor; THEY have less difficulty than might be expected.*)—Geeze he's *light* isn't he!

A.: Fasten litter straps at chest—(*THEY do so.*)—and just above the knees. (*Etc.*) Cover body with additional sheet.

B.: (*Immense sigh.*) Well—that's that.

A.: (*Continuing as before, with perhaps the slightest suggestion of sharing B.'s relief.*) PROCEDURE. Transfer body quietly and with dignity to the morgue, avoiding if possible public entrances and lobbies—

B.: (*As A. and B. pick up ends of the stretcher, in a loud, somewhat giddy voice.*)—"QUIETLY and with DIGNITY to the morgue—avoiding PUBLIC ENTRANCES AND LOBBIES." Yeah! You bet!

(*LIGHTS down as A. and B. exit with stretcher.*
LIGHTS up. A. and B. are alone, apparently in a nurses' lounge; both have cans of soda which THEY open, and drink from; A. lights a cigarette, and offers one to B.)

B.: (*Still shaky.*) I—uh, thanks but I—I'm not smoking now. I mean, I'm trying not to. (*Wipes face with tissue.*) Well. Sure glad I don't work in the *morgue*.

A.: (*Imperturbably.*) It's quiet in the morgue.

B.: I'll say!

A.: (*Regarding her quizzically; almost friendly.*) It wasn't so bad, was it?

B.: (*Laughing.*) To tell the truth, yes.

A.: Just following procedure.

B.: Procedure—! (*Shudders.*)

A.: Not the first time you saw a dead patient, was it?

B.: No, not exactly. But the first time I....touched one.

A.: (*Clinical interest.*) And how was it?

B.: (*Staring at A., perplexed.*) How was it? (*Pause.*) It was—something I won't forget.

A.: You won't?

B.: I sure *won't*.

(*A beat or two. A. regards B. as if bemused. BOTH sip from cans.*)

A.: (*Casually.*) That man—dead man I mean—he was my father. (*Picking tobacco off tongue, as B. stares at her.*) I mean—that man, when living, had been my father.

B.: (*Staring, blinking.*)—What?

A.: Him. Just now. My father.

B.: You're—joking!

A.: Why would I joke? (*Half-smile.*) It isn't my practice to joke.

B.: But—I don't believe it. Him—(*Points vaguely offstage.*)—us—*you*—

A.: (*Matter-of-factly.*) I should explain—I hadn't seen him in a while. We weren't close.

B.: Oh! You weren't "close."

A.: He left us when I was sixteen. Didn't remarry or anything, just left. He lived in the city—I'd run into him sometimes—we'd talk, sort of. Sometimes, he'd avoid me. (*Pause.*) Or I'd avoid him.

B.: Did you know he was here in the hospital?

A.: Sure.

B.: Did you know he was—dying?

A.: More or less.

B.: And you didn't tell anyone?

A.: (*As if genuinely baffled.*) Didn't tell anyone—?

B.: Oh—any of the nurses, or—

A.: Why should I?—I'm a professional. I do my job.

B.: And it didn't upset you to, to—

A.: I said, I'm a professional. He wasn't *my* first.

B.: (*Slight attack of dizziness.*) Oh—!

(*A. helps B., as B. leans forward, touching forehead to knees.*)

A.: You're all right.

B.: (*Recovering.*) I'm—all right. (*Pause.*) C'n I have a—?

(*A. passes the package of cigarettes to B., who takes one, lights it, exhales smoke gratefully.*)

B.: (*Emphatically.*) My God, I'm so—embarrassed. Here I was thinking of myself, mainly. My first—death. (*Pause.*) I wish I could go through it again, now. See how you did it. Knowing what you told me ....

A.: (*Moving off.*) Sorry! It's a scene that can't quite be repeated.

(*LIGHTS out.*)

THE END

 DISCUSSION

The key devices Oates uses are ones we have discussed before. Carefully shaped repetition of the "one, two, three..." sort draws the audience into any work (whether it is a poem, prose, or drama). The process of preparing the corpse builds tension. Where will all this end and what will be the upshot? What also builds tension is the triangle—A, B, and the body. Not every play, of course, is built on the pressures inherent in situations in which three or more characters rather than two or one occupy the stage. Most are. (For a classic work using more than one triangular situation see Henrik Ibsen's *Hedda Gabler.*)

Notice that Oates starts the play in medias res. Nurse A's father is already dead, they have been given the assignment of preparing the body, and they have gathered the "Death Pack." All this occurs before the point of attack. Other key pieces of information are contained in A's and B's first speeches. Oates establishes that A is matter-of-fact, experienced, and in charge. B is an apprentice and nervous, and her discomfort and inexperience is dramatized by her fumbling of some preparations. B's inexperience and ineptitude injects some humor that relieves the awful circumstances and punctuates the beats. Though it may appear that the revelation about the relationship between A and the corpse in the second scene is spur-of-the-moment, the audience will remember that A does appear almost too impatient, too cool, and too wedded to the procedures. Later, despite what she says about her indifference to her father, we sense that deeper emotions are operating. Notice how, as dramatists often do, Oates follows the dramatic revelation at the climax with another, lesser climax. B has been so focused on her own emotions that she hasn't learned the procedures.

● ● ● ● ●   *EXERCISES*   ● ● ● ● ● ●

1. Write the scene for A's last talk with her father.

2. Write a scene in which B is training a new nurse to prepare a corpse for the morgue.

3. Write a scene in which a supervisor assigns Nurse A the task of preparing the body.

◄━━━━━► OFF HAND

Michael Wallerstein's *Off Hand* is a quiet play, almost the dramatic equivalent of an epiphany in which the denouement is the characters' or an audience's sudden awareness of the true situation. Don't expect spectacular action.

The exposition or back story is simple. We find out the following:

1. The Woman and the Man are at the last night of an art show.
2. They are looking at two paintings, and one painting is more cheery and finished than the other.
3. Both characters are well-informed about art.
4. They are alone and lonely.
5. The Man is an unsuccessful artist who has struggled against family disapproval.
6. The Woman has lost her husband.

As you read, think about how much more the audience understands the situation than do the characters and about actions and states of mind you might suggest the actors consider when saying their lines. What is the key structural element that creates the tension?

Off Hand

MICHEL WALLERSTEIN

CHARACTERS

WOMAN: (early 60s). Tall, with a commanding presence. Still attractive. Dressed simply, yet elegantly. Wears just the right amount of expensive looking jewelry. There's a nervous energy about her, and her comments about art are quick and matter of fact. This is the first time she's out alone in public after her husband's death.

MAN, (late 20s). Medium build. Good looking. Charming. Passionate when he talks. Gets easily carried away. He appears to be self-confident but is vulnerable. Dressed in dark jeans and a dress shirt, trying to "fit in" the art world.

TIME

Today.

SETTING

An art gallery in New York City.

Lights up on Woman looking disapprovingly at a painting stage right (the paintings of the gallery are the audience). She is carrying a catalog, opens it and stares back at the painting.

Man sits on a gallery bench and observes Woman. She doesn't notice him. She is still examining the painting in front of her. She frowns.

WOMAN: Please.

She shrugs and moves on. She now stops (center stage) admiringly in front of the next painting. She clearly likes that painting.

WOMAN: Ahhh! Yes. (*Steps back for a better view.*)
MAN: So you like that one?
WOMAN: (*Annoyed, her back to him.*) Yes.
MAN: It's beautiful.
WOMAN: (*Still not facing him.*) Yes.
MAN: And you like it better than this one?
WOMAN: Without question.
MAN: Hmmmm. What do you like so much about it?
WOMAN: I don't know. I guess how the artist brings her soul to . . .
MAN: . . . her?
WOMAN: Yes. The artist is a woman.
MAN: Really? How do you know that? (*Reads the signature on the painting.*) R. Bastian. R could be for Robert or Ronald or a ton of other names.
WOMAN: I recognize a woman's depth and sensitivity. (*Pointing to the previous painting.*) This one, on the other hand, was definitely painted by a man. A man with a dark and twisted vision of the world.

MAN: (*Looking closely at the painting, defensively.*) At least he signed his full name. Andrew Barton. No ambiguity there.

WOMAN: No soul either. No surprise. Nothing. (*At the one she likes.*) Whereas this painting is filled with substance and meaning...It's far too spiritual and inspired to be the work of a man.

MAN: Oh, so Michelangelo or...Caravaggio or El Greco: they weren't spiritual or inspired because they were men?

WOMAN: Those great artists lived in different times. A man could not paint like that today. Not in a society only interested in the Dow Jones, MTV and dot coms...Now, if you'll excuse me.

Woman moves to the next painting. Man follows
Her. She wishes he'd leave her alone.

MAN: I'm sorry. I didn't mean to be so blunt.

WOMAN: (*Gentler.*) We're all entitled to our opinions.

MAN: That's right...So...How can you be so sure R. Bastian is a woman? There are no pictures in the bio. And no pronouns are ever used to describe her.

Woman now notices Man is attractive.

WOMAN: (*Girlish.*) Well, I don't like to brag...(*In a loud whisper.*)....but I know her personally.

MAN: Nothing wrong with a little bragging...So what does the R stand for?

WOMAN: (*With a perfect French pronunciation*). Renee. Renee Bastien.

MAN: (*Trying to sound as "French" as her.*) Renee Bastien...Hmmm? So what do you think Renee's trying to tell us with her painting?

Woman walks back to the previous painting.

WOMAN: Well, I...I'm not sure she's trying to tell us anything. The image is...magical, almost surreal, like the early works of Dali. The liberating hand...

MAN: (*Looking at the painting.*) That hand, yes. It's nice.

WOMAN: Nice? It's phenomenal. That hand is power. It's about to liberate the body from its imprisonment, to let it breathe finally, by throwing open the window. The window to freedom, to a new life!

MAN: (*Takes a closer look at the painting.*) Hmmm. Looks to me as if the hand is closing the window, not opening it.

WOMAN: Rubbish! Look at that light. The sun is shining outside the window. There's a gentle, westerly breeze. See how those branches swing to the left? And on the oak tree, a little bluebird is sticking out like in a Rousseau painting.

MAN: (*Trying to see.*) Oh, yeah. I see it.

WOMAN: And it's chirping.

MAN: You can't really tell it's chirping. It's too small.

WOMAN: It's chirping, alright? I know it is. And it's perfectly clear: the woman in the painting is opening the window. To get air. To begin again. There may be a slight hesitation in the movement, I'll grant you that, but the decision to open that window has been made years ago and now finally, she knows that nothing can stop her anymore. Not even her own fear.

MAN: Oh. So this is a woman's hand?

WOMAN: Of course it is.

MAN: Don't you think it's kind of square and rugged? And those veins.

WOMAN: Veins?!

MAN: You don't see veins like that on a woman's hand.

WOMAN: There are no veins on this hand.

MAN: And look, you can even see a few hairs.

WOMAN: Hair! Where?

MAN: (*Pointing.*) There.

WOMAN: That's no hair. That's just a . . . a careless brush stroke.

MAN: More like six or seven! No. I'm sorry. That is a man's hand.

WOMAN: This is my hand, alright? ! I posed for it. She painted *my* hand. (*Places her hand close up to the painting.*) And there is no hair on *my* hand.

MAN: Lady, that couldn't possibly be your hand.

WOMAN: And why on earth not?

MAN: Look at it! Yours is much prettier than that. So fragile and elegant. That is a hard working, tough man's hand. But if it's really yours, the artist should be shot. (*She turns her back on him.*) I'm sorry. I got carried away. A bad habit of mine . . . Let me make it up to you . . . smooth things over with a coffee across the street.

WOMAN: Thank you. I don't think so. I'd just like to enjoy this exhibition. Alone. If you don't mind.

MAN: Of course. I understand. I'm sorry.

Woman walks to the next painting. Man stares at her. She senses it.

WOMAN: (*Facing him.*) You're staring.

MAN: Sorry.

WOMAN: It's rude.

MAN: I just find you . . . interesting.

WOMAN: Young man, are you flirting with me?

MAN: Well, you are a very attractive woman.

WOMAN: And almost twice your age. (*Looks at one of the rings on her fingers.*) If you think I'm one of those rich ladies who spend their time lunching and attending every gallery opening in town, you're quite mistaken. I'm not rich. These rings are fake. All of them. Not worth a dime.

MAN: For heaven's sake, so now I'm after your money?

WOMAN: I'm sorry. I....it's just that men your age should be interested in younger women.

MAN: Sure. The young should stick together.

Woman walks away. He stares at her again.

WOMAN: You're staring again. Why?

MAN: Habit. I spend a lot of time in places like these and study whoever walks in. I make up stories about them. About their lives. About what brought them here today.

WOMAN: What do you think brought me here today?

MAN: Well, in your case, I already know: you came to see your hand.

WOMAN: Perhaps it isn't my hand after all.

MAN: So you didn't pose for it?

WOMAN: I did. Sort of. A friend of mine took pictures of my hand one day. (*Holds it out.*) He shot two entire rolls. Just of my hand. Imagine that...he said that a painter he knew was looking for the hand of perfect elegance and refinement. I was flattered. At my age, I couldn't believe that anything about my appearance could be "perfect." I was thrilled my friend thought of me, of my hand...(*Looks at the painting.*) Apparently Renee Bastien didn't agree with him. (*Faces Man, after a beat.*) But I needed to believe that was me up there, or at least a part of me. I've had a hard week. Month. Let's just say I've had a hard year and I wanted to feel special today.

MAN: And I blew all that for you, didn't I? What a jerk.

WOMAN: Don't worry about it.

MAN: There's nothing worse than robbing someone of their dream.

WOMAN: (*Walking away, decidedly.*) It was a small dream. A stupid one.

MAN: I lied to you.

WOMAN: My dear, young man, you haven't known me long enough to lie to me.

MAN: I wasn't really trying to figure you out. When I saw you looking at that painting, with your heart and not your mind, I knew I wanted your response.

WOMAN: Response?

MAN: I'm Andrew Barton. The painter with the "dark and twisted vision of the world."

WOMAN: Oh, my.

MAN: I painted the painting you hate.

WOMAN: I...I don't really hate it, just...

MAN: Yes, you do. Everybody does. This is my first exhibition. And I've been watching people ignore my work all week and go straight to R. Bastian's stupid hand. Sorry. And since the exhibit ends tonight, I just wanted to know what was wrong with my work? How come no one ever stops in front of my painting and goes: "Ah, yes."

WOMAN: So I robbed you of *your* dream?

MAN: Yeah, but I'm used to it.

WOMAN: No one ever gets used to that. No one ever should.

MAN: My art teachers told me I was wasting my time, that I should quit art school and get a job.

WOMAN: I'm sure someone must like your work or they wouldn't be showing it here. Someone obviously believes in you.

MAN: The owner of the gallery is my Aunt. (*She chuckles.*) My parents cut me off once they found out I was studying more art than law. So she felt sorry for me. I sold my car, my stereo, my t.v. and everything I own just to be able to paint and have this exhibition. Not a good move, I'd say. Wouldn't you?

WOMAN: I don't know what to say.

MAN: My mother didn't even show up.

WOMAN: I'm sure she's sorry.

MAN: You would have shown up, if...

He stops, feeling he's gone too far. They look at each other for a short, awkward moment.

WOMAN: (*Light.*) You're a nice, young man. And I do see talent in your painting...

MAN: ...despite my dark and twisted vision of the world, huh?

WOMAN: A great, big foot crushing Planet Earth. Yes. I'd say it's dark.

MAN: It was meant to be ironic.

WOMAN: You don't say.

An awkward silence.

MAN: Sorry you've had such a bad year.

WOMAN: Well, it's over now. My husband...he was very sick...I nursed him day in, day out. I wanted to, of course, but it was very...He...he finally died last month. Everyone says it's much better this way—no more pain. Maybe for them. Meanwhile, my whole world's collapsed, as if that foot of yours smashed it to pieces.

MAN: I'm sorry.

WOMAN: (*Studying his painting.*) Is there...Yes! Is there a hand holding that foot?

MAN: (*Excited.*) I knew it! I knew you'd finally see it! The hand is superimposed on top of the foot, lifting it away.

WOMAN: And...isn't there someone...trying to escape from that crushing foot?

MAN: Yes! That's right.

WOMAN: I think it's a woman...

MAN: (*Interjecting. Grinning.*)...or a man.

WOMAN: She's trying to pull herself out between the forth and fifth toe. Of course, I wouldn't see all this if I weren't looking from exactly this angle.

MAN: Exactly!

WOMAN: Very Magritte. (*Looking now, more intensely.*) And that hand...that hand is liberating the planet, isn't it?

MAN: You got it!

WOMAN: So the woman is struggling for nothing.

MAN: Or the man. Could be. It could be all in his or her mind. But the liberating hand is definitely a woman's hand. (*Takes her hand gently.*) Not unlike yours. As a matter of fact, it's just like yours.

WOMAN: (*Wanting to believe*). Do you think?

MAN: I'm positive. Look at it: the same fine, elongated fingers. The same elegance. This is your hand!

WOMAN: Extraordinary. Yes. Yes...I think I see it. I do.

Woman and Man stand close and look at the painting together.

Lights fade.

End

 DISCUSSION

The action begins *in medias res* on the last evening of the exhibit. Both characters are at the art show for personal reasons. The Woman because she believes she has provided a model hand for one of the pieces; the Man to discover if anyone understands his piece and likes it.

The tension between the characters is the result of their needs.

Notice the convention of assuming that the space between the audience and the characters is a wall and on that wall are paintings. Though in some plays the playwright pierces the fourth wall and characters talk directly to the audience (e.g., in *Equus*) or even engage the audience directly in the play, normally the drama occurs at an arm's length so that the audience can observe while participating emotionally. In *Off Hand*, Wallerstein relies on our recognition of certain actions as setting the scene. The characters behave in ways we expect art gallery patrons to act. They believe where they are and so also do we.

The Woman's first bit of dialogue, "Please," ironically indicates that she is not really pleased. In a single word Wallerstein tells us about her reaction to the painting that will create the conflict between the characters and that she has strong reactions (after all, she blurts her reaction out loud). In no more than nine lines of short dialogue we understand the basic situation.

Notice how the art at which they are looking creates two triangles: (1) Woman, Man, "good" painting; (2) Woman, Man, "bad" painting. Although the tension is finally resolved, it flows through the stage business of looking and reacting to the art. The discovery of the true situation is that each character has a personal connection to the art. The audience probably realizes quite early the reason for the Man's urgency; the Woman's urgency is revealed later, though it is hinted at earlier when she describes what she thinks is happening in the "better" painting.

Wallerstein's strategy is to give the audience first impressions of the characters, impressions that are not quite accurate. The Woman is presented as cool, patrician (her dress, her French) and with fixed attitudes; the Man as bumptious (the effects of youth) and challenging. As the play unfolds, however, we see that the Woman and Man actually are sensitive to each other's needs and share a common loneliness. The opposition of youth and age resolves itself through their underlying similarity. They need to give each other a hand.

Off Hand is a slim play, but like most effective plays, it contains more subtext than text. The Woman's interpretation of the painting she likes—"It's about to liberate the body from its imprisonment"—is really less a judgment than a reflection of her hope that somehow she can escape the imprisonment she has experienced in the years of tending a dying husband. The Man's statement to the Woman that "there's nothing worse than robbing someone of their dream" is really a reflection of his own feelings about the public's dislike of his painting, his parents' rejection of his desire to be a painter, and his instructor's criticism of his talent. In effect, his painting of a foot crushing the world is a reflection of his own situation. When the Woman finally sees the hand lifting the foot, her understanding resolves the needs both have.

●   ●   ●   ●   ●   *EXERCISES*   ●   ●   ●   ●   ●

1. Assuming that the Woman has recognized her need to give a hand to others, write a beat for what may happen between her and the Man at the end.

2. Write a play using the characters and situation in "Just Married" (Chapter 11).

◀━━━▶   A WORD ON PLAYS FOR FILM AND TELEVISION

If you want to write play scripts for film (whether to be presented in a movie theater or on television), you need to master special techniques and jargon. You must read about the media, see the media, and work in the media. Special subgenre, dramatic programs such as *CSI*, *Lost*, or sitcoms, require specialized knowledge about the television business. You are wasting your time writing a script for *The Simpsons* when the producers use only contract writers or the network intends to cancel the program for the next year. That is, you are wasting your time unless you are simply practicing television script-writing.

For those of you who do wish to try a filmscript, we have a brief list of suggestions that will be useful for all the subgenres. Please keep in mind that these are rules of thumb to which there are exceptions. Before reading on, you may wish to look at a film script on the Internet. (One source is http://www.simplyscripts.com/movie.html. You can also do a search for a particular script.)

1. Read as many complete original *film scripts* as you can, particularly of films that you can rent and study at home on your DVD or computer. When we say "film script," we are not speaking of "shooting scripts," which include detailed instructions for the cinematographer, nor of those scripts you may find printed in magazines. These often do not follow the author's original format. As you compare the writer's script with the final product, notice how short most scenes in a film script will be. A film scene is defined as any change in place or time. Put a stopwatch on the film and compare the time with the pages in your script. You will notice that a page of script is almost equal to a minute on the screen. In fact, a long scene (say three minutes or three pages long) in a film will usually be followed by several short scenes. Film scripts that the producer can't scan at jet speed are likely to land quickly in the return basket. Reading the scene will take the same amount of time as viewing it.

2. In a stage play, the dialogue tends to be the action that the characters are performing, or dialogue triggers an action that the characters will perform. In a film, the action triggers the dialogue. That is, someone does something and that causes a verbal response. Humphrey Bogart starts walking down the airport runway with Claude Raines and then says, "Louis, I think this is the beginning of a beautiful friendship." Or Dorothy lands in Oz and after looking around says, "Toto, I don't think we're in Kansas anymore." What she says is a reaction to both what she and we witness as part of the action. Not vice versa.

3. Remember that the camera can and will see details of actions and gestures in ways that a theater audience cannot see them. Therefore, not as much dialogue will be needed. In fact, what the camera can see, the characters will seldom discuss. A student gets his paper back. He turns it over. The camera shows a *C*. When the student pulls a long face as he looks at his grade, the teacher won't say, "Are you unhappy with your *C*, Mr. Wanagrade?" Rather, she'll frown and say, "You didn't even deserve that grade." Student rips paper in half. Teacher picks up gradebook and changes grade to *F*.

4. While novelists and playwrights often discover in the process of writing how the plot will turn out for the characters (remember that the characters are thinking of the plot as their lives), it is best in a screenplay to know exactly what choices the characters will have to make at the end. In other words,

you should begin your writing with a relatively clear notion of the plot and write rather mathematically toward the conclusion. Most films are driven by time. Because of limited audience endurance, they usually can be no more than two hours long. You have to fit everything that needs to be shown to understand the plot and characters within that time. Unlike books, movies are made to be experienced in one sitting; if you watch them in pieces, you lose the intended effect. The minute in a film is a minute in the viewer's life. When you have a clear picture of the plot, you will tend not to meander.

5. They call them *movies* because people move. Audiences do not expect characters to stand around and talk. They expect car chases and kisses (sometimes quite long car chases and kisses); and swinging, climbing, eating, and other actions (the verbs). Just as in a play, however, you do not have to worry about describing the details of the set or characters (the nouns). You have collaborators (set, costume designers, choreographers, explosives experts) and others who will provide the details. You should simply mention the place and get on with the action.

6. Do not waste your time writing a production script in which you indicate such directions as "favoring shot," "close two shot," "camera dissolves to," or tell the actors how to say the dialogue (e.g., "whispering," "with a whine in her voice"). Of course, on occasion you will want to suggest some details related to the action or acting but use such technical and directorial terms sparingly. One of the surest ways of having your script placed in your SASE and dropped off at the nearest mailbox is for the writer to usurp the tasks of the directors, actors, and the host of other collaborators who will spring into action when the producer chooses the screenplay. However, you will have to know the conventions about describing places, times, and the movement of characters; the general placement of dialogue and description; and such matters as when to use capital letters and when not.

Put your efforts into making a good story about the characters, one that exploits the possibilities within the medium. Your characters and their needs and desires will be no different from those in fiction or a play. Just how you let the viewer experience the story will be different because, just as in any other dramatic medium, you are providing a framework for others to perform.

Finally, film and television are such specialized ways of storytelling that you probably will want to take courses dedicated to writing for these media.

●   ●   ●   ●   ●   *EXERCISES*   ●   ●   ●   ●   ●

1. Using the pages from a script as a model, try to "write" the script for a film as you watch it on DVD. Notice how every change of location is a new "scene." Notice how little dialogue there is compared with a stage play.

2. Generally speaking, a film script will be about 120 pages long for a film that will run between 90 and 120 minutes. It will have about 120 scenes. Of course, you don't write to that measure. The measure is the result of the medium's demand for movement through space and time. And, as you know, many films are adaptations from previous works. An adaptation exploits the audience's familiarity with the plot and the characters; however, the chief reasons for the frequency of adaptations is that the scriptwriter (or producer) knows what will happen and so can concentrate on constructing the script. If you wish to gain experience constructing film scripts, one useful place to start would be by adapting a published story or stage play. Try a film script of the first ten scenes of a story from Chapter 11 or of a novel you have recently read.

Summary

A script is an occasion for a performance. The most effective ones are those written with an appreciation of both the freedoms and limitations of the medium's conventions. On the one hand, the playwright has only to indicate the presence of a chair, not describe it; on the other hand, the detail of the pettipoint will not be visible to most spectators and so it cannot be as important as it might be in a work of fiction. Because a performance is unstoppable, the effects cannot be as subtle as those in poetry and fiction. The audience must quickly grasp character and circumstance. The premise needs to be shaped so that the point of attack is late in the story. Above all, the playwright must master the craft of presenting both text and subtext in dialogue, the primary vehicle of character and plot.

> *"The subject of drama is The Lie. At the end of the drama THE TRUTH—which has been overlooked, disregarded, scorned, and denied—prevails. And that is how we know the drama is done."*
>
> David Mamet

PART FIVE

THE WRITER'S BUSINESS

e	delete; take it out out
⌒	close up; print as o ne word
e	delete and close up
∧	caret; insert here / text
#	insert aspace
stet	let marked text stand as set
tr	transpose; change order the
/	(used to separate two or more marks)
¶	begin a new paragraph
no¶	no paragraph
sp	spell out; change 15 to fifteen
cap	set in capitals
lc	set in lower Case
H	hyphen
M	dash
ˆ,	comma
ˇ	apostrophe
⊙	period
:	colon
;	semicolon
"	quotation marks
(/)	parentheses
[/]	brackets
Q	? or Q Is this really correct (content or form)

CHAPTER 15

FROM DRAFTING TO REVISION TO SUBMISSION

"Sorry, but I'm going to have to issue you a summons for reckless grammar and driving without an apostrophe."

> *"[Review by another] can show the writer that he has at some specific point written misleadingly or has failed to evoke some important element of a scene—mistakes the writer [may] not catch himself because, knowing what he intended, he thinks his sentences say more than they do. Seeing the effects of his mistakes makes the writer more careful, more wary of the trickery words are capable of."*
>
> John Gardner

◀▰▰▰▶   FEEDBACK

Just as a computer programmer writes code to enable someone else to accomplish something, so an author writes words that someone else will use (read) to achieve a result. In the early stages of creating your program, it is useful to perform a "beta test" of the product—that is, let select users try it so that, should some parts not work, you can change them. Workshops and writing groups that we mentioned in Chapter 1 are convenient places to try out your narrative. However, you should prepare yourself for both helpful and hapless feedback. The following are typical cases.

A. Let us say someone notes that at the end of every line your poem jolts to a stop. For her your poem feels chopped into tiny pieces. You may have intended the effect but all realized intentions as well as accidental ones may not produce an effective work. Listen to that comment. However, if someone else contends your "meaning" is too depressing and they'd like you to lighten up, he needs to write his own poem. Feedback that asks you to change the meaning can be safely ignored.

B. Someone notes that you called special attention to a picture on the mantel at the start of your story and he was waiting for something to happen because of it. Or, that you bring three characters into a scene and only two speak or do anything. Such comments are valuable because they can lead the writer to see a technical flaw that is easily correctable. However, if someone claims that "people never act or feel that way" and so your character is not believable, that commentator is measuring your work against his own observations about human nature or some statistical measure in the "real" world. For a variety of reasons, such criticism may be useless unless it is directed to the internal structure of your work. You can have a character who sees through walls. But if later in your work, for the plot's sake, he cannot see through walls, that inconsistency will annoy the reader. (You could of course, invent a reason for the character's loss of x-ray vision.) Listen to feedback that claims you have been inconsistent because inconsistency in your work raises issues of verisimilitude and coherence. On the other hand, if your reader insists on a worldview that fits his vision of reality, probably he is too literal minded. Those who can't suspend disbelief when they enter a narrative will never enjoy it; you can't please readers who will not allow themselves to be pleased.

C. You have written a play with thirty characters, or a two-thousand-page novel, or a ten-thousand-line poem, and someone points out that you may have difficulty getting it produced, published, or read. Realities of the marketplace you need to listen to. However, you must to write what you must write, and market considerations are hardly to be listened to as a criticism of the work unless you want a wide audience. *Necessary* length is not a flaw.

D. "That's how I felt" or "that's what I believe" is not an appropriate response when feedback indicates the work lacks something. The excuse is a non sequitor because the issue always is whether the writing works for someone else. Frequently, the writer has only managed to lay out emotions or ideas in such general or vague terms that they do not live for the reader. It's a fatal error to assume a reader will believe that merely setting down a personal experience or belief, in and of itself, has merit. The writer's job is to create experience in the reader through language. Of course the writer knows what he was getting at (or does he?). As readers of our own work, we are privileged in ways that make us poor critics of it. Remember that the reader doesn't care how the writer feels. The real question is: Has the writer made the reader feel? If you haven't, the feedback becomes the occasion for revision.

E. "But it really happened like that" doesn't tackle the issue of whether the writing is effective. Don't mistake accuracy in rendering events that are source materials with the needs of the work at hand. The mere fact that something really happened does not justify placing it in a narrative poem. Feedback can get bogged down in arguments about facts and often becomes a way for the writer to avoid problems with the presentation. Something may have happened but not be managed convincingly in the work itself. (This issue is trickier in creative nonfiction, in which the test of factual accuracy is higher.)

F. You can't avoid negative feedback by asking the following question: "Doesn't *creative* mean I can do what I want?" This response is frivolous. It is close to the immature belief that "freedom" means doing anything you want. The freedoms we have grow from our agreements to limit ourselves; we have responsibilities to others. Similarly, there are limitations—conventions of language and genre—that you must master as part of your responsibility to readers.

G. On occasion, feedback may come in the form of "you've broken the rules." It is wise to avoid responding to a work with a cookie cutter. The only rule for a work of art is this: "Has it been successful in moving or interesting an audience?" It may be conventional to avoid starting a sentence with "and" or "but." But a "but" at the start of a sentence may provide needed emphasis. Or, the "rule" that you ought not to repeat a word may not turn out to be the most useful practice if there is no better word (see Chapter 4, "Language Is Your Medium") or if you are setting up a poetic chant. If your sonnet is better for being fifteen instead of fourteen lines, so be it. The "rules" are distilled best practices, not commandments.

H. If your reader has not responded well to an aspect of your technique, it is no defense to say "well, Hemingway wrote short, choppy sentences." What worked for Hemingway may not work in your piece. A variation to this defense is: "In his recent bestseller, Clancy Stemingway did the same thing you didn't like in my work. If he can get away with it, why can't I?"

Sometimes poor writing gets published and sells well; sometimes famous writers get by on their reputations; sometimes other elements in a work are so effectively handled or the subject is so engrossing that the reader overlooks stretches of klutzy plotting or indifferent prose. That such writing gets published is not an excuse for shoddy practice, and the person giving you feedback should not in good conscience encourage bad habits.

I. If someone is puzzled by an aspect of your work or the work as a whole, explaining your intention is probably not a good strategy. Listen to the puzzlement. Does it come from ignorance of the subject, form, or manner? Actually, for ignorance the only cure is a wider education in life and literature than you may have time to give. If the lack of understanding occurs because you have "hidden" something or you have been unclear in your writing, your best response is not an explanation but a revision or acceptance that you work just isn't everyone's cup of reading.

J. The response to feedback that goes "Isn't it all a matter of taste?" is absolutely correct. Discussion ended. Well, almost ended. For a variety of reason, the feedback may come from someone more experienced or more sensitive to nuances or simply more disinterested. In any case, it may be a matter of taste, but the feedback warns you that your reader did not like something. You ignore the response at your peril. If the negative feedback comes from more than one reader, you are in double peril.

K. "I did it just like the book said." How-to books on writing everything from poetry to mysteries weigh down the shelves of your library and bookstore. Run an Internet search and you will get millions of hits, of which at least 25 percent are books and computer programs promising the recipe for writing success. If you follow a cookbook you may end up with a tasty soufflé, but in writing the ingredients and measurements are never the same. Each time out you have a new complex of problems to solve. A writer cannot be the slave to prescriptions, and the only formulas for success emerge from the individual struggle with the individual work. It's a new game every time. Some formula writing produces some kinds of popular literature, but most likely the formula was inside the person in the first place. Your job is to make thinking in the conventions second nature so that you draw on them spontaneously rather than reach for them like cookie cutters. There are no easy answers.

THE LOOK OF THE THING

"No one knows for certain how many good stories are passed over because the manuscripts containing them are formatted poorly, but it is certain that a properly

formatted manuscript will be more eagerly read by an editor than a poorly formatted one."

William Shunn

Ultimately, before readers read the words they will see your manuscript as an object. The teacher, friend, editor, producer...whoever will pick it up and see it all at once, as one might a painting or a person. Of course, appearances deceive, but in this less-than-perfect world, people do judge on first impressions. One might imagine a far-sighted editor who would see beyond those sonnets presented on paper towels and discern the next Shakespeare. But you are best off assuming most editors would toss the manuscript in your SASE and run it to the nearest mailbox.

Present your manuscript as your reader expects to see it.

Start using standard format conventions with the first word you put down. These conventions are relatively strict, though as you will see, some variations are acceptable. For example, usually each page of your manuscript should be printed only on one side of the paper. However, in the interests of green behavior, we have known some editors who ask writers to print on both sides. Nevertheless, unless told otherwise, follow these general practices (already preset in your word processing program):

1. Use standard 8 1/2 by 11 paper (20 pound).
2. Use standard margins: 1 1/2-inch margin at top and left, an inch at right and bottom.
3. Use standard fonts (Times, Courier) and font sizes (12 point).
4. Number multiple-paged manuscripts. (Teachers and editors do drop manuscripts and the pages scattter. One of the modern computer blessings is that you can set your word processor to paginate and enter your name and other information automatically.)
5. Print clear copies on one side only in black.
6. Follow the teacher's, publisher's, or theater's instructions for fastening pages together.
7. Avoid cute presentation with clip art.☺
8. Use special effects such as bold and italics with a light hand. (**Too** *many* are a real *turn off* for a teacher or editor.)
9. Don't format your manuscript as if it is a printed page. Present it with ragged right margins.
10. Double space unless told otherwise except for poetry. (This practice makes it easier for you to insert edits and moves the reading along.)

Beyond these basic and sensible practices, the various genres have individual conventions.

Poetry

Because the visual look of the poem is so important (see Chapter 5, "The Elements of Poetry"), give the person who will read it as much help as possible in seeing how the parts go together.

1. If the poem fits on one page, use the upper left corner for your address. Place your name after the poem, on a separate line and introduced by an em (short) dash. Nothing need go in the upper right corner.

2. Do not begin more than one poem on a page. Do not number the page or the successive pages that hold separate works.

3. If you like, use a wider left margin—2 inches or even a bit more—to bring the poem closer to the center of the page.

4. Keep the title in caps, centered above the poem or flush with its left margin.

5. In the case of longer, multipaged poems, take additional care. Since your byline can't follow the partial poem that appears on the first page, put your name above your address as you would for a fiction submission. Use the upper right corner to indicate how long the poem is *in lines*. Type the word *continued* on the bottom right of the first and successive pages as necessary. At the upper right of the following pages, provide a short title along with page number (e.g., "Wheelchair-7"). This system is more useful than your name when you are submitting a number of poems at once. To be even more cautious, you might provide your last name at the upper left of successive pages.

6. If you double-space your poetry manuscript (as some editors prefer), be sure to quadruple space for divisions between sections (stanzas).

7. Most important, indicate whether the last line on a page does or does not coincide with a stanza break. Don't leave it to the teacher, editor, or typesetter to guess about this important dimension of your work.

A one-page poetry manuscript might look like the sample shown on p. 100.

Prose

As with poetry, remember to check with the teacher or publisher for different or additional guideliness.

1. For multipage works, be sure your name, address, phone number, and e-mail address appear at the top left side of the first page.

2. Though not absolutely necessary, you may place the number of words in the upper right-hand top of the first page. (Another blessing of

word-processing programs is that you can get manuscript word counts automatically.)

3. Capitalize and center the title of your story about one-third to one-half way down the page.

4. Number successive pages—the upper right corner is a convenient place—with a short identifying tag, like your last name (e.g., "Writer/2").

5. Don't staple the pages together. Choose a clip that will hold your pages together securely. (Teachers and other readers often remove the clip so that they may read and flip the pages easily.)

On p. 174 we have printed a sample of the first page of a prose manuscript.

Drama

You must follow the conventions for production scripts, which differ from the printed appearance of plays in books and also differ among subgenres—stage plays, screenplays, and radio plays. The conventions can be complex, but the general principle is to separate dialogue from directions for the actors or camera. You can purchase a computer program that assists you in placing various elements in a script. If your wallet is thin or you are just experimenting with one of the dramatic subgenres, you can do as well with checking the Internet for various play formats. Here are sites we have found helpful.

Stage Plays: www.bbc.co.uk/writersroom/scriptsmart/stageus.pdf
Screen Plays: www.oscars.org/nichol/format.html
Radio Plays: www.bbc.co.uk/writersroom/scriptsmart/radious.pdf

On p. 292 we have printed a sample page from a stage play manuscript.

A few final words: Keep in mind that you don't want unconventional or sloppy presentation to divert your reader from entering the world you have created. And remember that, if you follow the basic formats as you are writing, you avoid having to reformat later, which creates both increased risk of creating additional errors and the loss of time better spent on other matters, such as revision.

The first principle of manuscript presentation is consistency. This is also the second. The third principle is to do everything in your power to make the task of reading and handling your manuscript as simple as possible.

REVISION

> *"Revision will almost always involve some cutting of repetitions, unnecessary explanations, and so on. Consider using revision consciously as a time to consider what could go if it had to.... You are allowed to cry and moan softly while you cut them."*
>
> Ursula K. Le Guin

To **revise** means literally to "see again." To **edit** means to bring into conformity with established standards. Though these two terms are often used interchangeably, they point to different concerns. In this chapter, we shift back and forth, sometimes focusing on one term, sometimes the other. Paradoxically, taking another look and honoring conventions become part of a single process as the author searches for ways to improve his or her work. The essential principle is to always be discontented with your manuscript but to accept the limits of the number of changes you can do before you tackle your next work.

When to Revise

The vast majority of writers agree that writing and revising by wholes leads to the best results. It makes sense to begin revising and editing your work only when you have a complete draft in front of you. After all, if a successful literary work is a web of interrelated parts, then changes cannot be made in isolation. A revision in one place almost invariably demands a revision somewhere else. Revising a work that is only partly completed is better than doing nothing at all, but it is inefficient. You can revise Chapter 1 more effectively once you know which materials coming later in the work will affect Chapter 1.

However, you should not completely ignore problems along the way. Your word processor will automatically signal most misspellings (and may even correct them) and a lack of agreement. It makes sense to take care of such problems right then. As for the more significant issues such as clutter and fogginess, at the end of each writing session, take informal notes for future revisions. If, as is most likely, you create on the computer, leave yourself notes in color (another benefit of the computer) as you go along. Then, when you have a draft of the whole work, or major portions of it in front of you, review those notes and determine what kind of revisions will satisfy your new concerns. For example, if you write your way into a situation that demands "backloading" of information, make yourself a revision note, but don't stop to do the actual revision: Push on.

How to Revise

Revising means taking a critical stance toward what you have done. Many writers need to take a vacation from their work for a while to see it clearly and objectively. Of course, the pressures of a deadline may mean a short vacation of only several hours. Whether dealing with large-scale structural issues or consistent spelling of a nickname, we see things more clearly when we have reduced the emotional charge that is part of the creative impulse. In a way, you have to take on another personality. You have to become someone who can read and evaluate critically what you actually wrote, not what you wanted to write or hoped you wrote. Don't rely on your beta reader.

We can consider three levels of rewriting:

1. For literary quality
2. For the conventions of mechanics, grammar, and manuscript form
3. For factual accuracy and consistency

When assessing the literary effectiveness of the work, consider its impact on the reader, its focus, its handling of the conventions of genre, its depth of characterization, and that elusive thing called "style." Don't rush the process and practice tough love.

Like a pilot preparing for a landing, keeping a checklist in mind will help you go through the process with greater thoroughness and efficiency than just "looking for things." Checklists such as the ones following are no more than a guide, however. Begin with the lists provided here, and then go on to develop your own based on your experience and work habits. Keep in mind that items in these checklists are not exclusive to one genre. You always need to be alert for ineffective diction choices, style, and coherence.

CHECKLIST FOR POETRY

1. Can the line breaks be justified?
2. Is the speaker's voice consistent?
3. Are the sounds and rhythms of language used expressively?
4. Do figures of speech (or any other devices) call too much attention to themselves at the expense of their function?
5. Have you eliminated stale language—especially clichés and unnecessary trite expressions?
6. Are the parts of the poem subordinated to an overall effect?
7. Are the parts (lines, images, stages, events) in the best possible order?
8. Have you let evocation and ambiguity turn into vagueness and unintelligibility?

9. If the poem is in sections, should it be?

10. Do you feel that each section has a proper relationship to the others and to the whole?

11. Do the visual and auditory levels of the poem complement each other?

———————●———————

CHECKLIST FOR FICTION AND NONFICTION

1. Is your point of attack effective? That is, have you begun the narrative too early (quite likely) or too late? A well-chosen point of attack will allow you to give exactly what the reader needs to follow the story through its climax and resolution.

2. Is the structure effective? Do you have the scenes you need (and only the scenes you need) to develop your material? Are the scenes in the best order? Is there a sense of inevitability about the ending that grows naturally out of the flow of events and information without sending out obvious signals?

3. Are the transitions between scenes clean and clear?

4. Are the sections of summary and exposition adequate? Are they over-done? Have you struck an effective balance between showing and telling?

5. Is the narrator's perspective, the point of view, the best choice for this story? Is the perspective consistently maintained?

6. Are the main characters developed sufficiently? Do they become more than mere types? Do they have sufficient interest as rounded or shaded individuals? Are their actions consistent without being overly predictable?

7. Are minor characters and walk-ons kept to a minimum and kept within the bounds of their functions in the story?

8. Is the dialogue natural? Is it plausible? Does it do more than merely impart information? Are the dialogue tags kept simple? Is it always clear who is speaking?

9. Do you have an energetic mix of the various storytelling elements? Generally, it is wise to avoid long stretches of anything—description, exposition, dialogue. Keep the story moving forward and engage the reader on many levels.

10. Is there an overall unity of effect—a controlling idea, mood, emotion, or thematic thrust that the various ingredients support?

———————●———————

CHECKLIST FOR PLAYS

1. Have you given your characters things to do while they are talking (thereby giving your actors something to do)? This is another way of ensuring that the play is visual.

2. Does each beat exist to advance the plot? Even if a beat or moment is interesting in itself, if it does not fit into the plot, you must remove it.

3. Have you removed or revised every beat that exists *only* for the purpose of giving exposition?

4. Does each character have an apparent want? Within moments after each character has appeared, something of his or her approach to life should be visible to the audience (even if the judgment will be modified later).

5. Are the character's wants in conflict with the other characters' wants? In most plays, meaningful conflict grows from these personal wants, not from ideas about how best to run the railroad.

6. Have you removed all stretches of dialogue that can be cut without the audience's missing anything of the plot? This type of revision requires line-by-line effort. If you sense that the dialogue (and therefore the plot) is dragging, go back to where the drag began and try deleting until the play begins to feel alive again.

7. Is the environment built into the characters' actions, beliefs, and dialogue? The characters can see, and the audience can see what the characters can see. Exploit the possibilities.

8. Have you eliminated all unnecessary designators (tags) and stage directions?

9. Have you checked to see that you have changed or eliminated elements that depended on scenes or characters you excised in the process of developing the script?

Checklist for Mechanics

If some of the terms in this checklist cause you to draw a blank, go back to your style manual and give yourself a quick refresher course in mechanics. Consult a dictionary or the Internet whenever in doubt. Trust any anxieties you feel about a word choice or expression and make sure you are in control of your decisions. Check any idiomatic constructions that you're not sure of as well as regionalisms that you have appropriated for your work. Read your work aloud (slowly) to test what you have written against your inner ear. If it doesn't "sound" right to your ear, don't let a problem go just because you are eager to get the manuscript into a publisher's or director's hands. In addition, those giving you feedback will note problems that you need to take care of.

1. Have you checked spelling carefully? (Don't guess and don't trust your word processing program to pick up everything.)

2. Have you checked punctuation to ensure that it does not confuse the reader? (*Note*: Stick to the conventions whenever you can. Variations for effect can be useful, but they can also be annoying. For example, multiple exclamation points, ampersands instead of "and," & ellipses that leave the reader.... lost in the dots!!!!! In poetry, special conventions adopted for a particular work should be used consistently so the reader can become

comfortable with how they are meant to operate. Be careful about what goes inside and what goes outside quotation marks. On the one hand, remember that punctuation is an opportunity to shape how the reader sees relationships among words. On the other hand, don't break punctuation conventions except for a significant creative purpose.)

3. Have you eliminated the common sins of writing dangling modifiers, incomplete comparisons, run-on sentences (usually a punctuation problem), or unintended sentence fragments (also usually a punctuation problem)? *Note*: Break with conventions for a good purpose, not out of ignorance or carelessness.

4. Have you checked for consistencies in tense, number, and agreement?

5. Are the pronoun references clear? *Note*: Avoid vague *this, that, it, she, he,* and other pronouns. Keep the distance between pronouns and their antecedents minimal. Make sure a pronoun does, in fact, refer to a noun or to a clause or phrase functioning as a noun.

6. Have you kept the modifiers near what they modify? Avoid "squinters," modifiers that can point in two directions and completely change sentence meaning.

7. Have you chosen precise, concrete nouns and verbs that will require minimal modification? *Note*: Reduce modifying phrases to single words and avoid circumlocutions.

8. Have you varied your sentence constructions or lengths? *Note*: Mix complex and simple, long and short. Don't overuse parallelism. Keep your prose moving through sentence variety, and be alert to sounds and rhythms.

Finally, *read the work aloud and have others read it aloud to you.* Hearing the work will give you a new perspective on its effectiveness and also help you catch errors such as typos that are often missed in silent reading.

Remember to break any "rule" to achieve clarity and power.

> *"The main rule of a writer is never to pity your manuscript."*
>
> Isaac Bashevis Singer

 ## PROOFING AND SUBMITTING

At this point in the first four editions, we wrote about the flexibility that word processing gives writers no matter how they write their first drafts. Even for us it is difficult to think of a time when writers had typewriters on their desks, not computers. Access is so universal now that you undoubtedly are aware of all the tools available for producing the copy that you will print for a teacher, writing group, or editor. Still, we need to point out a few dangers and suggest some strategies for presenting the best possible manuscript.

As we've pointed out, your word-processing program will not catch errors and inconsistencies in such things as the spelling of proper nouns, homonyms (e.g., to, too, two), correct spellings for words that are not the word you wanted to use (e.g., "place" instead of "plate"), accidental repetition of a sentence or entire paragraph, and similar matters. Also, none of the grammar or syntax checking programs are so flexibile that they will intuit when you really meant to write a fragment or have a character speak ungrammatically or any other departure from conventions. As long as you are aware and understand the nature of your departures, you can boss your word-processing program instead of being a slave to it. You are still smarter than the machine and, as we said in Chapter 1 ("Working Like a Writer"), readers will think of an error as an error no matter how it occurred and blame you. More important, distraction caused by errors either annoy readers or, even worse, trigger a total turn-off from your creation.

We should alert you again to some of the dangerous practices that the ease of word processing may encourage. Since you can play around with all sorts of design features—type styles, sizes, graphics, colors—you may be tempted to overdo italics and bold, different styles and sizes of fonts, clever clip art, and so on. Don't! All these features in the program detract from a reader's attention to the narrative. Keep the manuscript simple, and don't waste your time trying to be a designer unless, of course, you intend to publish the work yourself. Also, the very ease with which you can research material and paste it into your text may accidentally lead you to plagiarism. Be sure to put in the quotation marks or indicate in some way that you have used another writer's text.

PROOFREADING CHECKLIST

1. Do not rush **proofing**.
2. Proof several times, each for different elements—spelling, grammar, punctuation, typography.
3. Do a reverse proofing starting with the last sentence and going backward to the beginning. You will pick up errors in sentences that you might not otherwise because the tendency is to see what you expect to see.
4. Proof from hard copy, not from the computer screen. If you make a correction or change on the screen, you might well accidentally make another error. When you print out a page that you have revised or corrected, proof it again since new errors do tend to creep in.
5. Don't speed up after catching an error. Errors flock together and the next word or sentence may contain one also.
6. Read the work out loud with someone else who is following along on another copy of your text. You will both pick up mistakes.

7. Use a reading guide (like a ruler or three-by-five card) to lead your eye to each word and sentence.

8. Have someone else read the manuscript, but keep in mind that you are not released from proofing yourself. In fact, another person who proofreads may become interested in the content and so miss errors.

9. Do not proof and watch television at the same time. Turn off your cell phone.

10. Rest frequently, but clearly mark where you have stopped so you won't skip text when you begin again.

To keep track of your changes before you enter them, we find it handy to use basic proofreading symbols. They are also handy when revising, proofing, or editing work for someone else. We provide a short list of the most common on p. 358. (You can find more detailed lists on the Internet.)

Some Possible Problems

There are some drawbacks to writing with a word-processing program. Most monitors (screens) show you only a fraction of a page at a time, usually somewhere between a third and a half. This limitation leads to tunnel vision: the tendency to pay too much attention to the limited amount of material glowing before your eyes and not enough to the larger flow of content and style. Even as you flip back and forth among screens full of text, you lose continuity.

To compensate for this difficulty, we recommend that you print out your work often and do much of your revising and editing on the printed copy. It is much easier to work with whole sheets of text, especially since you can then lay three or four next to each other to get a feel for the flow of your work. Working on printouts of successive revisions allows you to refine your work efficiently and effectively. (We understand, however, that there may be a cost factor in printing multiple "editions" using some printers.)

Some writers get around the tunnel vision problem by single-spacing when they draft, so they can see twice as much material. Then, depending on their program, they either reformat to double-spacing before printing or command the printer to double-space. We find this a partial solution, especially since it is very difficult to read single-spaced material on the screen for a long time. Another partial solution is employing the "page preview" feature, which also crowds the screen. You'll have to discover what works best for you.

Proofreading, in particular, is best done on printed text. Staring at the monitor—any monitor—is more wearing on the eyes than is scrutinizing printed text. We find that our proofreading is less accurate when we read from the screen. Perhaps it's just a matter of an old habit dying hard, but most writers have had the same experience. Another advantage is the portability of the printed copy; you can work on it wherever you want to without lugging around your laptop.

Frequent printouts are also a safeguard against the vulnerability of electronic text. Not only should you save and back up your files regularly, but also you should print out hard copy as a final defense against computer or disk failure. Although these failures are infrequent, it takes only one to make you wish you had taken simple precautions.

▶ FINDING A HOME FOR YOUR WORK

Finding a proper outlet for your writing is often backbreaking and frustrating work that calls for the skills and energy of a salesperson and patience of a saint. The effort appears to be antithetical to the creative process, and it may well be. However, if you want to expand your audience beyond your voice, you need to get to marketing rather than moaning about the soul-destroying effort. No one is going to come knocking at your door, and if they do, you would be well advised to be suspicious. Even relatively successful writers have to face up to the submission process—and frequently the rejection slip. If that is true for them, then what for writers just starting to submit work for publication?

We do not intend to discourage you; rather we want to encourage you to have realistic expectations. Fortunately, you have a new tool for marketing—the Internet. Almost all literary magazines, publishers, theaters, newspapers, and film producers have a site, and usually, the site will contain information about submitting manuscripts. Morever, there are Web sites as well as books that gather information about markets, and the Internet also houses e-zines to which you can submit your work.

Many beginning writers are unrealistic. They send their work only to the most prestigious magazines, publishers, theaters, and movie studios, not realizing that such outlets can deal with only a tiny percentage of the thousands of manuscripts they receive. No beginning athlete would expect to go from a first lesson in how to swing a golf club to making the cut in the U.S. Open; that athlete would first try to make the golf team, then play in local and regional tournaments before taking on Tiger Woods.

In a sense, writing for publication—that is, to make something public—is a form of competition. Only a finite number of markets are available for the many writers seeking homes for their work. For example, the Source Festival's call for ten-minute plays in 2007 generated over 900 submissions for 24 slots. *Poet Lore,* which publishes about 150 poems a year, receives 2,000 poems a year. Therefore, sending manuscripts to inappropriate places only strains the system and lessens your chances of reaching an audience. Submit your work to those publishers and theatre and film producers who are likely to give it a sympathetic reading. Finding them requires researching the literary or dramatic marketplace after you honestly assess what you have to offer. Keep in mind, however, that lightening does strike, and it may strike you if you are persistent (and write well).

Publication Markets

It makes sense to take your first forays into submitting with your college and local literary magazines and theaters. Look for newly established publications and theaters since they are likely not to have piles of manuscripts waiting for consideration and to be open to considering beginners. Search in *The International Directory of Little Magazines & Small Presses* (Dustbooks), which lists almost 4,000 book and magazine publishers with descriptions of their interests and the percentage of received manuscripts that they publish. Look for contests in the various genres listed on the Internet, but first look at the "Test Kit for Scams" on pp. 376–377. If you are producing a good deal of work in a single genre—poetry let us say—look in the specialized annual market books for those genres. Here is a short list:

> *Directory of Poetry Publishers* (Dustbooks): Published annually
> *Novel & Short Story Writer's Market* (Writer's Digest): Published annually
> *Dramatist's Sourcebook* (Theatre Communications Group)

Many more printed books with publication markets exist, and some specialize on sub-genres such as science fiction, romance, creative nonfiction, writing for children, and religious markets. You can find them on the Internet or by searching an online book seller. Search the Internet for listings of e-zines (as of this writing, we found more than 100). Be sure to check their Web sites before submitting to any publisher.

Your survey efforts will make you familiar with many writers who appear with some regularity in the periodicals you are reading. If your work has something in common with theirs, find out where else they are being published. Contributors' notes often provide such information, as well as a way of gleaning something about the achievement and status of the writers appearing in these pages. Is this periodical *really* open to previously unpublished writers? Might it be open to me?

A useful and businesslike way to research the market for your poems and stories is to examine the acknowledgments pages of collections by writers whose work you admire, especially those whose style has some affinity with your own. Here you will find credited those periodicals that first published the individual stories or poems. Now you have a short list of possible markets for your own work. Get your hands on those magazines and target your submissions carefully.

Search the Internet and you can often find out about a recently announced contest, a special issue of an established literary magazine, or a call for submissions by a magazine just getting started. This last category is a reasonable place for a beginning writer to send work. You and the magazine have something in common.

Finally, there is nothing like the company of other writers to help you find your way into print. Many of them will have that bit of information or that suggestion without which your work either will remain unpublished or will be published in a periodical of lesser merit than it deserves. You might consider joining one of your local or national literary organizations. For resources close to you, go to your search engine and enter "writers' organizations" (plus your state or city). You may have to refine your search to find the exact group that fits your needs. If you are still associated with a college or university you should look into joining the Associated Writers Program (AWP). Check with your creative writing department or look at their Web site: awpwriter.org. The site also contains links to other sites and resources.

We have said nothing about marketing books. In the careers of most writers, publication in periodicals precedes book publication. Writers find their first congenial editors and their first audiences by submitting to magazines, especially the noncommercial literary magazines whose main purpose is to nurture writers who have not yet captured a public large enough to warrant investment on the scale of the commercial publishing houses. The publication credits earned in these periodicals can win you the attention of a university or commercial press. What has happened, in effect, is that by meeting the standards and pleasing the tastes of many periodical editors, you have made a case for yourself. Book publishers depend on such credits to help them sift through the thousands of manuscripts that come their way.

Though it is possible to break through with a first novel, most novelists begin by getting samples of their work published in periodicals. These samples, presented as short stories, are often relatively self-contained chapters of novels in progress.

Play and Film Markets

Drama presents (if you will excuse the pun) a special case, since "publication" of a play is most often the residual of success in the theater (or on film). As we have already said, be involved in theater (or with film), even if on a volunteer basis. Work with educational television, small acting groups, experimental theaters, and college and university theaters. Go to conferences and participate in programs at which you might have an opportunity to meet producers and directors. Enter contests for new plays. (They'll *have* to read the playscript.) *Note:* The Dramatist's Guild (dramatistsguild.org) is ambivalent about contests that charge entrance fees. We see no difficulty with small fees of $5–$10 so long as the reasons for the fee are stated clearly. After all, most theaters (like small literary magazines and pubishers) always operate in the red. (Still, read the "Test Kit for Scams" on pp. 376–377 before you write a check.) Finally, look for opportunities to have your play heard—at a staged reading, for example, or in a workshop group.

Just as we recommend that you not look to publish first in those few places in which everyone wants to appear, so we recommend that you have realistic expectations and not search for a Broadway production first time out. When you do submit to a theatrical company, be sure you have researched its requirements. There's no use wasting postage sending a play to a theater that either hasn't the means to produce it or is not interested in the premise. Look at their Web sites. You will notice that many companies now ask for a query letter, a synopsis, and dialogue samples. *Don't send more than they ask for* if you want an unbiased reading.

   ## BEFORE YOU WRITE THAT CHECK

The easy path to publication is paved with your dollars.

Beware of contests that charge excessive reading fees or that require the purchase of the "prize anthology" before a final decision can be made on your work. Too often these publishing ventures prey on naive authors who will succumb to their promises. Your work will appear in print, but no exercise of editorial judgment has taken place—just the exercise of the author writing a check.

Essentially, scams fall into three categories:

1. services to writers—from editing, through organizations, to agenting
2. education for writers—including correspondence schools
3. publication—including contests and "prizes"

Sometimes the three categories can run together. All these categories, of course, reflect legitimate concerns that the confidence man/woman exploits. It wouldn't be a confidence game if the attempt to ripoff the writer or would-be writer did not have the aura of truth.

It is in the nature of the pure racket that the minute it's found, its name changes. Many ripoffs are around for so little time that, rather than develop an ever-changing list of their names, we developed the following Test Kit for Scams.

Test Kit for Scams

[Adapted from "The Writer's Center Scam Identification Kit."]

NOTE: No single test necessarily damns the product. Two or more ought to make you pause before writing a check. Three or more probably calls for contacting the Better Business Bureau or the Criminal Complaints division of the Post Office. The tests are simple common sense in any situation in which someone asks you for money. Beware of the following:

1. Any agent or publisher who asks for money, no matter how little. Pay entry or reading fees (no matter how small) only after carefully checking the publication and agent.
2. Any literary activity or service that asks for money *after* you have responded to its ad, but did not indicate a charge in that ad. In brief, beware of advertisements for free services.

3. Anything that sounds like another well-known literary activity but isn't. For example, suspect a publication called *Prairie Schoonover* or Mcgrew-Hille.

4. Any organization (educational or professional), publication, editor, or publisher that only has a post office box number, no phone and/or personal name.

5. Any publications and organizations that clearly are one-person operations.

6. Any mail request for money or membership put out on tacky flyers. (However, fancy brochures do not a legitimate operation make.)

7. Any organizations, organizers, publications, publishers, instructors, judges—none of whom appear in any standard reference works. (However, a "name" does not mean quality or legitimacy. We know of organizations that use names without permission. And remember, the reference listings do not necessarily check bonafides.)

8. Any claims to be nonprofit that do not have the IRS 501(c)(3) tax-exempt status.

9. Any out-of-towners coming to give a service (e.g., a course, editing) who are not associated with a local organization.

10. Anything that smacks of vanity publication. One warning sign that a magazine or anthology is a vanity press is if it does not give contributors' copies. That is, it expects you to buy copies and, sometimes, to sell them.

11. Any "publisher" who advertises for authors. They want authors all right. And their money.

> "*The con artist plays on our lack of confidence in our work and, at the same time, our self-deception, perhaps even the con-person in us. Paying someone else to say we are writers or to publish us, present us, or to make our work publishable is—at some atavistic level—a wish for magic to do away with work. Abracadabras cost dollars and you still haven't paid your dues. Re-read "The Emperor's New Clothes" and check "writer's scams" on the internet for up-to-date information about frauds.*"
>
> Allan Lefcowitz from *The Writer's Carousel*

All work that you send out should be accompanied by a stamped, self-addressed envelope (**SASE**). Because a computer copy can be so easily created, many writers handle the SASE in the following way. In their cover letter, they say: "If the manuscript is not suitable, please destroy it and inform me of your decision in the enclosed SASE." It is often more expensive to send back a manuscript than it is to reprint it. If you are fortunate, a carefully pre-pared manuscript sent in an appropriate envelope with an equally appropriate return envelope will survive both the postal system and the perusal of editors. If the manuscript still looks fresh when returned, you can send it out again. If it is beginning to look worn, then it's time to send out a fresh copy. Put your-self in an editor's place.

For most editors, the concern about "simultaneous submissions" (sending to more than one market at the same time) still exists, in spite of the relaxed stance regarding the nature of the manuscript. Don't send a work to more than one place at a time unless you know that the publisher accepts this practice. Even then, you should always let editors know that a work is being considered elsewhere.

Finally, if they have one, always remember to check the Web site of the publication, theater, or contest for any special directions.

 ## Cover Letters

Editors have conflicting things to say about the value of accompanying your submission with a cover letter, though all agree that if you send one, it should be brief. Essentially, a cover letter is a letter of transmittal: Its job is to call attention to the manuscript as briefly and effectively as possible. A few sen-tences about yourself, a few about the manuscript, and a few about why you have sent it to this particular publication should do the job. Indeed, finding a way of showing your familiarity with the periodical certainly can't hurt; just don't get cute, abrasive, or overly humble.

You may be tempted to try to use the cover letter to "sell" the play, poem, or story. Not only is this tactic a waste of your writing energy, but also it will mark you as an amateur. Let your literary or dramatic work sell itself.

 ## A Manuscript Checklist

Here are some additional considerations when submitting to a publisher or producer:

1. Don't be cute or impolite. Manuscripts with clever drawings (not associated with the story), elegant printing (yes, we know you have fancy dingbats), calligraphy, or any of those other efforts to enhance the words by visual means will immediately mark you as an amateur.

2. Don't reverse pages to check whether or not your manuscript has been read. If your reader does not get far enough to read the reversed pages, they prob-

ably don't deserve reading or are not suitable for the publication (or theater). The reader who does get that far will recognize the trick and be insulted.

3. Check your manuscript to see that all the pages are there.

4. Make sure the manuscript will fit the SASE.

5. Don't call the editor(s). If you do, they will be sure to send the manuscript back, since they have better things to do than shepherd a Nervous Nelly.

6. Don't follow your submission with a revised manuscript. You should have sent the revision the first time!

7. Don't sit around waiting for the rejection slip or that beautiful letter saying they loved it. Keep writing.

 WHAT ABOUT COPYRIGHT?

"Copyright is a form of protection provided by the laws of the United States...to the authors of 'original works of authorship' including literary, dramatic, musical, artistic, and certain other intellectual works. This protection is available to both published and unpublished works." (*Copyright Basics,* Library of Congress Copyright Office, Circular R1.)

Here are the important points for any writer to know:

1. Your work is automatically copyrighted when you get it into a fixed form—on paper, a rock, or a computer disk.

2. You cannot copyright an idea for a work.

3. You cannot copyright a title. (You can trademark one, but the process is overkill 99.99% of the time.)

The key point about copyright is that you have to write something before you can claim copyright. And the minute you write it down (even a letter), you have copyrighted it.

If you want to *register* your copyright as evidence of when you wrote a work, request information and a form from the Copyright Office, Library of Congress, Washington, DC 20559. It has a Web site from which you can download detailed information and forms: www.copyright.gov. As we are writing this, the Copyright Office is testing a beta program to allow writers to register online. Some writers are registering copyright these days because the penalty for violation of copyright increases when the work is registered. This step is probably useful only for nonfiction articles, books, and block buster novels like *Gone with the Wind* or *Harry Potter.*

In any case, concern about copyright is usually premature for a beginning writer. Get your writing out to publishers. Start writing your next piece.

Good luck!

• • GLOSSARY OF KEY TERMS • •

ABSTRACT: Language is abstract when it refers to intangible attributes or qualities—love, freedom, ideas. *Abstract* does not point to the material, physical bases of experience. Abstractions appeal to the intellect rather than to the senses. See **concrete.**

ACCENT: In poetry, equivalent to *stress.* Accent occurs when a syllable receives greater emphasis in pronunciation than those around it.

ACCENTUAL-SYLLABIC VERSE: Equivalent to *metrical verse.* The poetic lines are based on counting units that in themselves systematically alternate stressed and unstressed syllables. See **meter.**

ACCENTUAL VERSE: Verse in which lines are defined by the number of stressed syllables, as in "iambic pentameter." See **meter.**

ACT: Major unit of a play containing a major division of the dramatic action. Acts are often marked by intermissions or a lowering of the curtain. Act divisions punctuate the emotional or logical development of the play. See **scene.**

ACTION: "What happens" in a literary or dramatic work. The events that constitute the **plot.**

ALLITERATION: Proximate repetition of identical consonant sounds at the beginning of words or emphasized syllables. Use with great care to avoid unintentionally comic effects and to avoid calling so much attention to the sound that the sense becomes submerged in the lilting lyrical lullabies of labial liquidities.

ALLUSION: **Figure of speech** making an implied reference to something, real or fictitious, outside the work. Effective allusions bring useful associations to the reader's mind. "She didn't exactly have his head brought in on a platter, but she might as well have," evokes in a short space a complex story from the Bible.

AMBIGUITY: In a word, passage, or complete text, ambiguity allows for multiple interpretations, none of which is allowed to prevail over the others. *Unintentional* ambiguity can result in confusion and distraction because the meaning is merely obscure. Purposeful ambiguity allows one meaning to enrich another or all plausible meanings to complicate an issue or observation. Ambiguity should arise because the subject and emotions are complex, not because the writer has failed to think deeply about the subject or express it well.

ANALOGY: Comparison, often figurative, that explains or describes an unfamiliar object or idea through characteristics it shares with a more familiar object or idea. "A dictator is like the captain of a ship who thinks his crew has no other purpose than to obey his commands."

ANAPEST: See **meter.**

ANAPHORA: Repetition of a word or phrase at the beginning of successive lines.

ANTICLIMAX: Sudden drop in dramatic tension or seriousness in a fiction or drama. Usually a falling off after the **climax,** allowing for a serene concluding note. Sometimes an unintentional failure to sustain interest, relevance, or power. It usually occurs because the writer wants to spell out what happened, leaving nothing to the reader's or viewer's imagination.

ARCHAIC: Relating to diction that is filled with obsolete words or word usage: "yore," "go thee hence." Archaisms in contemporary poetry are rarely tolerated, since they most often suggest the wish to receive unearned poetic status by a liberal sprinkling of terms and phrases from revered works of the past. Archaisms can be used successfully for special purposes, such as to capture the flavor of the past in a historical or fantasy narrative.

ASSONANCE: Repetition of identical or similar vowel sounds in close proximity, as in "fetch the message."

BACKGROUNDING: See **exposition.**

BALLAD STANZA: Popular quatrain in folk songs and poetry, in which the first and third lines are iambic tetrameter, and the second and fourth are iambic trimeter. The usual rhyme scheme is *abcb.*

BATHOS: Insincere or excessive pathos; a falling away from the sublime to the ridiculous or from the elevated to the banal or commonplace. Also, a miscalculation in which intended elevation is not attained.

BEAT: Working unit of dialogue in which a shift in the emotional dynamic between characters occurs.

BLANK VERSE: Unrhymed iambic pentameter. See **meter.**

CAESURA: Pause, usually punctuated, *within* a line of verse.

CHARACTER: Imagined personage in a literary or dramatic work.

CHARACTERIZATION: Means used to create a **character.** Includes what the character says and does as well as what the narrator or another character is given to say (or think) about the character. Presentation of a character's thoughts, fancies, and dreams are also means of characterization.

CHRONOLOGY: Relating of facts or events in the order of their occurrence. The temporal order of events, as distinguished from their rearrangement in memory or in a **plot.**

CLICHÉ: Stale phrase, usually figurative, that reveals the writer's unwillingness to work hard for something fresh. Such borrowed formulas of expression as "it takes two to tango" have lost their original strength through overuse (and even misuse). See also **dead metaphor.**

CLIMAX: Moment of greatest tension in a dramatic or narrative work; it is most often also the major turning point. The moment at which the reader or audience is moved to its highest pitch of excitement.

CONCRETE: Concrete diction points to particulars, and most often to material objects, their qualities, and their motions. The concrete fastens upon palpable experience. See **abstract.**

CONCRETE POETRY: Poetry in which the design of the line breaks imitates the subjects as in a poem about swans that is shaped like a swan or a religious poem shaped like a cross.

CONFLICT: Actions and tensions resulting from opposing forces set loose in a **plot.** These forces may be external or internal. For example: Jill and Beth want the same man. Arthur is torn between honor and greed. The shipmates pit themselves against the storm.

CONNOTATION: Suggestions or associations provoked by a word. Though connotations are subjective, totally private ones cannot be communicated. Even though you may associate "pain" with ice cream on a hot day, it is unlikely your reader will. It is because of connotation that there are no synonyms. If "rug" and "carpet" mean the same thing (see your dictionary), how come no one advertises "wall-to-wall rugging"? Contrast with **denotation.**

CONSONANCE: Loosely, the echoing of terminal consonants in end words. More narrowly, a kind of **slant rhyme** in which patterns of consonants surround contrasting vowels: *blood/blade.*

CONVENTION: Literary or dramatic convention is any recognized and accepted means of expression within a particular form—or the form itself. When we speak of *convention,* we are usually addressing those features or devices that are particularly unrealistic: for example, Shakespeare's characters speaking in **blank verse,** or a first-person narrator remembering a conversation word for word that happened twenty years before. Often, conventions embody "rules": the conventions of the **sonnet,** of the well-made play, of indicating a change of speakers (in fiction dialogue) by beginning a new paragraph. The language system itself is a body of conventions dealing with how words and phrases may be related, spelled, and punctuated. Informational and artistic communication depends on the conventions shared by artist and audience, writer and reader.

CONVENTIONAL: According to **convention.** Sometimes used pejoratively to suggest a lack of inventiveness, but most often meaning the tried-and-true way of doing something.

COUPLET: In poetry, a two-line unit of composition (sometimes a **stanza**). Couplet lines are usually matched in length, meter, and rhyme.

DACTYL: See **meter.**

DEAD METAPHOR: Overworked **metaphor** that has lost its figurative vividness and its image content. When we say "the constitution is the *bulwark* of the nation," we are using a dead metaphor because the meaning is now merely denotative. What was once concrete is in the process of becoming an abstraction. We no longer envision a wall or the side of a ship in a battle scene. A dead metaphor is often a **cliché.**

DENOTATION: Direct, specific meaning. Often called the "dictionary" meaning of a word, in contrast to **connotation.**

DESIGNATOR: See **dialogue tag.**

DEUS EX MACHINA: Literally, a god out of a machine. The abrupt and improbable appearance of a solution to a problem. The use of such devices (as a miracle cure that saves the young wife because the story must end happily) almost always reveals a deficiency in plotting.

DIALECT: Regional or cultural variation (in pronunciation, **idiom,** grammar, or **syntax**) within a language; for example, the Yorkshire dialect in England or the Cajun dialect in Louisiana.

DIALOGUE: Representation of speech in a literary or dramatic work. More strictly, the representation of conversation between two or more characters.

DIALOGUE TAG: In fiction dialogue, the terminology that identifies the speaker and (sometimes) describes the tone of the speech. For example, "William said," "she screamed," "Jim answered haughtily." Avoid the excessive and unnecessary, as in the last two.

DICTION: Refers to the choice of words in a particular work. Writers must consider the aptness of their word choices to the occasion. Conventionally, there are four levels of diction: formal, informal, colloquial, and slang. We have argued that diction should be accurate, precise, concrete, appropriate, and idiomatic. How words are characteristically chosen and combined by an author constitutes that author's **style.**

DONNÉE: Literally, "the given," the raw material—**premise, character, theme, setting,** or idea—on which the writer works toward the development of the finished work. Also, the assumption, not necessarily made explicit, out of which the work develops.

DRAFT: Unless prefaced by "final," an early version or state of a work in progress. The preliminary work, in writing, that will be revised and edited into the completed and "finished" work. As a verb: to compose; to write tentatively; to explore in writing without stopping for refinements.

DRAMATIC MONOLOGUE: In poetry, a speech by a single character, usually to an implied listener or audience, that reveals the speaker's personality. The speaker is an imagined character, clearly distinguished from the poet.

DRAMATIZE: To create a drama. In **fiction,** to render a scene in detail, stressing what the characters are saying and doing. *Showing* in contrast to *telling* or *summarizing.*

EDIT: To refine a piece of writing by (1) bringing it into conformity with accepted standards **(conventions)** of usage and genre, and (2) making adjustments of the relationships between parts. See **revise.**

ELEGANT VARIATION: Comes from fear of repetition and often results in elaborate searches for another word when the best choice has already been made. Usually, the attempt is to impress the reader with the range of one's vocabulary rather than to communicate; for example, using *scribe* or *maker* for *author.*

END RHYME: **Rhyme** that occurs at the end of lines.

END-STOPPED LINES: Lines that terminate with some degree of grammatical completeness and with punctuation, causing a definite pause or break when read aloud or "heard" silently.

ENJAMBEMENT: Also, *enjambment* and **run-on** line. No pause at the end of a line. The grammatical structure (and sense) "runs on" from one line to the next.

EPIPHANY: Sudden insight or moment of illumination in which an important truth is understood by a character (and, additionally, by the reader). Often, the epiphany is the climactic moment of a short story.

EPISTOLARY: Poem or stories that take the form and tone of a letter or letters. An epistolary novel is one in which the narrative is developed through an exchange of letters between characters.

EUPHONY: Pleasant combination of sounds.

EXPOSITION: Explanation. Presentation (by the narrator in fiction, through dialogue in drama) of essential information, especially what has happened prior to the ongoing present of the literary or dramatic work.

FABLE: Brief **narrative,** in prose or verse, composed to make a moral point. Fables often involve improbable or supernatural events and sometimes use animals as characters.

FARCE: In drama, a low form of comedy that depends on fast-paced, surprising twists of plot, physical frenzy, and misunderstandings. Farce aims at broad, unsubtle effects.

FICTION: Imagined happenings presented in the guise of history or biography—thus **narrative**—and usually in prose. The two principal types of fiction are the novel and the short story.

FIGURE OF SPEECH (FIGURATIVE LANGUAGE):   Expressing one thing in terms of something else. Figurative language exploits words for more than their literal meanings. Major figures of speech include **metaphor, simile, personification,** and **allusion.**

FIXED FORM: Poem whose structure is defined by a set pattern of meter, rhyme, and sometimes repetition of line or phrase. The **sonnet, villanelle,** sestina, rondeau, triolet, and limerick are among the more popular fixed forms.

FLASHBACK: **Scene** that interrupts ongoing action with prior action, usually triggered by a present event that jogs a character's memory.

FOIL: A **character,** set in similar circumstances to the protagonist, whose nature or behavior sharply contrasts to that of the protagonist. Thus, a foil is used for the **characterization** of the primary personage.

FOOT: In metrical poetry, a unit combining stressed and unstressed syllables in a set pattern. See **meter. Lines** are measured by the number of feet they contain.

FORESHADOWING: Manipulation of events and access to information so as to anticipate, without predicting, future events. Frequently the reader does not know that something has been foreshadowed until the events themselves happen. Foreshadowing is one way of creating **verisimilitude. Mood** is often used to foreshadow.

FORM: See **genre.** Also, the arrangement of component parts in a literary or dramatic work so as to ensure unity and coherence.

FORMAL: Following established custom, usage, or **convention.** Following the principles of the literary or dramatic type. In **diction,** serious or dignified.

FORMAT: General structure or plan; more specifically, the conventions of manuscript presentation or the layout of a page or book: the typographical design.

FREE VERSE: Lines that follow no fixed metrical pattern, though they are often loosely rhythmical. Free verse often employs parallel grammatical phrasing, verbal repetition, and typographical patterning as means of expression.

GENRE: Literary kind, species, or form. Each genre is defined and recognized by its **conventions.** Novel, short story, poem, and play are all such categories, as are subdivisions such as **sonnet** and **farce.**

HERO: Major character around whom the events occur. Loosely, a character held up for emulation because of his or her superior traits. See protagonist.

HEROIC COUPLET: Iambic pentameter rhymed **couplets.**

HYPERBOLE: **Figure of speech** in which exaggeration is used to make a point. Calling a prose style "hyperbolic" is usually a negative comment.

IAMB: See **meter.**

IDIOM: Particular usage peculiar to a language (or to a subgroup of a language) whose meaning does not logically grow out of the meanings of its parts. For example, when we say "the kettle is boiling," we are using an idiom we understand but that would not translate literally into another language. Indeed, the kettle is *not* boiling, though the water is. Most idioms have their roots in **metaphor.**

IDIOMATIC: Usage in accord with an **idiom.** Natural, vernacular, or normal expression of native speakers that may violate the school rules of the language. Write idiomatically.

IMAGE: **Concrete** representation of sensory reality. Thing or quality that can be experienced by one or more of the senses.

IMAGERY: Collective character of the **images** in a particular work: its sensory content and the suggestive nature of that content.

INDIRECT DISCOURSE: Paraphrase of dialogue without actually quoting.

IN MEDIAS RES: "In the middle of things." The strategy of beginning a literary or dramatic work in the midst of the action rather than at the beginning of the chronological sequence. See **point of attack.**

INTERIOR MONOLOGUE: Expression of a flow of thoughts through the mind of a single character, usually limited to a single event or occasion. A reproduction of interior experience. See also **stream of consciousness.**

INTERNAL RHYME: **Rhyme** words occurring *within* consecutive or proximate lines, rather than at the beginning (head rhyme) or at the end **(end rhyme).**

IRONY: Most forms of irony involve a contradiction (often only apparent) for what is at first taken to be true and then is discovered to be otherwise. *Verbal irony* contrasts statement and suggestion: Hemingway has Jake say "Isn't it pretty to think so," at the end of *The Sun Also Rises,* but it's really rather painful to think so. *Dramatic irony* involves a situation in which the truth is the tragic opposite of what the characters think it is, and the audience knows this truth before the character does. It is thought to be ironic when fate or luck pushes someone's life in an unexpected, undeserved direction *(cosmic irony).* Irony always involves an incongruity of some sort. It can be comic or tragic. Swift's *Modest Proposal* is ironic: His real intention is to make it clear that the English landlords are already, in effect, eating Irish children. The apparent prescription for a problem is really a description of the problem.

LINE: Unit of composition in poetry. Line as an expressive concern is one of the few absolute distinctions between poetry and prose.

LINE BREAK: Convention of how lines end in a particular poem or how a particular line ends. Line breaks may coincide with or counterpoint sense and syntax. They may be preset or unpredictable. They may or may not be reinforced by repeated sounds.

LITERAL: **Denotative,** without **figurative** suggestion or embellishment. "Jane looks like Mary" is a literal comparison; "Jane looks like a goddess" is figurative (a **simile**). In translation, a capturing of the exact meaning of the original: "Word for word."

LYRIC: Poem, usually brief, expressing subjective reality. Most often cast in the **first person,** lyric poetry is called the poetry of emotion.

MAGIC REALISM: Fantastic, magical, or illogical elements combined with realistic or even "normal" setting.

MASK: See **persona.**

MEASURE: See **meter.**

MELODRAMA: Form of **drama** in which sensational incident and audience thrills dominate over characterization. Melodrama disdains probability and **motivation** while insisting on cheaply won justice for one-dimensional heroes, heroines, and villains. Thus, *melodramatic* is often used as a pejorative term.

METAPHOR: **Figure of speech** that depends on an unexpected area of likeness between two unlike things that are said to be identical. Metaphors tend to be literally impossible assertions: "The moon is a gold doubloon."

METER: In poetry, the recurrence of a pattern of syllables **(syllabic verse),** stressed syllables **(accentual verse),** or feet **(accentual-syllabic verse).** Most often used to describe the latter, in which **lines** are defined by type and number of feet. There are four basic feet in English meter. The **iamb** is an unstressed syllable followed by a stressed ($\breve{}/$), the **trochee** is a stressed syllable followed by an unstressed ($/\breve{}$), the **anapest** is two unstressed syllables followed by a stressed ($\breve{}\breve{}/$), and the **dactyl** is one stressed syllable followed by two unstressed ($/\breve{}\breve{}$). Two other feet are used only for variation within lines. These are the **pyrrhic,** of two unstressed syllables ($\breve{}\breve{}$), and the **spondee,** of two stressed syllables ($//$). Line length is labeled as follows: monometer, dimeter, trimeter, tetrameter, pentameter, hexameter, and heptameter. Thus a line of four dactyls would be called "dactylic tetrameter." *Meter* means **measure.** See **prosody** and **scansion.**

METONYMY: **Figure of speech** in which the name of one thing is substituted for another with which it is associated in some way. When we read "The White House announced," we know that, in fact, the White House represents a spokesperson for the president or the executive branch of government.

MISE-EN-SCÈNE: (1) The scenery and properties used in a play to represent the **setting** (lights, costume, sound, and special effects), along with the positioning and gestures of the actors. Whatever is needed to stage a scene. (2) By extension, the surroundings in which something happens.

MIXED METAPHOR: **Metaphor** in which the terms of comparison are shifted, usually unintentionally. "I smell a rat, and I shall nip it in the bud."

MOOD: Emotional atmosphere of a literary or dramatic work. The state of mind produced in the reader or audience. See **tone.**

MOTIVATE/MOTIVATION: Causes, within a **character** and the circumstances surrounding the character, for the ensuing action. Literally, the character is *moved* to seek revenge because of some prior event or need. Without adequate motivation, the **action** will seem arbitrary and unconvincing.

MYTH: **NARRATIVE,** usually communally developed and transmitted, often involving supernatural events and gods. Myths tend to be stories of origination: of the universe, of a river, of the seasons, of an animal, of a royal family, of a nation, of a ceremony. Myths are grounded in the folk beliefs and ritual practices of tribes, nations, and races.

NARRATE: Act of reporting a story or a scene in a story. The result is the **narrative.**

NARRATIVE: See **narrate.**

NARRATOR: Person who tells the story to the audience. The narrator may be a character in the story (first person) or someone the author makes up to tell the story more objectively (third person). To speak of the story's "narrator" or "speaker" allows us to speak about the manner in which the story is being told without confusing that manner with the author's. A "naive narrator," for example, may take quite a bit of sophistication to create.

OBJECTIVE NARRATOR: See **point of view.**

ODE: **Lyric** poem generally celebrating a person, place, or event and usually employing a complex stanzaic pattern (see **stanza**). More loosely, any poem of commemoration.

OFF-RHYME: See **rhyme.**

OMNISCIENT NARRATOR: See **point of view.**

ONE-DIMENSIONAL CHARACTER: Character who is presented without an explanation of the reasons for his or her behavior and who behaves in a relatively predictable way (see **stock character**). The term is often used negatively. Many of the characters who have simple tasks in the plot need only to be one-dimensional.

ONOMATOPOEIA: Imitation in the sound of a word (or word combination) of the sound connected to the action or thing named or described. "Slap," "swish," and "ping-pong" are examples, as is Poe's invention "*tintinabulation* of the bells...."

OPERATOR(S):   Occur when the real action verb is turned into a noun behind another verb. "You should make a *decision*" hides the real action: "You should *decide*." When "Hospitals *provide isolation* for individuals with suspected or confirmed infectious TB," they *isolate* patients. Such constructions are not only wordy, they lack vigor. They often occur with passive constructions. See **passive.**

ORGANIC (FORM): Idea that a work of art should be seamless. Ideally, the work would be so integrated that no word, scene, character, line—not a period—could be changed or deleted without destroying the effect of the work. When form is organic, it seems to grow out of its content, that is, to be inseparable from it. This is an ideal that the writer should aim for.

OVERWRITING: Usually caused by excessive use of adjectives and adverbs in an attempt to impress the reader.

OXYMORON: Compressed **paradox** in which an apparent contradiction makes sense when one of the terms is reinterpreted, as in "the sound of silence." Most often an adjective-noun combination: "terrible beauty" or "fortunate fall" or (humorously) "jumbo shrimp."

PACE: Tempo of the unfolding action as it is felt by the reader. The writer controls pace through a careful blending of dialogue, narration, description, exposition, and other elements. Long, unbroken stretches of one or another method destroy pace in fiction. In plays, pace refers to the timing of emotional ebbs and flows.

PARADOX: Contradiction, as in "paradoxically, Mary's humor, the virtue that attracted people to her, kept her in hot water with her friends." Paradox creates tension in a work because the human mind wants to resolve the contradiction. For example, in the **oxymoron** "hateful love," the contradiction leads us to see that love (a good) is hateful (a bad) when it is unrequited. Paradox is not necessarily effective *unless you have provided a resolution or potential for a resolution* of that paradox.

PARODY: Imitation of the **style** of a literary or dramatic work, usually treating a contrasting subject.

PASSIVE: Grammatical constructions in which the action is not given an immediate actor or agent: The verb has no subject (in the expected place). For example, "The ball was hit out of the park." Who hit it? "It was discovered that...." Who discovered it? Passive constructions are often called weak because the energizing link of actor and action is either missing or weakly made: "The pail of water was fetched by Jack and Jill." Though legitimate for some purposes, passive constructions often give the impression of indecision, fuzzy thinking, or downright deceitfulness, as in bureaucratic and academic prose.

PERSONA: In poetry and prose fiction, the speaker or **narrator** of a literary work, especially as distinguished from the author. A figurative **mask** the author wears to tell a story. In drama, more simply a **character.**

PERSONIFICATION: Giving human characteristics to inanimate objects: "the sleeping sea." In contemporary writing, this figure of speech is used sparingly and with great care.

PETRARCHAN SONNET: See **sonnet.**

PLOT: Sequence in which an author arranges (narrates, dramatizes) events (actions). The order in which the reader or spectator receives information. Only when this sequence is chronological is plot equivalent to story. A *story* stresses the temporal connections among events; a *plot* stresses the causal connections, often by introducing causes after their effects (as in a **flashback**).

PLOT LINE: Metaphorical way of talking about a plot as if it were, for example, a clothesline on which the author hangs scenes.

POETIC DICTION: Refers to the belief that poetry is, in part, characterized by a special type of language composed of archaic grammar and diction ("thou," "erst," "yore," "finny prey") and the avoidance of common, unpoetic words ("fish," "toes," "sit," "crap"). Modern poetic practice is to avoid poetic diction as artificial and, therefore, unable to communicate real emotions.

POINT OF ATTACK: Moment in a literary or dramatic work at which the plot, but not necessarily the story, begins. See **in medias res.**

POINT OF VIEW: Vantage point from which the materials of a story are presented.

PREMISE: Combination of **character, setting,** and situation at the **point of attack.**

PROOF(READ):   To check your manuscript for grammatical, punctuation, and spelling errors. A manuscript with many proofing errors is unlikely to receive a favorable reading because the editor's attention is drawn to the manner rather than the matter.

PROSODY: Principle(s) of organization in a poem, especially those dealing with the **conventions** of **versification:** sound patterns, **rhyme, meter,** and **stanzas.** Also, the study of such principles. See also **scansion.**

PURPLE PROSE: Elaborately adjectival and adverbial descriptions torturing the reader's patience with high-sounding but often hollow verbiage. See **overwriting** and **hyperbole.**

PYRRHIC FOOT: See **meter.**

QUATRAIN: **Stanza** of four lines.

REDUNDANT: Unnecessary repetition of a word or idea.

REVISE/REVISION: To look at again. Of course, the idea is not to look at it but to make changes in what you look at. *Revision* is not the same as *proofing* or *editing*. The word is meant to suggest a more radical act in which the author rearranges, eliminates, and adds elements to the work.

RHYME: *True* rhyme is the agreement in the last vowel and final consonant (if there is one) of two or more words: "Terence this is stupid *stuff*/You eat your victuals fast en*ough*" (A. E. Housman). Rhyme is no longer considered a sure sign that you are in the presence of poetry. Contemporary poets tend to avoid the blatancy of true rhyme in favor of less intense echoes, known collectively as **off-rhyme** or **slant rhyme.** These include consonant echoes ("leaf/chaff") and even the more subdued mating of similar but not identical sounds ("meat/lad"). For some poets, the occurrence of the same sound(s) anywhere in the last syllable (or word) represents a rhyme ("lass/slip"). One special kind of off-rhyme is **consonance,** in which a pattern of identical consonant sounds surrounds any vowel: "kiss/case."

RHYTHM: Flow of stressed and unstressed syllables, pauses, line breaks, and other devices the writer can control for musical effects. While we most frequently speak of rhythm, or the lack thereof when considering poetry, prose also has rhythms that can add to or detract from your work. *Rhythm* can also be used more loosely to refer to how the parts of a work are patterned.

RUN-ON: See **enjambement.**

SARCASM: Type of bitter **irony** or cutting remark. It means literally "to tear flesh." A sarcastic tone in a character or narrator should be used with great care since it can easily be mistaken for mere nastiness.

SASE: Self-addressed, stamped envelope. To be included with all submissions to publishers.

SATIRE: Refers to those works (or parts of works) in which the actions or the statements of the characters ridicule contemporary behavior or fashion. Satiric writing relies for its effects on **irony.** Mishandled, satire falls off into mere **sarcasm.**

SCANSION: Analysis of the metrical features of a poem (accented and unaccented syllables, **feet, caesuras**). When we *scan,* we use graphic symbols to indicate and highlight the essential features. Scansion does not create these features; it only indicates what they are by conventional markings. Stressed syllables are indicated by slashes (/) placed over the syllables, unstressed syllables by hyphens (-) or breves (ˇ) over the syllables, feet by vertical lines between the syllables (|), and caesuras by doubled vertical lines (||) at the pauses. **Rhyme** schemes are described by equating the rhymed syllables to letter symbols. Thus a poem in rhymed **couplets:** *aa bb cc,* etc.; a poem in **terza rima:** *aba bcb cdc ded,* etc.

SCENARIO: In playwriting and screenwriting, an extended outline of the play's **action** used to convey (to a producer) what the completed script will contain. Less formal than **treatment.**

SCENE: Dramatic subdivision of a work, identified by a change of place or time. See **act.**

SENTIMENTAL (SENTIMENTALITY): Not to be confused with "sentiment" (feeling), *sentimental* refers to the expression of inappropriately excessive emotions. One writes sentimentally when the language demands from the reader more intense responses than the occasion really demands. Unless meant humorously or to reveal the self-indulgence of a character, the writer of the following is sentimental: "Did my itty bitty kitty hurt its poor sweet tail?" A mature audience is likely to laugh at or throw aside sentimental writing.

SET (SETTING): Physical place (and all the things in it) created for a play or film or parts of them in which the scene happens. It is the place the author mentions or describes in a story. See **mise-en-scène.**

SIMILE: Usually described as a comparison using "like" or "as," the simile is a type of analogy in which the quality of one thing is used to identify it with what is essentially a different thing: "A state is like a ship." "She is as beautiful as a rose." Effective similes give us a sense of an unknown through a known. See **figure of speech** and **metaphor.**

SLANT RHYME: See **rhyme.**

SOLILOQUY: Related to the **dramatic monologue,** this kind of poem or (in a play) speech represents the reflections or thoughts of a character, addressed to no one in particular. A speech to oneself.

SONNET: Poem in fourteen lines, usually iambic pentameter, rhyming in one or another of the major sonnet traditions or a variation thereof. The **Petrarchan** (Italian) sonnet rhymes *abbaabba/cdcdcd.* The first eight lines (octave) always use envelope rhymes on the same two sounds. The final six lines (sestet) have various schemes, including *cdecde* and *cddcdd.* The Shakespearean (English) sonnet has three **quatrains** of alternating rhyme followed by a **couplet:** *ababcdcdefefgg.*

SPONDEE: See **meter.**

STAGE BUSINESS: Refers to the actions of an actor that are usually *suggested* but sometimes stated in the script. For example, if coffee is being served, the actor may sip from the cup for a needed pause or to do something while another character is speaking.

STANZA/STANZAIC: Group of lines defined by a space break from another, usually equivalent, group of lines. Stanzas are frequently organized around metrical (see **meter)** and **end rhyme** patterns that are repeated from stanza to stanza. See **strophe.** Though both *stanza* and *paragraph* are divisions that assume there is some type of internal organization, we do not use the word *paragraph* when speaking of a stanza.

STEREOTYPE: From the process that printers use to produce many copies from a casting, by analogy this refers to a character type continued or repeated without change from one work to another. Though the word is often used with a negative connotation, writers often rely on stereotypes. See **stock character** and **one-dimensional character.**

STICHIC: Continuous, unbroken poem. Browning's "My Last Duchess" is stichic.

STOCK CHARACTER: Such characters lack a unique set of traits, but they are immediately recognizable from their past appearances: "the good-hearted whore," "the wise-cracking Brooklyn street kid," "the deaf but spry grandmother."

STOCK SITUATION: Conventional situations found frequently in fiction and drama. Examples are (1) a boarding house (dorm, boat, hotel) filled with quirky people and managed by one relatively sane person, and (2) two girls—best friends—falling in love with the same guy.

STORY: See **plot.**

STREAM of CONSCIOUSNESS: Type of **interior monologue** that pretends to imitate the unselected, chaotic, unorganized flow of real thought. Useful for writing works that invoke psychological realism.

STROPHE/STROPHIC: A strophe is a major division of a poem. A strophic poem is one that is divided into distinct, though not necessarily equivalent, units rather than being continuous **(stichic).** See **stanza.**

STYLE: Manner of expression typical of a writer or artist. Distinctive styles result from identifiable habits of **diction** and **syntax.** *Style* can also refer to typical choices of material or point of view. Everyone, of course, has a style, but that style may be dull or ineffective because the language is trite or inappropriate for poetry or storytelling.

SUBPLOT: Secondary series of actions that reflects and heightens the concerns of the main **plot.** Within a narrative that presents a group's struggle to survive a storm, a romance may spring up between two of the characters. The romance, as it complicates the survival plot, adds interest and point.

SUBTEXT: What is implied rather than stated in a communication. Whatever the words say on the surface, like an iceberg, most of the message lies beneath. At the simplest level, for example, "How did you like my poem?" contains a request for affirmation, a concern about your opinion, and an indication of insecurity (otherwise why ask?). It *is not* a request for an honest opinion, and the asker would be hurt if you gave a negative one. See **text.**

SYLLABIC VERSE: Verse in which lines are defined by the number of syllables.

SYMBOL: Concrete objects (or evocations of concrete objects through words) that stand for or evoke images of ideas, stories, or other things. *Natural symbols,* like water, may literally be life-giving and purifying, as well as suggesting spiritual purification. Both natural symbols and cultural symbols (the cross) or signs (a traffic light or these very words) can communicate relatively simple ideas (stop or you'll get a ticket) and extremely complex relationships (sacrifice, redemption, and salvation). Everyone, including writers, uses symbols for communication. For the most part it is a mistake to work consciously to create symbols for your works. In the process of creating precise images, symbols will naturally emerge. Usually people do not read or go to the theater for the symbolism.

SYNECDOCHE: Figure of speech in which a part refers to the whole: "Can I borrow your wheels tonight?"

SYNOPSIS: Summary of the plot. If you are asked for a synopsis, don't tell what the work is supposed to mean; tell what happens.

SYNTAX: Order in which you place the words. For example, in English syntax you normally place the modifier before the noun and the subject before the verb. (*Grammar* refers to how a word is changed to indicate number, time, and gender.) Unusual syntax in poetry or awkward syntax in prose tends to call attention to the order of the words and draws attention from their meaning.

TERCET: **Stanza** of three lines. A *triplet* rhymes *aaa*.

TERZA RIMA: Three-line stanza interlocked with adjoining **tercets** rhyming *aba bcb cdc* and so forth, as in Shelley's "Ode to the West Wind":

> Make me thy lyre, even as the forest is:
> What if my leaves are falling like its own!
> The tumult of thy mighty harmonies
>
> Will take from both a deep, autumnal tone,
> Sweet though in sadness. Be thou, Spirit fierce,
> My spirit! Be thou me, impetuous one!

TEXT: Either the written material under discussion ("Let's look at the text") or the surface meaning of the material. *Text* often refers to the **denotative** meaning, the vehicle for the **subtext.**

THEME: Paraphraseable *message* in a work. Literally "a proposition," the theme of a work is likely to involve the writer's view about society, nature, or some other system of relationships. A writer who has studied and thought most deeply about a subject and who has felt it most intensely is likely to have the most interesting things to say about it. Even if your wish to communicate a theme is the reason you start writing, your job is to write the work well. Don't push the theme; it will get in.

TONE: Refers to the narrator's (or speaker's) attitude toward the subject and/or the reader: haughty, playful, somber, nasty, or ironic, for example. Tone is related to **point of view** and **subtext** in that it results from choices in content and technique: images, symbols, rhythms, sentence structure, and so on. Metaphorically, "tone of voice." See also **mood.**

TREATMENT: Technical term for an extended synopsis that presents your idea for a film or television program. There are quite specific rules for doing a treatment, and you should read several treatments before trying your own. Compare **scenario.**

TRITE: Word for a figure of speech that no longer surprises because it is shopworn. Do not confuse trite ("that's the way the ball bounces") with idiomatic ("shopworn").

TROCHEE: See **meter.**

VERISIMILITUDE: *Like* reality. Distinguish between reporting real events and making up events that appear to be real. The creative writer's task is the latter, not the former.

VERSE/VERSIFICATION: Metrical aspect of poetry. Sometimes used synonymously for **line** or metrical, rhymed passages; for example, "in the following verses...." Also used pejoratively, as in "that's merely verse," suggesting the work in question only wears the costume of poetry.

VILLANELLE: Nineteen-line poem in which the first and third lines of the first **tercet** are alternately the last lines of the following four tercets and also form the couplet that ends the concluding **quatrain:** A_1bA_2 abA_1 abA_2 abA_1 abA_2 abA_1A_2. Thus, there are only two rhyme sounds. Most often in iambic pentameter.

WEAK PASSIVE: See **passive.**

ACKNOWLEDGMENTS AND CREDITS

We wish to thank the following authors and publishers for permission to reprint or publish for the first time the following:

Lines from the poetry exercise "Hope" by Wilma A. Alcala, used by permission of the author.

A. R. Ammons, "Muse." Copyright © 1964 by A. R. Ammons, from *Collected Poems 1951–1971* by A. R. Ammons. Used by permission of W. W. Norton & Company, Inc.

Susan Astor, "The Poem Queen" from *Dame* (Athens: The University of Georgia Press, 1980). Copyright © 1980 by Susan Astor. Reprinted with the permission of the author.

Krista Benjamin, "Letter from My Ancestors" as published in *Margie,* also appeared in *The Best American Poetry of 2006*, editor Billy Collins. Used by permission of the author.

Elizabeth Bennett, "Small Explosion" from *Poet Lore* (Fall 1986). Reprinted (along with an earlier draft) with the permission of the author.

Kate Blackwell, "You Won't Remember This" from *You Won't Remember This* by Kate Blackwell, published by Southern Methodist University Press. Copyright © 2007 by Kate Blackwell. Reprinted by permission of Southern Methodist University Press and Kate Blackwell.

Stephen Bluestone, "Isaac on the Altiplano" and "Moses Miamonides" from *The Laughing Monkeys of Gravity.* Mercer University Press © 1995 (Macon,

Georgia, 31207). Reprinted by permission of Mercer University Press, 1995. Prose commentaries used by permission of the author.

Christian Bök, "Vowels" from *Eunoia*, by Christian Bök. Published by Coach House Books, 2001. Reprinted by permission of the publisher.

Geoffrey Brock, "Flesh of John Brown's Flesh: Dec 2, 1859," first appeared in *Subtropics*, Spring 2006. Reprinted in *Best American Poetry 2007*, Heather McHugh, ed. Reprinted by permission of the author.

Sterling Brown, Thirteen lines of "Old Lem" from *The Collected Poems of Sterling A. Brown*, selected by Michael S. Harper. Copyright © 1980 by Sterling A. Brown. Reprinted by permission of HarperCollins Publishers.

Cecilia Cassidy, excerpt from "Dialysis and the Art of Life Maintenance" from *GW Forum* 42 (Spring 1994). Copyright © 1994 by Cecilia Cassidy. Reprinted with the permission of the author.

Siv Cedering, "Figure Eights" from *Letters from the Floating World: New and Selected Poems*. Copyright © 1984 by Siv Cedering. Reprinted with the permission of the author and the University of Pittsburgh Press.

Poetry exercise "January Thunder" by Sally Cheney, used by permission of the author.

Billy Collins, "The Brooklyn Museum of Art" from *The Apple That Astonished Paris*. Copyright © 1988, 1996 by Billy Collins. Used by permission of the University of Arkansas Press, www.uapress.com.

Robert Coover, "My Grandmother's Nose" by Robert Coover. Copyright © 2005 by Robert Coover. Originally appeared in *Daedalus* (June 22, 2005, Vol. 134, Issue 3). Reprinted by permission of Georges Borchardt, Inc., for the author.

Noel Coward, excerpts from *Blithe Spirit* (New York: Doubleday, 1942). Copyright 1942 by Noel Coward. Reprinted with the permission of Michael Imison Playwrights, Ltd.

Sandy Daniels, "Inside Out." Reprinted with the permission of the author.

Don DeLillo, excerpt from *Underworld*. (Scribner, 1997).

James J. Dorbin, "Dreams." Reprinted with the permission of the author.

Rita Dove, "Loose Ends" from *In Short: A Collection of Brief Creative Nonfiction* (New York: W. W. Norton & Company, 1996), Judith Kitchen and Mary Paumier Jones, eds., Adapted from "A Handful of Inwardness" by Rita Dove from *The Poet's World* (Washington: The Library of Congress, 1995). Copyright © 1995 by Rita Dove. Reprinted by permission of the author.

Tony Earley, "Just Married." Reprinted by the permission of Regal Literary, Inc. as agent for the author. Copyright © 1999 by Tony Earley. Story originally appeared in *Esquire*, May 1999.

Denise Edson, "Anatomy of Melancholy." Reprinted with the permission of the author.

Stanley Elkin, selection from *The MacGuffin*. (Simon and Schuster, 1991).

Annie Finch, "Thanksgiving" from *Eve*. Story Line Press, © 1997. (Three Oaks Farm, Brownsville, OR 97327). Reprinted by permission of the publisher.

Dorothy Canfield Fisher, "Sex Education" from *The Yale Review*, 35, (December 1945). Reprinted by permission.

Poetry exercises beginning "Summer came on slow" and "Kirk burned for a while" by Bruce Fleming, used by permission of the author.

Brendan Galvin, "Fog Township" from *Seals in the Inner Harbor*. Copyright © 1986 by Brendan Galvin. Reprinted with the permission of Carnegie Mellon University Press.

Philip Gerard, "The Fact Behind the Facts" first published in *Brevity*, 27 May 2008. Reprinted by permission of the author.

Margaret Gibson, excerpt from "Affirmations" from *Long Walks in the Afternoon*. Copyright © 1983 by Margaret Gibson. Reprinted with the permission of Louisiana State University Press.

Albert Goldbarth, "Stopping by Woods on a Snowy Evening" copyright © 2006, 2009 by Albert Goldbarth. From *To Be Read in 500 Years*. First published in *New Letters*, Vol. 72, Issue 3/4, pg. 74, 2006. It is printed here with the permission of *New Letters* and the Curators of the University of Missouri-Kansas City and the author.

Jessica Goodheart, "Advice for a Stagosaurus," copyright © 2005 by the Antioch Review, Inc. First appeared in *The Antioch Review*, Vol. 63, No. 1. Reprinted by permission of the Editors.

Ernest Hemingway, "A Very Short Story" reprinted with the permission of Scribner, a Division of Simon & Schuster, Inc., from *In Our Time* by Ernest Hemingway. Copyright © 1925 by Charles Scribner's Sons. Copyright © renewed 1953 by Ernest Hemingway. All rights reserved.

Ernest Hemingway, from *The Sun Also Rises* (Simon & Schuster, 1982).

Bob Hicok, "So I know" originally published in *The American Poetry Review*, Sept/Oct 2007, Vol. 36, No. 5. Reprinted by permission of the author.

A. E. Housman, "From the wash the laundress sends" from *The Collected Poems of A. E. Housman*. Copyright 1936 by Barclays Bank Ltd., Copyright © 1964 by Robert E. Symons, Copyright © 1965 by Henry Holt and Company. Reprinted by permission of Henry Holt and Company, LLC.

Vicki Hudspith, "Ants." Reprinted by permission of the author.

Lines from the poetry exercise "Desert Rain Poem" by Alice S. James, used by permission of the author.

James Jones, "The Beggar Woman" from *Viet Journal* by James Jones, copyright © 1974 by James Jones. Used by permission of Dell Publishing, a division of Random House, Inc.

Edward P. Jones, "The First Day" from *Lost in the City* (William Morrow, 1992). Reprinted with the permission of the author.

Bel Kaufman, "Sunday in the Park" from *The Available Press/PEN Short Story Collection* (New York: Ballantine Books, 1985). Copyright © 1985 by Bel Kaufman. Reprinted with the permission of the author.

Allison Klein, "A Gate-Crasher's Change of Heart" by Allison Klein from *Washington Post*, Friday, July 13, 2007. © 2007, The Washington Post. Reprinted with permission.

Maxine Kumin, "Stopped Time in Blue and Yellow" from *Our Ground Time Here Will Be Brief* (New York: Viking Penguin, 1982). Copyright © 1982 by Maxine Kumin. Reprinted with the permission of the author.

Lee Lawrence, "Journal Excerpts." Reprinted by permission of the author.

Philip Levine, "For Fran," from *New Selected Poems* by Philip Levine, copyright © 1991 by Philip Levine. Used by permission of Alfred A. Knopf, a division of Random House, Inc.

Audre Lorde, "A Litany for Survival." Copyright © 1978 by Audre Lorde, from *The Collected Poems of Audre Lorde* by Audre Lorde. Used by permission of W. W. Norton & Company, Inc.

Joanie Mackowski, "When I was a dinosaur" first published in *Pool 4* (2005): 57. Reprinted by permission of the author.

Poetry exercise, "Teen Mall Rats Die in Suicide Pact" by Rose MacMurray, used by permission of the author.

Karen Malloy, "Bagged Air." Reprinted with the permission of the author.

Excerpt from the short story exercise "GP" by Jerome Marr, used by permission of the author.

Alice McDermott, *Charming Billy*. New York: Farrar, Straus and Giroux, 1998.

James McLure, excerpt from *The Day They Shot John Lennon* (New York: Dramatists Play Service, 1984). Copyright © 1984 by James McLure. Reprinted with the permission of Bret Adams Ltd. Artists Agency.

E. Ethelbert Miller. *Fathering Words: The Making of an African American Writer*. New York: St. Martin's Press, 2000, pp. 1–2.

Marianne Moore, "The Fish" reprinted with the permission of Scribner, a Division of Simon & Schuster, Inc., from *The Collected Poems of Marianne Moore* by Marianne Moore. Copyright © 1935 by Marianne Moore. Copyright © renewed 1963 by Marianne Moore and T. S. Eliot. All rights reserved.

Richard Newman, "Briefcase of Sorrow" from *Borrowed Towns* by Richard Newman. Reprinted by permission of the author. (World Press, 2005).

Anaïs Nin, excerpt from *The Diary of Anaïs Nin, Volume VI: 1931–1934*. Copyright © 1966 by Anaïs Nin, reprinted by permission of Houghton Mifflin Harcourt Publishing Company.

Jean Nordhaus, "Gloves" from *A Language of Hands* (Adelphi, Maryland: SCOP Publicatons, 1982). Copyright © 1982 by Jean Nordhaus. Reprinted with the permission of the author.

Naomi Shihab Nye, "Mint Snowball" from *Mint*. Reprinted by permission of the author Naomi Shihab Nye, 2008.

Joyce Carol Oates. Play, *Procedure*, copyright by the Ontario Review, Inc., 2009. Reprinted by permission.

Pat Shelly, "French Movie" from *Bogg* #56 (1986). Copyright © 1986 by Pat Shelly. Reprinted with the permission of the author.

Dave Smith, "Night Fishing for Blues" (excerpt) from *Cumberland Station* (Champaign: University of Illinois Press, 1976). Copyright © 1973, 1974, 1975, 1976 by Dave Smith. Reprinted with the permission of the author.

"Sovran Bank Advertisement." Copyright © by Sovran Financial Corporation and Lawlor Advertising. Reprinted with the permission of Sovran Financial Corporation.

William Stafford, "What's in My Journal" from *Crossing Unmarked Snow: Further Views on the Writer's Vocation* by William Stafford. Copyright © 1998 by The University of Michigan Press. Used by permission of The University of Michigan Press.

Sue Standing, "A Woman Disappears Inside Her Own Life" from *Deception Pass* (Cambridge: alicejames books, 1984). Copyright © 1984. Reprinted by permission of the publishers.

John Steinbeck, from *Working Days: The Journals of The Grapes of Wrath, 1938–1941* by John Steinbeck, Introduction by Robert DeMott, copyright © 1989 by Elaine Steinbeck. Used by permission of Viking Penguin, a division of Penguin Group (USA) Inc.

Adrien Stoutenburg, excerpt from "A Short History of the Fur Trade" from *Land of Superior Mirages: New and Selected Poems*. Copyright © 1986 by The Johns Hopkins University Press. Reprinted with the permission of the publishers.

Karen Swenson "Time and the Perfume River" from *The Landlady in Bangkok*. Copyright © 1994 by Karen Swenson. Reprinted with the permission of Copper Canyon Press, www.coppercanyonpress.org

Hilary Tham, "Chinese Medicine" and "Father" from *Lane With No Name*. Copyright © 1997 by Hilary Tham. Reprinted with the permission of Lynne Rienner Publishers, Inc.

Dylan Thomas, excerpt from "Do Not Go Gentle Into That Good Night" from *The Poems of Dylan Thomas*, copyright © 1952 by Dylan Thomas. Reprinted by permission of New Directions Publishing Corp.

Michel Wallerstein. "Off Hand" by Michel Wallerstein, as appeared in *Perfect 10: Writing and Producing the 10-Minute Play* by Gary Garrison. Reprinted by permission of the author.

Poetry exercise "Land Lord Dharma" by Jerry Webster, used by permission of the author.

William Carlos Williams, excerpt from "The Dance" from *The Collected Poems: Volume II, 1939–1962*, copyright © 1944 by William Carlos Williams. Reprinted by permission of New Directions Publishing Corp.

Baron Wormser, "Soap Opera" from *Good Trembling* (Boston: Houghton Mifflin Company, 1985). Copyright © 1985 by Baron Wormser. Reprinted with the permission of the author.

●   ●   ●   ●   ●   *IMAGE CREDITS*   ●   ●   ●   ●   ●

INDEX

For Additional Notes

For Additional Notes

For Additional Notes

For Additional Notes

For Additional Notes